Using DacEasy

Stephen Nelson

Que® Corporation
Carmel, Indiana

Using DacEasy™

Copyright © 1988 by Que® Corporation

Library of Congress Catalog No.: 88-62748
ISBN 0-88022-391-X

92 91 90 89   8 7 6 5 4 3 2

Interpretation of the printing code: the rightmost double-digit number is the year of the book's printing; the rightmost single-digit number, the number of the book's printing. For example, a printing code of 88-1 shows that the first printing of the book occurred in 1988.

Using DacEasy is based on DacEasy Accounting Versions 3.0 and 2.0.

Screen reproductions in this book were created by means of the InSet program from INSET Systems Inc., Danbury, CT.

About the Author

Stephen Nelson

Stephen Nelson, a certified public accountant, provides financial consulting and computer-based financial modeling services to a variety of firms and investors—principally in the areas of real estate and manufacturing.

Nelson's past experience includes a stint as the Treasurer and Controller of Caddex Corporation, a venture-capital-funded start-up software development company and an early pioneer in the electronic publishing field, and, prior to that, as a senior consultant with Arthur Andersen & Co. There Steve provided financial and systems consulting services to clients in a variety of industries.

Steve has authored over 30 articles on financial management and modeling for national publications, including *Lotus Magazine* and *INC Magazine*, and is the author and architect of *Business Forecasting and Planning with Microsoft Excel*, a collection of spreadsheet templates published by Microsoft Press.

Nelson holds a Bachelor of Science in Accounting from Central Washington University and a Master's in Business Administration with a Finance emphasis from the University of Washington.

Publishing Manager

Scott N. Flanders

Product Director

Karen A. Bluestein

Senior Editor

Lloyd J. Short

Editors

Kelly Currie
Jeannine Freudenberger

Technical Editor

Alan L. Gray, C.P.A.

Editorial Assistant

Debra S. Reahard

Indexed by

Brown Editorial Service

Book Design and Production

Dan Armstrong
Brad Chinn
Cheryl English
Lori A. Lyons
Dennis Sheehan

Table of Contents

Trademark Acknowledgments

Introduction

If you're reading this introduction, one of the following three statements is probably true:

1. You're considering installation of a small-business accounting package like DacEasy™.

2. You've decided to install DacEasy and want a little extra help.

3. You're now using DacEasy and want a reference source that goes beyond the information provided in the DacEasy user's manual.

In any of these three cases, *Using DacEasy* will help. In this text, you'll find a wealth of information on the latest version of DacEasy™ Accounting: Release 3.0.

When you finish reading this introduction, you'll know what DacEasy Accounting 3.0 is and whether the program can suit your needs. This introduction also identifies the chapters that cover each of the pieces that make up the whole of DacEasy.

What Is DacEasy?

DacEasy is a complete set of accounting and financial management tools you can use to manage your business more profitably. The package includes modules to process purchasing, accounts payable, billing, accounts receivable, and inventory activities and also features a full general ledger with budgeting and forecasting capabilities and complete financial statements. DacEasy completely automates every area of your accounting process and provides you with pages and pages of financial information that can help you better manage most of your business activities. By using DacEasy, a small business can have the same quality financial information and management tools that were previously available only to large corporations with huge computers and extensive accounting staffs.

Don't be deceived by DacEasy's low price. This program provides the same accounting horsepower for which some of your competitors—and many larger corporations—are paying thousands of dollars. (Before you say to yourself that the author is probably exaggerating, let me add that in the past I've spent several thousand dollars on microcomputer-based accounting packages that aren't half as good as DacEasy.)

Unfortunately, the fact that DacEasy is a bargain causes some confusion among buyers and accountants. People think that DacEasy is similar to the other inexpensive small-business accounting packages on the market. Most of these other packages, however, amount to little more than automated checkbooks or collections of loosely integrated bookkeeping tools that help pay bills or generate customer invoices. I don't mean to say that these other packages aren't valuable or appropriate. You may need only a simple little system. In comparison, however, you should understand that DacEasy is a complete, integrated accounting system that wholesalers, retailers, and service firms with annual revenues of up to several million dollars should be able to use with confidence and success.

When To Use DacEasy

DacEasy is a powerful, integrated accounting system. Accordingly, if you want to track every transaction, automate nearly every bookkeeping task, and have access to reports on almost every financial facet of your business, you should consider DacEasy.

The package goes beyond simply keeping your books and generating standard accounting forms like purchase orders, checks, and invoices. DacEasy gives you the structure and tools to perform sophisticated accounting operations and produce comprehensive financial reports. If you want more than simple bookkeeping, if you want more than fast and easy forms generation, if you want a wealth of financial information literally at your fingertips, turn to DacEasy.

On the other hand, if you want something only to prepare invoices or write checks, or if you need a program that merely kicks out an income statement you can use to prepare your tax return, DacEasy isn't the solution for you. Less powerful and less complicated solutions are available.

I respectfully submit, however, that you should consider asking for more from your accounting system than forms generation and an annual profit-and-loss statement. You may feel that I, as a certified public accountant, feel obliged to make this statement. That's probably true. But most business managers echo my feelings. You *must* be able to monitor and measure the financial health and performance of your business. For some small businesses, the owners and managers can perform this monitoring and measuring on the backs of envelopes and in their heads. Unfortunately, most businesspeople who *think* they can manage their business's finances this way, *can't*.

As I mentioned earlier, you can probably use DacEasy to perform the accounting for a business that has as much as several million dollars in annual revenue. At some point, though, you may have more bookkeeping and accounting than one person, working eight hours at a computer, can perform. In that case, you probably need a system that allows two or more people to work simultaneously on accounting and bookkeeping tasks within the accounting package.

If you currently have several accountants and bookkeepers on your staff, you may still be able to use DacEasy, but you're probably a candidate for a multiple-user system. Talk to someone knowledgeable in business accounting packages if you think you may need such a system. This certain someone could be your certified public accountant, a salesperson at the store where you purchased your computer, another business owner who is using a multiple-user system, or a computer consultant.

About This Book

Using DacEasy is divided into 12 chapters and four appendixes.

Chapter 1, "A Review of Small-Business Accounting," covers the basics of accounting. Learning and using a business accounting system is much like learning to drive a car. A significant investment of time, and sometimes money, is involved. Just as you need to learn about speed limits, road signs, and driving laws before driving a car, you need to learn about bookkeeping and accounting in order to use any full-fledged accounting system. Chapter 1 describes what income statements and balance sheets are, discusses how double-entry bookkeeping works, and illustrates the standard bookkeeping transactions you use to record the financial activities of your business.

(*Using DacEasy* is written with the assumption that you're already familiar with your computer. If you're new to computerized systems and want to learn some computer basics, however, Que's *Using PC Dos*, 2nd Edition, and *MS-DOS User's Guide*, 3rd Edition, both by Chris DeVoney, provide excellent information about operating and maintaining your computer.)

Chapter 2, "Getting Started with DacEasy," outlines the steps necessary to install and begin using DacEasy successfully. The chapter discusses the important steps of ordering preprinted forms, learning the system, picking the conversion date, and installing the software and also describes some basic procedures for operating DacEasy once it is installed.

Chapter 3, "Defining the Chart of Accounts and System Options," describes why you need to and how you define a Chart of Accounts. The chapter also provides instructions for setting each of the system options, including such things as telling DacEasy which colors you want displayed on-screen and how much space the program should reserve on disk for storing accounting information.

Chapter 4, "Loading the Master Files," describes why you need to and how you load your system's master files. You'll create master files for frequently used information such as products you sell, vendors from whom you purchase, and customers to whom you sell. After you've defined the Chart of Accounts and loaded the master files, you're ready to begin using the system to record your accounting transactions.

Chapter 5, "Protecting Your System," lists the procedures you need to follow to protect your system from human and machine errors that can damage and destroy your accounting records. The chapter gives advice on what to do if your accounting records are accidentally erased and also lists some basic internal controls, or accounting checks, you should consider using to minimize opportunities for employee theft and embezzlement. Although this topic isn't a pleasant one to cover, it's important, particularly when you begin using a computerized accounting program.

Chapter 6, "Using the Purchase Order Module," begins the discussion of the screens and reports you'll use in your daily record keeping and decision making. This chapter covers the tools that support the purchasing of goods and services. The chapter begins with a review of the purchasing process and ends with detailed instructions for using this module to automate your firm's purchasing activities.

Chapter 7, "Using the Accounts Payable Module," overviews the accounts payable function and describes how it works with DacEasy. The chapter also provides suggestions and the instructions you'll need in order to use the accounts payable portion of DacEasy, including such topics as paying bills, summarizing amounts spent for various expenses, and tracking amounts owed to your vendors.

Chapter 8, "Using the Billing Module," provides you with background information on the bookkeeping involved in billing customers and describes the procedures for using the Billing module to perform this bookkeeping function, generate customer invoices, and update inventory records for sales.

Chapter 9, "Using the Accounts Receivable Module," describes the way the accounts receivable process typically works for firms and shows you how to use the tools in the Accounts Receivable module to manage your own receivables better and more easily. The chapter also discusses the generation of reports such as aging reports, customer lists, sales reports, and cash-flow reports.

Chapter 10, "Using the Inventory Module," discusses the importance of good inventory management and control and explains why a perpetual inventory system (such as the one DacEasy provides) is the best choice. The chapter describes how to use the Inventory module's screens and reports to maintain a perpetual inventory system. You'll also find an overview of the types of inventory reports you can create, including price lists, activity reports, and sales reports.

Chapter 11, "Using the General Ledger Module," explains how the general ledger collects information from the other modules. In this chapter, you'll learn how the general ledger allows you to record any additional financial information not available in one of the other modules and then uses this information to generate financial statements that summarize your business's financial condition and performance.

Chapter 12, "Using the Periodic Routines," describes the steps you follow to indicate to DacEasy that an accounting period—a month or year for which you're calculating net income—has ended and that you're beginning a new accounting period. This chapter describes also how to use DacEasy's forecasting features to construct a budget.

The four appendixes provide information on a variety of subjects.

Appendix A, "DacEasy Accounting 3.0 Files," lists the files that are contained on DacEasy's two program disks, shows what program disk DacEasy needs for each main menu option, and lists the files (and their contents) that DacEasy creates after you define the data files.

Appendix B, "Reviewing DacEasy's Sample Custom Report Formats," shows you the four custom reports that the program provides as samples for the Financial Statements Generator option on the Financials menu. You can use these sample formats as is, modify them to suit your own needs, or create entirely new formats of your own design.

Appendix C, "Converting Your Current DacEasy Accounting Files to DacEasy Release 3.0," discusses the utility program you can run to convert your Release 1.0 or 2.0 files to Release 3.0 format.

Appendix D, "Using This Book for DacEasy Release 2.0," points out the major and minor differences between Release 2.0 and Release 3.0. If you're working with Release 2.0 but are aware of the changes that have been included in Release 3.0, *Using DacEasy* can be just as helpful to you as to a 3.0 user.

In the back of the book are menu maps of Release 2.0 and 3.0 to help you find the option or screen you need in order to accomplish a task in DacEasy.

1

A Review of Small-Business Accounting

This chapter shows you that accounting can be simple if you remove the clutter with which accountants usually burden you. The purpose of the chapter is to provide you with a clear understanding of the basics—which is what you need in order to grasp the mechanics of DacEasy—and to change accounting and bookkeeping from burdens into powerful tools that can help you run your business more profitably. This chapter describes the two standard financial statements that businesses use and accounting systems like DacEasy typically generate: an income statement and a balance sheet. The chapter also describes the logic and steps for using a popular tool called double-entry bookkeeping. Finally, the chapter concludes with some brief explanations of how DacEasy's seven modules can help with these everyday bookkeeping and accounting tasks.

Introducing a Sample Business

Imagine that it's summertime and you're eight years old. Although much of your time has been spent climbing trees, collecting insects, and learning to ride a bicycle, you've not been so busy as to miss two quite remarkable features of this particular summer: the days are unusually hot and dry, and a parade of cars and people has been going by your house. After perfecting your bicycling balancing skills and getting the go-ahead from your mother, you decide that you need to acquire your own two-wheeled transportation. After several Sundays of checking the newspaper, however, you're disappointed to see that not many summer jobs are advertised for eight-year-olds. "No problem," a friend says. "Just start your own business." After some research and review of the summer's hot franchises, you decide to go with a standard: the lemonade stand.

Measuring Your Profits with an Income Statement

Your goal in operating the lemonade stand is simple. You want to make enough money to buy a bicycle. Although you could operate the lemonade stand for the entire summer and then hope you've made enough to purchase a new bicycle, you think monitoring your profits over the summer is a wiser method. The tool you use to measure whether you're making or losing money—and how much over a period of time—is called a *profit-and-loss statement*, or an *income statement*.

The first thing to realize about an income statement is that it measures your profit or loss for a certain period of time, called an *accounting period*. Businesses usually measure profits monthly and yearly, but you can pick any time interval you want. In the lemonade stand business, measuring profits at the end of each day may be best. Obviously, the bigger the time period, the longer you go between assessments of your profits. But the choice is yours.

Totaling Sales

The first step in determining your profits is to look at how much lemonade you've sold for the day (or for any other accounting period you use). If you've decided to measure profits daily, you need to keep track of your daily sales also. Thinking back over the first day, you recall that you sold eight glasses of lemonade—seven to the dwarves that live next door in Mrs. White's house and an eighth glass to little Billy Samuelson. The dwarves each paid you with a quarter, which is the price of a glass. Unfortunately, Billy was broke, so you let him sign an IOU for a quarter. What are your sales for the day? Figure 1.1 shows the total sales (8 × $.25 = $2.00).

Fig. 1.1

The first day's lemonade sales.

The First Day's Lemonade Sales	
The Seven Dwarves	$1.75
Billy Samuelson	$0.25
Total Sales	$2.00

You need to bear in mind two important points about this whole problem of measuring sales. First, if you use a longer accounting period—such as a month or a year—you need to maintain a list of your sales as you go along. Even in the lemonade stand business, getting to the end of the month and accurately remembering how many glasses of lemonade you sold would be difficult. Accountants and bookkeepers call such a list a *sales journal*. You can call it whatever you want. In any case, you need one.

Second, the cash you collect in an accounting period doesn't necessarily equal the sales for that accounting period. On the first day, for example, sales were greater than cash collected because Billy didn't have the quarter to pay for the lemonade. If Billy pays his IOU tomorrow, and you don't sell any lemonade for IOUs, the sales will be less than the cash collected. Keeping track of customer IOUs is easy if you issue only a few and customers quickly pay their IOUs. More often, however, you'll have many IOUs from many customers. You need to track closely these IOUs, called *accounts receivable*, so that you know which customers owe you, how much they owe, and what they're paying when they give you cash. Just as you keep track of sales in a list or journal, you also probably need to monitor your accounts receivable.

(***Note:*** Some accounting systems follow a cash basis of accounting, in which sales and expenses are measured only when cash is received or paid out. DacEasy, however, follows the accrual basis of accounting, in which sales are measured not only in cash but also in amounts owed to you, and expenses can be paid in cash or charged.)

Totaling Expenses

The second step in measuring your lemonade stand profits is to total your expenses. Suppose that you purchased from the corner grocery six lemons at $.30 apiece for a total of $1.80 and a one-pound box of sugar for $1.00. You also bought a large pitcher for $3.00. If you add up the cash spent for the day, the situation looks bleak, as figure 1.2 shows.

The First Day's Costs	
Lemons	$1.80
Sugar	$1.00
Pitcher	$3.00
Total Costs	$5.80

Fig. 1.2

The first day's costs.

Although you generated $2.00 in sales for the day, you spent $5.80 for supplies and equipment. "At this rate," you think, "I'm going backward—and fast." But what you spent doesn't necessarily equal your true expenses. Suppose that you use half a lemon for each glass of lemonade. Because you sold eight glasses of lemonade, you used only four lemons, which means the cost of lemons used amounts to 4 times $.30, or $1.20. In addition, you used only a tablespoon of sugar in each glass of lemonade, so you used only about 1/10 of your sugar, or $.10. Accountants and bookkeepers call costs such as the lemons and the sugar *costs of goods sold*.

The other cost is the $3.00 pitcher. "Wait a minute," you think. "This pitcher will last for the whole summer, which means approximately 12 weeks, or if I work 5 days a week, about 60 days." If you allocate the cost of the pitcher for each day, the result is a mere $.05 a day ($3.00 divided by 60 days). Accountants and bookkeepers call this allocation *depreciation*. The concept is simple: something you can use for several accounting periods shouldn't be an expense of just one period but of each period in which you can use the expenditure. Based on this accounting then, your income statement for the first day looks like the one shown in figure 1.3.

Fig. 1.3

The first day's income statement.

The First Day's Income Statement	
Lemonade Sales	$2.00
Expenses	
Lemons	($1.20)
Sugar	($0.10)
Pitcher	($0.05)
Profit	$0.65

In a nutshell, you've just learned how to measure the profit for a period. Here's a summary of the rules of thumb you need to remember when you apply the measurement tools to a lemonade stand—or to a billion-dollar business. First, you have to select the period of time for which you want to measure profits. Second, you need to keep track of total sales for the period, including both cash and credit sales. Third, you need to measure your expenses for the accounting period, which can be tricky. Some of the things you bought during the first accounting period aren't expenses of the current accounting period but of a future period. (In the case of the lemonade stand business, the lemons and sugar you still held as inventory at the end of the day fall into this category.) Additionally, the costs of certain items are costs for more than one accounting period, so you need to allocate, or depreciate, them over the number of periods used.

Measuring Your Assets and Liabilities with a Balance Sheet

The second traditional tool you use to monitor the financial health of your business is a *balance sheet*. A balance sheet lists the assets you own and liabilities you owe at a point in time. (The difference between assets and liabilities is called owner's equity.) Notice that a balance sheet is thus quite different from an income statement. An income statement is a summary of what has happened to your sales and expenses *over* a period of time. A balance sheet provides a snapshot of your business *at* a specific point in time.

The first decision is to pick a point in time at which you want to measure the assets and liabilities. Usually, the point in time for which you construct a balance sheet is the end of an accounting period. In the lemonade stand example, because you measure profits daily, you might want to construct a balance sheet at the end of each day.

Totaling Assets

Creating a balance sheet is a two-step process. The first step is to list your *assets*. Suppose that at the end of the first day you have the assets shown in figure 1.4.

Lemonade Stand Assets	
Currency and Change	$5.95
IOU from Billy Samuelson	$0.25
Lemons Remaining (worth $0.30 Each	$0.60
Sugar Remaining (9/10 of a box)	$0.90
Pitcher (59 days @ $0.05/day)	$2.95
Total Assets	$10.65

Fig. 1.4

Lemonade stand assets.

Although listing the assets for your lemonade stand is rather straightforward, you apply the same rules in larger businesses. List the cash you're holding, any accounts receivable, any items you're holding for resale to customers (usually called inventory), and the undepreciated portions of any costs you're allocating over several time periods (usually called fixed assets).

Totaling Liabilities and Owner's Equity

The second step is to list your *liabilities* and *equities*. Determining these items is a little tougher than listing assets. Liabilities and equities include essentially three items: those amounts that people have lent you (liability), those amounts you've invested in the business (owner's equity), and any profit you have left in the business (owner's equity). Suppose that in the lemonade stand business, you originally invested the $5.00 you'd accumulated in pennies in a large bowl on your dresser. Imagine also that your mother lent you $5.00—money that you have to pay back by the end of the summer. You also know that you made $.65 in profit on the first day of the lemonade stand's operation (sales of $2.00 less expenses of $1.35), which you decide to leave in the business. (The amount of profit you leave in the business is called *retained earnings*.) Accordingly, your liabilities and equities are as shown in figure 1.5.

Fig. 1.5

Lemonade stand liabilities and owner's equity.

Lemonade Stand Liabilities & Owners Equity	
Loan from Mother	$5.00
My Original Investment	$5.00
Profits Left in Business	$0.65
Total Liabilities & Owners Equity	$10.65

Notice that the total liabilities and equities equal the total assets. Is this a coincidence? Not if you've accurately listed your assets, liabilities, and equities. The liabilities/equities list identifies the sources of the money you've used for your assets. The assets list identifies the things in which you've invested the money you received from lenders, investors, and profits.

Constructing a Standard Balance Sheet

You might construct a balance sheet this way for your own use, but business owners usually restate the balance sheet to follow a standard format, as shown in figure 1.6.

In general, accountants and bookkeepers apply several conventions to the format and layout of a balance sheet. First, assets and liabilities are each segregated into two categories: current and noncurrent. *Current assets* for most businesses include cash, accounts receivable, and inventory. Other examples of current assets are listed in DacEasy's sample Chart of Accounts, which is shown in Chapter 3. In general, a current asset is an asset that will be converted to cash

Lemonade Stand Balance Sheet
at the end of the first day

Assets		
Current Assets		
Cash	$5.95	
Accounts Receivable	0.25	
Lemon & Sugar Inventory	1.50	
Total Current Assets		$7.70
Noncurrent Assets		
Original Cost – Pitcher	3.00	
Less: Accumulated Depreciation	0.05	
Total Noncurrent Assets		2.95
Total Assets		$10.65
Liabilities and Owner's Equity		
Current Liabilities		
Loan from Mother	$5.00	
Total Current Liabilities		$5.00
Owner's Equity		
Contributed Capital	5.00	
Retained Earnings	0.65	
Total Owner's Equity		5.65
Total Liabilities and Owner's Equity		$10.65

Fig. 1.6

Lemonade stand balance sheet at the end of the first day.

or expense within the next year. For example, the lemons held as inventory will be converted to expense, and the receivable from little Billy will be converted to cash.

Noncurrent assets include all your other assets, including long-term investments and your fixed assets, such as equipment, fixtures, and real estate. In the lemonade stand example, the pitcher was considered a noncurrent asset. (In your "real" business, a $3.00 item, even if it lasts for several periods, probably isn't significant enough that you need to depreciate it to get an accurate picture of profits.)

The lemonade stand example shows only one current liability—the $5.00 loan from your mother. In general, though, a *current liability* is any debt you will pay within one year of the balance sheet date, including such items as money owed suppliers (accounts payable), money owed the government for taxes (taxes payable), and money owed employees for wages (wages payable). Again, DacEasy's sample Chart of Accounts lists other current liabilities.

Noncurrent liabilities include the remaining liabilities, which logically are those you will pay some time after the next year. Typically, noncurrent liabilities are bank loans or other loans that might extend for one or more years.

For a large business, the standard format usually presents the information in a highly summarized, easy-to-understand way. With the lemonade stand business, however, using the standard balance sheet format may only confuse the reader. A review of the formats that other businesses use may be interesting and helpful, particularly if you're preparing income statements and balance sheets for the first time. Publicly held corporations (those that sell stock to the public) usually distribute annual reports that include balance sheets and income statements. Public libraries often have copies of the annual reports for many of the larger public corporations.

Finally, recognize that as your business becomes more and more complex, you need to learn more about balance sheets and income statements. Complexity doesn't just equate to transaction volume. The lemonade stand might be selling thousands of glasses of lemonade each day and still not require accounting that's any more complex than the example given here. Basically, the numbers just get bigger. But some small businesses have complicated financial transactions and ownership structures. For example, you may transact business in multiple currencies or use exotic financing alternatives like financing leases and different kinds of owner's equity.

Understanding Double-Entry Bookkeeping

Do you need to understand double-entry bookkeeping to use DacEasy? Yes, you do. For several hundred years, people have used double-entry bookkeeping to record the financial information needed to construct a balance sheet and profit-and-loss statement. But don't despair if you don't already know this method of bookkeeping. The next few paragraphs provide an overview of its mechanics and logic, which should be enough to get you started if your business's financial affairs aren't too complicated. (If your finances *are* extremely complex, you need more information than I can provide in a chapter. Refer to an introductory college accounting text, such as a recent edition of *Fundamentals of Financial Accounting*, written by Glenn A. Welsch and Robert N. Anthony and published by Richard D. Irwin, Inc.)

Double-entry bookkeeping reflects the fact that when you enter into any financial transaction, you're either moving dollars around on your balance sheet or doing something that simultaneously affects both your balance sheet and your income statement. For example, if you pay an employee wages, you affect the balance sheet because you decrease cash, and you affect the income statement because of the wages expense. If you sell a glass of lemonade, you increase either cash or accounts receivable and increase sales. If you collect a receivable, you decrease accounts receivable and increase cash. If you pay a bill you owe, you decrease accounts payable and decrease cash.

Recognizing Debits and Credits

Double-entry bookkeeping is simply a formal approach for recognizing that for any financial transaction, two things are happening. One of the things is called a *debit*, and the other a *credit*. This terminology is probably familiar to you. You may have heard accountants and bookkeepers talk about debits and credits, and your bank has probably mentioned crediting your account. In each of these cases, people are referring to a transaction recorded by double-entry bookkeeping. Basically, debits and credits refer to whether an asset or equity, or a revenue or an expense, is increasing or decreasing as a result of a transaction. Figure 1.7 shows what accountants mean by debits and credits. Notice that for assets and expenses a debit indicates an increase, and a credit is a decrease. The opposite is true for equities and revenue: a debit signals a decrease, and a credit is an increase.

What Debits and Credits Mean:	Debit	Credit
Balance Sheet Items		
Assets	Increase	Decrease
Liabilities and Owner's Equity	Decrease	Increase
Income Statement Items		
Revenues	Decrease	Increase
Expenses	Increase	Decrease

Fig. 1.7

The meaning of debits and credits.

No magic is involved with this debit and credit business. It's just a way of describing whether you increase or decrease an asset, an equity, a revenue, or an expense. But notice a little trick: the meanings of debits and credits are flip-flopped for assets and equities and for revenues and expenses, so when you correctly reflect the economics of a transaction, the total debits *always* equal the total credits.

Keeping the Books for the Sample Business

To demonstrate this trick, the following examples show the debits and credits for transactions you may have recorded as you started and operated the lemonade stand business. The outline and description of the debits and credits of a transaction is called a *journal entry* because traditionally the debits and credits were first listed in a journal. (You always enter debits on the left side of an account and credits on the right side.)

1. You invested $5.00 from your savings. Accordingly, you increase (debit) cash for $5.00 and increase (credit) contributed capital for $5.00.

	Debit	Credit
Cash	$5.00	
Contributed Capital		$5.00

2. Next, you borrowed $5.00 from your mother because you felt you needed extra money on your trip to the grocery store for supplies and equipment. Accordingly, you again increase (debit) cash for $5.00 and increase (credit) a liability labeled "Loan from Mother" for $5.00.

	Debit	Credit
Cash	$5.00	
Loan from Mother		$5.00

3. Your next step was to trot down to the grocery store and spend $1.80 on lemons, $1.00 on sugar, and $3.00 on a pitcher. You need to record these three purchases. First, you increase (debit) your lemon inventory for $1.80 and decrease (credit) cash for the purchase of the six lemons. Second, you increase (debit) your sugar inventory for $1.00 and decrease (credit) cash for the purchase of the box of sugar. Third, you increase (debit) a new asset labeled "Pitcher" for $3.00 and decrease (credit) cash for that amount.

	Debit	Credit
Lemon Inventory	$1.80	
Cash		$1.80
Sugar Inventory	$1.00	
Cash		$1.00

Pitcher	$3.00	
Cash		$3.00

4. Suppose that the next transaction was the sale of the seven glasses of lemonade to the dwarves who live next door. To record the sale, you increase (debit) cash for $1.75 and increase (credit) revenue for $1.75.

	Debit	*Credit*
Cash	$1.75	
Sales		$1.75

5. Next, you sold a glass of lemonade to little Billy Samuelson. You remember Billy. Because he didn't have a quarter, you let him give you an IOU rather than cash. For this sale, you increase (debit) accounts receivable for $0.25 and increase (credit) revenue for $0.25.

	Debit	*Credit*
Accounts Receivable	$0.25	
Sales		$0.25

6. You also need to recognize that you used 4 lemons from your lemon inventory, 1/10 of the box of sugar, and 1/60 of the cost of the pitcher. Therefore, you decrease (credit) the lemon inventory for $1.20 and increase (debit) the costs of lemons sold for $1.20. Similarly, you decrease (credit) the sugar inventory for $0.10 and increase (debit) the costs of sugar sold for $0.10. Finally, you pull a little piece of the pitcher's cost into the daily expense by depreciating 1/60 of the $3.00 purchase price (because you'll use the pitcher for 60 days this summer). To depreciate the pitcher, you increase (debit) the pitcher depreciation expense for $0.05 and decrease (credit) the accumulated depreciation for the pitcher for $0.05.

	Debit	*Credit*
Lemon Inventory		$1.20
Costs of Goods Sold—Lemons	$1.20	
Sugar Inventory		$0.10
Costs of Goods Sold—Sugar	$0.10	
Pitcher Depreciation Expense	$0.05	
Accumulated Depreciation—Pitcher		$0.05

You'll notice two handy features of this double-entry bookkeeping. First, in a transaction that's correctly recorded, the debits equal the credits. The totals act as a double check on your logic and arithmetic. Second, if you begin with your beginning balances for assets, equities, revenues, and expenses, and add all the increases and subtract all the decreases (debits and credits), you're left with the correct ending totals for each of your assets, equities, revenues, and expenses.

Figure 1.8 shows a list of the debits and credits you've accumulated. Such a list of accounts and their balances is called a *trial balance*. You can use the trial balance to create both a balance sheet and an income statement. Notice that by using the revenue and expense totals, you can easily prepare the income statement shown in figure 1.3, and that by using the asset, creditor's equity, and owner's equity totals, you have everything you need (except the profits remaining in the business, or retained earnings) to prepare the balance sheet shown in figure 1.6.

Fig. 1.8

The lemonade stand trial balance used to prepare the balance sheet and income statement.

Lemonade Stand Trial Balance	Debits	Credits
Assets		
Cash	$5.95	
Accounts Receivable	0.25	
Lemon Inventory	0.60	
Sugar Inventory	0.90	
Pitcher	3.00	
Accumulated Depreciation – Pitcher		0.05
Liabilities		
Loan from Mother		5.00
Owner's Equity		5.00
Retained Earnings		0.00
Revenue		
Sales		2.00
Expenses		
Cost of Lemons Sold	1.20	
Cost of Sugar Sold	0.10	
Pitcher Depreciation	0.05	
Total Debits and Credits	$12.05	$12.05

Once you've prepared the income statement for the accounting period and determined the income or loss for that period, you need to *close the books*. In this process, you reduce to zero, or close out, the revenue and expense accounts. To close out a revenue account, you debit the revenue account an amount equal to its current credit balance. To close out an expense account, you credit the expense account an amount equal to its current debit balance. The debit or credit needed to zero out the balance (net income) is recorded as an adjustment to the retained earnings account. Here's the appropriate journal entry:

	Debit	*Credit*
Sales	$2.00	
Costs of Goods Sold—Lemons		$1.20
Costs of Goods Sold—Sugar		$0.10
Pitcher Depreciation Expense		$0.05
Retained Earnings		$0.65

Figure 1.9 shows what the trial balance looks like after you make this closing entry. With the revenue and expense accounts zeroed out, and the difference recorded as an adjustment to retained earnings, you're ready to begin recording the revenues and expenses for the next accounting period.

Lemonade Stand Trial Balance	Debits	Credits
Assets		
Cash	$5.95	
Accounts Receivable	0.25	
Lemon Inventory	0.60	
Sugar Inventory	0.90	
Pitcher	3.00	
Accumulated Depreciation – Pitcher		0.05
Liabilities		
Loan from Mother		5.00
Owner's Equity		5.00
Retained Earnings		0.65
Revenue		
Sales		0.00
Expenses		
Cost of Lemons Sold	0.00	
Cost of Sugar Sold	0.00	
Pitcher Depreciation	0.00	
Total Debits and Credits	$10.70	$10.70

Fig. 1.9

The lemonade stand trial balance after revenue and expenses are zeroed out.

Double-entry bookkeeping is that simple. The main thing to remember is that you must always record the complete effect of a transaction on the balance sheet or record the dual effect of a transaction that impacts both the balance sheet and the income statement. Reviewing a few more example lemonade stand transactions may help to cement the double-entry mechanics a little more firmly in your mind.

First, you usually have some expenses that you don't pay with cash but with an IOU to the person providing the good or service. Suppose that in the lemonade stand example, you incur a rent expense of $0.20 for using your neighbor's yard as the lemonade stand location. The neighbor, however, recognizing the cash-flow problems inherent in starting any new business, kindly agrees to allow you to pay the rent later in the summer. You need to increase (debit) rent expense for $0.20 and increase (credit) accounts payable.

	Debit	Credit
Rent Expense	$0.20	
Accounts Payable		$0.20

To later record payment of the rent you owe your neighbor, you decrease (credit) cash for $0.20 and decrease (debit) accounts payable.

	Debit	Credit
Cash		$0.20
Accounts Payable	$0.20	

When you collect the IOU from Billy Samuelson, you need to increase (debit) cash for $0.25 and decrease (credit) accounts receivable for $0.25.

	Debit	Credit
Cash	$0.25	
Accounts Receivable		$0.25

How DacEasy Helps

If you use DacEasy in your lemonade stand business, the program provides a complete set of accounting tools to help you keep track of each of the transactions described in the preceding paragraphs and prepare both a balance sheet and an income statement. You can use all six modules: Purchase Order, Accounts Payable, Billing, Accounts Receivable, Inventory, and General Ledger. Also available is a set of periodic routines that support the six modules.

The following sections describe the types of benefits provided by each module and provide examples of how you can apply the modules to the lemonade stand operations.

Examining DacEasy's Modules

The *Purchase Order* module generates formal purchase orders and purchase returns as you order items from and return items to your suppliers. *Purchase orders* are forms you generate and then sign to tell a vendor that you agree to purchase items at a certain price. Purchase orders are, quite literally, contracts for the purchase of goods and services. *Purchase returns* are forms that describe items you previously purchased but are now returning to the vendor because you no longer want them, you are overstocked, or the items are defective in some way. As part of the return procedure, you print a purchase return to tell the vendor exactly what you're returning, how many, how much credit you expect, and why you're requesting the return. The Purchase Order module also provides a set of reports that enhance your ability to record and monitor purchasing activity.

The *Accounts Payable* module simply collects information about amounts you owe vendors, summarizes that information so that you can profitably use it, and automatically generates checks to pay the amounts you owe. This module provides detailed reports of all the accounts payable transactions and produces special summary reports, such as "agings." An aging shows the amounts you owe separated into groups based on the dates the payments are due. For example, an aging may show those debts you should have paid last month (current), those you must pay this month (in 0 to 30 days), and those you will pay next month (in 31 to 60 days).

You use the *Billing* module to record sales of products or services. The Billing module updates inventory and customer files, generates customer invoices, and collects the customer invoice information that the Accounts Receivable module requires. The Billing module also generates sales returns (you may call these customer credit memos) and journals, or lists, of Billing module transactions. With this module, you can keep up to three years of sales history information.

The *Accounts Receivable* module tracks the amounts that customers owe you, produces monthly customer statements, and records customer payments. Special reports, such as the accounts receivable agings, allow you to watch customer credit and collections closely. An accounts receivable aging shows the amounts customers owe you separated into groups based on when payment is expected (for example, 0 to 30 days, 31 to 60 days, 61 to 90 days, and over 91 days).

The *Inventory* module provides all the tools you need to maintain a perpetual inventory system. With this type of system, you know at all times the quantity of each item you have on hand, what the item cost, and whether you've ordered additional stock. Even if your business doesn't involve the sale of goods, you can benefit by the Inventory module because it collects and summarizes information about the services you sell.

The *General Ledger* module is the information depot that automatically collects all the transaction information from each of the modules and combines this data with other special transactions that weren't recorded in one of the other modules. (Because each of the other modules is summarized into a single account balance on the general ledger, the other modules are called subsidiary modules.) These special transactions include such things as asset depreciation, borrowing from a lender, and additional investments in the business by owners. From this information, the General Ledger module prepares your financial statements: a balance sheet and an income statement.

DacEasy also provides a set of *periodic routines*, or utilities, that support the six modules. The periodic routines clean up your accounting files at the end of an accounting period by resetting counters of that period's activity, make the end-of-period closing entry, and can forecast the activities and results of future accounting periods.

Applying the Modules to the Sample Business

The Billing module allows you to prepare customer invoices, or bills, which show the customers how much they owe for their glasses of lemonade. With a lemonade stand, you might not need invoices for cash-paying customers like the dwarves. You probably want invoices for customers like Billy Samuelson, however, so that they have a piece of paper that shows for what and why they owe you. The Billing module can also prepare a list of the sales you made, or a *sales journal*, and send a list of customer IOUs to the Accounts Receivable module. You can then use the Accounts Receivable module to maintain the list of customer IOUs and to record payments from customers when the payments are received.

The Purchase Order module and the Accounts Payable module recognize that when you purchase items like the lemons, the sugar, and the pitcher, you increase either assets or expenses, and that when you ultimately pay amounts owed your vendors and suppliers, cash decreases.

The Inventory module collects information from the Billing and Purchase Order modules and uses this data to keep track of exactly how many lemons and how much sugar you hold as inventory.

You can use the General Ledger module to record the journal entries that aren't recorded as part of a purchase or sale, such as the depreciation of the pitcher, your initial contribution of capital, and that loan from your mother. You can use the general ledger also to print automatically a trial balance, an income statement, and a balance sheet.

Finally, you can use the periodic routines to clean up your accounting files. These routines make the entry that zeros out the revenue and expense totals at the end of an accounting period and puts the difference between revenues and expenses into the retained earnings account.

Chapter Summary

By using a lemonade stand as an example of a simple small business, this chapter explained how to create and why you use the profit-and-loss statement and the balance sheet. You also learned the mechanics and logic of double-entry bookkeeping and discovered how DacEasy can simplify your accounting and bookkeeping tasks. In the next chapter, you learn how to get started with DacEasy.

2

Getting Started
with DacEasy

Implementing a new computer-based accounting system presents a unique set of challenges and opportunities, particularly if you used manual accounting systems in the past. Unfortunately, using a new system often turns into a major headache for the people attempting to shut down an old manual system and simultaneously start up a new automated system. But the transition doesn't have to be that way. By applying some of the tactics others have learned through trial and error, you can ease considerably the installation of any computer-based accounting system, including DacEasy. This chapter covers the following topics:

- Ordering any preprinted forms you'll need
- Learning to use the system
- Picking the conversion date
- Installing the software
- Operating the software

Readying Your Business
for DacEasy

Getting your business ready for DacEasy requires that you order any preprinted forms you'll need, train the people who will use the new system, and pick the conversion date. By spending a few minutes to review this section of *Using*

DacEasy, you can save yourself from the traditional errors that new users of computer-based accounting packages make in implementing and installing new systems. Common mistakes include such things as forgetting to order a business form that is needed immediately in order to do business, failing to verify that the new system will perform necessary tasks, and beginning to use a new system in the middle of an accounting period.

Ordering Preprinted Forms

Many of the modules allow or require you to order preprinted business forms. (Nearly all automated accounting systems require such forms.) Table 2.1 summarizes the forms required or recommended for each of DacEasy's modules and indicates whether having the form simply makes things easier or is truly a requirement.

Table 2.1
Preprinted Forms Recommended or Required for Modules

Module	*Preprinted Forms Required/Recommended*
Purchase Order	Purchase order forms are recommended, but you may use blank paper.
Accounts Payable	Preprinted, continuous-form checks are required for automated check writing.
Billing	Preprinted forms are recommended for economy and professional appearance, but you may use blank paper or continuous-form letterhead.
Accounts Receivable	Customer statement forms are recommended if you send monthly customer statements.
Inventory	This module uses no forms.
General Ledger	This module uses no forms.

You can order the preprinted, continuous-feed, multipart forms you need from a local commercial printer. But you probably should order your forms from Dac Software, Inc. The prices are reasonable, and Dac Software will include your company name and address—and a logo, too, if you have one—on the forms. One of the other nice features of using Dac Software's preprinted forms is that you're assured that the forms are fully compatible with DacEasy.

Dac Software, Inc., also provides Quick Forms, which are generic business forms that don't include your company name or address and are thus less expensive. (You can find examples of Quick Forms in the DacEasy package.)

Learning To Use the System

You need to devote some resources toward training either yourself or the people who will use the system. Don't expect to be able to spend a few minutes with the system and be off and running. Just as you enjoy greater benefits from using a computer-based accounting system, such as DacEasy, as compared to spreadsheets and word processing packages, you must exert greater efforts to learn the system and begin tapping into those benefits.

To use any accounting package, including DacEasy, you need to focus on two separate steps. First, you must learn the accounting and bookkeeping conventions on which the software designers have relied. Although DacEasy employs standard accounting and bookkeeping practices—and that's exactly what you want from the program—you may have had your own special techniques. Or you may not have paid much attention to your accounting and bookkeeping. Your first step amounts simply to reconciling the way DacEasy will keep your books with the way you keep your books now.

Second, you need to learn how to use DacEasy as a bookkeeping tool—how to get it to do the things you need it to do. This step is easy because accounting with DacEasy is easy. But nonetheless, you still need to spend time learning both how DacEasy does its work (for example, with double-entry bookkeeping) and how you can use the program to do your work. You can approach the learning process in several ways.

Read the user's manual and this book—or at least the chapters that apply to those modules you think you'll use. Understanding both the underlying accounting and the software's operation is essential if you are to enjoy all the benefits that DacEasy provides. Reading this book and the DacEasy user's manual should give you a sturdy foundation.

Talk to other DacEasy users in your locality. Formal and informal user groups provide excellent support networks. The users are often working through the same problems that you're encountering and, hopefully, enjoying the same benefits that you're seeking. The store that sold you DacEasy, the consultant who helped you install DacEasy, or the C.P.A. who prepares your annual financial statements or tax return may be able to direct you to other DacEasy users.

Spend some time just playing with the software. Try different transactions and transaction volume levels, explore the menus and screens, and pore over the reports. Far from being wasteful or superfluous, this activity (called a user test) produces important benefits. Experimenting increases your confidence in the system, gives you experience in working with live business data, and, most important, allows you to confirm that a module can accomplish the tasks for which you need it.

Successfully implementing an automated accounting and financial management system delivers tremendous benefits. Once you have your new DacEasy system installed and operating, you'll wonder how you ever ran your business without it.

Picking the Conversion Date

Picking the conversion date—the day on which you plan to stop using your old manual system and begin using your new DacEasy system—is another critical decision you must make before you can enjoy the many advantages of an automated accounting system. You need to weigh carefully the time involved in several preliminary steps, including selecting the modules you need, ordering and receiving the preprinted forms, learning to use the system, and preparing all the modules for operation.

Accounting period cutoffs usually represent the other major business issue that affects the timing of the conversion date. To begin using a new accounting system, you must be able to summarize the existing data. You therefore need a trial balance to show the dollar amounts of each asset, liability, owner's equity, revenue, and expense account. (A trial balance is a list of all the accounts and their current balances. For more information, refer to Chapter 1.) You must record the beginning (or opening) balance of each account either when you set up your accounts or with an opening entry in the general ledger (see Chapter 3).

If you're lucky enough to be installing DacEasy as you're starting your business, that's great. Because no previous financial activities are involved, you don't need to worry about letting the system know where you stand. In other words, every amount in your trial balance is 0.

Usually, the best time to begin using a new computer-based accounting system is at the beginning of the accounting year, called a fiscal year, when the revenue and expense amounts are equal to 0. The next best time is at the beginning of an accounting period. For example, if you prepare balance sheets and income statements monthly, you can begin a new system at the beginning of a month.

If you don't use an accounting period with a clean cutoff, you risk counting the same sale twice or the same expense twice—errors that destroy the accuracy and reliability of your accounting records. Additionally, and just as destructive, you may neglect to record a transaction because you think you've recorded it in the other system.

You may encounter these same problems of double or missing entries if you don't stop using the old system on the conversion date. You probably don't want to maintain two accounting systems anyway, because doing so is a surefire method of getting overworked and then deciding not to use the system that's more difficult—inevitably the new system you're trying to learn.

Installing the Software

To use DacEasy, you must meet the following minimum hardware requirements:

- IBM® personal computer or compatible
- 256K of memory (or 384K if used with DacEasy Mate)
- Two floppy disk drives or a single floppy disk drive and a hard disk
- MS-DOS® or PC DOS Version 2.0 or later
- 80-column printer capable of printing 132 columns in compressed mode
- Color or monochrome monitor

The steps for installing the DacEasy system vary, depending on whether your computer uses only floppy disks or has both a floppy and a hard disk drive.

C.P.A. Tip: Before you continue, estimate the number of customers you invoice, the number of invoices you create daily, the number of vendors from whom you purchase, the number of products you sell, and the number of services offered. You need to supply this information during installation, and you can save time if you gather the information now rather than stop to do so during the installation.

Installing DacEasy on a Hard Disk System

To install DacEasy on a hard disk system,

1. Turn on your computer and monitor. Make sure that your system has the correct date and time set. (Type *DATE* at the C› prompt.)

2. Place Disk No. 1 from the DacEasy system in drive A. Type *A:* and press Enter. At the A› prompt, type *INSTALL* and press Enter.

3. Follow the on-screen instructions and place Disk No. 2 in drive A. The program reads that disk and then tells you when to return Disk No. 1 to drive A.

4. The introductory install screen appears and asks whether you're installing DacEasy on a floppy disk system or a hard disk system (see fig. 2.1). (Notice that the screen says you can cancel the install program at any time by pressing Esc.) Press *H* to tell DacEasy that you want to install on a hard disk.

```
┌──────────────────────────────────────────────────────────┐
│                  DAC-EASY INSTALLATION                     │
├──────────────────────────────────────────────────────────┤
│                                                            │
│                                                            │
│             WELCOME TO DAC-EASY ACCOUNTING!                │
│                                                            │
│   This routine is used to install Dac-Easy onto your hard  │
│   disk or to create working copies of your program files   │
│   if you are using a dual-floppy system. This process will │
│   also configure your hardware to take full advantage of   │
│   Dac-Easy's features.                                     │
│                                                            │
│   If you are installing Dac-Easy for a floppy drive system,│
│   you will need two blank formatted diskettes (in addition │
│   to the disks found in your Dac-Easy Accounting Package). │
│   Label these disks PROGRAM-1 and PROGRAM-2. If you do     │
│   not have these disks ready, press ESC to exit this       │
│   routine. Use the FORMAT command to prepare the blank     │
│   disks (see your DOS manual for more information          │
│   on FORMAT).                                              │
│                                                            │
│                                                            │
│     Is Dac-Easy to be installed on a Floppy or Hard Disk   │
│     (F/H)?                                                 │
│                                                            │
└──────────────────────────────────────────────────────────┘
```

Fig. 2.1

The initial DacEasy installation screen.

5. DacEasy informs you that it may need to modify your DOS CONFIG.SYS file so that the file contains statements setting the number of files open at 20 and the number of buffers at 16 (see fig. 2.2). The program must reset these statements because it runs with many files open and performs many reads from the hard disk. (For more information on the FILES and BUFFERS settings, see your DOS manual.) To continue, press Enter.

6. Now the system is ready to copy the DacEasy program files to a directory on your hard disk. The default drive and directory specification is C:\DEA3 (see fig. 2.3). If for some reason you don't want the DacEasy directory named DEA3, you can specify another hard disk directory, such as DAC, by editing the path name shown on the screen. To edit the path, first check the cursor's position. If the cursor rests on the C:, simply type over the default directory and

```
╔══════════════════════════════════════════════════════════════╗
║                   DAC-EASY INSTALLATION                        ║
╠══════════════════════════════════════════════════════════════╣
║ For maximum performance, Dac-Easy requires that the following two statements
║ exist in the CONFIG.SYS file of the boot (DOS) disk:
║
║   FILES=20
║   BUFFERS=16
║
║ If the CONFIG.SYS file does not exist, it will be created at this time.  If
║ CONFIG.SYS exists but these statements are either not found or do not have
║ the minimum settings, the file will be modified accordingly (no other
║ statements will be changed).
║
╚══════════════════════════════════════════════════════════════╝
```

Press ←┘ to continue, ESC to exit.

Fig. 2.2

Setting the FILES and BUFFERS statements.

press Enter. If the cursor rests at the end of the default directory, use the Backspace key to erase the existing path name, type the path name you want to use, and press Enter.

```
╔══════════════════════════════════════════════════════════════╗
║                   DAC-EASY INSTALLATION                        ║
╠══════════════════════════════════════════════════════════════╣
║ The Dac-Easy Program files will now be copied to your hard disk.  Specify
║ the path name for the directory where you would like the program files
║ stored.  If the path name does not exist, the system will create it for you.
║
║ Enter path name: C:\DEA3
║
╚══════════════════════════════════════════════════════════════╝
```

Fig. 2.3

Specifying the DacEasy program directory.

If the directory does not exist, the install program asks whether you want to create the directory. Press *Y* for yes. The install program then copies the contents of the install disk (Disk No. 1) to the specified directory of your hard disk.

7. When the screen prompts you, remove Disk No. 1 from drive A and insert Disk No. 2, which the program then copies to the specified hard disk directory. The install program then displays a message saying that the installation is complete (see fig. 2.4). You should remove the disk from drive A and reboot your system.

```
        The installation process has been successfully completed.
        Remove the disk from the drive A: and re-boot your system.

                  Thank you for using Dac-Easy Accounting.




A:\>
```

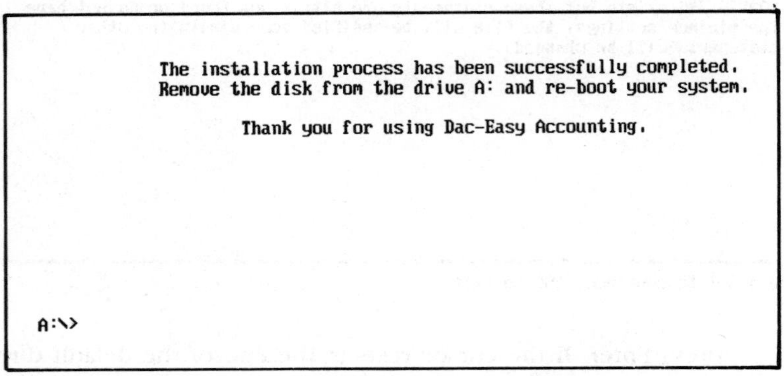

Fig. 2.4
The "installation complete" message.

You're not quite finished with the installation procedure. Now you must define the files that you will use.

8. Type *C:* to return to the C› prompt. Next type *CD DEA3* to change from the current directory to the directory where you've stored DacEasy. (If you used a directory name other than DEA3, substitute that name in the CD command.) To start DacEasy, type *DEA3* at the C› prompt. The first time you start DacEasy after you've installed it, the program prompts you to indicate whether you have a color monitor. After this initial screen, the copyright screen appears. When the copyright screen shown in figure 2.5 appears, press any key to continue. From now on, you start DacEasy this way (by changing to the DacEasy directory and typing *DEA3* at the C› prompt).

9. You need to tell DacEasy where to store your data files, or accounting information. The program supplies the default directory name FILES (see fig. 2.6). If for some reason you don't want the directory for your data files named FILES, you can specify another hard disk directory by editing the path name shown on the screen. To edit the default directory name, simply type over it.

10. DacEasy then displays a new screen that asks a series of questions relating to the amount of space needed on your hard disk to store your accounting information. As shown in figure 2.7, DacEasy first asks whether you want to use the sample Chart of Accounts. Press *Y* for

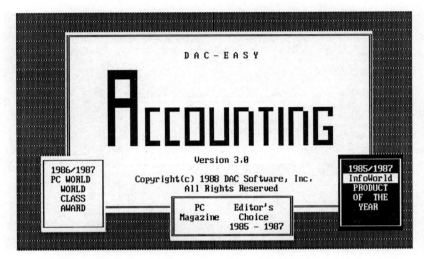

Fig. 2.5

*The DacEasy
copyright screen.*

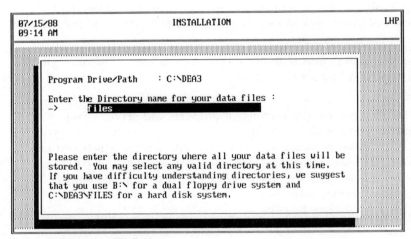

Fig. 2.6

*Specifying the
DacEasy data files
directory for a
hard disk system.*

yes, and press Enter. (Chapter 3 explains the Chart of Accounts, why
you need it, and how to modify it.) The next screen prompts you to
put Disk No. 1 in drive A so that the program can retrieve the sample
Chart of Accounts. Do so and press Enter.

Note: The next steps involve providing information about your business. You
probably should add 20 percent to each of your estimates to allow for error
and growth.

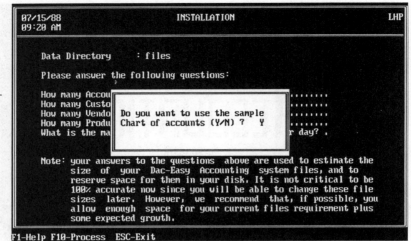

Fig. 2.7

Choosing whether to use the DacEasy sample Chart of Accounts.

11. Tell DacEasy the number of customers you have. Customers, for purposes of this question, include those to whom you send invoices and customer statements.

12. The next question asks how many vendors you have. Vendors include those to whom you send purchase orders and computer-produced checks.

13. Indicate the approximate number of products and services you offer. DacEasy's definition of products includes those items for which you need to maintain perpetual inventory records and for which you may produce purchase orders. Services include those items for which you want to maintain detailed financial histories that show amounts of each kind of service sold.

14. Tell DacEasy the maximum number of invoices you plan to create each day.

    Figure 2.8 shows a completed file sizes screen. (By the way, don't worry if you exceed the file sizes specified. Chapter 3 describes a special option, Rehash, that allows you to increase the specified file sizes.)

15. DacEasy estimates the total hard disk space required, verifies that the required hard disk space exists, and asks whether the program can start creating files. Answer *Y* for yes. If you select file sizes that require more disk space than is available, DacEasy alerts you that insufficient space exists and then restarts you at the point at which you specified the name of the data files subdirectory (step 9).

```
07/15/88                    INSTALLATION                         LHP
09:52 AM


    Data Directory      : files

    Please answer the following questions:

    How many Accounts in your chart of Accounts? ............. 275
    How many Customers do you have? ........................... 50
    How many Vendors do you have? ............................. 50
    How many Products and/or Services do you have? ........... 25
    What is the maximum number of Invoices you have per day? . 2


    Note: your answers to the questions  above are used to estimate the
          size  of  your  Dac-Easy  Accounting  system files, and to
          reserve space for them in your disk. It is not critical to be
          100% accurate now since you will be able to change these file
          sizes later.  However, we recommend  that, if possible, you
          allow  enough  space  for your current files requirement plus
          some expected growth.

F1-Help F10-Process  ESC-Exit
```

Fig. 2.8

A completed file sizes screen.

16. DacEasy next prompts you to complete the company name table—the place where you define the name, address, and telephone and facsimile numbers of the company for which you're going to use DacEasy. The first line of the company name table appears on every screen in the DacEasy system. All four lines appear on the reports and on most of the other printed output generated by the system.

Type on each line the appropriate information, press F2 to center the information on the line, and then press Enter to continue to the next line. You can use any of the keyboard keys that produce a character: upper- and lowercase letters, numbers, and symbols. If you make a typing mistake, use the Backspace key or the Del key to remove the error. When you're finished typing and centering the last line, verify that the information is correct and as you want it to appear on screens and printouts. Then press Enter or F10 to save and begin using your company identification. Figure 2.9 shows the company name table for a company called Acme Marbles Company.

Don't worry if later you want to change some part of the company name table. You can easily modify the table without going through the entire installation process. Simply follow the steps outlined in Chapter 3 for setting the company identification.

At this point, you've finally completed the installation, and the DacEasy main menu appears (see fig. 2.10). Whenever you start DacEasy in subsequent sessions, you briefly see the copyright notice screen and then this menu.

You're now ready to define the Chart of Accounts and set the system options (see Chapter 3).

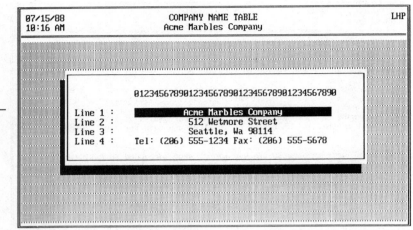

Fig. 2.9

*The company
name table.*

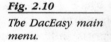

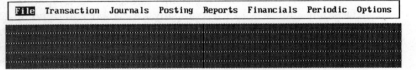

Fig. 2.10

*The DacEasy main
menu.*

Installing DacEasy on a Floppy Disk System

To install DacEasy on a floppy disk system,

1. Turn on your computer and monitor. Leaving your DOS disk in drive A, make sure that your system has the correct date and time set. (Type *DATE* at the A› prompt.) Then format three blank floppy disks. (Refer to the information in your DOS manual on the FORMAT command if you're unsure of how to format.) Label the three disks *Program Disk 1*, *Program Disk 2*, and *Data Disk*.

2. Place Disk No. 1 from the DacEasy system in drive A. At the A› prompt, type *INSTALL* and press Enter.

3. Follow the on-screen instructions and place Disk No. 2 in drive A. The program reads that disk and then tells you when to return Disk No. 1 to drive A.

4. The introductory install screen appears and asks whether you're installing DacEasy on a floppy disk system or a hard disk system (see fig. 2.11). Press *F* for floppy disk.

```
╔══════════════════════════════════════════════════════════════════╗
║                      DAC-EASY INSTALLATION                        ║
╠══════════════════════════════════════════════════════════════════╣
║                                                                  ║
║                                                                  ║
║                  WELCOME TO DAC-EASY ACCOUNTING!                  ║
║                                                                  ║
║  This routine is used to install Dac-Easy onto your hard disk or to create ║
║  working copies of your program files if you are using a dual-floppy system. ║
║  This process will also configure your hardware to take full advantage of ║
║  Dac-Easy's features.                                            ║
║                                                                  ║
║  If you are installing Dac-Easy for a floppy drive system, you will need two ║
║  blank formatted diskettes (in addition to the disks found in your Dac-Easy ║
║  Accounting Package).  Label these disks PROGRAM-1 and PROGRAM-2.  If you do ║
║  not have these disks ready, press ESC to exit this routine.  Use the FORMAT ║
║  command to prepare the blank disks (see your DOS manual for more information ║
║  on FORMAT).                                                     ║
║                                                                  ║
║                                                                  ║
║      Is Dac-Easy to be installed on a Floppy or Hard Disk (F/H)? ║
║                                                                  ║
╚══════════════════════════════════════════════════════════════════╝
```

Fig. 2.11

The initial DacEasy installation screen.

5. DacEasy informs you that it may need to modify your DOS CONFIG.SYS file so that the file contains statements setting the number of files open at 20 and the number of buffers at 16 (see fig. 2.12). The program must reset these statements because it runs with many files open and performs many reads from the disk. (For more information on the FILES and BUFFERS settings, see your DOS manual.) To continue, press Enter. If the CONFIG.SYS file does need to be modified, the install program directs you to insert the DOS disk in drive A and press Enter.

6. The program then tells you that it will make copies of your program disks so that you can use the copies to operate the accounting system (see fig. 2.13). Follow the instructions on the screen to replace your DOS disk in drive A with the DacEasy Disk No. 1, and put the blank formatted disk labeled Program Disk 1 in drive B. Press Enter to make a working copy of Disk No. 1. Follow the instructions on the screen to place the DacEasy Disk No. 2 in drive A and the blank, formatted disk labeled Program Disk 2 in drive B. Press Enter to make a working copy of Disk No. 2. After you've made copies of the original DacEasy disks, put the originals in a safe place. Restart your computer with your DOS disk in drive A.

```
                    DAC-EASY INSTALLATION

 For maximum performance, Dac-Easy requires that the following two statements
 exist in the CONFIG.SYS file of the boot (DOS) disk:

     FILES=20
     BUFFERS=16

 If the CONFIG.SYS file does not exist, it will be created at this time.  If
 CONFIG.SYS exists but these statements are either not found or do not have
 the minimum settings, the file will be modified accordingly (no other
 statements will be changed).
```

Fig. 2.12

*Setting the FILES
and BUFFERS
statements.*

Press <┘ to continue, ESC to exit.

```
                    DAC-EASY INSTALLATION

 Dac-Easy will now make working copies of your program disks.  These copies
 should be used for the day-to-day operation of the program.  Once this
 process is completed, the original program disks should be put away in a
 safe place.

 Place Dac-Easy Disk-1 in drive A:

 Place the blank, formatted disk labeled "Program-1" in drive B:
```

Fig. 2.13

*Beginning to
make working
copies of your
program disks.*

Press <┘ to continue, ESC to exit.

7. To complete the installation and start the DacEasy software for the
   first time, put Program Disk 1 in drive A and the disk labeled *Data
   Disk* in drive B. Then type *DEA3* at the A› prompt. The program
   prompts you to insert Disk No. 2 in drive A, and then tells you to
   replace Disk No. 2 with Disk No. 1. Then the copyright screen
   appears (see fig. 2.14).

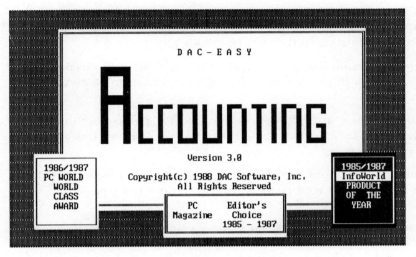

Fig. 2.14

The DacEasy copyright screen.

8. You need to tell DacEasy where to store your accounting information (see fig. 2.15). The default selection is for a dual floppy system is drive B.

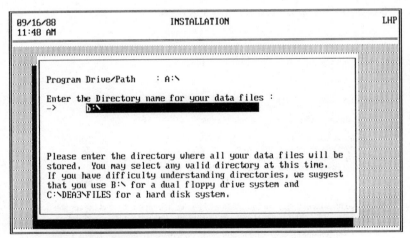

Fig. 2.15

Specifying the DacEasy data files directory for a floppy disk system.

9. DacEasy displays a new screen that asks a series of questions which you need to answer so that the program can set aside enough space to store your accounting information. The program first asks whether you want to use the sample Chart of Accounts. Answer *Y* for yes and

press Enter. (Chapter 3 explains the Chart of Accounts, why you need it, and how to modify it.) The program then copies the Chart of Accounts information to the Data Disk in drive B.

Note: The next steps involve providing information about your business. You probably should add 20 percent to each of your estimates to allow for error and growth.

10. Tell DacEasy how many customers you have. For purposes of this question, customers include those to whom you send invoices and customer statements.

11. The next question asks how many vendors you have. Vendors include those to whom you send purchase orders and computer-produced checks.

12. Indicate how many products and services you have. Products include those items for which you need to maintain perpetual inventory records and for which you may produce frequent purchase orders. Services include those items for which you want to maintain detailed financial histories that show amounts of each kind of service sold.

13. Tell DacEasy the maximum number of invoices you plan to create each day.

Figure 2.16 shows a completed file sizes screen.

Fig. 2.16

A completed file sizes screen.

```
09/16/88                        INSTALLATION                          LHP
11:49 AM


   Data Directory      : b:

   Please answer the following questions:

   How many Accounts in your chart of Accounts? ............. 275
   How many Customers do you have? .......................... 25
   How many Vendors do you have? ............................ 25
   How many Products and/or Services do you have? ........... 5
   What is the maximum number of Invoices you have per day? . 5


   Note: your answers to the questions  above are used to estimate the
         size  of  your  Dac-Easy  Accounting  system files, and to
         reserve space for them in your disk. It is not critical to be
         100% accurate now since you will be able to change these file
         sizes  later.  However,  we  recommend  that, if possible, you
         allow  enough  space  for your current files requirement plus
         some expected growth.
```

F1-Help F10-Process ESC-Exit

14. DacEasy estimates the total disk space required, verifies that the required space exists, and asks whether the program can start creating files. Answer *Y* for yes. If you select file sizes that require more disk space than is available, DacEasy alerts you that insufficient space exists and then restarts you at the point at which you specified the data files drive (step 8).

15. DacEasy next prompts you to complete the company name table—the place where you define the name, address, and telephone and facsimile numbers of the firms for which you'll be using DacEasy. The first line of the company name table appears on every screen in the DacEasy system. All four lines appear on the reports and on most of the other printed output generated by the system.

    On each line, type the appropriate information, press F2 to center the information on the line, and press Enter to continue to the next line. You can use any of the keyboard keys that produce a character: upper- and lowercase letters, numbers, and symbols. If you make a typing mistake, use the Backspace key or the Del key to remove the error. When you're finished typing and centering the last line, verify that the information is correct and as you want it to appear on screens and printouts. Then press Enter or F10 to save and begin using your company identification. Figure 2.17 shows the company name table for the Acme Marbles Company.

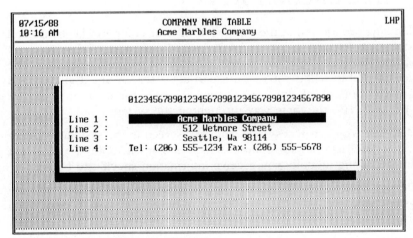

Fig. 2.17

The company name table.

Don't worry if later you want to change some part of the company name table. You can easily modify the company name table without going through the entire installation process. Simply follow the steps outlined in Chapter 3 for setting the company identification.

At this point, you've finally completed the installation, and the DacEasy main menu appears (see fig. 2.18). From now on, whenever you start DacEasy, you briefly see the copyright notice screen and then this menu.

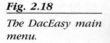

Fig. 2.18

The DacEasy main menu.

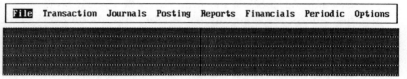

Operating the Software

The following general operating rules apply to the entire DacEasy system. Basically, you need to understand three rough categories of operations: using function keys, selecting menu options, and editing data on the screen.

Using the Function Keys

The function keys are located at the top or left of your computer keyboard and are labeled F1, F2, F3, and so on. Software manufacturers use these function keys to provide shortcuts—quicker, simplified ways of program operation. The function keys available while you're on a particular screen are displayed and described at the bottom of the screen. DacEasy uses three of the function keys—F1, F4, and F10—the same way throughout the system.

F1 is the Help key. You can access help from any screen in the system by pressing F1. Within DacEasy, help is context-sensitive. For example, if you select help within the Billing module, you receive information specific to billing.

F4 is the Change Date key. Although you should always begin DacEasy with the correct system date set, you can use F4 to override the system date once you've started DacEasy.

F10 is the Save Data key. You can save information you've just entered or changes you've just made by pressing F10.

The operations of the remaining function keys are specific to whatever module you're using. To learn about these special function keys, refer to the chapters that describe each of DacEasy's modules.

Selecting Menu Options

DacEasy provides two alternatives for selecting menu options. The first method is to type either the first letter or the number of the option you want to execute or access. For example, from the main menu (see fig. 2.18) you can type an *F* to access the File menu. From the File menu (see fig. 2.19) you might type the number *2* to choose the Customers option. If an option is preceded by a number, you cannot access that option by typing the first letter. You must either type the option's number or use the cursor-movement keys to highlight the option.

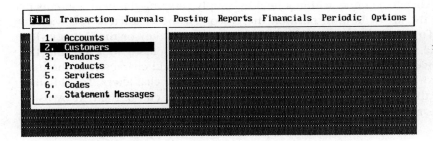

Fig. 2.19

The File menu.

A second method for selecting menu options is to use the cursor-movement keys to highlight the appropriate menu selection. For example, if you press the left- and right-arrow keys, the highlight moves across the main menu options. Once a menu option is highlighted, press Enter to access that option's items. You can then move the highlight down the list of options by pressing the down-arrow key. When the option you want is highlighted, press Enter.

To exit any screen and return to the preceding, higher level of the menu, press Esc.

Editing Data on the Screen

Editing data on a screen involves both moving between fields and editing within a field. You can move from one field to the next by pressing Enter. You can move to the next field also by pressing the down-arrow key and to the preceding field by pressing the up-arrow key. Simultaneously pressing the Ctrl and Home keys (Ctrl-Home) moves you to the first field on a screen; pressing Ctrl-End moves you to the last field on a screen.

Within a field, you simply type the appropriate characters. Whether DacEasy lets you enter only numeric or both alphabetic and numeric data depends on the module you're using (see the chapters that correspond to the modules). In general, however, you type dollar amounts as numeric data by using the number keys on your keyboard. If an amount represents a negative number, you precede the number with a hyphen, as in -2.47. If you don't enter the cents, the system assumes that the number is an even dollar amount.

Most of the remaining data stored in the system (data other than dollar amounts) can be either alphabetic, numeric, or both. In cases where alphabetic characters are allowed, you can generally use both upper- and lowercase characters. Exceptions to these general rules are noted in the chapters describing the modules where an exception arises.

You can change an entry within a field by simply retyping the field contents or by using the arrow keys to position the cursor on the characters you want to change. To delete characters, use either the Backspace key or the Del key. The Backspace key removes the character preceding the cursor location; the Del key removes the character at the cursor location. To add characters in the middle of text, press the Ins key and then type the needed characters. To add characters to the end of the text, position the cursor at the end of the text by using the right-arrow key and then simply type the necessary characters.

Chapter Summary

This chapter described both the steps for readying your business for a new computer-based accounting system and the procedures for installing the software on your computer. Getting your business ready includes selecting the modules you want to use, ordering any preprinted forms, learning to use the system, and picking an appropriate conversion date. In this chapter, you also learned some basics of DacEasy operations, such as how to use the function keys, choose menu options, and edit data on the screen. Chapter 3 explains the next steps in using DacEasy: defining the Chart of Accounts and setting the system options.

CHAPTER 3

Defining the Chart of Accounts and System Options

This chapter describes why you need to and how to define the Chart of Accounts and how to set the system options and defaults. You need to complete both tasks so that you can begin loading the master files. That procedure is described in Chapter 4.

Defining the Chart of Accounts

The Chart of Accounts simply lists the classifications you use to keep track of your assets, liabilities, owner's equities, revenues, and expenses. Your Chart of Accounts represents the most important building block of your DacEasy accounting system. No matter which modules you've decided to use, you need to set up some kind of a Chart of Accounts. Even the lemonade stand example in Chapter 1 used a simple Chart of Accounts, which comprised the various line items shown on both the income statement and the balance sheet.

Choosing Detail and General Accounts

Essentially, you want to consider two accounting issues when constructing your own Chart of Accounts. The first issue is the level of detail at which you want to accumulate financial data. Every classification that you want to be able to debit and credit, and therefore derive an individual balance for, needs to have its own account. If you want to see how much you're spending on electricity, for example, you need an electricity expense account. DacEasy calls these *detail accounts*. They are the only accounts that the program allows you to debit and credit.

A second accounting issue involves deciding what subtotals and totals you want to show on your balance sheet and income statement. DacEasy calls these *general accounts*. Every line on your balance sheet and income statement on which you want to show dollar amounts needs an account number in the Chart of Accounts.

These two requirements mean that you must list in your Chart of Accounts both the accounts to which you'll make your debits and credits and the accounts you want to subtotal and total on your financial statements. For example, if you want to construct the income statement shown in figure 3.1, your Chart of Accounts must include the accounts listed in figure 3.2.

Fig. 3.1

Sample income statement for Acme Marbles Company.

Sample Income Statement for Acme Marbles Company			
REVENUE			
Cats eye revenue		$12,500	
Bumble bee revenue		$12,500	
Cleary revenue		$12,500	
Yellow swirls revenue		$12,500	
Total Revenue			$50,000
EXPENSES			
Cost of Marbles Sold			
Cats eye marbles cost	$5,000		
Bumble bee marbles cost	$5,000		
Cleary marbles cost	$5,000		
Yellow swirls marbles cost	$5,000		
Total Cost of Marbles Sold		$20,000	
Operating Expenses			
General Expenses			
Supplies Expense	$4,000		
Rent Expense	$1,000		
Total General Expenses		$5,000	
Sales Expenses			
Travel Expenses	$8,000		
Commissions	$7,000		
Total Sales Expenses		$15,000	
Total Operating Expenses		$20,000	
Total Expenses			$40,000
PROFIT			$10,000

First determine your general accounts (those you want to contain totals and subtotals). Then add the detail accounts below the general level to achieve a satisfactory degree of detail for your business and tax records.

```
┌─────────────────────────────────────────────────┐
│ Accounts Required for Income Statement           │
├─────────────────────────────────────────────────┤
│              Cats eye revenue                    │
│              Bumble bee revenue                  │
│              Cleary revenue                      │
│              Yellow swirls revenue               │
│              Total Revenue                       │
│              Cats eye marbles cost               │
│              Bumble bee marbles cost             │
│              Cleary marbles cost                 │
│              Yellow swirls marbles cost          │
│              Total Cost of Marbles Sold          │
│              Supplies Expense                    │
│              Rent Expense                        │
│              Total General Expenses              │
│              Travel Expenses                     │
│              Commissions                         │
│              Total Sales Expenses                │
│              Total Operating Expenses            │
│              Total Expenses                      │
│              PROFIT                              │
└─────────────────────────────────────────────────┘
```

Fig. 3.2

The accounts required for the sample income statement.

In addition to deciding at what level of detail you want to keep your books, you probably should consider the classifications by which you report profits and losses to the Internal Revenue Service, the classifications you use for budgeting or cost control, and any special classifications you need in order to show reports to lenders or investors.

For example, if you're a sole proprietor, your Chart of Accounts should reflect the same level of detail as the IRS schedule C, which is the form sole proprietors use to report their profits and losses to the federal government. Your accounting system should provide the information you need for your tax returns. Otherwise, you may have to construct manually an income statement to report your taxable profits.

The installation instructions in Chapter 2 directed you to use DacEasy's sample Chart of Accounts because it provides a useful starting point for your own Chart of Accounts. Examine the sample Chart of Accounts, which is shown in figure 3.3, and identify those detail and general accounts that give you the level of detail you need for reporting to the IRS, controlling your costs, and reporting appropriate details and summaries on your financial statements. You'll probably find yourself primarily crossing off unnecessary accounts, but you may need to add an account or two. If you don't want to use this Chart of Accounts, reinstall the software and select not to use the sample Chart of Accounts.

```
                        Acme Marbles Company              Page no. 1
                          512 Wetmore Street
                          Seattle, Wa  98114
                 Tel: (206) 555-1234 Fax: (206) 555-6789

                        CHART OF ACCOUNTS

                                      Acct.
         Acct. #  Account Name        Type  Level  Type     General
         -------  -----------------   ----- -----  -------  --------
         1        Assets              ASSET   1    GENERAL
         11         Current Assets    ASSET   2    GENERAL  1
         1101         Petty Cash      ASSET   3    DETAIL   11
         1102         Cash In Banks   ASSET   3    GENERAL  11
         11021          Checking Account    ASSET  4  DETAIL  1102
         11022          Payroll Account     ASSET  4  DETAIL  1102
         11023          Savings Account     ASSET  4  DETAIL  1102
         1103         Cash Register Fund    ASSET  3  GENERAL 11
         11031          Cash Register # 1   ASSET  4  DETAIL  1103
         11032          Cash Register # 2   ASSET  4  DETAIL  1103
         1104         Mktable Securities    ASSET  3  GENERAL 11
         11041          Cert. of Deposit    ASSET  4  DETAIL  1104
         11042          US Gover. Securities ASSET 4  DETAIL  1104
         11043          Other Securities    ASSET  4  DETAIL  1104
         1105         Accounts Receivable   ASSET  3  GENERAL 11
         11051          Accts Rec'ble Module ASSET 4  DETAIL  1105
         11052          Allow Doubtful Accts ASSET 4  DETAIL  1105
         1106         Other Receivable      ASSET  3  GENERAL 11
         11061          Affiliated Company  ASSET  4  DETAIL  1106
         11062          Employee Loans      ASSET  4  DETAIL  1106
         11063          Officers Loans      ASSET  4  DETAIL  1106
         11064          Other Receivable    ASSET  4  DETAIL  1106
         1107         Inventory             ASSET  3  GENERAL 11
         11071          Inventory - Module  ASSET  4  DETAIL  1107
         11072          Allow Damage/Obsol. ASSET  4  DETAIL  1107
         12         Fixed Assets      ASSET   2    GENERAL  1
         1201         Autos & Trucks Net    ASSET  3  GENERAL 12
         12011          Original Value      ASSET  4  DETAIL  1201
         12012          Accum. Depreciation ASSET  4  DETAIL  1201
         1202         Furniture & Fixt.Net  ASSET  3  GENERAL 12
         12021          Original Value      ASSET  4  DETAIL  1202
         12022          Accum. Depreciation ASSET  4  DETAIL  1202
         1203         Office Equipment Net  ASSET  3  GENERAL 12
         12031          Original Value      ASSET  4  DETAIL  1203
         12032          Accum. Depreciation ASSET  4  DETAIL  1203
         1204         Machinery & Eq. Net   ASSET  3  GENERAL 12
         12041          Original Value      ASSET  4  DETAIL  1204
         12042          Accum. Depreciation ASSET  4  DETAIL  1204
         1205         Building Net          ASSET  3  GENERAL 12
         12051          Original Value      ASSET  4  DETAIL  1205
         12052          Accum. Depreciation ASSET  4  DETAIL  1205
         1206         Other Fixed Assets    ASSET  3  GENERAL 12
         12061          Original Value      ASSET  4  DETAIL  1206
         12062          Accum. Depreciation ASSET  4  DETAIL  1206
         1207         Land-Original Value   ASSET  3  DETAIL  12
         13         Deferred Assets   ASSET   2    GENERAL  1
         1301         Organization Expense  ASSET  3  GENERAL 13
         13011          Original Value      ASSET  4  DETAIL  1301
         13012          Accum. Amortization ASSET  4  DETAIL  1301
         1302         Leasehold Improv.Net  ASSET  3  GENERAL 13
         13021          Original Value      ASSET  4  DETAIL  1302
```

Fig. 3.3

DacEasy's sample Chart of Accounts.

```
Date : 10/20/88              Acme Marbles Company              Page no. 2
Time : 01:42 PM              512 Wetmore Street
                             Seattle, Wa  98114
                   Tel: (206) 555-1234 Fax: (206) 555-6789

                             CHART OF ACCOUNTS
```

Acct. #	Account Name	Acct. Type	Level	Type	General
13022	Accum. Amortization	ASSET	4	DETAIL	1302
1303	Prepaid Expenses	ASSET	3	GENERAL	13
13031	Insurance	ASSET	4	DETAIL	1303
13032	Rent	ASSET	4	DETAIL	1303
13033	Interest	ASSET	4	DETAIL	1303
13034	Taxes	ASSET	4	DETAIL	1303
14	Other Assets	ASSET	2	GENERAL	1
1401	Deposits	ASSET	3	GENERAL	14
14011	Rent	ASSET	4	DETAIL	1401
14012	Leases	ASSET	4	DETAIL	1401
14013	Utilities	ASSET	4	DETAIL	1401
14014	Security	ASSET	4	DETAIL	1401
1402	Long Term Investment	ASSET	3	GENERAL	14
14021	Cert. of Deposit	ASSET	4	DETAIL	1402
14022	Other Long Term Inv.	ASSET	4	DETAIL	1402
2	Liabilities	LIAB.	1	GENERAL	
21	Short Term Liability	LIAB.	2	GENERAL	2
2101	Accts Payable-Module	LIAB.	3	DETAIL	21
2102	Notes Payable	LIAB.	3	DETAIL	21
2103	Accrued Payable	LIAB.	3	DETAIL	21
2104	Taxes Payable	LIAB.	3	GENERAL	21
21041	Payroll Taxes	LIAB.	4	GENERAL	2104
210411	Federal Income W/H	LIAB.	5	DETAIL	21041
210412	Fica W/H Employee	LIAB.	5	DETAIL	21041
210413	Fica W/H Employer	LIAB.	5	DETAIL	21041
210414	Futa	LIAB.	5	DETAIL	21041
210415	Suta	LIAB.	5	DETAIL	21041
210416	State Income W/H	LIAB.	5	DETAIL	21041
210417	City Income W/H	LIAB.	5	DETAIL	21041
210418	Disability Insurance	LIAB.	5	DETAIL	21041
21042	Sales Tax Payable	LIAB.	4	DETAIL	2104
21043	Property Tax	LIAB.	4	DETAIL	2104
21044	Franchise Tax	LIAB.	4	DETAIL	2104
21045	Foreign Tax	LIAB.	4	DETAIL	2104
21046	Income Tax Payable	LIAB.	4	GENERAL	2104
210461	Federal Income Tax	LIAB.	5	DETAIL	21046
210462	State Income Tax	LIAB.	5	DETAIL	21046
210463	City Income Tax	LIAB.	5	DETAIL	21046
21047	Other Tax Payable	LIAB.	4	DETAIL	2104
2105	Other Pyroll Payable	LIAB.	3	GENERAL	21
21051	Union Dues	LIAB.	4	DETAIL	2105
21052	Employee Charity	LIAB.	4	DETAIL	2105
21053	X'mas Fund Accrued	LIAB.	4	DETAIL	2105
2106	Dividends Payable	LIAB.	3	DETAIL	21
2107	Other Payable	LIAB.	3	DETAIL	21
22	Long Term Liability	LIAB.	2	GENERAL	2
2201	Mortgages Payable	LIAB.	3	DETAIL	22
2202	Notes Payable	LIAB.	3	DETAIL	22
2203	Current L/Term Liab.	LIAB.	3	DETAIL	22
2204	Other Long Term Liab	LIAB.	3	DETAIL	22
23	Deferred Liability	LIAB.	2	GENERAL	2

CHART OF ACCOUNTS

Acct. #	Account Name	Acct. Type	Level	Type	General
2301	Commit & Contingency	LIAB.	3	DETAIL	23
2302	Deferred Income	LIAB.	3	DETAIL	23
2303	Profit/Instalm.Sales	LIAB.	3	DETAIL	23
2304	Unearned Interest	LIAB.	3	DETAIL	23
3	Stockholders Equity	CAP.	1	GENERAL	
31	Capital Stock	CAP.	2	GENERAL	3
3101	Common Stock	CAP.	3	GENERAL	31
31011	Par Value	CAP.	4	DETAIL	3101
31012	Surplus	CAP.	4	DETAIL	3101
3102	Preferred Stock	CAP.	3	GENERAL	31
31021	Par Value	CAP.	4	DETAIL	3102
31022	Surplus	CAP.	4	DETAIL	3102
3103	Treasury Stock	CAP.	3	DETAIL	31
32	Retained Earnings	CAP.	2	GENERAL	3
3283	1983 Profit/(Loss)	CAP.	3	DETAIL	32
3284	1984 Profit/(Loss)	CAP.	3	DETAIL	32
3285	1985 Profit/(Loss)	CAP.	3	DETAIL	32
3286	1986 Profit/(Loss)	CAP.	3	DETAIL	32
3287	1987 Profit/(Loss)	CAP.	3	DETAIL	32
33	Current Earnings	CAP.	2	DETAIL	3
4	Revenues	REV.	1	GENERAL	
41	Sales	REV.	2	GENERAL	4
4101	Sales Dept. 01	REV.	3	DETAIL	41
4102	Sales Dept. 02	REV.	3	DETAIL	41
42	Sales Returns	REV.	2	GENERAL	4
4201	Returns Dept. 01	REV.	3	DETAIL	42
4202	Returns Dept. 02	REV.	3	DETAIL	42
43	Shipping	REV.	2	GENERAL	4
4301	Freight	REV.	3	DETAIL	43
4302	Insurance	REV.	3	DETAIL	43
4303	Packaging	REV.	3	DETAIL	43
4304	Surcharge	REV.	3	DETAIL	43
44	Financial Income	REV.	2	GENERAL	4
4401	Ints. Investments	REV.	3	DETAIL	44
4402	Finance Charges	REV.	3	DETAIL	44
4403	Dividends	REV.	3	DETAIL	44
4404	Purchase Discounts	REV.	3	DETAIL	44
45	Other Revenues	REV.	2	GENERAL	4
4501	Recovery Bad Debt	REV.	3	DETAIL	45
4502	Gain in Sale/Assets	REV.	3	DETAIL	45
4503	Miscellaneous	REV.	3	DETAIL	45
5	Total Expenses	EXP.	1	GENERAL	
51	Cost of Goods Sold	EXP.	2	GENERAL	5
5101	COGS Dept. 01	EXP.	3	DETAIL	51
5102	COGS Dept. 02	EXP.	3	DETAIL	51
52	Gen & Admin Expenses	EXP.	2	GENERAL	5
5201	Payroll	EXP.	3	GENERAL	52
52011	Wages	EXP.	4	GENERAL	5201
520111	Salaries	EXP.	5	DETAIL	52011
520112	Hourly	EXP.	5	DETAIL	52011
520113	Commisions	EXP.	5	DETAIL	52011

Fig. 3.3—Continued

```
Date : 10/20/88              Acme Marbles Company              Page no. 4
Time : 01:42 PM              512 Wetmore Street
                            Seattle, Wa  98114
                    Tel: (206) 555-1234 Fax: (206) 555-6789

                            CHART OF ACCOUNTS
```

Acct. #	Account Name	Acct. Type	Level	Type	General
520114	Overtime	EXP.	5	DETAIL	52011
520115	Compensations	EXP.	5	DETAIL	52011
520116	Bonuses	EXP.	5	DETAIL	52011
520117	Other Wages	EXP.	5	DETAIL	52011
520118	Contract Labor	EXP.	5	DETAIL	52011
52012	Benefits	EXP.	4	GENERAL	5201
520121	Health Insurance	EXP.	5	DETAIL	52012
520123	Dental Insurance	EXP.	5	DETAIL	52012
520124	401(k) Plan	EXP.	5	DETAIL	52012
520125	Other Benefits	EXP.	5	DETAIL	52012
52013	Taxes	EXP.	4	GENERAL	5201
520131	Fica Employer	EXP.	5	DETAIL	52013
520132	Futa	EXP.	5	DETAIL	52013
520133	Suta	EXP.	5	DETAIL	52013
520134	Disability Insurance	EXP.	5	DETAIL	52013
520135	Other Payroll Taxes	EXP.	5	DETAIL	52013
5202	Maintenance	EXP.	3	GENERAL	52
52021	Autos & Trucks	EXP.	4	DETAIL	5202
52022	Furniture & Fixtures	EXP.	4	DETAIL	5202
52023	Office Equipment	EXP.	4	DETAIL	5202
52024	Machinery & Equip.	EXP.	4	DETAIL	5202
52025	Building	EXP.	4	DETAIL	5202
52026	Other Assets	EXP.	4	DETAIL	5202
5203	Depreciation	EXP.	3	GENERAL	52
52031	Autos & Trucks	EXP.	4	DETAIL	5203
52032	Furniture & Fixtures	EXP.	4	DETAIL	5203
52033	Office Equipment	EXP.	4	DETAIL	5203
52034	Machinery & Equip.	EXP.	4	DETAIL	5203
52035	Building	EXP.	4	DETAIL	5203
52036	Other Assets	EXP.	4	DETAIL	5203
5204	Amortization	EXP.	3	GENERAL	52
52041	Organization Expense	EXP.	4	DETAIL	5204
52042	Leasehold Improv.	EXP.	4	DETAIL	5204
5205	Rents and Leases	EXP.	3	GENERAL	52
52051	Autos & Trucks	EXP.	4	DETAIL	5205
52052	Furniture & Fixtures	EXP.	4	DETAIL	5205
52053	Office Equipment	EXP.	4	DETAIL	5205
52054	Machinery & Equip.	EXP.	4	DETAIL	5205
52055	Building	EXP.	4	DETAIL	5205
52056	Other Leases or Rent	EXP.	4	DETAIL	5205
5206	Assets Insurance	EXP.	3	GENERAL	52
52061	Autos & Trucks	EXP.	4	DETAIL	5206
52062	Furniture & Fixtures	EXP.	4	DETAIL	5206
52063	Office Equipment	EXP.	4	DETAIL	5206
52064	Machinery & Equip.	EXP.	4	DETAIL	5206
52065	Building	EXP.	4	DETAIL	5206
52066	Other Assets Insur.	EXP.	4	DETAIL	5206
5207	Travel & Entertain	EXP.	3	GENERAL	52
52071	Lodging	EXP.	4	DETAIL	5207
52072	Transportation	EXP.	4	DETAIL	5207
52073	Meals	EXP.	4	DETAIL	5207

```
Date : 10/20/88           Acme Marbles Company                Page no. 5
Time : 01:42 PM           512 Wetmore Street
                          Seattle, Wa  98114
              Tel: (206) 555-1234 Fax: (206) 555-6789

                          CHART OF ACCOUNTS

                              Acct.
Acct. # Account Name         Type   Level  Type    General
------- -------------------- -----  -----  ------- --------
52074        Entertainment        EXP.    4    DETAIL    5207
52075        Other Travel Expense EXP.    4    DETAIL    5207
5208     Shipping             EXP.    3    GENERAL   52
52081        Freight              EXP.    4    DETAIL    5208
52082        Insurance            EXP.    4    DETAIL    5208
52083        Packaging            EXP.    4    DETAIL    5208
52084        Duties               EXP.    4    DETAIL    5208
52085        Other Shipping Exp.  EXP.    4    DETAIL    5208
5209     Taxes (other)        EXP.    3    GENERAL   52
52091        Sales Tax/Purchases  EXP.    4    DETAIL    5209
52092        Property Tax         EXP.    4    DETAIL    5209
52093        Franchise Tax        EXP.    4    DETAIL    5209
52094        Other Taxes          EXP.    4    DETAIL    5209
5210     Consulting Fees      EXP.    3    GENERAL   52
52101        Accountants          EXP.    4    DETAIL    5210
52102        Legal                EXP.    4    DETAIL    5210
52103        Other                EXP.    4    DETAIL    5210
5211     Office Supplies      EXP.    3    DETAIL    52
5212     Telephone & Telegrph EXP.    3    DETAIL    52
5213     Mail/Postage         EXP.    3    DETAIL    52
5214     Utilities            EXP.    3    DETAIL    52
5215     Alarms               EXP.    3    DETAIL    52
5216     Contribution/Donat.  EXP.    3    DETAIL    52
5217     Licenses/Permits     EXP.    3    DETAIL    52
5218     Memships/Dues/Subscr EXP.    3    DETAIL    52
5219     Advertising          EXP.    3    GENERAL   52
52191        Broadcast Advert.    EXP.    4    DETAIL    5219
52192        Print Advertising    EXP.    4    DETAIL    5219
5220     Promotion            EXP.    3    GENERAL   52
52201        Catalogues           EXP.    4    DETAIL    5220
52202        Brochures            EXP.    4    DETAIL    5220
52203        Other Promotions     EXP.    4    DETAIL    5220
5221     Public Relations     EXP.    3    DETAIL    52
5222     Marketing Research   EXP.    3    DETAIL    52
5223     Bad Debt Loss        EXP.    3    DETAIL    52
5224     Inventory Losses     EXP.    3    DETAIL    52
5299     Other Expenses       EXP.    3    DETAIL    52
53       Financial Expenses   EXP.    2    GENERAL   5
5301     Credit Card Discount EXP.    3    DETAIL    53
5302     Interest             EXP.    3    DETAIL    53
5303     Bank Charges         EXP.    3    DETAIL    53
5304     Sales Discounts      EXP.    3    DETAIL    53
5305     Agents Commisions    EXP.    3    DETAIL    53
5399     Other Financial Exp. EXP.    3    DETAIL    53
54       Other Expenses       EXP.    2    GENERAL   5
5401     Cash Short           EXP.    3    DETAIL    54
5402     Loss on Sale/Assets  EXP.    3    DETAIL    54
5403     Miscellaneous Losses EXP.    3    DETAIL    54
55       Income Tax           EXP.    2    GENERAL   5
5501     Federal Income Tax   EXP.    3    DETAIL    55
5502     State Income Tax     EXP.    3    DETAIL    55
```

Fig. 3.3—Continued

```
Date : 10/20/88              Acme Marbles Company              Page no. 6
Time : 01:42 PM               512 Wetmore Street
                              Seattle, Wa  98114
                   Tel: (206) 555-1234 Fax: (206) 555-6789
                          CHART OF ACCOUNTS

                                       Acct.
 Acct. # Account Name                  Type   Level  Type    General
 ------- -----------------------------  -----  -----  -------  --------
 5503           City Income Tax         EXP.     3    DETAIL   55
 D          Journal Difference          OTHER    1    DETAIL

           Number of Accounts printed 257
```

Entering a New Account

If you've just completed the installation procedure described in Chapter 2, your screen displays DacEasy's main menu (see fig. 3.4). If you're at some lower level of the program—because you selected a menu option, for instance—you can return to the main menu by pressing Esc, which backs you through each menu level.

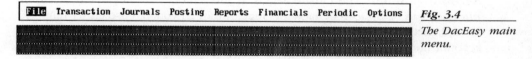

Fig. 3.4

The DacEasy main menu.

From the main menu, select File. Then select the first option, Accounts, to call up the Accounts File Maintenance screen (see fig. 3.5). On this screen, you can enter, edit, and delete Chart of Accounts information. Figure 3.6 shows the empty Accounts File Maintenance screen ready for your use.

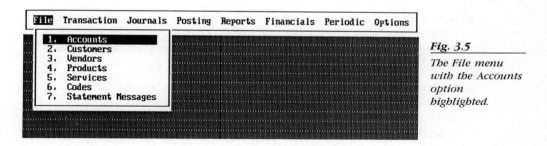

Fig. 3.5

The File menu with the Accounts option highlighted.

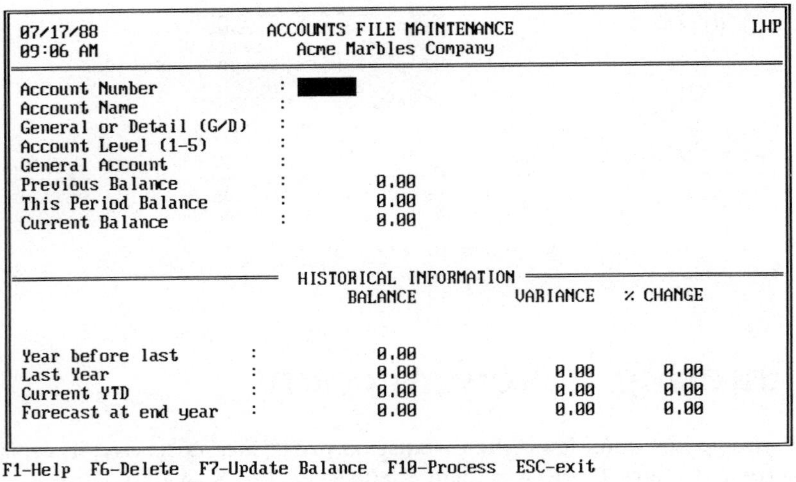

```
07/17/88              ACCOUNTS FILE MAINTENANCE            LHP
09:06 AM                 Acme Marbles Company

Account Number        : ████
Account Name          :
General or Detail (G/D) :
Account Level (1-5)   :
General Account       :
Previous Balance      :        0.00
This Period Balance   :        0.00
Current Balance       :        0.00

                  ═══ HISTORICAL INFORMATION ═══
                       BALANCE      VARIANCE    % CHANGE


Year before last   :        0.00
Last Year          :        0.00        0.00      0.00
Current YTD        :        0.00        0.00      0.00
Forecast at end year :      0.00        0.00      0.00
```

F1-Help F6-Delete F7-Update Balance F10-Process ESC-exit

Fig. 3.6

The Accounts File Maintenance screen ready for data entry.

The following paragraphs describe the fields on the Accounts File Maintenance screen in which you enter data.

Account Number: The cursor begins at the Account Number field. *Account numbers* can be up to six characters long. Although you can use either numeric or alphabetic characters for your account numbers, you'll find that numeric account numbers simplify data entry within the DacEasy modules. By including only numbers, you can use the numeric keypad for almost all your data entry.

After entering a new account number, press Enter. The cursor then moves to the Account Name field.

C.P.A. Tip: You have several ways to create easy-to-use account numbers:

■ Start each of the five categories of accounts with a different number. For example, start asset account numbers with a 1, liability account numbers with a 2, capital account numbers with a 3, revenue account numbers with a 4, and expense account numbers with a 5.

■ Use only as many places in your account numbers as you need in order to differentiate accounts. Extra numbers only slow your data entry. For example, if all your account numbers end in 0, you've wasted a character and unnecessarily increased your data entry time.

■ Leave intervals between the account numbers you assign so that you have room to add new accounts. For example, numbering the expense accounts 5011, 5012, 5013, 5014, and so on, means that you can't insert a new number between accounts 5011 and 5012 without changing the account number length. But if you number the same expense accounts 5010, 5015, 5020, and 5025, you have several spaces between account numbers for inserting additional accounts.

■ Even if you don't want to use DacEasy's sample Chart of Accounts as the foundation for your own, you should carefully examine the sample. It may give you many good ideas for structures and accounts.

Account Name: The *account name* can include as many as 20 characters. You may want to develop and use standard abbreviations in your Chart of Accounts so that you can easily fit names within the 20-character limit. By planning ahead and being consistent with your abbreviations, you make your Chart of Accounts easier for other users to understand. Note the consistent abbreviations within DacEasy's sample Chart of Accounts: Accumulated Depreciation is always abbreviated "Accum. Depreciation," Cost of Goods Sold is abbreviated "COGS," and Machinery & Equipment is always abbreviated "Machinery & Equip."

After correctly entering the account name, press Enter. The cursor moves to the General or Detail (G/D) field.

General or Detail (G/D): In this field you enter a code that describes whether an account can receive direct debits and credits (a detail account) or whether the account is just a subtotal or total account that accumulates the debits and credits (a general account). If you study figures 3.1 and 3.2, you can see that they include accounts representing the revenue and expense classifications you might debit and credit. These accounts are the detail accounts. You can also see that some accounts simply act as subtotals. These accounts are the general accounts. Figure 3.7 lists the accounts shown in figure 3.2 and specifies which are detail and which are general.

After correctly coding the account as general or detail, press Enter. The cursor moves to the Account Level (1–5) field.

Account Level (1–5): The *account level* code indicates the level of an account number. The level 1 accounts represent the five major account categories: assets, liabilities, capital, revenue, and expense, which are always general accounts. Level 2 accounts are those that are summed to compute level 1 accounts. For example, current assets and noncurrent assets are level 2 accounts that are totaled to calculate assets, a level 1 account.

Level 3 accounts are those that are summed to compute level 2 accounts. Similarly, level 4 accounts are summed to compute level 3 accounts, and level 5 accounts are summed to compute level 4 accounts. Figure 3.8 shows the sample income statement for the Acme Marbles Company with the account levels identified.

Detail and General Accounts Identified	
Cats eye revenue	detail
Bumble bee revenue	detail
Cleary revenue	detail
Yellow swirls revenue	detail
Total Revenue	general
Cats eye marbles cost	detail
Bumble bee marbles cost	detail
Cleary marbles cost	detail
Yellow swirls marbles cost	detail
Total Cost of Marbles Sold	general
Supplies Expense	detail
Rent Expense	detail
Total General Expenses	general
Travel Expenses	detail
Commissions	detail
Total Sales Expenses	general
Total Operating Expenses	general
Total Expenses	general
PROFIT	general

Fig. 3.7

The detail and general accounts for the sample income statement.

Sample Income Statement for Acme Marbles Company	account level 4	account level 3	account level 2	account level 1
REVENUE				
Cats eye revenue			$12,500	
Bumble bee revenue			$12,500	
Cleary revenue			$12,500	
Yellow swirls revenue			$12,500	
Total Revenue				$50,000
EXPENSES				
Cost of Marbles Sold				
Cats eye marbles cost		$5,000		
Bumble bee marbles cost		$5,000		
Cleary marbles cost		$5,000		
Yellow swirls marbles cost		$5,000		
Total Cost of Marbles Sold			$20,000	
Operating Expenses				
General Expenses				
Supplies Expense	$4,000			
Rent Expense	$1,000			
Total General Expenses		$5,000		
Sales Expenses				
Travel Expenses	$8,000			
Commissions	$7,000			
Total Sales Expenses		$15,000		
Total Operating Expenses			$20,000	
Total Expenses				$40,000
PROFIT				$10,000

Fig. 3.8

The sample income statement with account levels identified.

You need to create a level 1 account before you can enter a level 2 account below that level 1. Similarly, you need to create the level 2 account before you can enter a level 3, the level 3 before you can enter a level 4, and the level 4 before you can enter a level 5. For each branch of the level chart, the lowest level must be the detail account, and the higher level accounts into which the lower levels are accumulated must be general accounts. (By design, Dac Software has made the PROFIT account an owner's equity/capital account rather than a revenue/expense account. Although figure 3.8 seems to indicate that the PROFIT account is a level 1 account, just like the Total Revenues and Total Expenses accounts, it's not. You must enter the PROFIT account as a detail account for the owner's equity/capital account.)

When you're entering accounts, you cannot skip levels. For example, you cannot add a detail account at level 5 if the general account to which it applies is a level 3. You also must pay attention to which general account you assign the detail account, because you can assign it to any general account within the range.

General Account: This field describes the general account into which the account is accumulated. Obviously, the only account levels without a General Account field are the level 1 accounts. You must specify a general account for all other accounts so that account balances are included in the subtotals and totals.

Historical Information: You can enter historical information in the Year before Last, Last Year, and Forecast at End Year fields. Developing these figures will be time-consuming, however, unless you're converting from another automated system that used the same account numbers. The Year before Last amount is the balance this account showed two years ago. The Last Year amount is the balance this account showed last year. The Forecast at End Year amount shows what you estimate the account balance will be at the end of the current year. I suggest you postpone entering this information until next year. Then DacEasy will generate the data for you.

Entering the Trial Balance

As stated in Chapter 2, you must load your trial balance when you define your Chart of Accounts. If you've timed your conversion date to occur at the beginning of an accounting year, you need to load your assets, liabilities, and owner's equities. If you're converting to DacEasy in the middle of an accounting year, you also must load the revenue and expense balances and then run the end-of-month periodic routine for the general ledger (see Chapter 12).

To load the balances of these accounts, enter them in the This Period Balance field of the level 1 accounts for assets, liabilities, and so on. Set the This Period Balance by pressing F7 and entering the current balance. Remember to enter the decimal point for cents.

If you use the Inventory, Accounts Payable, and Accounts Receivable modules, don't enter inventory, accounts payable, or accounts receivable totals here; enter them as part of setting up the product, vendor, and customer master files (see Chapter 4).

Examining the Other Account Fields

The system calculates the data for the rest of the fields presented on the Accounts File Maintenance screen. The Previous Balance field shows the account amount at the end of the preceding accounting month. The This Period Balance field shows the changes to the account during the current accounting period. The Current Balance field shows the account balance to date and equals the sum of the Previous Balance and the This Period Balance. The Current YTD field shows the balance accumulated in this account since the beginning of the accounting year. The VARIANCE and % CHANGE fields calculate the dollar change and the percentage change from the Year before Last amount to the Last Year amount to the Forecast at End Year amount.

Now you're ready to add the account. To do so, press either F10 or Enter. If the new account is a level 1 account, DacEasy asks you to indicate the type of account. Enter *A* for asset, *L* for liability, *C* for capital, *R* for revenue, *E* for expense, and *O* for other. Figure 3.9 shows the Accounts File Maintenance screen after a new payroll expense account for officers' salaries has been added to the sample Chart of Accounts.

Editing an Account

The steps for editing an account are simple. You need to know only the account number. For example, if you decide to change the name of an existing account, type the account number. The program retrieves the information for that account number. You can then press Enter until the cursor highlights the field you want to edit.

Deleting an account also requires only that you know the account number. For example, if after further consideration you decide to delete the account you just added, simply type the account number. After the program has retrieved

```
07/17/88                 ACCOUNTS FILE MAINTENANCE                      LHP
09:06 AM                    Acme Marbles Company

Account Number        : 520119
Account Name          : Officer's Salaries
General or Detail (G/D) : D
Account Level (1-5)   : 5
General Account       : 52011
Previous Balance      :           0.00
This Period Balance   :           0.00
Current Balance       :           0.00


                    ───── HISTORICAL INFORMATION ─────
                            BALANCE        VARIANCE    % CHANGE

Year before last      :          0.00
Last Year             :          0.00          0.00        0.00
Current YTD           :          0.00          0.00        0.00
Forecast at end year  :          0.00          0.00        0.00


F1-Help  F6-Delete  F7-Update Balance  F10-Process  ESC-exit
```

Fig. 3.9

The Accounts File Maintenance screen with sample data.

the account information, press F6 (Delete). DacEasy then asks you, Are you sure you want to delete this record. (Y/N)? To delete the record, press *Y* and Enter.

If you've previously used an account, DacEasy does not allow you to delete it. You cannot delete an account that contains a nonzero balance. If you need to change (or zero out) the balance of an account, press F7 (Update Balance). Then enter the negative (or opposite) amount and press F10 or Enter. The next time you recall the account, it will have a zero balance.

Setting System Options

To begin setting options, simply select Options from the DacEasy main menu. The Options menu then offers seven choices (see fig. 3.10):

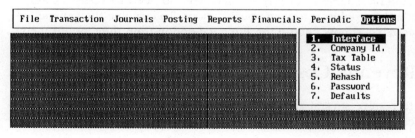

```
 File  Transaction  Journals  Posting  Reports  Financials  Periodic  Options

                                                  1.  Interface
                                                  2.  Company Id.
                                                  3.  Tax Table
                                                  4.  Status
                                                  5.  Rehash
                                                  6.  Password
                                                  7.  Defaults
```

Fig. 3.10

The Options menu.

Interface	Describes which accounts in the Chart of Accounts the other modules should debit and credit
Company Id.	Holds the company name and address that appear on screens, reports, and forms
Tax Table	Stores the various sales tax rates that the program uses to generate invoices
Status	Shows the number of records you defined and the number of records you used in each of the master files
Rehash	Allows you to increase the number of records defined for each of the master files
Password	Sets the system passwords
Defaults	Represents the five system defaults you should review to verify that DacEasy operates appropriately

Defining the General Ledger Interface Table

You use the general ledger interface table so that the subsidiary modules—such as Billing, Purchase Order, Accounts Receivable, Accounts Payable, and Inventory—can automatically send, or post, accounting information to the general ledger. You need the general ledger interface table if you plan to use the General Ledger module with any of the other modules.

One handy feature of using DacEasy's sample Chart of Accounts is that the general ledger interface table is already defined. You do need to verify, however, that the definition conforms to your specifications. To examine the general ledger interface table, simply choose the Interface option from the Options menu.

Using Revenue/Cost Departments

You need to resolve several accounting issues before defining the general ledger interface table. First, you must decide what your Chart of Accounts should look like.

Second, you need to decide whether to use revenue/cost departments. Suppose that Acme Marbles Company sells its marbles to both wholesalers and retailers. In addition, Acme purchases marbles both from offshore manufacturers located in Asia and from domestic manufacturers. Given these facts, you can classify revenues and product costs by either customer or product type, because customers may be either wholesale or retail, and products may be either imported or domestic. Figure 3.11 highlights the differences among using a revenue/cost classification based on customer type, using a revenue/cost classification based on product type, and using no revenue/cost classification.

Alternative Revenue/Cost Departments

BY CUSTOMER:	Wholesale	Retail
Revenue	20000	30000
Marble Costs	10000	10000
Gross Margin	10000	20000

BY INVENTORY:	Offshore	Domestic
Revenue	40000	10000
Marble Costs	15000	5000
Gross Margin	25000	5000

BY NONE:	
Revenue	50000
Marble Costs	20000
Gross Margin	30000

Fig. 3.11

Differences among alternative revenue/cost departments.

Setting up revenue/cost departments results in both your revenues and costs being grouped according to customers or products. To use a revenue/cost classification, you'll need to define a department number later, when loading your customer or product master file. (For more information on master files, see Chapter 4.) For example, you might define a department code of 01 for wholesale customers and a department code of 02 for retail customers, or a department code of 01 for imported marbles and a department code of 02 for domestic marbles. In this way, you give yourself the opportunity to examine revenues and direct costs by customer or product type.

After you've chosen Options Interface, the GL Interface Table screen appears, with the cursor at the Revenue/Cost Department field. You select the revenue/cost department by toggling the space bar to select INVENTORY, CUSTOMER, or NONE and then pressing Enter. Because you can't select both INVENTORY and CUSTOMER, think about which method is more valuable to you. After you select the revenue/cost department method and identify the revenue/cost departments in the customer, product, or service master files, you cannot change them.

Entering and Editing the Data

If you use revenue/cost departments (INVENTORY or CUSTOMER), DacEasy requires that the sales, sales returns, and cost of goods sold accounts specified in the general ledger interface table be general accounts. If you specify no revenue/cost department (NONE), the accounts specified in the table must be detail accounts.

The other master files use the general ledger interface table. For example, the customer file needs bank checking, accounts receivable, sales discounts, and finance charges accounts; the vendor file needs bank checking, accounts payable, purchase tax, and purchase discounts accounts; and the service file needs bank checking, accounts receivable, sales tax, finance charges, and sales discounts accounts. Each of these accounts must be a detail account.

To complete the general ledger interface table as shown in figure 3.12, enter the account numbers into the table as follows (the system warns you if you've selected an invalid account number or entered a general account number when a detail number is required):

1. **Bank Checking:** Enter the Chart of Accounts number of the checking account against which you plan to write both manual and computer-generated checks.

2. **Accounts Receivable:** Enter the account number that the Accounts Receivable module should debit (to record sales) within the Chart of Accounts.

3. **Accounts Payable:** Enter the account number that the Accounts Payable module should credit (to record purchases) within the Chart of Accounts.

4. **Purchase Tax:** Enter the sales tax account number that the Accounts Payable module should debit within the Chart of Accounts.

5. **Sales:** Enter the sales revenue account number that the Billing module should credit within the Chart of Accounts to show the sales revenue generated.

6. **Purchase Discount:** Enter the account number you want the Accounts Payable module to credit within the General Ledger module to show purchase discounts received for making early payments.

7. **Sales Tax:** Enter the current liability account number for the Billing module to credit within the Chart of Accounts to show sales tax payable as a result of making a sale or collecting on a sale.

8. **Finance Charges:** Enter the revenue account number you want the Accounts Receivable module to credit as a result of accruing a finance charge when your customer's payment is overdue.

9. **Inventory:** Enter the asset account number for the inventory you want the Billing module to credit and the Purchase Order module to debit within the General Ledger module to show changes in the inventory balances.

10. **Sales Returns:** Enter the revenue account number for the Billing module to debit within the General Ledger module to show the sales returns made by customers.

11. **Cost of Goods Sold:** Enter the expense account number you want the Billing module to debit within the General Ledger module to show the inventory items sold to customers.

12. **Sales Discounts:** Enter the expense account number you want the Accounts Receivable module to debit within the General Ledger module to show the discounts that customers took when paying you—discounts perhaps stemming from early payment.

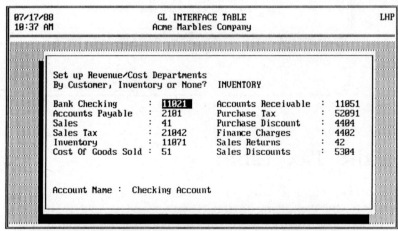

Fig. 3.12

The General Ledger Interface Table screen.

When you've completed the general ledger interface table, press Enter or F10. The program saves your results and returns you to the Options menu.

Defining the Company Identification

When you installed DacEasy, you defined the company identification. If you want to revise that identification, perhaps because the company name or address has changed, you can use the second option on the Options menu, Company Id.

DacEasy provides four lines that appear at the tops of screens and reports. Each line is up to 40 characters long. Typically, you put your full company name on the first identification line, and your address, phone number, and related data on the lines that follow. To center the text entered on a line, press F2 when you've finished typing on that line. After you've completed your revisions, press F10 to save your work and return to the Options menu. Figure 3.13 shows the company name table you use to identify the company.

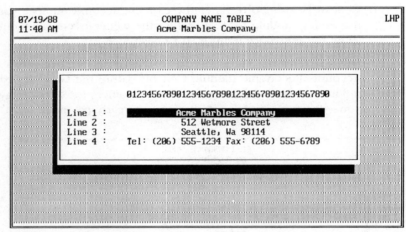

Fig. 3.13

The Company Name Table screen.

Loading the Tax Table

The Tax Table option, number 3 on the Options menu, sets up 10 sales tax rates in a tax table. By identifying in the customer and vendor master files (described in Chapter 4) which of these sales tax rates are applicable to a specific customer or vendor, you can automatically calculate sales tax when generating purchase orders and customer invoices.

To set up the tax table for your system, choose Tax Table from the Options menu. To define the first sales tax percentage, Tax Rate 0, enter the appropriate rate as a percent. For example, figure 3.14 shows the tax rates table with tax rate 0 set to 7.8 percent, or .078, which you enter as 7.8. Press Enter to move to subsequent tax rate fields. When you finish setting tax rate codes, you can save your entries either by pressing F10 or by pressing Enter when the last data entry field on the screen (Tax Rate 9) is highlighted. Either approach returns you to the Options menu.

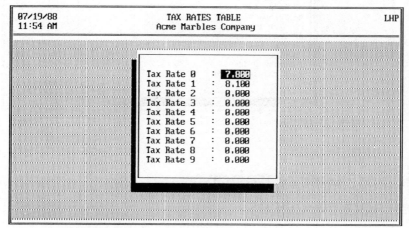

```
07/19/88                    TAX RATES TABLE                          LHP
11:54 AM                   Acme Marbles Company


                  Tax Rate 0   :   7.800
                  Tax Rate 1   :   8.100
                  Tax Rate 2   :   0.000
                  Tax Rate 3   :   0.000
                  Tax Rate 4   :   0.000
                  Tax Rate 5   :   0.000
                  Tax Rate 6   :   0.000
                  Tax Rate 7   :   0.000
                  Tax Rate 8   :   0.000
                  Tax Rate 9   :   0.000




F1-Help F10-Process  ESC-Exit
```

Fig. 3.14

The Tax Rates Table screen.

Viewing the Status

The Status option, number 4 in the Options menu, shows you the number of records defined and the number of records used in each of your files. The defined amounts are all based on your entries during installation when the program asked for your estimates of the numbers of customers, vendors, purchase orders, products or services, and invoices you would have. The used amounts show the actual number of records you've used for each category.

Although you enter no data with this option, you should view this screen occasionally to make sure that you're not running out of reserved space within the DacEasy files. Figure 3.15 shows the File Status screen that appears when you select the Status option.

If, when entering transactions, you exceed the number of defined records, DacEasy prevents you from making any other entries until you modify the definition by using the Rehash option.

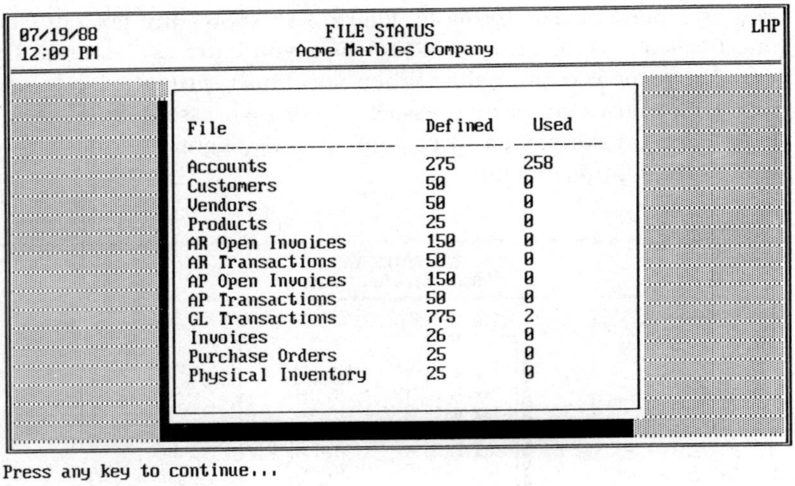

```
07/19/88                    FILE STATUS                        LHP
12:09 PM                 Acme Marbles Company


          File                    Defined      Used
          ----------------------  -------      --------
          Accounts                   275        258
          Customers                   50          0
          Vendors                     50          0
          Products                    25          0
          AR Open Invoices           150          0
          AR Transactions             50          0
          AP Open Invoices           150          0
          AP Transactions             50          0
          GL Transactions            775          2
          Invoices                    26          0
          Purchase Orders             25          0
          Physical Inventory          25          0


```

Press any key to continue...

Fig. 3.15

The File Status screen.

Modifying the Number of Defined Records

Rehash, the fifth option on the Options menu, allows you to update your descriptions of the number of defined records reserved in each of your accounting files. You might use this option either because you've viewed the File Status screen and realize that you want to reserve more space or because DacEasy alerts you that it has run out of space in one of the files and needs additional space to continue. Figure 3.16 shows the File Rehash screen. As with other data entry screens, you can save your changes and return to the Options menu either by pressing F10 or by pressing Enter when the last field on the screen is highlighted.

Setting Passwords

The sixth option on the Options menu is Password. Setting the system passwords relates to your system's overall security and so is discussed in Chapter 5, "Protecting Your System."

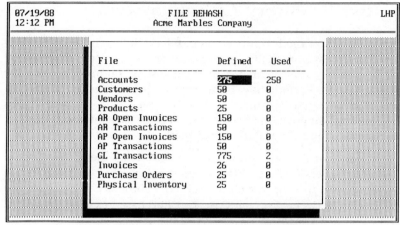

Fig. 3.16

The File Rehash screen.

Setting the Option Defaults

Choosing Defaults from the Options menu produces five other options that you need to review or set (see fig. 3.17). With these options, you can choose the inventory cost system; assign starting purchase order, purchase order return, invoice, and sales return numbers; define printer control codes; change your screen colors (if you have a color monitor); and write customer and vendor messages.

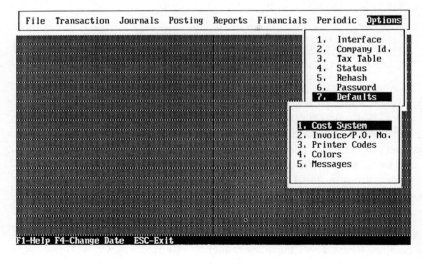

Fig. 3.17

The Defaults submenu under the Options menu.

Choosing the Inventory Costing System

Accounting for the costs of the inventory you purchase, hold, and then resell is probably one of the most potentially complicated areas of accounting for the small business. You need to realize that with the decision you make about your inventory costing, you also decide how to determine the costs of the items you sell—the cost of goods sold. Fortunately, DacEasy provides you with three options for accounting for inventory costs: the average cost method, the last purchase price method, and the standard cost method.

After you select the Cost System option from the Defaults menu, the Define Cost System screen appears (see fig. 3.18). Press the space bar until the inventory method you want to use appears on the screen. (The space bar toggles the inventory cost system between Average Cost, Last Purchase Price, and Standard Cost.) To select the cost system, press F10 or Enter.

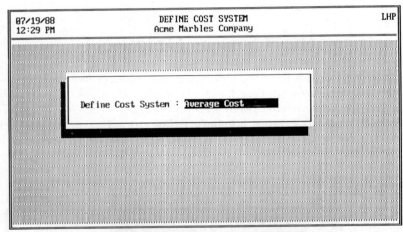

Fig. 3.18

The Define Cost System screen.

Most likely, you'll want to use the *average cost* method for calculating your inventory costs. With this method, DacEasy computes the total costs of your inventory, computes the total number of units you have on hand, and then calculates the cost per unit by dividing the total costs by the total number of units. The program uses this calculated average cost per unit for valuing both the inventory you're holding and the cost of goods sold. The impact of selecting this method isn't all that apparent until you find yourself in a situation where prices are changing.

For example, suppose that you operate a fruit stand and that the price of one of your most popular items, fresh Florida oranges, is rising. If you've been purchasing oranges for $2.00 a box and you currently have 20 boxes in your cooler, your inventory costs are easy to calculate—$2.00 × 20. And if you sell a box to a customer, the cost of that box is clear too—it's $2.00. But what happens if you purchase 15 more boxes at $2.25 a box and then sell 10 of the boxes? You need to answer two questions: What's the value of the inventory you're still holding (the 25 boxes of oranges left in the cooler)? And what's the cost of goods sold for the 10 boxes you just sold?

Here's how the average cost method answers the questions. First DacEasy calculates the total purchases in dollars: $2.00 × 20 boxes + $2.25 × 15 boxes = $73.75. Then the program calculates the total units purchased: 20 boxes + 15 boxes = 35. Finally, the program calculates the average cost per box by dividing the total purchase amount ($73.75) by the total units purchased (35). The result, rounded to the nearest penny, is $2.11. This average cost per unit allows you to answer easily the two basic questions regarding your inventory. The value of the inventory you still hold is 25 times $2.11, or $52.75, and the cost of goods sold is 10 times $2.11, or $21.10.

This fruit stand example is also helpful for illustrating the other two inventory costing methods provided by DacEasy. The *standard cost* method uses for the unit cost the standard cost amount specified in the product file—which may or may not be close to the actual inventory unit cost. You select the standard cost after careful consideration of what you think the unit cost should be. Then you calculate both inventory and cost of goods sold based on your estimation of unit cost. Why would you want to use standard costs? Doing so means that you need to develop standard costs for each product. When you do use standard costs, however, something interesting happens.

Suppose that you're back at the fruit stand, but this time you're using the standard cost method of costing inventory. If the standard cost for oranges is $2.00 a box, then your inventory of 20 boxes is carried at $2.00 a box, and your cost of goods sold is calculated as $2.00. And what happens when you go out and buy 10 boxes of oranges at $2.25 a box? You record the transaction like this:

	Debit	*Credit*
Inventory	$30.00	
Overspending/Variance—oranges	$ 3.75	
Cash		$33.75

The fact that you overspent is immediately apparent at the time you make the purchase, because you report a variance. Underspending also immediately shows up. Standard inventory costing represents an aggressive cost management tool. It allows you to specify the exact cost and the standard cost of items you're buying for resale and then compare the purchase price to the standard cost. Notice that, compared to the average cost method, the standard cost method gives you a much better handle on the overspending of $.25 a box. The average cost method lumps everything together and shows both the inventory and cost of goods sold at $2.11.

One major problem with the standard cost inventory system, however, is that it's unacceptable for income tax and financial accounting purposes. Neither tax laws nor financial accounting standards allow this costing method.

The other inventory costing assumption is the *last purchase price* method. This method uses the last purchase price as the inventory cost per unit and the cost of goods sold per unit. To continue with the fruit stand example, if you've been buying oranges for $2.00 a box but then start spending $2.25 a box, DacEasy adjusts the per unit cost of your inventory to $2.25 a box and calculates the cost of goods sold for any oranges you sell at $2.25 a box. The advantage of using this inventory costing assumption is that your inventory is always calculated in terms of replacement cost, and your cost of goods sold is based solely on what it last cost you to buy the inventory.

The importance of this advantage is simple. Suppose that you've been selling boxes of oranges for $2.20 a box. Under the average cost method, you calculate both your inventory and your cost of goods sold as $2.11 a box, which means you think you're still making money ($2.20 is greater than $2.11). Under the last purchase price method, however, you show the inventory and cost of goods sold at $2.25. You're thus selling each box of oranges at a nickel less than what you paid for it! The last purchase price method has shown you that you probably need to raise your prices.

Despite its benefits, the last purchase price method, like the standard cost method, is usually unacceptable for income tax and financial accounting purposes.

Most accountants would advise you to use the method that allows you to make the best decisions. Although outsiders like the Internal Revenue Service, your bank, or your investors may require specific accounting conventions, you can always adjust the results produced by your new accounting system so that they conform to external rules and requirements.

Assigning Initial Invoice and Purchase Order Numbers

In any accounting system, you use numbers to identify many transactions and documents. Invoices have numbers. Purchase orders have numbers. If you use purchase order returns and sales returns, these too have numbers. If you've been in business long and have high transaction volumes, you've probably already been using numbers to identify transactions. That way, any time you, a customer, or a vendor wants to talk about a particular transaction, you need to mention only the invoice number, and everyone knows exactly to which invoice you're referring.

You need to identify four of these numbers. When you choose Invoice/P.O. No. from the Defaults menu, DacEasy asks you for the latest number you assigned to a purchase order, a purchase order return, an invoice, and a sales return (see fig. 3.19). Type each number and press Enter.

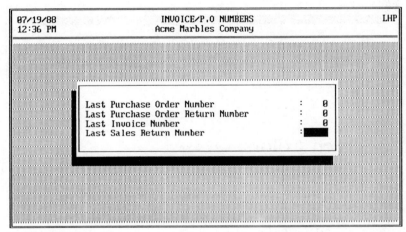

Fig. 3.19

Specifying the latest purchase order, purchase return, invoice, and sales return numbers.

Once DacEasy knows the latest number you assigned to each of these categories, the program can add 1 to each of these numbers to get the next numbers it should use. Accordingly, if you haven't been using numbers to identify purchase orders, purchase order returns, invoices, and sales returns, enter *0* as the latest number for each. DacEasy then assigns 1 as the next number.

Setting Printer Codes

You choose the Default menu's Printer Codes option to set printer control codes so that DacEasy can operate your printer correctly. The program needs to know which codes it must send to your printer to produce normal, 10-characters-per-inch, print or condensed, 15-characters-per-inch, print. DacEasy also needs to know how many lines to print per page. You can define printer codes for up to 12 printers, as shown in figure 3.20. The correct printer control codes, sometimes called escape sequences, should be listed in your printer's user manual.

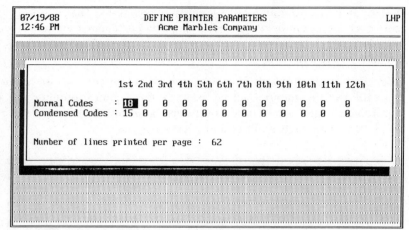

Fig. 3.20

Setting printer codes.

```
07/19/88                DEFINE PRINTER PARAMETERS              LHP
12:46 PM                   Acme Marbles Company


            1st 2nd 3rd 4th 5th 6th 7th 8th 9th 10th 11th 12th
Normal Codes    : 18  0   0   0   0   0   0   0   0   0   0   0
Condensed Codes : 15  0   0   0   0   0   0   0   0   0   0   0


Number of lines printed per page :  62



F1-Help F10-Process   ESC-Exit
```

Changing Screen Colors

If you have a monitor that displays multiple colors, you can use the Colors option, which is the fourth option on the Defaults menu, to assign different colors to the various components of the DacEasy screens.

As shown in the top section of the Color Definition screen in figure 3.21, the DacEasy screens are composed of up to 12 separate parts: Horizontal Menu, Vertical Menu, Menu Selector, Background, Window, Titles/Headers, Help Window, Prompt, Active Field, Inactive Field, Line Status, and Urgent Status. You may assign to each of these items one of the colors shown in the Colors box on the screen. On a color monitor, each lowercase a appears in a different color.

To "paint" one of the screen components, use the arrow keys to highlight the screen component and press Enter. An example of that screen component then appears in the Examples box. Use the arrow keys to highlight the color you want to assign to the selected screen component. After you've highlighted the color, press Enter. The example in the Examples box changes to the color you selected. Repeat these steps to paint each separate screen component.

If you have a color monitor, spend a few minutes painting the components of your screens in some interesting colors. A variety of colors usually makes your screens more visually interesting and easier on your eyes.

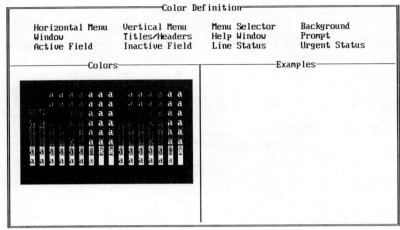

```
┌─────────────────────────Color Definition─────────────────────────┐
│                                                                   │
│    Horizontal Menu   Vertical Menu    Menu Selector   Background   │
│    Window            Titles/Headers   Help Window     Prompt       │
│    Active Field      Inactive Field   Line Status     Urgent Status│
│     ┌──────────Colors──────────┐      ┌──────────Examples─────────┐│
│     │                          │      │                          ││
│     │                          │      │                          ││
│     │                          │      │                          ││
│     │                          │      │                          ││
│     │                          │      │                          ││
│     │                          │      │                          ││
│     │                          │      │                          ││
│     └──────────────────────────┘      │                          ││
│                                        │                          ││
└───────────────────────────────────────┴──────────────────────────┘
F1-Help F10-Process   ESC-Exit
```

Fig. 3.21

Defining colors for screen components.

Loading the Messages File

The messages file, which is accessed from the Messages option of the Defaults menu, relates to the message codes you can set in each customer and vendor record. (The customer and vendor master files and the steps for loading each file are described in Chapter 4.) You use the message code and the messages file to remind you of important information when you're dealing with a customer or a vendor. Perhaps you need to remember that you must always get a purchase order number from a particular customer, or that you always get a discount from a certain vendor simply by asking for a better price. You may have dozens of special pieces of information that would be helpful for you to remember at the appropriate times.

Each message code can access a message that has as many as 39 characters. For each customer or vendor, you can plant one message code within the customer or vendor record so that the corresponding message appears when you reference that customer or vendor. The credit limit and current balance for a customer or vendor also appear. In fact, that information is displayed only if you've entered a message code. For that reason, you may want to create and use some standard message even if you don't need a special message for a customer or vendor.

To enter or edit a message, select the Messages option from the Defaults menu. You then see the Special Messages Table screen, which includes the messages and the corresponding codes. You can store in the messages file as many as 40 messages—each identified by the number of the slot in which you store the message. Simply move the cursor to the slot you want to use and then type the message. Within each message, you can use the Home and End keys to move the cursor to the beginning and end of the message. The special messages table comes with four sample messages, the first four shown in figure 3.22.

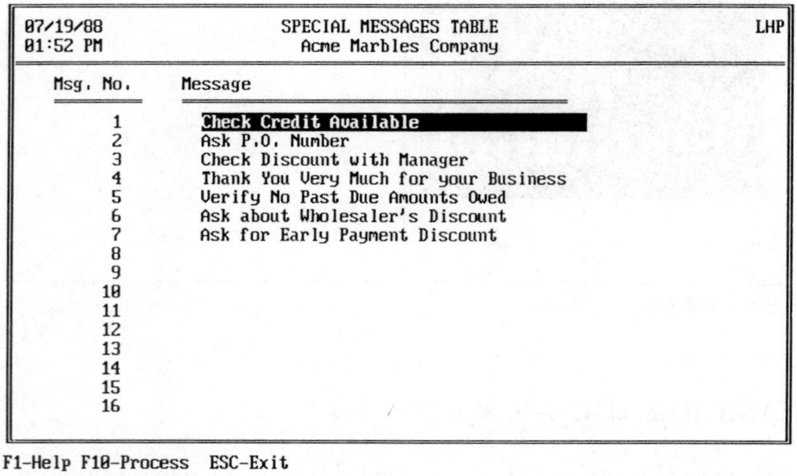

Fig. 3.22

The Special Messages Table screen.

```
07/19/88                    SPECIAL MESSAGES TABLE              LHP
01:52 PM                      Acme Marbles Company

    Msg. No.      Message

        1         Check Credit Available
        2         Ask P.O. Number
        3         Check Discount with Manager
        4         Thank You Very Much for your Business
        5         Verify No Past Due Amounts Owed
        6         Ask about Wholesaler's Discount
        7         Ask for Early Payment Discount
        8
        9
       10
       11
       12
       13
       14
       15
       16


F1-Help F10-Process  ESC-Exit
```

Notice that only 16 messages are displayed on the screen at one time. You can use the arrow keys to move up and down the list. To save the messages you've added or the edits you've made, press F10, or press Enter when the highlighted message slot is number 40.

Chapter Summary

This chapter describes the intermediate steps you need to take after you've installed DacEasy but before you load the master files. These steps include defining the Chart of Accounts you'll use to keep your books and setting the system options and defaults. In Chapter 4, you learn how to load the master files.

CHAPTER 4

Loading the Master Files

Master files serve three general purposes:

1. *Master files store information you use again and again.* For example, suppose that you use a vendor's complete name and address each time you send the vendor a purchase order or a check. If you make hundreds of purchases a year, you'll be typing the name and address hundreds of times. By storing the text in a master file and assigning an abbreviation or a code to the vendor, however, you can type the vendor's abbreviation or code to access the entire name and address. You can use master files for such tasks as including customer names and addresses on invoices and customer statements and typing product descriptions on purchase orders and invoices.

2. *Master files collect and store data that summarizes certain key bits of information.* For example, within the vendor master file, you might store information about how much you've purchased from the vendor this year and last year. In the customer master file, you might store information about how much you've sold a particular customer this year and last year. All the DacEasy master files collect and store this type of summary information.

3. *Master files provide an internal control function.* Internal controls are procedures or verifications you use to minimize clerical errors and prevent other users from tampering with or stealing your data. For example, the master files list the customers and vendors with whom you can transact business. By limiting and controlling the addition and deletion of customers and vendors to master files, you limit and control with whom you (and the people who work for you) can transact business. Chapter 5, "Protecting your System," tackles the subject of internal controls in more detail.

75

This chapter describes which master files are required for each of DacEasy's modules and explains how to load each of the master files.

Determining Which Master Files You Need

Six master files are available for you to load: customer, vendor, product, service, codes, and statement messages. Refer to table 4.1 to see which master files you need in order to operate the modules you've decided to use.

Table 4.1
Master Files Used in Each Module

Module	Master Files Used
Purchase Order	product, vendor, service, purchase order codes
Accounts Payable	vendor
Billing	customer, product, service, billing codes
Accounts Receivable	customer, statement messages
Inventory	product, service
General Ledger	none
Forecasting	customer, vendor, product, service

Figure 4.1 shows the choices that are included in the File menu, which you access from the main DacEasy menu. You used the first option, Accounts, to enter and edit your Chart of Accounts (see Chapter 3). The remaining options—Customers, Vendors, Products, Services, Codes, and Statement Messages—help you load the master files.

Before you begin loading the master files, you should probably gather all the pertinent information about your customers, products, vendors, and so on. Spend some time familiarizing yourself with each File Maintenance screen before you enter any important data so that you have a general understanding of what information you'll need. Give yourself plenty of time to set up each type of file.

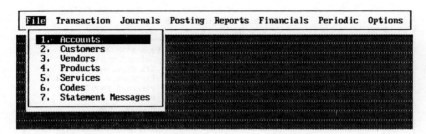

File Transaction Journals Posting Reports Financials Periodic Options

```
1.  Accounts
2.  Customers
3.  Vendors
4.  Products
5.  Services
6.  Codes
7.  Statement Messages
```

Fig. 4.1

The File menu.

Loading the Customer Master File

You use the customer master file to store frequently needed information about customers, such as their names, addresses, and phone numbers; special instructions for dealing with particular customers; and historical information.

If you're planning to use the Billing or Accounts Receivable module, you need the customer master file. In this file, you describe each customer to whom you send invoices and each customer you monitor in monthly statements and aging reports. You need to enter a customer record for each customer with whom you transact business.

Entering and Editing Customer Data

To access the Customer File Maintenance program, choose the Customers option from the File menu. Figure 4.2 shows the Customer File Maintenance screen as it appears before you enter any data.

The following paragraphs describe the fields in which you enter information for customer records on the Customer File Maintenance screen.

Customer Code: The *customer code* is an abbreviation for identifying customers within the Billing and Accounts Receivable modules. You can use up to six characters or numbers to enter your code when you're entering a customer record.

Before you begin assigning codes, spend some time thinking about how you want to organize your customers. One point to keep in mind is that the system uses the customer codes as one of the fields upon which you can sort the records in the customer master file. You therefore want to use customer codes that group the customers in a meaningful order that can help you as you're poring over the customer information lists and reports. To ease data entry and

```
07/20/88                CUSTOMER FILE MAINTENANCE                    LHP
09:50 AM                   Acme Marbles Company

   Customer Code  : ■■■■■■        Type (O=Open B=Balance):    0
   Name           :                    Sales Person    :
   Contact        :                    G/L Department  :
   Address        :                    Discount %      :      0.00
   City           :            State :  Discount Days  :         0
   Zip Code       :         Tel :     -  Due days       :         0
   Tax Id. Number :                    Message Code    :
   Credit Limit   :        0.00   Previous Balance  :           0.00
   Credit Available :      0.00   This Period Bal.  :           0.00
                                  Current Balance   :           0.00
   Last Sale Date  :  / /      Last Payment Date :    / /
   Month Int. Rate :  0.00     Sales Tax Code    :    0 Rate:
   ═════════════════════ STATISTICAL INFORMATION ═════════════════════
                 Yr.Bef.Lst Last Year This Year Forecast  Variance    %

   # Invoices :      0        0        0        0        0      0.0
   $ Sales    :      0        0        0        0        0      0.0
   $ Costs    :      0        0        0        0        0      0.0
   $ Profit   :      0        0        0        0        0      0.0

   F1-Help  F2-Add Tax Rate  F6-DELETE  F7-Enter Invoice F10-Process  ESC-exit
```

Fig. 4.2

The Customer File Maintenance screen before you enter data.

minimize errors, assign the shortest code possible. And remember to allow room to insert additional customers in the customer master file in the appropriate order.

To edit a customer record, you simply enter that customer's code. The Customer File Maintenance program then retrieves the appropriate customer record.

Name, Contact, Address, City, State, Zip Code, and Tel: You store the customer's business name, the name of the contact person, and the customer's complete address and telephone number in these fields.

Type (O = Open B = Balance): The *type* identifies the detail at which you want customer invoice information stored. You have two choices: *O* (open invoice) and *B* (balance forward). "Open invoice" means that each open invoice is kept in the accounting information files until the customer pays and you run the end-of-the-month accounting routines. "Balance forward" means that only the total invoice amount for the preceding month—rather than all unpaid invoices—is kept in the accounting information files.

In general, you should probably use the open invoice method. Although the balance forward method minimizes the level of detail with which you're deluged as you review reports, you'll have difficulty applying customer payments to specific invoices and keeping close watch on overdue amounts. The balance forward method is helpful only if you don't need detailed information at the invoice level, perhaps because you don't usually carry many invoices from one month to the next or because customers always pay the outstanding balances without needing to know what the total amounts represent.

An example of a large company that bills on a balance forward basis is the phone company. The preceding month's amount is never detailed but only carried forward as a balance still owed. Like the phone company, you may want to carry only the beginning balance for those situations that involve too much detail to maintain. In these cases, your customer statements become almost like invoices, and what were invoices appear as line items on the statement. If you do use the balance forward approach, you should keep one copy of the customer statements in your files so that you have a record of the detail that comprises the balance forward.

Sales Person: You may want to identify the salesperson who is handling the customer. Although this field doesn't affect processing, it does provide a sort order for reports. For example, you can group and subtotal customer information, including billing and accounts receivable data, by salesperson. You can use up to five characters for the salesperson code, so you should have plenty of space to enter either a code or perhaps the person's first name.

G/L Department: This field is used to show which revenue/cost department sales, cost of goods sold, and sales returns are included for a certain customer. You need to define a G/L department if you set the revenue/cost department to CUSTOMER in the general ledger interface table. If you set the revenue/cost department to INVENTORY or NONE, leave the G/L Department field blank. If you're using the sample Chart of Accounts, you've already been given two departments to use: 01 and 02. Simply identify the appropriate department for the customer.

The department code appended to the account number prefix described in the general ledger interface table must equal a real revenue account number in the Chart of Accounts. For example, a sales revenue account number *41* combined with a department code *01* concatenates to *4101*, which must be a revenue account number. (You may want to review Chapter 3's discussion of the revenue/cost department definition in the general ledger interface table to help you decide how to assign department codes.)

Discount %: You use the *discount percent* to determine the amount of discount you allow a customer to deduct from an invoice if the customer pays within the defined number of discount days. The discount equals the discount percent multiplied by the invoice amount (not including freight and insurance).

Discount Days: The *discount days* is the number of days that sets the period within which the customer may deduct the discount percent from a payment.

C.P.A. Tip: Although early payment discounts are standard in many industries, recognize that early payment discounts are an extremely expensive way to borrow money from your customers. For example, suppose that normal payment terms require customers to pay within 30 days. Because you're in a tight cash flow situation, you start offering customers a 2 percent discount if they pay you within 10 days. You essentially pay them a 2 percent interest charge if you get your money 20 days early. With roughly 18 20-day periods in one year, the 2 percent for 20 days equates to approximately 36 percent annually!

Due Days: The *due days* is the number of days within which you require the customer to pay the invoice. Obviously, setting a due date doesn't mean that you'll always receive payments from the customer within or by that date. But you *can* begin assessing finance charges and sending collection letters to customers who are delinquent in their payments to you.

Tax Id. Number: The Tax Id. Number field is a 12-character alphanumeric field in which you can store a customer's federal tax identification number. You may, for example, want to collect and store this information if you sometimes pay customers, because you must report such payments to the Internal Revenue Service on a 1099 form.

Message Code: The *message code* identifies any special message you want to see whenever you enter the customer number. The two-character code is the preassigned code for the message you've included in the messages file (see Chapter 3). You need to have a copy of the messages you previously entered in that file so that you can enter the appropriate message code on the Customer File Maintenance screen.

Credit Limit: The Credit Limit field is an internal control tool you use to limit the credit extended to a customer. For example, you probably don't want to give new customers much credit because they haven't proved themselves to be responsible customers who pay you on time. Additionally, you may not want to extend any customer more than a specified amount of credit—you don't want to depend on any one customer for too large a piece of your receivables. Think carefully about this field. It basically amounts to your lending decision for each customer.

Month Int. Rate: The *monthly interest rate* is the percentage that, when multiplied by the past due balance, calculates the monthly finance charge a customer has incurred by missing the invoice due date. For example, if you plan to charge customers 1.5 percent per month on past due amounts, you enter *1.5* in the Month Int. Rate field. Be aware, however, that some state usury laws limit the interest rates you can charge.

Sales Tax Code: The *sales tax code* is the tax rate code that represents the correct sales tax percentage for the customer and the sale. When the Sales Tax Code field is highlighted, the tax rates table appears in the upper right corner of the screen (see fig. 4.3). When you select the correct sales tax code, DacEasy automatically pulls the sales tax rate into the Rate field of the customer record.

```
07/20/88              CUSTOMER FILE MAINTENANC  TAX RATES TABLE
09:50 AM                 Acme Marbles Company
                                                Tax Rate 0   :   7.800
  Customer Code :  C10                 Type (   Tax Rate 1   :   8.100
  Name          :  Columbus Glass Works, Inc.   Tax Rate 2   :   0.000
  Contact       :  Mr. Christopher Columbus      Tax Rate 3   :   0.000
  Address       :  East 57th Avenue              Tax Rate 4   :   0.000
  City          :  Seattle          State :  W   Tax Rate 5   :   0.000
  Zip Code      :  98104-    Tel ; (206)555-90   Tax Rate 6   :   0.000
  Tax Id. Number:                                Tax Rate 7   :   0.000
  Credit Limit       :     5000.00  Previous Bal Tax Rate 8   :   0.000
  Credit Available :       5000.00  This Period  Tax Rate 9   :   0.000
                                    Current Bala
  Last Sale Date    :               Last Payment Date :
  Month Int. Rate  :   1.50         Sales Tax Code    :    0 Rate:  7.800
                                    STATISTICAL INFORMATION
```

Fig. 4.3

The tax rates table in a pop-up window.

Statistical Information: You can use the Yr. Bef. Lst, Last Year, This Year, Forecast, Variance, and % fields to enter statistical information about a customer. For example, you can note the number of invoices to this customer; the sales revenue and cost of goods sold for the year before last year, last year, and this year; and your forecast for this year. If you enter these amounts, DacEasy calculates the resulting profit margin (the sales revenue minus the cost of goods sold) and the variance in dollars and percent between this year's amount and your forecast amount.

Unless you're converting from another automated system and have this information at your fingertips, however, these figures are tedious to develop. I suggest that you postpone using the statistical information until your second year of using DacEasy. By then, the program will have automatically developed the data for you.

Examining the Remaining Fields

You may have noticed that the Customer File Maintenance screen includes six other fields. DacEasy skips the cursor over and doesn't let you enter data in the Credit Available, Previous Balance, This Period Bal., Current Balance, Last Sale Date, and Last Payment Date fields. The system automatically collects and updates this data for you. Here are brief descriptions of these fields:

Previous Balance	The total invoices owed by the customer at the end of the preceding accounting period
This Period Bal.	The total invoices owed by the customer in the current accounting period
Current Balance	The total of all invoices owed by the customer; equals the Previous Balance plus the This Period Bal.

Credit Available   The unused portion of the customer's credit limit; calculated as the Credit Limit minus the Current Balance

Last Sale Date   The month, day, and year of the last time an invoice was prepared for this customer

Last Payment Date   The month, day, and year of the last time this customer made a payment to you

Using the Special Function Keys

In addition to the F1 (Help), F4 (Change Date), and F10 (Save Data) keys, three special function keys are available on the Customer File Maintenance screen. F2 (Add Tax Rate) allows you to add sales tax percentage rates to the tax rates table. When you press F2, a pop-up window appears, allowing you to specify a tax code number and a tax rate (see fig. 4.4).

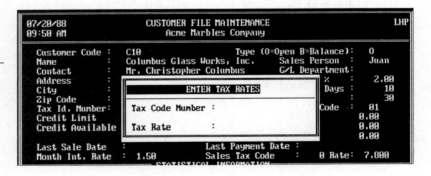

Fig. 4.4

The pop-up window for entering a new tax rate.

F6 (Delete) allows you to delete a customer record while that record is displayed. To delete the record for an existing customer in the master file, simply enter the customer's code in the Customer Code field of the Customer File Maintenance screen. The Customer File Maintenance program retrieves the record for that customer. Then press F6. A pop-up window appears and confirms that you want to delete the record. Press Y and Enter to delete the record. (Note, however, that DacEasy does *not* allow you to delete a customer record that has a current balance.)

With F7 (Enter Invoice), you can enter existing invoices for the customer whose record is displayed on the screen. This option provides a quick way to set up your starting accounts receivable balances. When you press F7, a pop-up window appears at the bottom of the screen (see fig. 4.5). The window prompts you to enter the invoice number, invoice code, invoice date and amount, discount date and amount, due date, and a cross-reference for each open invoice. (The total dollar amount of customer invoices you enter with F7 should equal the total accounts receivable in your trial balance at your conversion date, because this Enter Invoice option is where you set your initial accounts receivable balance.)

```
┌──────────────────────────────────────────────────────────────────────┐
│            Transaction:          Discount Available:    Due   Reference│
│ Invoice # Code   Date   Amt. Balance  Date     Amount   Date   Number  │
│ ───────── ──── ──────── ──────────── ──────── ──────── ────── ────────│
│ 88001      I   07/20/88     235.78 07/30/88       4.72 08/19/88 PO9056  │
│ 88002      D   07/15/88     450.13 07/25/88       9.00 08/14/88 PO9001  │
│ 88003      C   07/10/88     123.45 07/20/88       0.00 08/09/88 verbal  │
├──────────────────────────────────────────────────────────────────────┤
│ F1-Help  F2-Add Tax Rate  F6-DELETE  F7-Enter Invoice F10-Process  ESC-exit │
└──────────────────────────────────────────────────────────────────────┘
```

Fig. 4.5

The pop-up window for entering existing customer invoices.

Although only three invoices display in the pop-up window at a time, you can enter as many as you want and move through the list by using the up- and down-arrow keys. The Invoice # field holds up to nine digits for uniquely identifying open invoices. The Code field shows whether the item entered is an invoice (code "I"), a credit memo (code "C"), or a miscellaneous debit memo (code "D"). DacEasy includes invoices and miscellaneous debit memos as positive amounts and credit memos as negative amounts in the calculation of the Current Balance.

If you have existing open invoices with a customer, use F7 so that when the customer's payments arrive, you can describe which invoices the payments satisfy.

When you finish entering or editing a customer record, press F10 to save your work or press Enter when the last field (Sales Tax Code) is highlighted. To exit the Customer File Maintenance screen without saving your work, press Esc. Figure 4.6 shows the Customer File Maintenance screen filled with sample data.

Loading the Vendor Master File

The vendor master file is similar in use and layout to the customer master file. You use the vendor master file to store frequently used information about the vendors from whom you purchase goods and services and to accumulate historical information about vendors. You need to enter a vendor record for each vendor with whom you transact business regularly. In addition, you must enter a "dummy" vendor record that you can use to generate purchase orders and invoices for vendors with whom you deal infrequently.

Fig. 4.6

*The completed
Customer File
Maintenance
screen.*

```
07/20/88                  CUSTOMER FILE MAINTENANCE                        LHP
01:53 PM                     Acme Marbles Company
      Customer Code :   C10              Type (O=Open B=Balance):   0
      Name          :   Columbus Glass Works, Inc.   Sales Person :  Juan
      Contact       :   Mr. Christopher Columbus    G/L Department:
      Address       :   East 57th Avenue            Discount %    :     2.00
      City          :   Seattle       State :  WA   Discount Days :       10
      Zip Code      :   98104-    Tel : 206 555-9000 Due days      :       30
      Tax Id. Number:                               Message Code  :     01
      Credit Limit      :      5000.00  Previous Balance  :        0.00
      Credit Available  :      4437.54  This Period Bal.  :      562.46
                                        Current Balance   :      562.46
      Last Sale Date    :               Last Payment Date :
      Month Int. Rate   :   1.50        Sales Tax Code    :    0 Rate: 7.000
                          ══════════ STATISTICAL INFORMATION ══════════
                      Yr.Bef.Lst Last Year This Year Forecast  Variance      %
      # Invoices :        0         0        0        0         0       0.0
      $ Sales    :        0         0        0        0         0       0.0
      $ Costs    :        0         0        0        0         0       0.0
      $ Profit   :        0         0        0        0         0       0.0

  F1-Help  F2-Add Tax Rate  F6-DELETE  F7-Enter Invoice F10-Process  ESC-exit
```

Entering and Editing Vendor Data

To access the Vendor File Maintenance program, choose the Vendors option
from the File menu. Figure 4.7 shows the Vendor File Maintenance screen as it
appears before you enter any data.

Fig. 4.7

*The Vendor File
Maintenance
screen before you
enter data.*

```
07/20/88                   VENDOR FILE MAINTENANCE                         LHP
01:58 PM                     Acme Marbles Company
      Vendor Code   :                   Type (O=Open B=Balance):   0
      Name          :                             Territory     :
      Contact       :                             Type          :
      Address       :                             Discount %    :     0.00
      City          :               State :       Discount Days :        0
      Zip Code      :          Tel :       -      Due days      :        0
      Tax Id. Number:                             Message Code  :
      Credit Limit      :         0.00  Previous Balance  :        0.00
      Credit Available  :         0.00  This Period Bal.  :        0.00
                                        Current Balance   :        0.00
      Last Purch. Date  :    /  /       Last Payment Date :     /  /
                                        Sales Tax Code    :    0 Rate:
                          ══════════ STATISTICAL INFORMATION ══════════
                      Yr.Bef.Lst Last Year This Year Forecast  Variance      %
      # Invoices :        0         0        0        0         0       0.0
      $ Purchases:        0         0        0        0         0       0.0

  F1-Help  F2-Add Tax Rate  F6-DELETE  F7-Enter Invoice F10-Process  ESC-exit
```

The following paragraphs describe the fields in which you enter information for
vendor records on the Vendor File Maintenance screen.

Vendor Code: The *vendor code* is an abbreviation for identifying a vendor within the Purchase Order and Accounts Payable modules. When entering a vendor record, you can use up to six characters or numbers for your code. You can use vendor codes, like customer codes, to sort the records in the master file. You therefore may want to use codes that group the vendors in a meaningful order.

To edit a vendor record, simply enter that vendor's code. The Vendor File Maintenance program retrieves the appropriate vendor record.

Name, Contact, Address, City, State, Zip Code, and Tel: You store the vendor's business name, the contact person's name, and the vendor's complete address and telephone number in these fields.

Type (O = Open B = Balance): The *type* identifies the detail at which you want vendor invoice information stored. You have two choices: *O* for open invoice, and *B* for balance forward. "Open invoice" means that each open invoice is kept in the accounting information files until you pay the vendor and run the end-of-the-month accounting routines. "Balance forward" means that only the total invoice amount for the preceding month—rather than all unpaid invoices—is kept in the accounting information files.

In general, you should use the open invoice method. Although the balance forward method minimizes the level of detail with which you're deluged as you review amounts you owe, you'll have difficulty paying specific invoices. You may want to use the balance forward method when you don't need detailed information at the invoice level, for example, if you seldom carry over unpaid invoices from the prior month.

Territory: You probably won't find much of a reason to use this field. If you prefer, however, you can use the Territory code in almost the same way you use the Sales Person code in the customer master file—to sort and subtotal the vendors. The user's manual suggests storing the purchasing agent's name in this field. That's one idea. You may be able to think of a better one.

Type: The Vendor File Maintenance screen contains a second Type field, which you can use to sort and subtotal vendor information on reports that the DacEasy system doesn't already provide. For example, the user's manual suggests using this field to flag or identify those vendors who will require a 1099 form at the end of the calendar year. Taking that approach, you merely need to sort your vendors by Type to see a list of those vendors that require 1099s.

Discount %: The *discount percent* determines the amount of discount the vendor allows you to deduct from an invoice if you pay within the defined number of discount days. The discount equals the discount percent multiplied by the invoice amount (not including freight and insurance).

Discount Days: The *discount days* is the number of days that sets the period within which you can deduct the discount percent from your payment.

C.P.A. Tip: You should recognize that *not* taking early payment discounts is an extremely expensive way to borrow money from your vendors. For example, suppose that a vendor normally requires payment within 30 days but allows a 2 percent discount for payments received within 10 days. If you pay within 30 rather than 10 days, you essentially pay the vendor a 2 percent interest charge for paying 20 days later. Because one year contains roughly 18 20-day periods, the 2 percent for 20 days equals approximately 36 percent annually.

Although you may need to be "borrowing" this money, you can probably find a much cheaper lender. As rough rules of thumb, if a vendor gives you a 1 percent discount for paying 20 days early, you're borrowing money from him at about 18 percent annual interest. A 3 percent discount works out to a whopping 54 percent a year.

Due Days: The *due days* is the number of days within which the vendor requires you to pay invoices.

Tax Id. Number: The Tax Id. Number field is a 12-character alphanumeric field in which you can store a vendor's federal tax identification number. You need to collect and store this number for those vendors for whom you must prepare the Internal Revenue Service form 1099.

Message Code: The *message code* identifies any special message you want to see whenever you enter the vendor number. The two-character code is the pre-assigned code you assigned to the message in the messages file (see Chapter 3). You need to have a copy of the messages you previously entered so that you can enter the appropriate message code.

Credit Limit: The Credit Limit field shows the credit limit a vendor has agreed to extend you.

Sales Tax Code: The *sales tax code* is the tax rate code from the tax rates table that represents the correct sales tax percentage for the vendor and the sale. When the Sales Tax Code field is highlighted, the tax rates table appears in the upper right corner of the screen. When you select the sales tax code, DacEasy automatically pulls the sales tax rate into the Rate field of the vendor record.

Statistical Information: You can use the Yr. Bef. Lst, Last Year, This Year, Forecast, Variance, and % fields to enter statistical information about a vendor, such as the number of invoices and purchases from that vendor. DacEasy calculates the variance in dollars and percent between the actual amount and the forecast amount for the current year based on your entries. As with the customer statistical information, you may want to postpone using this information until your second year of operation with DacEasy. By then, the program will have automatically developed the data for you.

Examining the Remaining Fields

The Vendor File Maintenance screen includes six fields in which DacEasy doesn't let you enter data: Credit Available, Previous Balance, This Period Bal., Current Balance, Last Sale Date, and Last Payment Date. The system automatically collects and updates this information for you. Here are brief descriptions of these six fields:

Previous Balance	The total invoices owed to the vendor at the end of the preceding accounting period
This Period Bal.	The total invoices owed to the vendor in the current accounting period
Current Balance	The total of all invoices owed to the vendor; equals the Previous Balance plus the This Period Bal.
Credit Available	The unused portion of the vendor's credit limit; calculated as the Credit Limit minus the Current Balance
Last Purch. Date	The month, day, and year of the last time a purchase order was prepared for this vendor
Last Payment Date	The month, day, and year of the last time you made a payment to this vendor

Using the Special Function Keys

You can use the same three special function keys on the Vendor File Maintenance screen that you used on the Customer File Maintenance screen—and with essentially the same results. F2 (Add Tax Rate) allows you to add sales tax percentage rates to the tax rates table. When you press F2, a pop-up window appears, allowing you to specify a tax code number and a tax rate. With F6 (Delete), you can delete a vendor record while that record is displayed. (You can delete a vendor record only if that vendor does not have a current balance.)

F7 (Enter Invoice) allows you to enter existing invoices owed to the vendor whose record is displayed on the screen. When you press F7, a pop-up window appears at the bottom of the screen and prompts you to enter the invoice number, code, date, and amount; the discount date and amount; the due date; and a cross-reference for each open invoice. (The total dollar amount of vendor invoices you enter with F7 should equal the total accounts payable balance in your trial balance at your conversion date, because this Enter Invoice option is where you set your initial accounts payable balance.)

Although only three invoices display at a time in the pop-up window, you can enter as many as you want and move through the list on the window by using the up- and down-arrow keys. The Invoice # field holds a vendor invoice number that can be as many as nine digits. The Code field shows whether the item entered is an invoice (code "I"), a credit memo (code "C"), or a miscellaneous debit memo (code "D").

DacEasy includes invoices and credit memos as positive amounts and miscellaneous debit memos as negative amounts, when calculating the Current Balance. Although this accounting seems backward at first, DacEasy assumes that when you indicate a credit memo, you're entering what amounts to a credit to accounts payable from your perspective. Thus the balance owed increases just as it does for an invoice, which also produces a credit to the accounts payable account. Conversely, DacEasy assumes that by indicating a debit memo, you're entering what amounts to a debit to accounts payable, meaning that the balance owed decreases.

If you have existing open invoices with a vendor, you should use F7 when you set up the vendor master file. Then, when you pay a vendor, you can describe which invoices you're paying.

When you finish entering or editing a vendor record, press F10 to save your work or press Enter when the last field on the screen (Sales Tax Code) is highlighted. To exit the Vendor File Maintenance screen without saving your work, press Esc. Figure 4.8 shows the Vendor File Maintenance screen filled with sample data.

Loading the Product Master File

You use the product master file to keep track of the items you purchase, hold, and then resell to customers. You need the product file if you want to use inventory to maintain a perpetual inventory system for your product inventory.

```
07/20/88                  VENDOR FILE MAINTENANCE                        LHP
12:52 PM                     Acme Marbles Company

   Vendor Code   :   F10              Type (O=Open B=Balance):   O
   Name          :   First Class Marble Mfg. Inc.  Territory  :
   Contact       :   Isaac Newton             Type          :
   Address       :   5150 Mukilteo Speedway   Discount %    :     2.00
   City          :   Mukilteo      State :  WA Discount Days :       10
   Zip Code      :   98210-    Tel : (206)555-3212 Due days   :       30
   Tax Id. Number:                          Message Code   :     06
   Credit Limit  :      10000.00  Previous Balance :          0.00
   Credit Available :    3549.89  This Period Bal. :       6450.11
                                  Current Balance  :       6450.11
   Last Purch. Date :             Last Payment Date :
                                  Sales Tax Code   :   1 Rate: 8.100
===================== STATISTICAL INFORMATION =====================
                Yr.Bef.Lst Last Year This Year  Forecast  Variance      %

 # Invoices :   [          ]      0       0        0         0        0.0
 $ Purchases:          0          0       0        0         0        0.0
```

F1-Help F2-Add Tax Rate F6-DELETE F7-Enter Invoice F10-Process ESC-exit

Fig. 4.8

The completed Vendor File Maintenance screen.

Excluding Some Products

Using the product master file doesn't require any difficult accounting decisions. The master file simply represents an automatically maintained list of what you purchase and resell. In some businesses, however, many of the inventory items have minimal value, are easy to replenish, and don't need to be monitored too closely. Consider excluding these kinds of items from your product master file and from your inventory records in general. The reason is simple: Often, much of the work you do to manage your inventory is related to these small, almost insignificant items. Unfortunately, you then have less time to spend on the more important inventory items and on your other business duties.

If you do have inventory items of minimal value for which you don't want to maintain perpetual inventory records, the accounting is pretty basic. You simply account for these items as expenses when you purchase them. Although you still need to keep track of your on-hand quantities and know when to reorder these materials, you can easily check quantities by periodically glancing at the shelf on which you store the items.

Entering and Editing Product Data

To create a product master file, choose Products from the File menu. Figure 4.9 shows the Product File Maintenance screen as it appears before you begin entering product data.

```
 07/20/88                 PRODUCT FILE MAINTENANCE              LHP
 02:50 PM                    Acme Marbles Company
  Product Code  :  ███████      Description :
  Measure       :               Fraction    :    0      Dept.  :
  Bin           :               Vendor      :
  Sales Price   :     0.000     Taxable(Y/N): Y
  Last Sale Date:    /  /        Minimum     :    0      Reorder :     0
  Last Purch. Date :  /  /   Lst.Purch.Price :    0.000
  Std. Cost     :     0.000     Avg. Cost   :    0.000
  On Hand  Units :              0.000  Dollars    :     0.000
  Committed Units :             0.000
  On Order Units  :             0.000
 ═══════════════════════ STATISTICAL INFORMATION ═══════════════════
                  Yr.Bef.Lst Last Year This Year Forecast Variance    %
  Units Purch. :      0         0        0         0        0       0.0
  $ Purchase   :      0         0        0         0        0       0.0
  Units Sold   :      0         0        0         0        0       0.0
  $ Sales      :      0         0        0         0        0       0.0
  $ Cost       :      0         0        0         0        0       0.0
  $ Profit     :      0         0        0         0        0       0.0
  Times Turn   :    0.0       0.0      0.0       0.0      0.0       0.0
  Gross Return :      0         0        0         0        0       0.0

  F1-Help  F6-Delete  F7-Enter Stock  F10-Process  ESC-exit
```

Fig. 4.9

The Product File Maintenance screen before you enter data.

To develop a product record, you need to enter information in 12 fields: Product Code, Description, Measure, Fraction, Dept., Bin, Vendor, Sales Price, Taxable (Y/N), Minimum, Reorder, and Std. Cost. You must complete each of these fields for every product you define in the system. In addition, you need to tell DacEasy the starting balances and the unit prices for those products held at the beginning of the accounting period. The following paragraphs describe the fields in which you enter information for each product.

Product Code: The *product code* is an abbreviation you can use within the system to refer to the product. The field allows up to 13 characters, which gives you enough room to use either the universal product code or the European product code.

Description: The Description field gives you up to 20 characters of free text to describe the product.

Measure: You use the Measure field, which can contain up to four characters, to describe the unit of measure you use to describe the product on reports, invoices, purchases, and so on. For example, if you sell eggs by the dozen, your unit of measure equals dozen, which you might abbreviate *dozn*. If you sell fish by the pound, your unit of measure equals pound, which you might abbreviate *lbs*.

Fraction: The Fraction field applies to the Measure field and allows you to specify the fractional units in each unit of measure. For example, if you purchase eggs with a unit of measure specified as *dozn*, your fraction equals *12* because the fractional units of a dozen eggs are the 12 single eggs that comprise the dozen. Similarly, if you specified fish with a unit of measure of *lbs*, your fractional unit might be *16* because 1 pound contains 16 ounces. Using fractional units makes specifying purchases and sales much easier. For example, if you sell 15 eggs, you can specify the quantity as 1.3 (calculated as one dozen eggs and three single eggs). If you can't buy and sell fractional units of the product (for example, if your product is marbles), enter *1* in the Fraction field.

Dept.: The Dept. field relates to the revenue/cost departments specified as part of the general ledger interface table definition. You need to define a department if you set the revenue/cost department to INVENTORY in the general ledger interface table. If you set the revenue/cost department to CUSTOMER or NONE, leave the Dept. field blank. You must enter the Dept. code exactly as you set it up in the general ledger interface table. Otherwise, DacEasy displays an error message. If you're using the sample Chart of Accounts, DacEasy has already provided two departments: 01 and 02. You simply identify which department applies to the product.

The account number prefix (described in the general ledger interface table) combined with the department code must equal a real revenue account number in the Chart of Accounts. For example, a sales revenue account number of *41* combined with a department code of *01* concatenates to *4101*. The number 4101 must be a revenue account number. (You may want to review Chapter 3's discussion of revenue/cost departments in the general ledger interface table.)

Bin: The Bin field allows you to use up to four characters to identify where the product is stored. For example, perhaps you store your eggs in bins in a cooler. You may then want to use this field to identify the exact cooler and bin. Alternatively, you might use the Bin field to identify the warehouse shelf on which the item is stored. If you don't have trouble keeping track of the storage locations of your various products, you don't need to use this field. In fact, using it in that case only adds to your work load and doesn't deliver any special benefits.

Vendor: The Vendor field is simply an information field that allows you to specify the most preferred vendor from whom you purchase this item. Although DacEasy doesn't verify that the vendor code you enter is defined in the vendor master file, the program does allow you to use the Vendor field to sort some product files. If you have already loaded your vendor master file, you may want to keep a copy of it on hand so that you can easily enter the correct vendor codes.

Sales Price: The *sales price* is the price at which you are currently selling this product. For example, if you're selling eggs for $1.39 a dozen, enter *$1.39* in the Sales Price field.

Taxable (Y/N): The Taxable (Y/N) field denotes whether you are charged sales tax when you purchase this item. You simply enter *Y* or *N*.

Minimum: The Minimum field represents the minimum number of units of the product you want to keep in inventory. You don't have to make an entry in this field, but if you do, inventory items whose balances on hand fall below the specified minimum appear on the inventory alert report, a special report identifying understocked products.

Reorder: The Reorder field represents the number of units of the product you want to buy whenever you place a purchase order for this item. This field does not display on the purchase order screen as the default number of units ordered. But the Reorder field *is* included on the inventory alert report—the special report that identifies which inventory items have units on hand below the minimum quantity you specified.

Std. Cost: The *standard cost* is the cost at which an individual unit of this product is listed in your inventory records if you use a standard costing inventory method. If you use average or last purchase price costing, do *not* use this field.

Statistical Information: You can use the Yr. Bef. Lst, Last Year, This Year, Forecast, Variance, and % fields to enter statistical information about a product. For example, you can record the number of units purchased, the dollar cost of purchases, the units sold, the dollars of units sold, and the cost in dollars of units sold for the year before last, last year, this year, and as forecast for the current year. If you enter these amounts, DacEasy calculates the resulting profit margin (the sales minus the costs), the resulting inventory turnover ratio, which the program labels "Times Turn" (the units sold divided by the units on hand), and the resulting gross return (the units on hand multiplied by the profit divided by the times turn).

(Independently, these last two calculations may not have much meaning to you. By comparing these ratios to those of similar businesses, however, you may gain insight into the profit margins and inventory turnovers of your peers and competitors. Such information should help you make better inventory purchasing, holding, and pricing decisions.)

The Product File Maintenance program also calculates the variance both in absolute amounts and in percentages between the This Year amount and the Forecast amount.

Unless you're converting from another automated accounting system that provides this statistical information, postpone using this information until DacEasy begins to collect and calculate it for you. Developing reasonable estimates of these amounts on your own will probably involve hours of work.

Examining the Remaining Fields

Notice that the Product File Maintenance screen contains eight other fields in which DacEasy doesn't let you enter data. The system collects and updates this information for you. Here are brief descriptions of these eight fields:

Last Sale Date	The month, day, and year of the last time an invoice was prepared for this product
Last Purch. Date	The month, day, and year of the last time a purchase order was prepared for this product
Lst. Purch. Price	The cost per unit of the most recent purchase of this product
Avg. Cost	The average cost per unit of the product items currently on hand; calculated as the total purchase costs of the on-hand units divided by the total number of units on hand
On Hand Units	The total number of units of this product you currently hold
Committed Units	The total number of units of this product for which invoices have been prepared but not yet posted
On Order Units	The total number of units of this product for which purchase orders have been prepared
Dollars	The total on-hand cost of this product computed with the inventory costing system you selected as part of setting the system options and defaults (see Chapter 3)

Figure 4.10 shows the Product File Maintenance screen filled with data. But the screen is missing one important piece of information: the starting inventory balances. You enter these balances with the F7 key, which is discussed in the next section.

Using the Special Function Keys

In addition to using the function keys that are available on all screens (F1, F4, and F10), you can use two special function keys on the Product File Maintenance screen: F6 and F7.

```
┌─────────────────────────────────────────────────────────────────┐
│ 07/20/88              PRODUCT FILE MAINTENANCE                 LHP │
│ 02:50 PM                Acme Marbles Company                      │
│  Product Code  : C10        Description : Cat's Eye               │
│  Measure       : each       Fraction    :    1      Dept.  : 01   │
│  Bin           : E12        Vendor      : F10                     │
│  Sales Price   :       0.020  Taxable(Y/N): Y                     │
│  Last Sale Date:            Minimum     :  10000    Reorder : 1000│
│  Last Purch. Date :         Lst.Purch.Price :   0.000            │
│  Std. Cost      :    ███████  .    Avg. Cost :   0.000           │
│  On Hand   Units :         0.000  Dollars   :      0.000          │
│  Committed Units :         0.000                                  │
│  On Order  Units :         0.000                                  │
│ ═══════════════════ STATISTICAL INFORMATION ════════════════════ │
│              Yr.Bef.Lst Last Year This Year  Forecast Variance  % │
│  Units Purch. :      0        0        0        0        0    0.0 │
│  $ Purchase   :      0        0        0        0        0    0.0 │
│  Units Sold   :      0        0        0        0        0    0.0 │
│  $ Sales      :      0        0        0        0        0    0.0 │
│  $ Cost       :      0        0        0        0        0    0.0 │
│  $ Profit     :      0        0        0        0        0    0.0 │
│  Times Turn   :    0.0      0.0      0.0      0.0        0    0.0 │
│  Gross Return :      0        0        0        0        0    0.0 │
└─────────────────────────────────────────────────────────────────┘
    F1-Help  F6-Delete  F7-Enter Stock  F10-Process  ESC-exit
```

Fig. 4.10

The partially completed Product File Maintenance screen.

F6 (Delete) allows you to delete a product record while that record is displayed on the screen. To delete the record for an existing product in the master file, enter the product code. The Product File Maintenance program then retrieves the record for that product. When you press F6, a pop-up window appears and confirms that you want to delete the record. Press *Y* and Enter to delete the record. Note that DacEasy does *not* allow you to delete a product record that has a nonzero balance.

F7 (Enter Stock) allows you to enter information about any inventory you have on hand. You use this option to set your initial inventory balances. When you press F7, a pop-up window appears in the middle of the screen (see fig. 4.11). The screen prompts you to enter the Units, Unit Cost, and Dollars for the product currently in stock. Enter the number of units on hand and the unit cost. DacEasy calculates the Dollars amount automatically, but you can edit this field if the program doesn't round the figure to your preference. (The total dollar amount of inventory you enter with F7 should equal the total inventory balance in your trial balance at your conversion date, because this Enter Stock option is where you set your initial inventory balance.)

If you have the on-hand balances of an inventory item, use F7 to record your inventory so that the automatically updated balances are always correct.

After you've entered or edited a product, press F10 to save your work, or press Enter when the $ Cost field in the Forecast column is highlighted. To exit from the Product Maintenance File screen without saving your data, press Esc. Figure 4.12 shows the Product File Maintenance screen filled with sample data.

```
 On Hand   Units   :    12000.000  Dollars  :     240.000
 Committed Units   :        0.000  ┌─────────────────────────────────────┐
 On Order  Units   :        0.000  │  Enter Additional Stock :           │
 ══════════════════STATISTI        │                                     │
                    Yr.Bef.Lst Last│  Units      :     12000.000         │   %
 Units Purch. :         0          │  Unit Cost  :         0.020         │  0.0
 $ Purchase   :         0          │  Dollars    :       240.00          │  0.0
 Units Sold   :         0          └─────────────────────────────────────┘  0.0
 $ Sales      :         0       0         0         0         0              0.0
 $ Cost       :         0       0         0         0         0              0.0
 $ Profit     :         0       0         0         0         0              0.0
 Times Turn   :       0.0     0.0       0.0       0.0         0              0.0
 Gross Return :         0       0         0         0         0              0.0

 F1-Help  F6-Delete  F7-Enter Stock  F10-Process  ESC-exit
```

Fig. 4.11

The pop-up window you use to enter stock on hand.

```
┌─────────────────────────────────────────────────────────────────────────┐
│ 07/20/88              PRODUCT FILE MAINTENANCE                        LHP  │
│ 04:26 PM                 Acme Marbles Company                             │
│  Product Code  : C10         Description  : Cat's Eye                     │
│  Measure       : each        Fraction     :     1        Dept.  : 01     │
│  Bin           : E12         Vendor       : F10                           │
│  Sales Price   :     0.020   Taxable(Y/N) : Y                            │
│  Last Sale Date:             Minimum      : 10000      Reorder : 1000    │
│  Last Purch. Date :      Lst.Purch.Price  :     0.020                    │
│  Std. Cost     :     0.000   Avg. Cost    :     0.020                    │
│  On Hand   Units   :   12000.000  Dollars  :     240.000                  │
│  Committed Units   :       0.000                                          │
│  On Order  Units   :       0.000                                          │
│ ════════════════════ STATISTICAL INFORMATION ═══════════════════════════ │
│               Yr.Bef.Lst Last Year This Year  Forecast  Variance    %    │
│  Units Purch. :       0        0        0         0         0      0.0   │
│  $ Purchase   :       0        0        0         0         0      0.0   │
│  Units Sold   :       0        0        0         0         0      0.0   │
│  $ Sales      :       0        0        0         0         0      0.0   │
│  $ Cost       :       0        0        0         0         0      0.0   │
│  $ Profit     :       0        0        0         0         0      0.0   │
│  Times Turn   :     0.0      0.0      0.0       0.0         0      0.0   │
│  Gross Return :       0        0        0         0         0      0.0   │
└─────────────────────────────────────────────────────────────────────────┘
 F1-Help  F6-Delete  F7-Enter Stock  F10-Process  ESC-exit
```

Fig. 4.12

The completed Product File Maintenance screen.

Loading the Service Master File

You use the service master file to keep track of the services you provide to your customers or clients. Although this master file isn't a requirement, using the file provides you with statistical information similar to that collected and stored in the product master file. The service master file may also ease your use of the Billing and Accounts Receivable modules.

Defining and Classifying Your Services

The service master file, which is a simplified version of the product master file, doesn't require any significant bookkeeping decisions. This file just lists the services you offer. You need to consider, however, a couple of points. First, the definition you provide for a service appears on invoices to customers, so you want something that's descriptive but not confidential.

Second, you want to assure that your service definitions are mutually exclusive. For example, suppose that you are a partner in the three-person law firm Adams, Bobbins, and Carter. If you and your partners provide tax, contract, and personal injury counsel, you can select one of two service classification schemes. You can classify the partners' time: Adams's time, Bobbins's time, and Carter's time. Or you can classify by the type of counsel: tax advice, contract advice, and personal injury advice.

Because you can use only one of these classification schemes, you may want to spend some time considering which one provides you with information that best allows you and your partners to manage service revenues and costs.

Entering and Editing Service Data

You need to complete seven fields to create a service record in the service master file: Service Code, Description, Measure, Fraction, Dept., Sales Price, and Taxable (Y/N). To access the Service File Maintenance program, choose the Services option from the File menu. Figure 4.13 shows the Service File Maintenance screen as it appears before you enter any data.

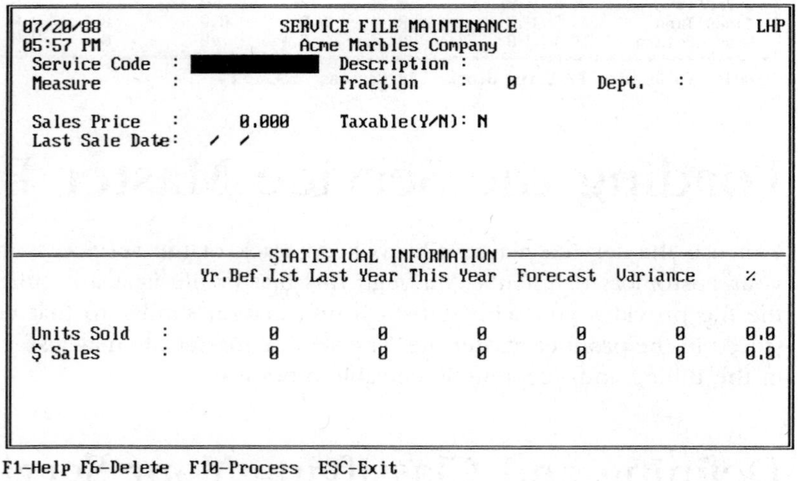

Fig. 4.13

The Service File Maintenance screen before you enter data.

```
07/20/88                   SERVICE FILE MAINTENANCE                    LHP
05:57 PM                      Acme Marbles Company
 Service Code   : ███████████  Description :
 Measure        :              Fraction    :   0      Dept.  :

 Sales Price    :     0.000    Taxable(Y/N): N
 Last Sale Date:   /  /




════════════════════════ STATISTICAL INFORMATION ════════════════════════
                  Yr.Bef.Lst Last Year This Year  Forecast  Variance    %


 Units Sold   :       0         0         0         0         0       0.0
 $ Sales      :       0         0         0         0         0       0.0




─────────────────────────────────────────────────────────────────────────
     F1-Help F6-Delete  F10-Process  ESC-Exit
```

The following paragraphs describe the fields in which you provide information for each service.

Service Code: The *service code* is an abbreviation you use within the system to refer to the service. This field's maximum length is 13 characters, which gives you plenty of room.

Description: The Description field allows you up to 20 characters of free text to describe the service.

Measure: You use the Measure field, which accommodates up to four characters, to describe the unit of measure with which you describe the service on reports, invoices, purchases, and so on. For example, if you sell legal services by the hour, your unit of measure equals *hour*.

Fraction: The Fraction field applies to the Measure field and allows you to specify the fractional units in each unit of measure. For example, if you always bill for your services in minimum time increments of 15 minutes (1/4 of an hour), enter *4* in the Fraction field.

Using fractional units makes specifying sales of fractional units much easier. If, for example, you sell 1 hour and 2 15-minute portions of time to a client, you can specify the quantity as *1.2.*

Dept.: The Dept. field relates to the revenue/cost departments specified as part of the general ledger interface table definition. You use this field exactly as you use the Dept. field in the product master file. If you want to break service revenues into revenue departments, see the discussion of Dept. in "Loading the Product Master File."

Sales Price: The Sales Price field holds the price at which you currently sell this service. For example, if you're currently offering one hour of legal advice for $90.00, enter the sales price as *$90.00.*

Taxable (Y/N): In this field, you indicate whether you charge sales tax. Simply enter *Y* or *N.*

Statistical Information: You can use the Yr. Bef. Lst, Last Year, This Year, Forecast, Variance, and % fields to enter statistical information about a service. For example, you can enter the units and dollars sold for the year before last, last year, this year, and as forecast for the current year. In addition, the Service File Maintenance program calculates the variance both in absolute amounts and in percentages between the This Year amount and the Forecast amount.

If you don't want to expend the effort necessary to collect and enter this information now, you can wait until DacEasy accumulates and calculates it for you after your first year of operation.

Examining the Remaining Field

The Service File Maintenance screen includes one other field. DacEasy doesn't permit you to enter data in the Last Sale Date field. The system collects and updates this information for you. The Last Sale Date shows the month, day, and year of the last time an invoice was prepared for this service.

To save the service record you've created, press F10. DacEasy saves the service information and then presents you with a fresh screen on which you can enter information for another service. Figure 4.14 shows the Service File Maintenance screen filled with sample data.

Fig. 4.14

The completed Service File Maintenance screen.

```
07/20/88                    SERVICE FILE MAINTENANCE                    LHP
05:57 PM                       Acme Marbles Company
   Service Code  : P10        Description :  polish marbles
   Measure       : hour       Fraction    :     4       Dept.  : 01

   Sales Price   :     0.005  Taxable(Y/N): N
   Last Sale Date:


                        ═══ STATISTICAL INFORMATION ═══
                        Yr.Bef.Lst Last Year This Year  Forecast  Variance    %


   Units Sold  :           0         0        0          0         0      0.0
   $ Sales     :           0         0        0          0         0      0.0




          F1-Help F6-Delete  F10-Process  ESC-Exit
```

Defining the Purchase Order and Billing Codes

The codes master file is not one but two short files that you access by selecting the Codes option from the File menu. Figure 4.15 shows the two options that display after you've selected Codes.

Not every item you purchase needs to be set as a specific product in the product master file. Similarly, not every item for which you bill a customer needs to be defined as a specific product or service in the product or service master file. You define a product in the product file so that you can maintain an accurate count of the number of units you're holding in inventory and the value of these

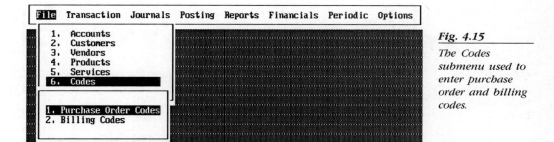

Fig. 4.15

The Codes submenu used to enter purchase order and billing codes.

units. You define a service record in the service file to maintain a history of the units and dollar amounts of the service sold.

Creating special product and service records for some items probably represents more work than the benefits warrant. DacEasy provides an alternative: what amounts to shorthand product and service files that provide codes similar to the product or service code. These brief files contain only a code, a description, the amount, the Chart of Account number to which these entries are recorded, and a flag that shows whether the item is taxable. You can list in these abbreviated files any products or services that don't meet the prerequisites for inclusion in the product and service master files.

After you provide a description, an amount, an account number (which must be defined as a detail account), and the taxable status on either the Purchase Order Codes or Billing Codes screen, you can use the code just as you would use any product or service master file code. If the amount varies, leave that field as 0. You can input the correct amount when you create the invoice or purchase order that uses the code. Figure 4.16 shows the predefined purchase order codes provided as examples by DacEasy. Figure 4.17 shows the predefined billing codes. You can toggle between these two screens by pressing F2.

To enter or edit one of these codes, simply use the arrow keys to move the cursor to the field you want to change. Although you have only 20 characters within this file to describe a general category of product or service, you can expand these short descriptions on the purchase orders and invoices to 50 characters.

To exit from either the Purchase Order Codes or Billing Codes program, press F10. DacEasy saves your work and returns you to the File menu. Pressing Esc returns you to the File menu but doesn't save your work. You can also save your entries and return to the File menu by pressing Enter or the down-arrow key when you're at the end of either codes list (at code 40). If you want to delete a purchase order code or billing code, place the cursor on that code and simultaneously press the Alt key and the letter *D*.

```
07/    ****  PURCHASE ORDER CODES  ****                      LHP
08:
       Code No.      Description        Amount    Account No.   Taxable
       ---------    -------------      --------  -------------  -------
          1         Freight              0.00      52081          N
          2         Insurance            0.00      52082          N
          3         Packaging            0.00      52083          N
          4         Advertising Radio/TV 0.00      52191          Y
          5         Advertising Print    0.00      52192          Y
          6         Autos & Trucks       0.00      12011          Y
          7         Furniture & Fixtures 0.00      12021          Y
          8         Office Equipment     0.00      12031          Y
          9         Machinery & Equip.   0.00      12041          Y
         10         Other Fixed Assets   0.00      12061          Y
         11         Office Supplies      0.00      5211           Y
         12                              0.00
         13                              0.00
         14                              0.00
         15                              0.00
         16                              0.00

   F1-Help   F2-Toggle PO/Billing   F10-Process   ALT D-Delete   ESC-Exit
```

```
07/    ****  BILLING CODES  ****                             LHP
08:
       Code No.      Description        Amount    Account No.   Taxable
       ---------    -------------      --------  -------------  -------
          1         Freight              0.00      4301           N
          2         Insurance            0.00      4302           Y
          3         Packaging            0.00      4303           Y
          4         Surcharge            0.00      4304           Y
          5                              0.00
          6         Autos & Trucks       0.00      12011          Y
          7         Furniture & Fixtures 0.00      12021          Y
          8         Office Equipment     0.00      12031          Y
          9         Machinery & Equip.   0.00      12041          Y
         10         Other Fixed Assets   0.00      12061          Y
         11                              0.00
         12                              0.00
         13                              0.00
         14                              0.00
         15                              0.00
         16                              0.00

   F1-Help   F2-Toggle PO/Billing   F10-Process   ALT D-Delete   ESC-Exit
```

Loading the Statement Messages File

This file generates standard messages, based on the status of a customer's account, at the bottom of the customer statements generated by the Accounts Receivable module. If you're not using the Accounts Receivable module or not planning to generate the customer statements, you don't need to enter statement messages in this file.

A customer's accounts can fall into one of five categories:

Inactive	The customer owes you no money
Current Bal.	None of the amounts this customer owes you are past due
Due 1–30 Days	Some portion of the amount a customer owes is past due by at least 1 day or as many as 30 days
Due 31–60 Days	Some portion of the amount a customer owes is past due by at least 31 days or as many as 60 days
Due Over 60	Some portion of the amount a customer owes is more than 60 days past due

Planning Messages

Think about what you want to communicate to customers based on the status of their accounts. Remember that the computer shows no discretion when generating these messages. If the test condition is met (for example, the most overdue invoice to a customer falls within the account classification), then the customer gets the message. The computer doesn't recognize that the customer may not have paid because you told him not to pay, because your product was defective, or because you forgot to send the invoice. And the customer usually doesn't recognize that the statement messages aren't personal communications from you.

Obviously, this whole situation can work to your benefit. Nice, friendly messages get generated even when you don't feel friendly. But a danger is inherent in this system. Suppose that you have a customer that purchases thousands of dollars of goods and services from you each month. Everything's current except one $40.00 invoice that you forgot to send and is now 60 days overdue. Do you want this customer's next statement to include a message like "Your account will be turned over to our legal department if your payment is not received immediately"?

Entering and Editing Statement Messages

If you want to include statement messages on your customer statements, choose the File menu's last option, Statement Messages. The Customer's Statement Texts screen appears (see fig. 4.18). To enter a two-line message for each customer account category, use the arrow keys to move the cursor to the first line of the message and then make your changes. Then move to the second line and make your changes. Within each line, use the F2 key to center the message. The message you type will appear on the statements of all customers whose oldest balance falls in the category that corresponds to the message.

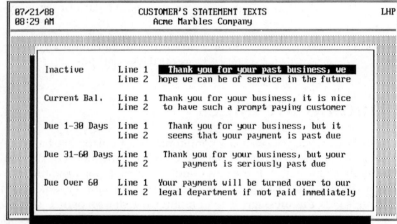

Fig. 4.18

The Customer's Statement Texts screen.

To save your changes to the statement messages file, press F10, or press Enter while you're on the second line of the Due Over 60 message. To exit without saving your changes, press Esc.

Note that the definition of "Due" is based on the Due Days field defined in the customer master file. If the Due Days field for a particular customer equals 30 days, for example, Due 1–30 Days means the invoice was billed between 31 and 60 days ago (calculated as 1 + 30 = 31 and 30 + 30 = 60). Due 31–60 Days means the invoice was billed between 61 and 90 days ago (calculated as 31 + 30 = 61 and 60 + 30 = 90), and so on.

Chapter Summary

This chapter described the steps for loading the six master files needed to operate the DacEasy accounting package: customer, vendor, product, service, codes,
and statement messages. Loading these master files is the final step in your
DacEasy preparations. Now you're ready to begin using the system. The next
chapter, "Protecting Your System," describes the steps for implementing internal controls within your system and for backing up and recovering your data.

CHAPTER 5

Protecting Your System

By this point, you've installed the DacEasy software on your computer, defined the Chart of Accounts and system options, and loaded the master files. You may have even polished your accounting skills a bit if they were rusty. But before you begin using the DacEasy system, you should know two things about protecting your system.

First, you should know how to back up your accounting files and how to recover the backups if your accounting files are lost or damaged. You can thus protect your system from power failures, hardware malfunctions, and software errors. Second, you should know a thing or two about internal controls, which are ways you can operate your DacEasy system to minimize human errors and unauthorized transactions. Internal controls protect the accuracy and reliability of your accounting files.

Note: In addition to practicing the procedures described in this chapter, you can use a simple device called a *surge protector* to protect your equipment from surges of electricity that can damage the fragile electronic components. Talk to your local computer supplier to see which type of surge protector is best for your system.

Learning Backup and Recovery Procedures

You use *backup* procedures to copy all your accounting information files so that you can still prepare financial statements and accounting forms if your original accounting files are lost or damaged. *Recovery* procedures are the steps you take to return your accounting information files to the condition they were in immediately before you lost or damaged the files.

Backing Up Your Files

The steps for backing up your accounting data files are essentially the same whether you're using a hard disk system or a floppy disk system. You simply use the DOS BACKUP command, a versatile command that can back up either a floppy disk or a hard disk. (BACKUP is most frequently used to back up a hard disk on floppy disks.) A unique feature of BACKUP is that if the data fills your backup disk, DOS prompts you to insert another blank formatted disk. BACKUP performs a sequential copy of your data. The command takes the following form:

BACKUP C:\DEA3\FILES A: /S

(The /S switch tells DOS to back up all subdirectories, starting with the current directory and working downward. For more information on switches, refer to your DOS manual.)

Backing up your data files is that simple. But you also need to make two important decisions. First you must decide how often you need to back up. Opinions vary regarding how frequent is frequent enough. My feeling is that you should back up your data files immediately after you complete any session in which you enter or change any accounting data. For example, if you've just finished installing the software, defining your Chart of Accounts, or loading your master files, you should back up your files. Most people back up their accounting records daily, weekly, or monthly.

After you've read the paragraphs on recovery procedures and worked with the program for a while, you can better estimate how often you need to back up your accounting files. For example, if you discover that backing up your files requires as much effort as re-creating six months of accounting activity, you might decide to back up your accounting files only every six months. (If your accounting is this light, however, I question why you're even using a computer-based system.)

A related question involves the number of old backup copies you should keep. Usually, two or three copies are adequate. (This rule of thumb is known as the "grandfather, father, and son" scheme.) For example, suppose that you back up your accounting files every day. On Thursday, while you're entering billing transactions, a power outage damages the accounting files. If you kept two old backup copies in addition to the most recent backup copy, you have not only a Wednesday backup but also Tuesday and Monday backups. If the Wednesday copy is somehow damaged (an unlikely but possible situation), you still have the Tuesday and Monday copies to restore. Obviously, the more recent a backup copy, the easier it is to recover. But using even an *old* backup copy is easier than recovering your accounting files with *no* backup copy. (See "Recovering Files If You've Never Backed Up.")

Be sure to store the backup copy of your accounting records in a safe place. You should not keep all the backup copies in the same location. If your business suffers a fire, for instance, you might lose all copies—no matter how many backups you kept. Store at least one copy at an off-site location, such as your safety deposit box at the bank.

Recovering the Backed-Up Files

Eventually, someone will trip over the computer power cord, or a power outage will occur because of a storm or brownout. You may even be so unfortunate as to have your computer malfunction, or have someone spill the contents of the pencil sharpener or a cup of coffee on the floppy disk that contains the accounting files. The only way to retrieve the data you copy with BACKUP is to use the DOS RESTORE command, which has this format:

    RESTORE A: C:\DEA3\FILES /S

After you've restored all your accounting files, you may notice one small problem. If you've worked with your files since the last backup, the restored versions aren't quite the same as the files that were damaged. The second part of recovering from damaged or destroyed accounting files involves reentering all the data that you had entered since you last backed up. You also need to reprint any accounting forms, such as invoices, purchase orders, and checks, and rerun any of the postings or periodic routines you ran after the last time you backed up. (Chapter 12 describes these periodic routines.) After completing this second step, your accounting files should mirror the way they looked immediately before they were damaged or destroyed. Back up your files before proceeding further.

Recovering Files If You've Never Backed Up

If some disaster befalls your accounting files but you didn't back them up, you must essentially go through each of the steps described in Chapters 2, 3, and 4. You need to reinstall the software, redefine the Chart of Accounts, and reload the master files. The trial balance amounts you enter should be from the trial balance at the end of the most recently completed accounting period. For example, if you lose your accounting files in the middle of August, use the July end-of-month trial balance to enter the assets, liabilities, owner's equities, revenue, and expenses. (Chapters 3 and 4 describe the steps for loading the trial balance into the Chart of Accounts.)

The trial balance acts as your "backup copy" of the accounting files. Then you must reenter all the transactions and data that you had entered since the date of the trial balance. You also need to reprint any accounting forms, such as invoices, purchase orders, and checks, and rerun any of the postings or periodic routines you ran after the trial balance date. After you complete the recovery, back up your files before proceeding further.

Using Internal Controls

A second important component in protecting your system is to use internal controls: rules and procedures to protect your business assets and the accuracy and reliability of accounting records. You must safeguard your system not only from power failures and system malfunctions but also from human errors and irregularities. Errors, in this context, are unintentional mistakes—such as accidentally transposing numbers or miscalculating an amount. Irregularities include intentional misrepresentation, fraud, theft, and embezzlement.

To help protect your system from such problems, you can do four things: leave a paper trail, retain documents, segregate accounting duties, and create passwords.

Creating Paper Trails of Transactions

One of the most important internal control procedures is making sure that as part of each transaction you create paper evidence which accurately describes and documents the transaction. The capability to produce this paper evidence is one of DacEasy's real strengths. You should try to take advantage of this strength as much as possible.

For example, for every sale or sales return, create an invoice or a sales return form. For every purchase or purchase return, create and keep a purchase order or purchase return form. These forms, far from being unnecessary paperwork, provide you with solid descriptions and documentation about a transaction —both at the time of the transaction and later.

The extensive journals that DacEasy maintains provide you with another important piece of the paper trail, or *audit trail*, of a transaction. Audit trails tie the individual transactions to the trial balance in the general ledger. For example, suppose that you notice a much larger than expected balance in some expense account. Using the journals, you can study each of the individual transactions that affected the expense account in question. The journals point you directly to the vendor invoice, check, or customer bill that started and now provides the best evidence and explanation of a transaction.

An irony of using a computer-based accounting system is that these types of systems probably use and generate more paper than any manual system. From an internal control perspective, this fact is comforting. The clean, easy-to-read, and well-organized information produced by DacEasy makes reviewing transactions, checking account balances, and researching suspicious conditions much easier.

Retaining Documents

After looking at all the paper a computer-based accounting system can generate (forms, audit trails, financial statements, and other special reports), you're probably wondering how long you need to hold on to that paperwork. Figure 5.1 provides some guidelines on how long you should keep the accounting forms, audit trails, and reports generated by DacEasy. These guidelines are based on statutory and regulatory requirements and statutes of limitations. If you have more questions about other accounting or business documents, talk to your tax advisor or attorney.

Segregating Accounting Duties

Segregating accounting duties is often difficult in a small business but is important nonetheless. You always want to have at least two people work on a transaction. For example, if one person places an order for some merchandise, another person should pay the bill. If one person collects and deposits customer payments, somebody else should apply the payments to accounts receivable. If one person writes the checks, another person should balance the checkbook.

Enacting such a division of labor has two reasons. First, co-workers may be able to catch each other's errors if they are directly or indirectly reviewing each other's work. And fewer errors means more accuracy in your accounting records.

How Long Should You Retain Accounting Documents?				
DacEasy Reports & Forms	1 yr	3 yrs	7 yrs	Permanent
Accounts Payable Journals			X	
Accounts Receivable Journals			X	
Backup Floppies of Accounting Files	X			
Billing Journals				X
Canceled Checks				X
Cash Receipts and Payments Journals				X
Chart of Accounts				X
Financial Statements – Monthly		X		
Financial Statements – Yearly				X
General Ledger Documents				X
Inventory Records			X	
Invoices – Customer & Vendor (1)			X	
Owner's Equity Documents				X
Purchase Orders & Returns (exc purchas'g copy)	X			
Purchase Orders & Returns (purchasing dept copy)			X	
Purchasing Journals				X
Sales Returns		X		
Trial Balance – Month End		X		
Trial Balance – Year End				X

Fig. 5.1

Document retention guidelines.

A second reason for having two people handle transactions relates to the problem of irregularities. Most often, when people are stealing they work alone. Collusion—two employees working together to steal from you—is rare. Accordingly, by having two or more workers involved in a transaction, you make any illicit activities difficult.

If you have a choice, the best way to split responsibility is to make sure that the person who performs the accounting for a transaction isn't the same person who has physical custody of the asset or management of the event. For example, you shouldn't have one individual both collect the cash and record the collection; or another person who both writes checks and records the purchase or expense. As an aid to dividing duties, DacEasy gives you the ability to create passwords.

Setting Passwords

You can set five passwords that limit what the password holders can do within the system. To set passwords, choose Options from the main menu. Then choose Password. Figure 5.2 shows the Password Table screen as it appears when you first choose the option.

The level 1 password allows its holders to use the accounts receivable transaction entry and cash receipt screens and the accounts receivable journals (described in Chapter 9), the accounts payable transaction entry and accounts payable journals (described in Chapter 7), the Purchase Order module and its

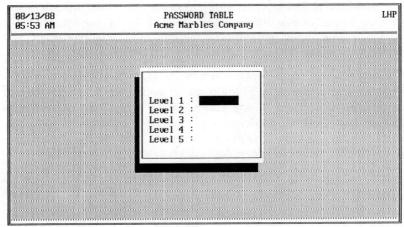

```
08/13/88                PASSWORD TABLE                    LHP
05:53 AM              Acme Marbles Company


              Level 1 : ████████
              Level 2 :
              Level 3 :
              Level 4 :
              Level 5 :


F1-Help  ESC-Exit
```

Fig. 5.2

*The Password
Table screen
before you set the
passwords.*

screens and reports (described in Chapter 6), and the Billing module and its screens and reports (described in Chapter 8). The first level does *not* allow holders to add customers, vendors, products, and accounts with the "on the fly" routine nor to post or run the periodic routines. (The "on the fly" routine refers to the ability to add customers, vendors, products, and accounts to the master files directly from the transaction screens. These techniques will be discussed in later chapters.)

By not letting a user run the posts or periodic routines, you prevent accidental transactions or routines and thus may avoid time-consuming recovery procedures. Additionally, by not allowing first-level password holders to add customers or vendors, you prevent these users from creating invoices or purchase orders or generating computer checks for companies that aren't already defined in the customer and vendor master files. You thus limit the password holder's access to transactions with already established customers and vendors and prevent an unscrupulous employee from selling items to, purchasing items from, or preparing computer checks for fictitious or unacceptable companies.

The level 2 password permits its holders to access everything that level 1 password holders can access plus the general ledger transaction entry and transaction journals, the accounts payable print checks routine, and the inventory reports and Enter Physical Inventory screen (described in Chapter 10).

In addition, second-level password holders can add customers, vendors, products, and accounts with the "on the fly" routine (but not through the File menu) and can use the Options Status option to see the number of defined and used records in each of the master files. You might allow more experienced DacEasy users to hold this level of password. You should realize, however, that a second-level password holder has the ability to create fictitious customers and vendors and then begin transacting business with them by buying phantom goods and services from them, generating computer checks to pay them, and billing them.

The level 3 password holder can perform any of the tasks that level 1 and level 2 password holders can perform. In addition, a user with a level 3 password can change the purchase order and billing codes tables, the statement messages table, the tax rate table, and option defaults; use the price assignment and entry routine in the Inventory module, the posting routines, and the file rehash routine; and create custom financial statements (described in Chapter 11).

From an internal control perspective, you won't find many reasons why a level 2 password holder shouldn't also be a level 3 password holder. In your business, however, you may encounter a unique situation in which the subtle differences between these two levels may be significant and may provide some additional protection for your system. For example, you may want to prevent some users from posting.

The level 4 password holders can perform every task that level 1, 2, and 3 password holders can perform. In addition, the fourth-level password holders can modify the general ledger interface table and the company name table and run all the closing processes. Remember that the general ledger interface table essentially describes how the pieces of the DacEasy system fit together. To minimize errors, consider preventing people—even trusted employees—from accidentally modifying that table. Similarly, because the closing or periodic routines (described in Chapter 12) erase and modify accounting data, you may also want to prevent people who don't run the periodic routines from accidentally stumbling on and running these routines.

The level 5 password permits access to everything that the lower level passwords do and includes one additional operation: the ability to set passwords. Even if you don't want to limit people's ability to use certain modules, you should set the fifth-level password immediately. The reason is that even if you don't want to limit other people's options in the system, you don't want them to limit yours either.

Table 5.1 summarizes which menu options are accessible at each password level. An *N* indicates that the option is not available at that level, and a *Y* indicates that the option is available.

Table 5.1
Password Holders' Accessibility to Menu Options

Menu Option	Password Level				
	1	2	3	4	5
File					
Accounts	N	N	Y	Y	Y
Customers	N	N	Y	Y	Y
Vendors	N	N	Y	Y	Y
Products	N	N	Y	Y	Y
Services	N	N	Y	Y	Y
Codes	N	N	Y	Y	Y
Statement Messages	N	N	Y	Y	Y
Transaction					
General Ledger	N	Y	Y	Y	Y
Accounts Receivable	Y	Y	Y	Y	Y
Accounts Payable	Y	Y	Y	Y	Y
Purchasing	Y	Y	Y	Y	Y
Billing	Y	Y	Y	Y	Y
Inventory	N	N	Y	Y	Y
Journals					
G/L Journal	N	Y	Y	Y	Y
G/L Activity	N	Y	Y	Y	Y
A/R Transactions	Y	Y	Y	Y	Y
A/R Cash Receipts	Y	Y	Y	Y	Y
A/P Transactions	Y	Y	Y	Y	Y
A/P Payments	Y	Y	Y	Y	Y
Purchase Journal	Y	Y	Y	Y	Y
P.O. Status Report	Y	Y	Y	Y	Y
Sales Journal	Y	Y	Y	Y	Y
Posting					
General Ledger	N	N	Y	Y	Y
Accounts Receivable	N	N	Y	Y	Y
Accounts Payable	N	N	Y	Y	Y
Purchase Orders	N	N	Y	Y	Y
Billing	N	N	Y	Y	Y
Physical Inventory	N	N	Y	Y	Y
Reports					
Accounts Receivable	N	Y	Y	Y	Y
Accounts Payable	N	Y	Y	Y	Y
Inventory	N	Y	Y	Y	Y

Table 5.1—*Continued*

Menu Option	Password Level				
	1	2	3	4	5
Financials					
Chart of Accounts	N	Y	Y	Y	Y
Trial Balance	N	N	Y	Y	Y
Balance Sheet/Income Statement	N	N	Y	Y	Y
Changes in Fin. Conditions	N	N	Y	Y	Y
Financial Statements Generator	N	N	Y	Y	Y
Periodic					
General Ledger	N	N	N	Y	Y
Accounts Receivable	N	N	N	Y	Y
Accounts Payable	N	N	N	Y	Y
Inventory	N	N	N	Y	Y
Options					
Interface	N	N	N	Y	Y
Company Id.	N	N	N	Y	Y
Tax Table	N	N	Y	Y	Y
Status	Y	Y	Y	Y	Y
Rehash	N	N	Y	Y	Y
Password	N	N	N	N	Y
Defaults	N	N	Y	Y	Y
"On the Fly" Routines	N	Y	Y	Y	Y

As you begin using and learning more about the modules and functions that the various password levels affect, you may want to change the passwords. One obvious but crucial warning is to remember your password—particularly if it's the level 5 password. If you set and later forget the level 5 password, you'll never be able to change passwords again.

Figure 5.3 shows the Password Table screen filled with sample passwords. You can use up to eight characters for creating each password. The more characters you use, the better you protect the password from accidental detection. Notice that the passwords shown in the figure have no rhyme or reason. Neither should your passwords have a pattern. If you use the color "blue" as the level 1 password, for example, a curious employee may soon guess that the higher level passwords are also colors. And then it's only a matter of time before the user figures out the level 5 password—even if it's "mauve."

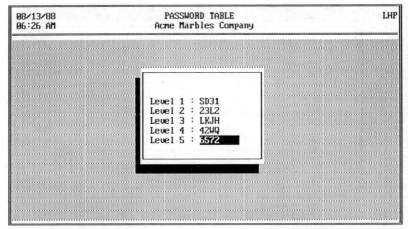

Fig. 5.3

The Password Table screen after you set the passwords.

Once you've assigned passwords, DacEasy requires a password from a user before the user can move past the copyright screen. Figure 5.4 shows the pop-up window that appears in the middle of the copyright notice screen, asking for your password.

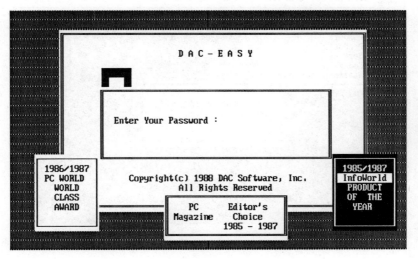

Fig. 5.4

The pop-up window that asks for your password.

Although you type your password to move past the screen, the password doesn't appear on-screen. Figure 5.5 shows how the window appears after you type the password.

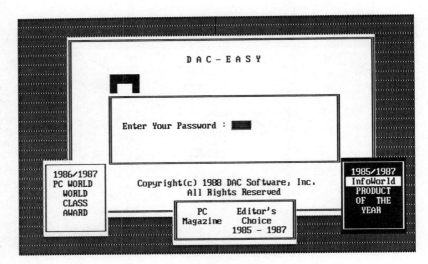

Fig. 5.5

The screen after you type the password.

If a password holder attempts to access a menu option for which a higher-level password is required, DacEasy displays a message that says the password holder cannot access the menu option (see fig. 5.6).

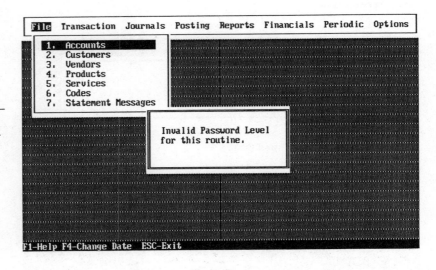

Fig. 5.6

The Invalid Password Level *message.*

Chapter Summary

This chapter described actions you can take to protect your system from both power and system failures and human errors and irregularities. You learned how to back up your data, the steps you can follow to recover your accounting files if your data is lost or damaged, and the internal controls—including the DacEasy passwords feature—you can implement to improve the accuracy and reliability of your accounting information. Now you're finally ready to put DacEasy to work for you. The rest of the book describes each module of the package.

6

Using the Purchase Order Module

The Purchase Order module provides a set of tools that allow you to order easily the goods and services you need and to track these orders until you receive the goods and services. You use the Purchase Order module in concert with the Accounts Payable module to recognize amounts you owe vendors for providing products or services. If you purchase inventory for resale, you use the Purchase Order module combined with the Inventory and Billing modules to maintain a perpetual inventory system.

This chapter reviews the purchasing process, discusses when you should use the Purchase Order module, and describes the decisions and tasks you need to complete before you begin using the purchasing system. For each purchase order menu selection, the chapter explains the event or transaction recorded, the steps you take to complete the menu selection, and ways to handle common errors.

Reviewing the Purchasing Process

The purchasing process, which consists principally of simple record keeping, begins when you decide that you need some item—a particular good or service. Perhaps after some research into the prices and services provided by alternative vendors, you place an order with the best vendor you can find. Placing an order typically means that you prepare a hard-copy purchase order, which you send to the vendor as paper proof of your intention to purchase an item. This purchase order details information about the vendor, the vendor payment terms, the specific items and quantities you're ordering, and any incremental

119

costs such as freight, insurance, and sales tax. The purchase order probably also identifies any special instructions for the order, such as delivery by a certain date or to a special address.

You send the purchase order to the vendor. The vendor often returns some written confirmation of your order—perhaps noting that the price has changed slightly from what you thought it was or maybe estimating a shipping date. Then you wait until you receive the ordered items. (Until you receive the goods, you usually want to monitor and check on unfilled purchase orders, verifying that you will receive the required items with the agreed-upon conditions.)

When you receive the goods, your purchasing system acknowledges that the goods have been received and verifies that the purchase terms and quantities match your purchase order. At this point, the purchasing process is complete. Information about the items ordered and received is passed to the inventory records to update the new units-on-hand balance for the goods ordered and to the accounts payable records to indicate that you now owe payment to the provider of the goods.

Although this summary only briefly describes the process, the mechanics are the same regardless of whether your purchasing system is manual or computer-based. By using DacEasy's Purchase Order module, however, you automate many of the steps in the cycle.

When To Use the Purchase Order Module

You should consider using the Purchase Order module if your purchasing volumes run at levels you find difficult or impossible to manage. Do you find yourself missing sales because an item you ordered arrives weeks late? Do you find yourself disagreeing with vendors about the prices and terms of your purchases? Are you often unsure about which of your ordered items you've already received? Do you frequently stock out-of-inventory items because you didn't realize your inventory balances were so low? If you answer "yes" to any of these questions, you may be able to improve profits by more formally managing your purchasing of goods and services. Usually, manufacturers, wholesalers, and retailers can profitably implement automated purchasing systems.

In some businesses, the operations don't warrant a formal, automated purchasing system. If you have such low purchasing volumes that you can easily place, remember, and monitor all orders yourself, or if you have wide diversity in both the vendors from whom you purchase and the products you purchase, you probably don't need the Purchase Order module. In these cases, maintaining large vendor and product master files for minimal purchasing volumes may not make sense. Many small service firms find themselves in this position.

Accessing the Menu Options for Purchasing

You can find purchasing menu selections in three places: the Transaction menu (Purchasing), the Journals menu (Purchase Journal and P.O. Status Report), and the Posting menu (Purchase Orders).

The Transaction Purchasing option provides you with screens to create and print purchase orders, record and print reports of merchandise received, and create and print purchase returns. The Purchasing submenu is shown in figure 6.1.

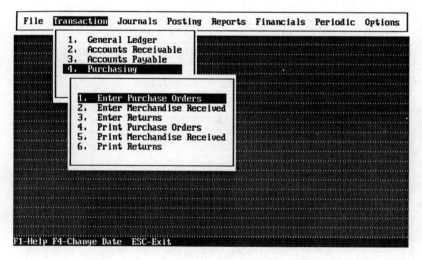

Fig. 6.1

The Purchasing submenu.

From the Journals menu (see fig. 6.2), you use the Purchase Journal option to print the purchase journal, which lists your purchase orders and returns. Another option on the Journals menu is P.O. Status Report, which you use to print the P.O. status report, which identifies unfilled or partially filled purchase orders.

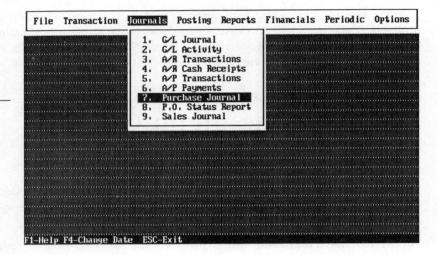

Fig. 6.2

The Journals menu.

The Posting Purchase Orders option (see fig. 6.3) posts, or passes, information to the Accounts Payable and Inventory modules to reflect orders, receipts, and returns of merchandise.

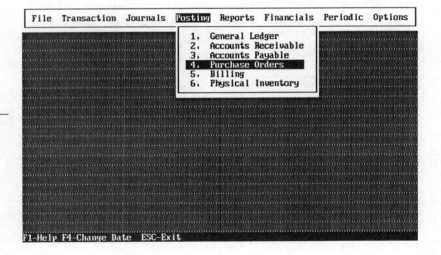

Fig. 6.3

The Posting Purchase Orders option.

This chapter describes in detail each of these menu options.

Entering Purchase Orders

You use the Enter Purchase Orders menu option to collect and calculate the information required to produce a purchase order. To access the Purchase Order screen, select the Transaction option from the main menu; choose the fourth option, Purchasing, from the Transaction menu; and then select option 1, Enter Purchase Orders, from the Purchasing submenu. Figure 6.4 shows the Purchase Order screen as it appears before you begin entering data.

```
                              Purchase Order #   ████████
   Vendor Code:                Remark:
                                                 Via
                                                 FOB
                                                 Your Ref.
                                                 Our Ref.
   Disc. Days      0 Disc. % 0.00  Due Days      0  Tax Code:    Rate:  0.000
   ┌──────────────────────────────────────────────────────────────────────┐
   │ Item #      Desc. Ordered                    Price    Disc. Extended   │
   ├──────────────────────────────────────────────────────────────────────┤
   │                                                                        │
   │                                                                        │
   │                                                                        │
   │                                                                        │
   │                                                                        │
   │                                                                        │
   ├──────────────────────────────────────────────────────────────────────┤
   │   Sub Total    Sales Tax    Total                                      │
   │     0.00         0.00        0.00                                      │
   └──────────────────────────────────────────────────────────────────────┘
F1-Help  F6-CANCEL  F10-Process  ALT D-Delete Line
```

Fig. 6.4

The Purchase Order screen before you enter data.

You can enter data in several fields to complete the Purchase Order screen: Purchase Order #, Vendor Code, Remark, Via, FOB, Your Ref., Our Ref., and for each product ordered the Item #, Ordered (quantity ordered), and Disc. (purchase discount) fields. You also have the option of editing the vendor's name and address, telephone number, discount days, discount percent, and due days, which are pulled from the vendor master file; and the product price, which is pulled from the product master file or purchase order codes file. The following paragraphs describe the data you enter and edit on the Purchase Order screen.

Purchase Order #: DacEasy Accounting assigns the *purchase order number* by adding 1 to the last purchase order number used. This number uniquely identifies the purchase order for both you and the vendor. For the first purchase order you create, the system adds 1 to the Last Purchase Order Number you entered as part of setting the system options and defaults (see Chapter 3).

You may choose to override the calculated purchase order number by entering your own previously unused number. If you enter a number that has already

been used, the Purchase Order screen retrieves the purchase previously identified by that purchase order number.

Vendor Code: This field holds the abbreviation you assigned in the vendor
master file to the vendor with whom you are now placing an order. When you
enter this code, the Purchase Order screen retrieves and displays the following
data under the vendor code: vendor name and address, discount days, discount
percent, due days, and sales tax code and rate. You may edit these fields if, for
this order, these values differ from the usual vendor name, address, and payment terms. If you specified a message code for the vendor, that code's message
and the vendor's credit limit, current balance, and remaining credit available
appear in a pop-up window (see fig. 6.5).

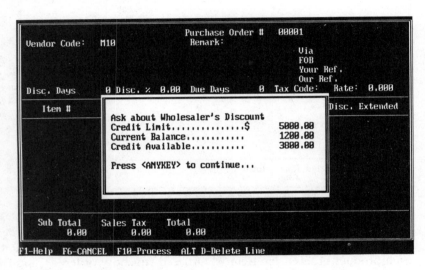

Fig. 6.5

*The pop-up
window that
appears if you set
a special message
for the vendor.*

If you want to prepare a purchase order to send to a vendor that you haven't
defined in the vendor master file, enter an unused vendor code. When you do
so, a pop-up window appears, telling you that the vendor does not exist and
asking you whether you want to create one. If you answer *Y* for yes, DacEasy
displays a short window that allows you to access an abbreviated Vendor File
Maintenance screen (see fig. 6.6).

Remark: These are three, 20-character fields you can use to enter any special
instructions or comments regarding this purchase order. You might, for example, specify a "required by" date or a different "ship to" address.

Via: You use this field to describe the method you want the vendor to use
when shipping the merchandise. You have up to 15 characters in which to
describe shipping methods (by overnight air, by land, and so on).

```
                          Purchase Order #    00001
 Vendor Code:    M20       Remark:
                                            Via          0

                        *** VENDORS ***
 Disc, Days        Vendor Code  : M20                              000
                   Vendor Name  :
     Item #        Contact      :                              nded
                   Address      :
                   City         :
                   State        :
                   Zip Code     :
                   Telephone    : (   )
                   Tax Code     : 0
                   Account Type : 0    (0-Open Invoice B-Bal. Forward)
                   Territory    :
                   Vendor Type  :

                   Disc Percent  : 0.00   Credit Limit :    0.00
 Sub Total         Discount Days : 0      Vendor Balance:   0.00
     0.00          Due Days      : 0      Credit Avail. :   0.00

 F1-Help  F2-Add Tax Rate  F10-Save  ESC-Exit
```

Fig. 6.6

The abbreviated Vendor File Maintenance screen.

FOB: In this field, you designate who pays the freight and shipping insurance and who bears the risks of ownership while the merchandise is in transit. *FOB shipping point* indicates that the merchandise is "free on board" at the shipping point. Therefore the purchaser pays the freight and shipping insurance and bears the risks of ownership while the goods are in transit. *FOB destination point* indicates that the merchandise is "free on board" at the destination point. In that case, the seller pays the freight and shipping insurance and bears the risks of ownership while the goods are in transit. Or, rather than use "shipping point" or "destination point," you can specify the actual location, as in "FOB Seattle."

Your Ref.: The Your Ref. field provides up to six characters to enter any code or number the vendor may be using to identify your order. Typically, you enter the vendor's invoice number here. You may not have this number until you receive the merchandise, so you often have to leave this field blank when creating the purchase order.

Our Ref.: The Our Ref. field provides up to six characters to enter any special code or number you are using in addition to the purchase order number to identify this order. Although the field is optional, you may find it helpful for referencing the person, department, or request that resulted in the purchase order.

Item #: You use the Item # field to specify what you're ordering. (DacEasy does not limit the number of items you can list on a single purchase order.) If you're ordering a product defined in the product master file, enter the product code. If you're ordering an item defined in the purchase order codes file, you can use one of the purchase order codes by typing the letter *C* (for codes), a space, and the purchase order code number.

When you complete the Item # field, DacEasy retrieves the description and price from the product or purchase order codes file and places that data in the Desc. and Price fields.

To include messages from the messages file, type in the Item # field the letter *M* (for messages), a space, and the message number. You can include your own description (using up to 40 characters) in the Desc. field by typing (in the Item # field) the letter *D* (for descriptions) and then the text of the description.

If you want to include a product that you haven't defined in either the product master file or the purchase order codes file, enter an unused item number. When you do so, a pop-up window appears, telling you that the item does not exist and asking whether you want to create one (see fig. 6.7).

Fig. 6.7

The pop-up window that tells you an item doesn't exist.

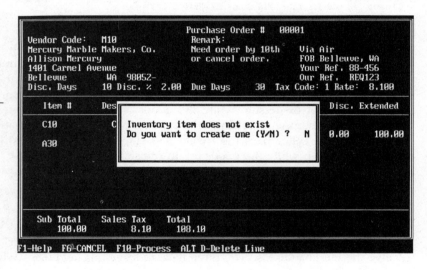

When you answer *Y* for yes, DacEasy displays a pop-up window in which you indicate whether you want to add products, services, or codes or return to data entry (see fig. 6.8). You can select options 1, 3, and 4. If you select option 1, an abbreviated Product/Service File Maintenance screen appears (see fig. 6.9). If you select option 3, the Add P.O. Service Codes screen appears (see fig. 6.10). You can return to the Purchase Order screen by selecting option 4.

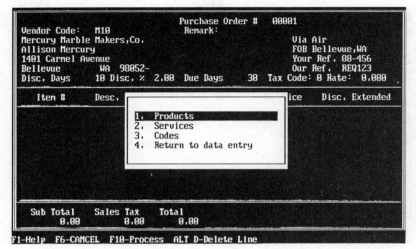

Fig. 6.8

The menu for adding products, services, and codes.

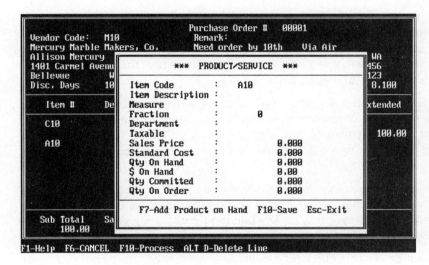

Fig. 6.9

The abbreviated Product/Service File Maintenance screen.

(Notice that DacEasy doesn't allow you to access option 2, Services, to enter a service into the service master file. The reason is that services don't appear on purchase orders.)

You may want to use this "on the fly" feature to add products to the product master file or purchase order codes file as you create purchase orders for the item for the first time.

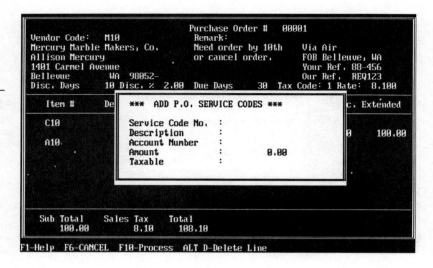

```
                            Purchase Order #    00001
  Vendor Code:   M10          Remark:
  Mercury Marble Makers, Co.  Need order by 10th    Via Air
  Allison Mercury             or cancel order.      FOB Belleuve, WA
  1401 Carnel Avenue                                Your Ref. 88-456
  Belleuve    WA  98052-                            Our Ref.  REQ123
  Disc. Days      10 Disc. % 2.00  Due Days     30  Tax Code: 1 Rate:  8.100

    Item #     De| *** ADD P.O. SERVICE CODES *** |c. Extended
    C10          | Service Code No.  :             |
                 | Description       :            |0    100.00
    A10          | Account Number    :            |
                 | Amount            :       0.00 |
                 | Taxable           :            |


      Sub Total   Sales Tax    Total
        100.00       8.10     108.10

 F1-Help  F6-CANCEL  F10-Process  ALT D-Delete Line
```

Ordered: In this field, you specify the quantity of an item you want to order. You can enter a quantity that includes fractions of a unit only if you specified fractional units in the product master file. Otherwise, the system permits only whole numbers. When you enter the Ordered quantity, the Purchase Order screen calculates the Extended amount.

You can edit the unit Price, the Disc., and the Extended fields if the system rounds these figures differently than you would. Keep in mind that this Disc. field is not an early payment discount field but a purchase discount field that you might use if you order items based on a price which then has a discount applied to it.

You enter an item number and an ordered quantity for each item you want included on the purchase order to this vendor. To delete an item from the list of goods you're ordering, press Alt-D while the item you want to delete is highlighted. To delete the entire purchase order, press F6.

After you enter on the Purchase Order screen each of the items you want included on the purchase order, press F10, which allows you to edit the calculated sales tax amount. You may need to correct the sales tax amount if you've specified some item as taxable in the product or purchase codes file when the item should be nontaxable—or vice versa. To save the purchase order, press F10 again. To save and print the purchase order you've just created, press F7. To continue editing, press any other key. Figure 6.11 shows the Purchase Order screen filled with sample data.

```
                         Purchase Order #   00001
   Vendor Code:  M10        Remark:
   Mercury Marble Makers, Co.   Need order by 10th    Via Overnight Air
   Allison Mercury         or cancel order.      FOB Seattle, WA
   1401 Carmel Avenue                            Your Ref.
   Bellevue     WA  98052-                       Our Ref.  REQ123
   Disc. Days    10 Disc. % 2.00  Due Days   30 Tax Code: 1 Rate: 8.100

      Item #        Desc. Ordered              Price   Disc. Extended

      C10           Cat's Eye
                      5000.000                 0.020  0.00     100.00
      C 1           Freight
                                                                20.00
      C 2           Insurance
                                                                 2.00
      D             Allison, Please rush this order. Thanks!




   Sub Total    Sales Tax    Total
     122.00        8.10     130.10
F1-Help  F6-CANCEL  F10-Process  ALT D-Delete Line
```

Fig. 6.11

The completed Purchase Order screen showing sample data.

Correcting Purchase Orders

If you enter a purchase order incorrectly, your reaction depends on whether you've already posted the purchase orders. (The posting process is described at the end of this chapter.) Correcting unposted purchase orders is easiest. To do so, access the Purchase Order screen, and retrieve the erroneous purchase order by typing its purchase order number. Then simply change the wrong entries and resave the purchase order. Because you've changed the purchase order, you also need to reprint it.

Correcting purchase orders you've already posted requires two steps. First, enter an entirely new purchase order, using the next purchase order number available. The new purchase order should look exactly like the incorrect one, except that you should specify the Ordered field as a negative amount. For example, if you originally created an incorrect purchase order for 10,000 cat's eye marbles, enter a new purchase for − 10,000 cat's eye marbles. Saving and then posting this new purchase order reverses your first, incorrect purchase order. Second, enter a third purchase order, this time using the data and amounts that you should have used in the first purchase order.

C.P.A. Tip: Always follow these two steps to correct transactions that have already been posted—don't combine the two steps. The reason is that as you (or others) later review purchasing activity, you can more easily determine what happened. You can easily spot two identical transactions that cancel each other and another independent transaction that represents the final, correct purchase order. To clarify the correction even further, you can use the Desc. field to document that one of the purchase orders is reversing an incorrect purchase order and that the other is the revised version of an incorrect purchase order. (See the discussion of the Item # field for information on how to add descriptions.)

Recording the Receipt of Goods

You use the Enter Merchandise Received menu option to record the receipt of goods, or merchandise, you ordered. To access the Merchandise Received screen, select the Transaction option from the main menu; choose option 4, Purchasing, from the Transaction menu; and then select option 2, Enter Merchandise Received, from the Purchasing menu. Figure 6.12 shows the Merchandise Received screen as it appears before you begin entering data.

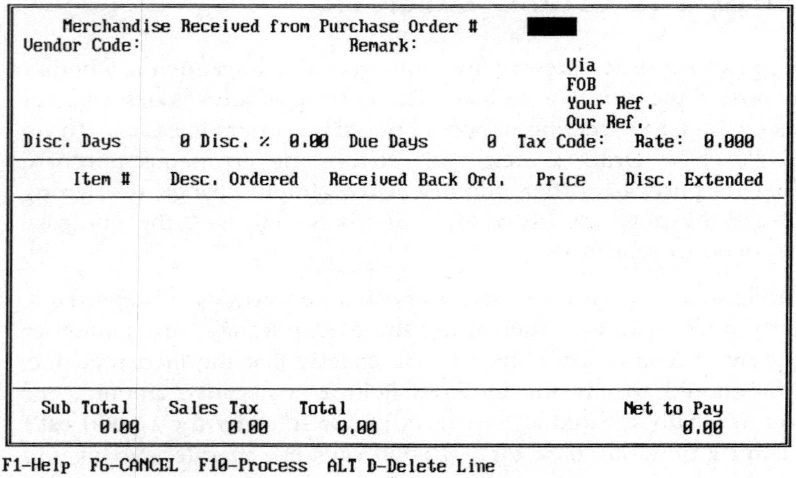

Fig. 6.12

The Merchandise Received screen before you enter data.

```
        Merchandise Received from Purchase Order #     ███
     Vendor Code:                        Remark:
                                                   Via
                                                   FOB
                                                   Your Ref.
                                                   Our Ref.
     Disc. Days      0 Disc. %  0.00  Due Days      0 Tax Code:   Rate:  0.000

        Item #    Desc. Ordered   Received Back Ord.   Price   Disc. Extended




     Sub Total    Sales Tax    Total                          Net to Pay
        0.00         0.00       0.00                             0.00

     F1-Help  F6-CANCEL  F10-Process  ALT D-Delete Line
```

You may need to fill only four fields to complete the Merchandise Received screen: Purchase Order #, Your Ref., Item #, and Received. But you can also enter and edit each of the fields you entered and edited on the Purchase Order screen. The reason is that you can use the Merchandise Received screen to record the receipt of items for which you never created a purchase order, or items that you didn't include on the purchase order. (To record merchandise received when you never created a purchase order for that merchandise, simply assign a new purchase order number, or allow the system to assign one for you. Then enter data in each of the fields you would have completed to create a purchase order: Remark, Via, FOB, Your Ref., Our Ref., and for each product an Item #, the Ordered quantity, and any purchase Disc.)

You again have the option of editing the vendor's name and address, telephone number, discount days, discount percent, and due days, which are pulled from the vendor master file, and the product price, which is pulled from the product master file or purchase order codes file. The following paragraphs describe the fields you use to record the receipt of merchandise.

Purchase Order #: This number uniquely identifies the purchase order for which you're recording the receipt of merchandise. If you're using the Merchandise Received screen to both create a purchase order and record the receipt of merchandise, you can assign a purchase order number by pressing Enter.

You type a number in this field only when you want DacEasy to retrieve a previously created purchase order. If you enter a number that hasn't been used yet, DacEasy tells you that the P.O./Merchandise Received/Purchase Return does not exist.

Your Ref.: The Your Ref. field provides up to six characters to enter any code or number the vendor may be using to identify your order. Typically, you enter the vendor's invoice number in this field.

Received: In this field, you specify the quantity of the item you received. When you enter the received quantity, the Merchandise Received screen calculates the back ordered (Back Ord.) quantity as the Ordered quantity minus the Received quantity, and calculates the Extended amount as the Received quantity times the Price. You can edit the unit Price, Disc., and Extended fields if the vendor's invoice differs from your calculations (and the vendor's version is correct). (As mentioned previously, this Disc. field is not an early payment discount field but a purchase discount, which you might use if you order items based on a price and then apply a discount.)

You complete the Item # and Received fields for each item you receive from this vendor. To delete an item from the list of goods on the purchase order, press Alt-D while the item you want to delete is highlighted. Note that you shouldn't delete an item from the list simply because you didn't receive the item. Deleting an item from this list completely removes the item from the purchase order. To delete the entire purchase order, press F6.

After you enter each of the items you received, press F10, which allows you to edit the calculated sales tax amounts. To save your work, press F10 again. To save your work and print the merchandise receipt form (the system's calculation of what you owe the vendor based on the merchandise received on the purchase order), press F7. To continue editing, press any other key. Figure 6.13 shows the Merchandise Received screen filled with sample data.

Fig. 6.13

The completed Merchandise Received screen showing sample data.

```
┌─────────────────────────────────────────────────────────────────────┐
│     Merchandise Received from Purchase Order #    00001               │
│ Vendor Code:   M10            Remark:                                 │
│ Mercury Marble Makers, Co.    Need order by 10th   Via Overnight Air  │
│ Allison Mercury               or cancel order.     FOB Seattle, WA    │
│ 1401 Carmel Avenue                                 Your Ref. 880089   │
│ Bellevue      WA  98052-                           Our Ref. REQ123    │
│ Disc. Days    10 Disc. % 2.00  Due Days    30 Tax Code: 1 Rate: 8.100 │
├─────────────────────────────────────────────────────────────────────┤
│    Item #    Desc. Ordered   Received Back Ord.   Price   Disc. Extended │
│                                                                       │
│   C10        Cat's Eye                                                │
│              5000.000    4000.000  1000.000       0.020   0.00   80.00 │
│   B10        Bumble Bee                                               │
│              0.000       4000.000  0.000          0.015   0.00   60.00 │
│   C 1        Freight                                                  │
│                                                                  20.00 │
│   C 2        Insurance                                                │
│                                                                   2.00 │
│                                                                       │
├─────────────────────────────────────────────────────────────────────┤
│   Sub Total   Sales Tax    Total                    Net to Pay        │
│    162.00       11.34      173.34                    173.34           │
└─────────────────────────────────────────────────────────────────────┘
 F1-Help  F6-Cancel  F7-Print Invoice  F10-Process
```

Correcting Merchandise Receipts

If you enter a merchandise receipt incorrectly, your reaction depends on whether you've already posted the merchandise receipts. (The posting process is described at the end of this chapter.) Correcting unposted merchandise receipts is easiest. To do so, access the Merchandise Received screen, and retrieve the erroneous purchase order by typing its purchase order number. Then simply change the wrong entries and save your work. Because you've changed the merchandise receipt, you also need to reprint it.

Correcting merchandise receipts you've already posted requires two steps. First, enter an entirely new merchandise receipt. The new receipt should look exactly like the incorrect one, except that you should specify the Received field as a negative amount. For example, if you created an incorrect merchandise receipt that recorded receipt of 2,500 Bumble Bee marbles, enter a new receipt for −2,500 Bumble Bee marbles. Saving and then posting this new merchandise receipt reverses your first, incorrect merchandise receipt. Second, enter a third merchandise receipt—the correct version of the receipt you were originally trying to enter.

Entering Purchase Returns

You use the Enter Returns menu option to collect and calculate the information required to return items you've previously purchased. To access the Purchase Return screen, select the Transaction option from the main menu; select option 4, Purchasing, from the Transaction menu; and then choose option 3, Enter Returns, from the Purchasing menu. Figure 6.14 shows the Purchase Return screen as it appears before you begin entering data.

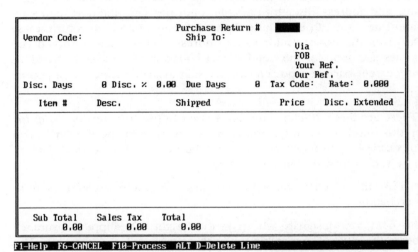

```
                            Purchase Return #    ████████
   Vendor Code:                 Ship To:
                                                    Via
                                                    FOB
                                                    Your Ref.
                                                    Our Ref.
   Disc. Days      0 Disc. %  0.00  Due Days     0  Tax Code:   Rate:  0.000

    Item #      Desc.        Shipped          Price    Disc. Extended




    Sub Total     Sales Tax     Total
       0.00          0.00        0.00
 F1-Help  F6-CANCEL  F10-Process  ALT D-Delete Line
```

Fig. 6.14

The Purchase Return screen before you enter data.

You need to enter data in several fields to complete the Purchase Return screen: Purchase Return #, Vendor Code, Ship To, Via, FOB, Your Ref., Our Ref., and for each product ordered an Item # and the Shipped quantity.

You have the option also of editing the vendor's name and address, discount days, discount percent, and due days (which DacEasy pulls from the vendor master file); the product price (which is pulled from the product master file or purchase order codes file); and any discount you received when you purchased the items you're returning. (You'll probably need to edit the product price, especially if you're using the average cost or standard cost inventory costing method.) The following paragraphs describe the fields in which you enter data on the Purchase Return screen.

Purchase Return #: DacEasy Accounting assigns the *purchase return number* by adding 1 to the last purchase return number used. Similar to the purchase order number, this return number uniquely identifies the purchase return for both you and the vendor. For the first purchase return you create, the system adds 1 to the Last Purchase Order Return you entered as part of setting the system options and defaults (see Chapter 3).

You enter a number in this field only when you want to retrieve a previously created purchase return. If the number you enter has not been used, DacEasy tells you that the P.O./Merchandise Received/Purchase Return does not exist.

Vendor Code: This field holds the abbreviation you assigned to the vendor to whom you are now issuing a purchase return. When you enter this code, the Purchase Return screen retrieves and places on the screen the following data: vendor name and address, discount days, discount percent, due days, and sales tax code and rate. You can edit these fields if, for this purchase return, these values differ from the usual vendor name, address, and payment terms. If you specified a message code for this vendor, that code's message and the vendor's credit limit, current balance, and remaining credit available appear in a pop-up window.

Ship To: These are three 20-character fields you can use to enter the "ship to" address for this purchase return if the address differs from the vendor's main address. For example, you might be returning the items to the vendor's factory or warehouse rather than the business office.

Via: You can use this 15-character field to describe the method you're using to ship the merchandise.

FOB: In this field, you designate who pays the freight and shipping insurance and who bears the risks of ownership while the merchandise is in transit. The FOB field is described in more detail in the section on "Entering Purchase Orders."

Your Ref.: The Your Ref. field provides up to six characters to enter any code or number the vendor may be using to identify your order. This number is probably the vendor invoice number used to bill you originally for these items, or perhaps a return authorization number.

Our Ref.: The Our Ref. field provides up to six characters to enter any special code or number you're using in addition to the purchase return number to identify this order. For example, you can enter in this field the purchase order number you used on your original order.

Item #: You use the Item # field to indicate what you're returning. If you're returning a product defined in the product master file, use the product code. If you're returning an item defined in the purchase order codes file, you can use one of the purchase order codes by typing the letter *C* (for codes), a space, and the purchase order code number. You can also include messages from the messages file by typing the letter *M* (for messages), a space, and the message number, and include a description with as many as 40 characters by typing the letter *D* (for descriptions) and the text of the description.

When you enter the item number, the Purchase Order screen retrieves the description and price from the product or the purchase order codes file or the message text from the messages file.

As with the Purchase Order and Merchandise Received screens, you can return a product that you haven't defined in either the product master file or the purchase order codes file by entering an unused item number. A pop-up window appears, telling you that the item does not exist and asking whether you want to create one. You should never need to use this feature, however, because if you're returning merchandise previously received, you already have defined a product or purchase order code.

Shipped: You specify in the Shipped field the quantity of the item you're returning. You may enter a quantity that includes fractions of a unit only if you specified fractional units in the product master file. Otherwise, the system allows you to enter only whole numbers. When you enter the quantity shipped, the Purchase Return screen calculates the Extended amount.

You can edit the unit Price, Disc., and Extended fields if the system doesn't round these amounts to your satisfaction. Again, remember that Disc. represents not an early payment discount but a purchase discount.

You enter an item number and a quantity shipped for each item you want to return to this vendor. To delete an item from the list, press Alt-D while the item you want to delete is highlighted. To delete the entire purchase return, press F6.

After you enter all the items you want to return, press F10 to edit the calculated sales tax amounts. To save the purchase return, press F10 again. To save and print the purchase return form you've just created, press F7. To continue editing, press any other key. Figure 6.15 shows the Purchase Return screen filled with sample data.

Correcting Purchase Returns

If you incorrectly enter a purchase return, your reaction depends on whether you've already posted the purchase return transaction. (The posting process is described at the end of this chapter.) To correct an unposted purchase return, access the Purchase Return screen, and retrieve the erroneous purchase return by typing the purchase return number. Make your corrections and then save your work. Because you've changed the purchase return, you also need to reprint it.

Fig. 6.15

*The completed
Purchase Return
screen showing
sample data.*

```
                           Purchase Return #   00001
 Vendor Code:   M10        Ship To:
 Mercury Marble Makers, Co.  Mercury Marble      Via land
 Allison Mercury           3400 Industrial Blvd  FOB Bellevue
 1401 Carmel Avenue        Bellevue WA 98052   Your Ref. 000089
 Bellevue     WA  98052-                       Our Ref. 000001
 Disc. Days     10 Disc. % 2.00 Due Days     30 Tax Code: 1 Rate: 8.100

   Item #      Desc.          Shipped         Price   Disc. Extended

   C10        Cat's Eye
                             2000.000               0.020  0.00     40.00
   B10        Bumble Bee
                             4000.000               0.015  0.00     60.00




   Sub Total   Sales Tax    Total
     100.00        8.10     108.10

 F1-Help  F6-Cancel  F7-Print Invoice  F10-Process
```

To correct a purchase return that you've already posted, first enter an entirely new purchase return. The new return should be identical to the incorrect purchase return, except that you must specify the Shipped field as a negative amount. For example, if you originally created an incorrect purchase return that showed a return of 7,000 Yellow Swirls marbles, enter a new purchase return for −7,000 Yellow Swirls marbles. Saving and then posting this new purchase return reverses your first incorrect purchase return. Next, reenter without errors the purchase return you were originally trying to enter.

Printing Purchase Order, Merchandise Received, and Purchase Return Forms

You use the last three options on the Transactions Purchasing menu to print purchase order, merchandise received, and purchase return forms. You can print a single form by pressing F7 after you create a purchase order, merchandise receipt, or purchase return. But the menu printing options allow you to print several forms at once, reprint previously printed forms, exclude certain data from printing, and modify the date that appears on the forms.

You print all three forms by using the same steps and the same print request fields, so the three options are discussed together. Figure 6.16 shows the Print Purchase Orders screen; figure 6.17, the Print Merchandise Receipts screen; and figure 6.18, the Print Purchase Returns screen. Notice that the only difference from screen to screen is the change of title. The parallel structure makes these menu options easier to use. Knowing how to use any one of the three means that you also know how to use the other two.

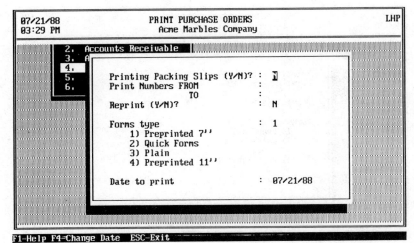

```
07/21/88              PRINT PURCHASE ORDERS                    LHP
03:29 PM               Acme Marbles Company

      2.  Accounts Receivable
      3.  A
      4.
      5.        Printing Packing Slips (Y/N)? :  Y
      6.        Print Numbers FROM             :
                          TO                   :
                Reprint (Y/N)?                 :  N

                Forms type                     :  1
                  1) Preprinted 7''
                  2) Quick Forms
                  3) Plain
                  4) Preprinted 11''

                Date to print                  :  07/21/88



F1-Help  F4=Change Date  ESC-Exit
```

Fig. 6.16

The Print Purchase Orders screen.

```
07/21/88            PRINT MERCHANDISE RECEIPTS                 LHP
03:32 PM               Acme Marbles Company

      2.  Accounts Receivable
      3.  A
      4.
      5.        Printing Packing Slips (Y/N)? :  Y
      6.        Print Numbers FROM             :
                          TO                   :
                Reprint (Y/N)?                 :  N

                Forms type                     :  1
                  1) Preprinted 7''
                  2) Quick Forms
                  3) Plain
                  4) Preprinted 11''

                Date to print                  :  07/21/88



F1-Help  F4-Change Date  ESC-Exit
```

Fig. 6.17

The Print Merchandise Receipts screen.

The fields you use to control printing forms are described in the following paragraphs.

Printing Packing Slips (Y/N)?: Answering this field *N* for "no" prints the form with the unit price and extended price. Entering *Y* for "yes" in this field prints the form without the unit price and extended price. For purchase orders and merchandise receipts, you almost always want the unit price and extended price to show. For some purchase returns, you may not want these amounts to show until you receive a credit memo from the vendor that specifies the amounts. The default answer to this question is *N*.

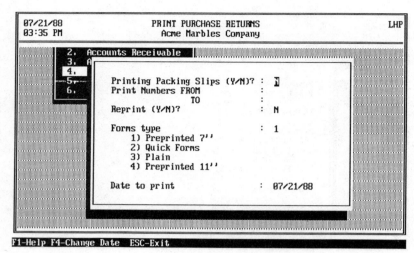

Fig. 6.18

The Print Purchase Returns screen.

Print Numbers FROM TO: By specifying the beginning and ending purchase order numbers when you're printing purchase orders and merchandise receipts and the beginning and ending purchase return numbers when you're printing purchase returns, you control which forms print. If you don't complete these fields, the system assumes that you want all forms printed that you haven't previously printed. If you want to print only one form, enter in both the FROM and TO fields the purchase order or purchase return number of the form you want to print.

Reprint (Y/N)?: Typically, you produce or print a form only once. This field allows you to reprint forms. Setting this flag to *N* lets you print only those forms that fall within the Print Numbers FROM TO range and have not been previously printed. Setting this flag to *Y* allows you to print *all* forms that fall within the Print Numbers FROM TO range. If you previously printed a form but subsequently modified it, the form reprints once regardless of whether you set the Reprint (Y/N)? field to *N* or *Y*.

Forms Type: You use this field to indicate what type of form you're using. DacEasy needs this information so that the system knows both the size of the form and whether to print your company name and address on the form and label the information such as item #, quantity, price, and extended price. Enter the number that corresponds to the form type you're using. Both the Preprinted 7″ and Preprinted 11″ forms (options 1 and 4) mean that you've ordered custom business forms which include your name, address, and form labels. Quick Forms (option 2) refers to DacEasy's generic forms, which contain form labels but not your company name or address. Plain (option 3) means that you're using plain, 8 1/2-by-11-inch, continuous-form computer paper.

Date To Print: This date appears on the forms as the date the form is generated. The system automatically fills this field with the system date. You may substitute another date if you want a different date to print on the forms.

Figure 6.19 shows a sample purchase order; figure 6.20, a sample merchandise receipt form; and figure 6.21, a sample purchase order return. All three samples are printed on plain paper.

Acme Marbles Company
512 Wetmore Street
Seattle, Wa 98114
Tel: (206) 555-1234 Fax: (206) 555-6789
P u r c h a s e   O r d e r

M10
Mercury Marble Makers, Co.
Allison Mercury
1401 Carmel Avenue
Bellevue WA 98052

Ship to/Remarks

Date 11/02/88   No. 00002 Page 1   Due Date 12/02/88

Via Best   FOB Seattle   Disc.days 10 Disc.% 2.00 Net Days 30 Your #   Our #Bob

Inventory #	Description	Ordered	Unit Price	Disc.%	Extended Price
C20	Cleary	3000.000	0.025		75.00
Y10	Yellow Swirls	1500.000	0.004	5.00	5.70

Sub-total	80.70
Tax	6.54
Total	87.24
Net to Pay	87.24

Fig. 6.19
A sample purchase order form.

Acme Marbles Company
512 Wetmore Street
Seattle, Wa 98114
Tel: (206) 555-1234 Fax: (206) 555-6789
M e r c h a n d i s e   R e c e i v e d

M10
Mercury Marble Makers, Co.
Allison Mercury
1401 Carmel Avenue
Bellevue WA 98052

Ship to/Remarks
Need order by 10th
or cancel order.

Date 11/02/88   No. 00001 Page 1   Due Date 12/02/88

Via Overnight Air   FOB Seattle, WA   Disc.days 10 Disc.% 2.00 Net Days 30 Your #880089 Our #REQ123

Inventory #	Description	Ordered	Received	Backorder	Unit Price	Disc.%	Extended Price
C10	Cat's Eye	5000.000	4000.000	1000.000	0.020		80.00
B10	Bumble Bee	0.000	4000.000	0.000	0.015		60.00
	Freight						20.00
	Insurance						2.00

Sub-total	162.00
Tax	11.34
Total	173.34
Net to Pay	173.34

Fig. 6.20
A sample merchandise received form.

Fig. 6.21

A sample purchase order return form.

Printing the Purchase Journal and the P.O. Status Report

You use the Journals menu to print the purchase journal and the P.O. status report. After you select Journals from the main menu, you choose Purchase Journal to print the purchase journal, or P.O. Status Report to print the P.O. status report.

The Purchase Journal

The purchase journal simply lists and describes the purchase orders and purchase order returns you've created since the last time you posted purchasing transactions. (The posting process is described in the next section.) You use the purchase journal in two ways: as a review for errors, and as a summary of items purchased.

First, before you post purchase orders, you review the purchase journal for possible errors in the purchase orders and returns you've created. If you do find errors, return to the screen you used to enter the order or return and make the necessary changes. Then print another copy of the purchase journal to review. When you find no errors, you can post these orders, receipts, and returns. Save the last, error-free copy of the purchase journal as your audit trail of purchasing transactions. A sample purchase journal is shown in figure 6.22.

```
Date : 11/02/88                        Acme Marbles Company                    Page no. 1
Time : 02:10 PM                        512 Wetmore Street
                                       Seattle, Wa 98114
                               Tel: (206) 555-1234 Fax: (206) 555-6789

                                       PURCHASE JOURNAL REPORT

        Vend.  PO.   Vendor
 Type   Dept.  Number Code        Name          Date       Gross       Tax        Total
-------- -----  ------ ------  ------------  ----------  ----------  ---------  -----------
PURCHASE       00001  M10    Mercury Marble Makers, Co 11/02/88   162.00     11.34       173.34
                             Purchase Total :             162.00     11.34       173.34
RETURN         00002  M10    Mercury Marble Makers, Co 11/02/88  -100.00     -8.10      -108.10
                             Purch.Returns Total  :       -100.00     -8.10      -108.10
                             Department Total :             62.00      3.24        65.24

                             Grand Totals :                 62.00      3.24        65.24
```

Fig. 6.22

The purchase journal report.

Notice that only three of the fields appearing on the purchase journal haven't been already defined in this chapter: Gross, Type, and Vend. Dept.

The Gross field refers to the Sub Total field shown on the Purchase Order, Merchandise Received, and Purchase Return screens. These subtotals include the individual line items on a purchase order but not the sales tax on the total purchases.

Unfortunately, DacEasy hasn't used the Type and Vend. Dept. fields consistently throughout the program, which makes their meanings a little difficult to explain. On the purchase journal, Type identifies whether the transaction listed is a PURCHASE or RETURN. Vend. Dept. shows the Type you entered for the vendor in the vendor master file. The purchase journal uses its Type (of transaction) field as the primary sort key for ordering the transactions on the journal and uses the Vend. Dept. field (the vendor Type defined in the vendor master file) as the secondary sort key. The purchase journal also shows subtotals by Vend. Dept. (vendor type). Notice that because the Acme Marbles Company doesn't use the field, the Vend. Dept. field and Department Total for this field show as blanks.

The purchase journal also prepares a summary of items purchased with each purchase order, listing these purchases by purchase order codes and product codes (see fig. 6.23). This summary, which is part of your audit trail, shows you the debits and credits made to the various general ledger accounts by the Purchase Order module.

On this portion of the journal, Type refers to those items you included on the purchase order or return by using a product code from the product master file (these items are labeled PRODUCT), and to those items you included on the purchase order or return by using a purchase order code from the purchase order codes file (these items are labeled CODE).

Fig. 6.23

The purchase journal report summary.

```
Date : 11/02/88                          Acme Marbles Company                       Page no. 2
Time : 02:10 PM                            512 Wetmore Street
                                           Seattle, Wa 98114
                              Tel: (206) 555-1234 Fax: (206) 555-6789

                                        PURCHASE JOURNAL REPORT
                                      SUMMARY BY INVENTORY AND CODE
Dept.  Type   Item/Acct #   Description              Units      Amount   Avg./Unit Last P.Price % Variance
-----  ----   ----------    -----------           --------    --------   --------- ------------ ----------
       CODE   52082         Insurance                            2.00
       CODE   52081         Freight                             20.00
                            Code total :                        22.00
                            Department Total :                  22.00

01     PRODUCT B10          Bumble Bee              0.000        0.00       0.00       0.02      -100.00
01     PRODUCT C10          Cat's Eye            2000.000       40.00       0.02       0.02         0.00
                            Product total :                     40.00
                            Department Total :                  40.00

                            Grand Totals :                      62.00
```

On the summary, the Dept. field refers to the revenue/cost department you defined in the product master file if you specified the revenue/cost department as INVENTORY. (You set the revenue/cost department as either CUSTOMER, INVENTORY, or NONE when you set the system options and defaults, as described in Chapter 3.) The Dept. field is the primary sort key that orders the items on the report. Because the purchase order codes do not use a revenue/cost department, these items appear first on the summary, with the Dept. field showing blank. This summary also calculates totals by department (meaning the revenue/cost department) and computes a grand total.

The P.O. Status Report

You use the P.O. status report, shown in figure 6.24, to monitor unfilled and partially filled purchase orders. This report lists open purchase orders sorted by vendor type (Vend. Type). For this report, Vend. Type means the type you entered in the vendor master file. Remember that on the purchase journal report, the field was labeled Vend. Dept. Try not to let all the inconsistencies confuse you.

The P.O. status report includes only four fields you've not yet used. The Status field indicates whether a purchase is 100 percent unfilled (identified as "On Order") or partially filled (identified as "Back Order"). The Tax and Total fields (representing sales tax and totals) apply to only the unfilled portion of the order and don't include any purchase discount you may have specified. The Printed field shows whether you have printed the purchase order or return. The other fields on the P.O. status report are used in the same way as they are on the other purchasing screens and reports.

```
Date : 11/02/88                      Acme Marbles Company                    Page no. 1
Time : 02:11 PM                       512 Wetmore Street
                                       Seattle, Wa 98114
                            Tel: (206) 555-1234 Fax: (206) 555-6789

                                      PO STATUS REPORT

Vend.  PO.    Vendor
Type   Number Code         Name        Date      Gross     Tax      Total    Status    Printed
-----  ------ ------  ---------------- -------- -------- -------- --------  --------  -------
       00002  M10     Mercury Marble Makers, Co 11/02/88   75.00     0.00    75.00   Backorder  YES
                      Department Total :           75.00     0.00    75.00

                      Grand Totals :               75.00     0.00    75.00
```

Fig. 6.24

The P.O. status report.

Posting Purchase Orders

Posting simply means passing information collected on the Purchase Order, Merchandise Received, and Purchase Return screens to the modules and files that need the information. Information from the Purchase Order screen updates the units-on-order quantity shown in the product master file and used by the Inventory module. Information from the Merchandise Received screen increases the units-on-hand quantity shown in the product master file and used by the Inventory module, increases the amounts spent for various expense classifications in the General Ledger module's trial balance, and increases the amounts you owe your vendors, as stored in the Accounts Payable module. Information from the Purchase Returns screen reduces the units-on-hand quantity shown in the product master file and used by the Inventory module, reduces the amounts spent for various expense classifications in the General Ledger module's trial balance, and reduces the amounts you owe vendors, as stored in the Accounts Payable module.

To post the purchasing activity to the general ledger, select the Posting option from the main menu. Then select the fourth option, Purchase Orders, from the Posting submenu. When you select Purchase Orders, a warning screen appears, as shown in figure 6.25. DacEasy asks you to be sure that you have entered the purchase orders and returns that you want to post; printed the journal, orders, and returns; and backed up your files in case your files are damaged during the posting process. (The process for backing up and restoring your files is discussed in Chapter 5, "Protecting Your System.") Press *Y* if you want to continue. DacEasy then automatically posts all your purchasing activity to the general ledger.

Caution: Be particularly careful if you're posting when other software programs are concurrently residing in memory. The results are unpredictable, and DacEasy may not be able to start or complete successfully the posting process if you have any programs running in memory. Memory-resident programs are

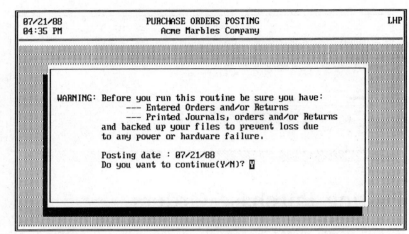

```
07/21/88                PURCHASE ORDERS POSTING              LHP
04:35 PM                   Acme Marbles Company


        ┌──────────────────────────────────────────────────┐
        │                                                   │
        │  WARNING: Before you run this routine be sure you have: │
        │           --- Entered Orders and/or Returns       │
        │           --- Printed Journals, orders and/or Returns │
        │       and backed up your files to prevent loss due │
        │       to any power or hardware failure.           │
        │                                                   │
        │       Posting date : 07/21/88                     │
        │       Do you want to continue(Y/N)? Y             │
        │                                                   │
        │                                                   │
        └──────────────────────────────────────────────────┘


F1-Help ESC-Exit
```

Fig. 6.25

*The Purchase
Orders Posting
screen's warning.*

those you can call up while you're operating DacEasy and then use to make a note, check your calendar, or make a quick calculation.

Chapter Summary

This chapter described using the Purchase Order module. You learned how to enter and print purchase orders, merchandise receipts, and purchase return forms. You also learned how to print and use the purchase journal and the P.O. status report and how to post the activity recorded in the Purchase Order module to the other modules that need information, such as the General Ledger, Accounts Payable, and Inventory modules. In the next chapter, you'll become familiar with the Accounts Payable module.

7

Using the Accounts Payable Module

You use DacEasy's accounts payable tools to record amounts you owe people, generate checks to pay these people, and record the payments. At the very least, the tools automate your check writing. Used in full, they allow you to control and account for all the amounts you owe vendors, all your disbursements, and the financial effect of these debts and disbursements.

This chapter reviews the accounts payable process, illustrates some sample accounts payable transactions, and describes why you might use DacEasy's Accounts Payable module to automate these transactions. In addition, for each accounts payable menu selection, this chapter describes the transaction recorded or report produced, the steps necessary to complete each selection, and ways to correct mistakes you make while using the Accounts Payable module.

Reviewing the Accounts Payable Process

In its simplest form, the accounts payable process amounts to no more than keeping records of the amounts you owe, why you owe these amounts, and other details of paying your debts. The process begins when you receive some merchandise (perhaps inventory you plan to resell or new furniture for your office) or service (perhaps legal advice or cleaning services). At this point, you need to recognize two events: First, you owe someone money. Second, you've acquired some good or service, and your books should therefore reflect the fact that you've increased assets or incurred expense.

145

Sometimes, you need to pay the vendor or supplier of the good or service immediately. More often, the vendor allows you either a few days or a few weeks to pay. In effect, the vendor gives you a short-term loan. If the vendor provides goods or services several times within a short period of time, the total you owe the vendor may include several separate amounts.

To pay the vendor, you write a check. In a manual accounts payable system, you get out your checkbook, find a pen, sift through your unpaid invoices, group invoices owed to the same vendor or supplier, and then write out a check to each vendor for the total owed to that vendor. In a computerized system such as DacEasy, the same steps occur. The system, however, does the work of sifting through the unpaid invoices, grouping by vendor or supplier the invoices that must be paid, and then printing the checks for the total amounts owed. But even in an automated system, *you* have to sign the checks. You then deduct the amount of the check from your checkbook balance, and, finally, recognize that you no longer owe the vendor on the invoices you've paid.

C.P.A. Tip: The person responsible for signing checks should always review the underlying documents—including invoices, purchase orders, and packing slips—to verify that the products were ordered, supplied, and not previously paid for.

That's the accounts payable process in a nutshell. Using a computer to help doesn't change the basic cycle but only makes it easier.

Examining Some Sample Accounts Payable Transactions

The Accounts Payable module is easier to understand if you first become familiar with the basic bookkeeping performed in an accounts payable system. This section reviews those procedures. Don't worry if you're not an accountant or if your first experience with debits and credits was in Chapter 1 of this book, however, because the Accounts Payable module records basically only three types of transactions.

The first type of transaction is buying a good or service on credit. To record either type of purchase, you use the same basic steps: you record the liability or debt you now owe the person who provided the good or service, and you recognize either the expense or asset that the received good or service represents.

If you remember Chapter 1's discussions of debits and credits, the balance sheet, and the income statement, you may be able to construct the debits and credits yourself. Because an increase in a liability (an amount you owe) is shown as a credit, you credit the accounts payable account. But what should you debit? Well, because you're probably also increasing either an expense or an asset, the debit part of the transaction is one of these.

A couple of sample transactions may clarify this concept for you. Suppose that you purchase 100,000 marbles of assorted styles from one of your offshore vendors for $2,000. You now owe the vendor $2,000 and have increased the marbles in your inventory by $2,000. You might make the following entry:

	Debit	Credit
Accounts Payable		$2,000
Inventory	$2,000	

For your information, this transaction is the one that the Purchase Order module automatically makes for you if you use that module to keep track of your purchases and receipts. If you aren't using that module, you make entries such as this one manually. You might also notice that both of these accounts are balance sheet items. The Accounts Payable account shows up on the liabilities portion of your balance sheet and the Inventory account on the assets portion. (When you enter the transaction in DacEasy, you also give the system Chart of Accounts numbers so that the assets and expenses are shown exactly where you want them. You'll see how to do that later in this chapter.)

Here's a second, similar transaction. Suppose that you received some legal advice—you've been considering incorporating your business and discussed the matter with your daughter, who's an attorney. After much pleading on your part, she agrees to bill you $150 for her services. You owe your daughter $150 and have increased your legal expenses by the same amount. You might make the following entry:

	Debit	Credit
Accounts Payable		$150
Legal Expense	$150	

You may wonder why you need to recognize the increase in legal expenses. But remember from Chapter 1 that you need to collect information for preparing an income statement—the calculation of how much revenue you've earned and expense you've incurred. You need to be tracking all expenses so that when you get to the end of the accounting period, you can calculate your profit or loss. (Here again, you need to enter a Chart of Accounts number so that the expense and liability are shown exactly where you want them on your income statement and balance sheet.)

Both the inventory purchase and the legal advice transactions fall into the first of the three rough categories of accounts payable transactions: recording a debt and an expense or asset when someone provides you with either a good or service.

The second type of accounts payable transaction involves returning an item that someone previously sold you. If you never recorded the credit and debit in the first place, you have no problem. Your records don't reflect that a transaction ever occurred. But even if you recorded the original transaction, you can easily account for the financial effect of the return. For example, suppose that you return the 100,000 marbles you received only a few paragraphs ago. You have 100,000 fewer marbles, so you reduce your inventory by $2,000. You also owe $2,000 less, so you reduce the accounts payable balance. If you remember that to reduce a liability you make a debit and to reduce an asset you make a credit, you already know the transaction to record this return:

	Debit	Credit
Accounts Payable	$2,000	
Inventory		$2,000

Maybe you've noticed that this transaction looks identical to the one used to record the marbles purchase, except that the debits and credits are reversed. If you think about it, this transposition makes sense, because you're reversing the original purchase journal entry.

The third type of accounts payable transaction is even easier. When you pay a vendor a debt you owe, you record the decrease in cash and the related decrease in your debts. For example, suppose that you pay the legal services bill you received from your daughter. Your debit and credit look like this:

	Debit	Credit
Accounts Payable	$150	
Cash		$150

The transaction to record payment of a debt always involves a debit to accounts payable and a credit to cash. Because the transaction is simple and always looks the same, DacEasy can easily record it—and does so whenever the system prints the checks. If you write any manual checks, you need to record the transaction by debiting the appropriate expense or asset account and crediting cash.

When To Use the Accounts Payable Module

Do you find tracking what and who you owe a chronic problem? Do you have days when your fingers ache from the writer's cramp induced by writing several hundred checks by hand? Do you find yourself needlessly missing early payment discounts or incurring late payment and finance charges? If you're nodding your head "yes," the DacEasy Accounts Payable module provides the answer to at least one of your problems: tracking and paying your bills.

Accessing the Menu Options for Accounts Payable

You can find the accounts payable tools grouped under five of the main DacEasy menus. From the Transaction menu, you can select the Accounts Payable option (see fig. 7.1) to access four accounts payable screens. The Accounts Payable Transaction Entry screen allows you to enter owed amounts that haven't been previously recorded by another module, such as the Purchase Order module. The Payments and Adjustments screen helps you record manual (handwritten) checks. The Checks to Print Journal screen lists the owed amounts, identified by invoice and grouped by vendor, for which DacEasy generates a check if you select the Print Checks option. The Print Checks screen allows you to generate checks automatically.

From the Journals menu, which is shown in figure 7.2, you can print two accounts payable reports. Choose the fifth option, A/P Transactions, to print the accounts payable transaction journal, which lists amounts you owe that have been recorded by the Purchase Order module and those amounts you recorded with the Accounts Payable Transaction Entry screen. To generate the accounts payable payments journal, which lists the paid invoices grouped by the checks that paid them, choose option 6, A/P Payments, from the Journals menu. These two journals—the transaction journal and the payments journal—provide you with the audit trails with which you can document all transactions recorded through the Accounts Payable module.

You use the Posting menu to update the general ledger for the accounts payable activity that has occurred since the last time you posted. Figure 7.3 shows the Posting menu with the Accounts Payable posting choice highlighted.

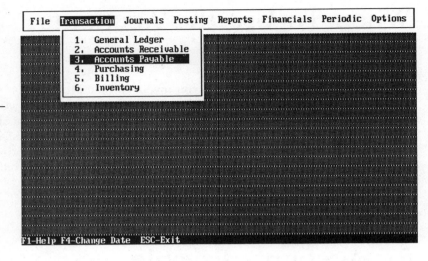

Fig. 7.1

The Transaction menu.

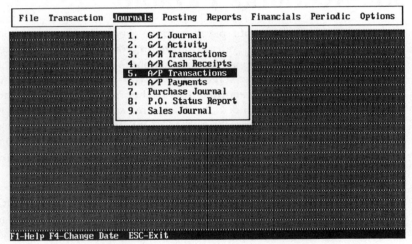

Fig. 7.2

The Journals menu.

From the Reports menu, you can print statements of what you owe vendors, an aging of amounts owed, a vendor directory, vendor mailing address labels, a report of payments made to vendors, and the Internal Revenue Service form 1099. Figure 7.4 shows the Reports menu with the Accounts Payable option highlighted.

Finally, the Periodic menu provides an Accounts Payable option (see fig. 7.5). You need to run periodic, or end-of-the-period, routines monthly and annually to close out old transactions and generate forecasts of the next year's accounts payable volumes and amounts. All the periodic routines are discussed in Chapter 12, "Using the Periodic Routines."

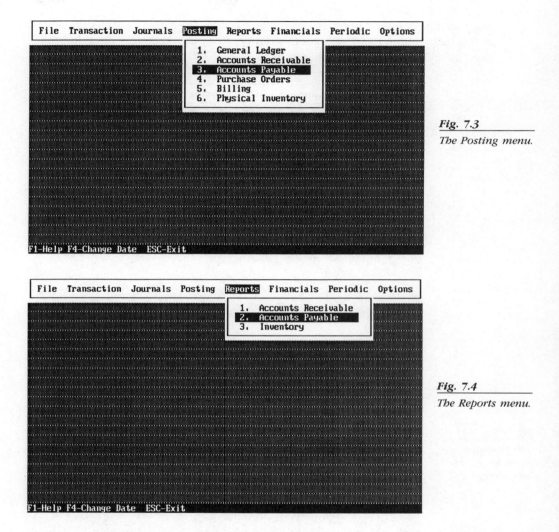

Fig. 7.3
The Posting menu.

Fig. 7.4
The Reports menu.

The rest of this chapter is devoted to walking you through the steps for using—and profiting from—DacEasy's accounts payable tools.

Entering Accounts Payable Transactions

Use the A/P Transaction Entry option to record amounts you owe for those purchases you didn't record in the Purchase Order module. To access the Accounts Payable Transaction Entry screen, first select Transaction from the main menu; choose option 3, Accounts Payable, from the Transaction menu; and select option 1, A/P Transaction Entry, from the Accounts Payable menu. See figure 7.6 for the menu hierarchy.

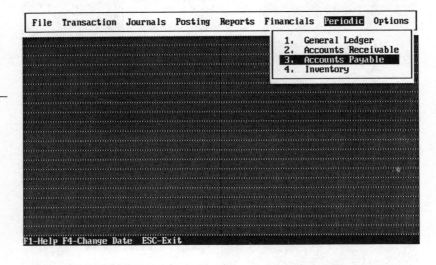

Fig. 7.5

The Periodic menu.

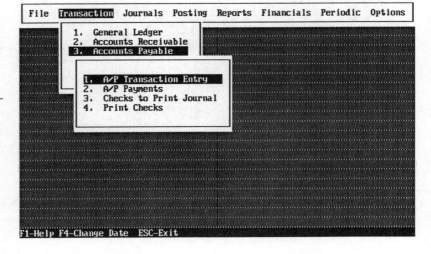

Fig. 7.6

The Transaction Accounts Payable submenu.

Figure 7.7 shows the Accounts Payable Transaction Entry screen before you begin entering data. Although at first glance you may think the screen requires you to enter a great deal of information, DacEasy completes most of the blanks for you. The following paragraphs describe each of the fields you either must enter or may edit.

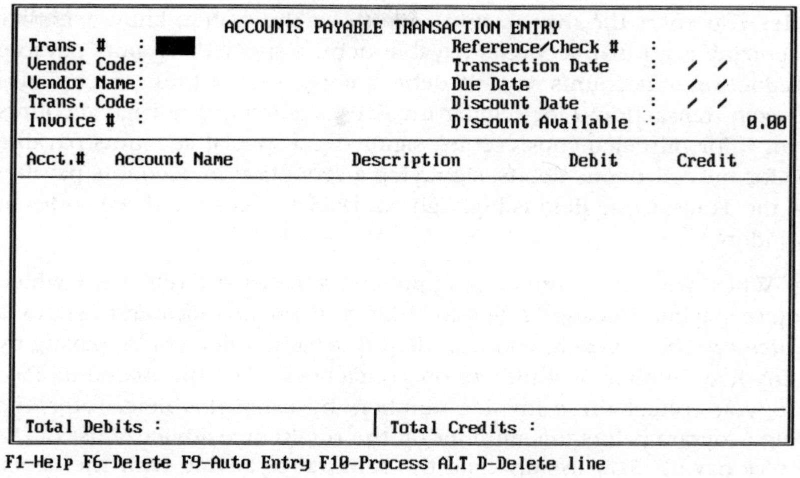

```
                    ACCOUNTS PAYABLE TRANSACTION ENTRY
      Trans. #  : ████              Reference/Check #  :
      Vendor Code:                  Transaction Date   :   / /
      Vendor Name:                  Due Date           :   / /
      Trans. Code:                  Discount Date      :   / /
      Invoice #  :                  Discount Available :        0.00

      Acct.#  Account Name          Description        Debit      Credit




















      Total Debits :              Total Credits :
```

Fig. 7.7

The Accounts
Payable
Transaction Entry
screen before you
enter data.

F1-Help F6-Delete F9-Auto Entry F10-Process ALT D-Delete line

Trans. #: The *transaction number* is the unique identifier that you use to reference the transaction until you post it to the general ledger. Press Enter while the cursor is in this field, and the system automatically assigns the next sequential transaction number.

If you want to edit a transaction you haven't posted yet, you can type the transaction number for that transaction. The Accounts Payable Transaction Entry screen then retrieves the transaction. But you can't modify transactions you've already posted. (If you need to correct an error, see this chapter's section on "Correcting Accounts Payable Transactions.") In fact, the Accounts Payable module resets the transaction number to 1 each time you post accounts payable transactions and payments.

Vendor Code: The *vendor code* identifies a vendor to the system and instructs the Accounts Payable Transaction Entry screen to retrieve the vendor's name and payment terms from the vendor master file.

As on the other screens in the DacEasy accounting system, if you find in the midst of entering a series of accounts payable transactions that you have an invoice for a new vendor, you can enter an unused vendor code. A pop-up window then appears, tells you that the code doesn't exist, and asks whether you want to create the code. By answering *Y*, you can access an abbreviated Vendor File Maintenance screen with which you can enter the new vendor into the master file.

After you enter a valid vendor code, any message you specified for the vendor also appears, along with your credit limit, current balance, and remaining available credit with that vendor.

Trans. Code: You enter the *transaction code* to let the system know whether you're recognizing a normal accounts payable debt, a special accounts payable debt, or a reduction in accounts payable debt. You use one of these three codes to describe each transaction: *I* for regular invoices, signifying a normal accounts payable debt; *C* for miscellaneous credits, signifying a special accounts payable debt; and *D* for miscellaneous debits, signifying a reduction in accounts payable debt. When the Trans. Code field is highlighted, DacEasy lists the three codes in a pop-up window.

Invoice #: When you pay vendors or suppliers, you usually tell them which invoices you're paying. Because a vendor bills you on invoices and assigns a unique *invoice number* to each, you can identify what invoice you're paying by noting the invoice number or numbers on your checks. For the Accounts Payable module, you collect these invoice numbers by using this field. Later, the check-writing program prints this number on the remittance advice, a list of the invoices you're paying. You usually mail the remittance advice with the check so that the vendor understands which invoices you're paying with the check.

Reference/Check #: This six-character field can be either alphabetic or numeric but not blank. The system forces you to enter data in this field so that you reference the transaction to the source document that creates or authorizes the transaction. (The cursor won't move to the next field until you complete the reference number.) Most often, you use the purchase order number, purchase request number, or maybe the name of the person who requested the good or service for which the invoice bills. If you're recording some amount the vendor owes you rather than a debt you owe to a vendor, you can use this field to note why the vendor owes you money.

Transaction Date: The *transaction date* is the date you want to show for the recording of the transaction in the Accounts Payable module. Because this date is typically the same as the system date, DacEasy places the system date in this field. You may change the date if you prefer.

Due Date: DacEasy calculates the *due date* by adding to the transaction date the due days specified for this vendor in the vendor master file. Although this figure is the best estimate that the system can make, you'll probably need to change the due date. When specifying the number of days within which payment is due, the vendor usually means the number of days since the vendor invoiced you or the number of days since the vendor shipped the goods or provided the services. In any of these cases, these dates probably don't correspond to your transaction date.

Discount Date: DacEasy calculates the *discount date* by adding to the transaction date the discount days specified for this vendor in the vendor master file. Here again, you usually need to change the system-calculated date because your transaction date is probably not the starting date the vendor uses for calculation of the early payment discount period.

Discount Available: This field shows the calculated early payment discount you received by paying the invoice early. You don't enter this field on the Accounts Payable Transaction Entry screen. DacEasy calculates the discount for you, based on the discount percent, if you pay the invoice by the discount date.

Acct. #: This field shows the *account number* from the Chart of Accounts, that should be debited or credited as part of the accounts payable transaction. Because you're making debits and credits to these accounts, they must be detail accounts. The system provides half of the transaction, based on the transaction code you entered. For example, if you're creating a transaction with a code of *I* for invoice or *C* for miscellaneous credit, DacEasy knows it should credit the accounts payable account number. If you're creating a transaction with a code of *D* for miscellaneous debit, DacEasy knows it should debit the accounts payable number. (In either case, the accounts payable account credited or debited is the one you defined in the general ledger interface table. Setting up this table is described in Chapter 3.) You enter the account number or numbers for the other half of the transaction.

If you want to debit or credit an account that you haven't set up in the Chart of Accounts, simply enter an account number that hasn't been previously defined. A pop-up window appears, alerts you that your entry is invalid, and asks whether you want to add the entry to the appropriate master file. When you answer *Y*, another pop-up window appears, which provides access to an abbreviated Chart of Accounts File Maintenance screen.

Account Name: When you enter an account number, the Accounts Payable Transaction Entry screen retrieves the name of the account from the Chart of Accounts. This important feature helps you verify that you're debiting or crediting the correct accounts.

Description: The 24-character Description field allows you to describe briefly either the transaction or the debit or credit component of the transaction.

Debit: If the account you've entered on a line represents the debit component of the transaction, you enter the amount of the debit in this field. If the account you've entered on a line represents the credit component, press Enter to move the cursor to the Credit field.

Credit: If the account you've entered on a line represents the credit component of the transaction, you enter the amount of the credit in this field.

To delete a debit or credit component of your transaction, press Alt-D while highlighting the Debit or Credit field. Press F6 to delete a transaction. To balance the transaction (so that the total debits equal the total credits), press F9 to enter the required debit or credit amount into the account number highlighted. For example, if you've just entered the account number for salaries expense, and the remaining debit should be to this account, press F9. F9 inserts only the amount required to balance a transaction.

After you finish recording the accounts payable transaction, you simply press F10, which saves the transaction, clears the screen, and positions the cursor at the Trans. # field. Then you're ready to enter another transaction.

Figure 7.8 shows the Accounts Payable Transaction Entry screen completed to record a sample rent bill. Notice that the credit is to the accounts payable detail account number from the sample Chart of Accounts and that the debits are to two expense accounts. The portion for the base rent is debited to the building rent expense detail account, and the portion representing the tenant's common area maintenance is debited to the utilities expense detail account. The invoice represents a debt for two kinds of expense: rent and utilities.

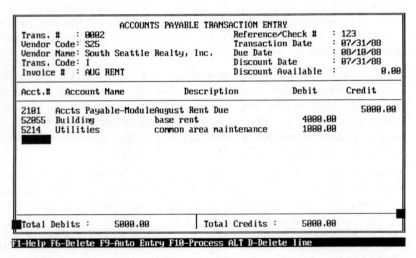

Fig. 7.8

The Accounts Payable Transaction Entry screen showing a sample transaction: recording monthly rent.

Although many transactions show only a single debit and credit, you may enter as many debits and credits as you need to complete your transaction. Remember that if you've correctly recorded a transaction, the total debits equal the total credits. The Accounts Payable Transaction Entry screen reflects this balance at the bottom of the screen. You can't save a transaction that doesn't balance, so if you need to make corrections to fields, you can use the arrow keys to move through each of the fields on the screen. If you begin to enter accounts payable transactions with many—say dozens of—debits and credits, you probably need to use the File Rehash option to increase the number of accounts payable transactions defined.

Figure 7.9 shows a debit accounts payable transaction—an entry that records a transaction when a vendor owes you money. In the example shown, this slightly unusual circumstance stems from an old legal bill that was paid twice. Adjusting for the amount of the overpayment requires a decrease in both the accounts payable balance and the legal expenses. You therefore debit accounts payable and credit legal expense.

```
                  ACCOUNTS PAYABLE TRANSACTION ENTRY
 Trans. #   : 0001              Reference/Check #  : 32889
 Vendor Code: H25               Transaction Date   : 07/22/88
 Vendor Name: Jimmy Hughes, Attorney at law Due Date : 08/21/88
 Trans. Code: D                 Discount Date      : 07/22/88
 Invoice #  : APR 234           Discount Available :        0.00

 Acct.#  Account Name          Description        Debit      Credit

 2101   Accts Payable-Modulelegal bill overpay    750.00
 52102  Legal              legal bill overpay                 750.00
 ▄▄▄▄▄


 Total Debits :      750.00   │  Total Credits :   750.00
```

F1-Help F6-Delete F9-Auto Entry F10-Process ALT D-Delete line

Fig. 7.9

The Accounts Payable Transaction Entry screen showing a sample transaction: recording a legal bill overpay.

Correcting Accounts Payable Transactions

Don't be discouraged if you find yourself making errors when you enter transactions. Finding and correcting erroneous transactions is part of the accounting and bookkeeping process. If you make a mistake when you enter an accounts payable transaction, and you haven't already posted the transaction, you can retrieve the incorrect transaction by typing its transaction number and then edit the fields you need to change. (Posting accounts payable transactions is described later in this chapter.)

If you have posted the accounts payable transactions, however, the correction procedure differs slightly. First, reverse the incorrect entry by entering a transaction that looks exactly like the incorrect one, except that you should reverse the debits and credits. For example, if you debited legal expense and credited accounts payable the first time, credit legal expense and debit accounts payable in the new entry. Use the Description field to document that this transaction is intended to reverse a previous transaction, and use the Reference/Check # field to tie this reversing transaction to the entry you're correcting. Save the new transaction by pressing F10.

To complete the error corrections, reenter the first transaction as you should have entered it the first time. Then save the transaction. The next time you post the accounts payable transactions, the second transaction will reverse the effects of your first entry, and the third, correct transaction will properly record the transaction.

C.P.A. Tip: Follow these two distinct steps for correcting transactions that you have already posted. Don't ever combine the two steps and merely create one transaction that adjusts the old incorrect entry so that it looks right. Canceling the incorrect entry with a reversing transaction and entering a new, correct transaction makes your procedures easier to understand when you view your records in a few weeks or a few months. You'll be able to see exactly what the error was and what the correction transaction was.

Recording Accounts Payable Payments

To record checks you've written by hand or to direct the DacEasy accounting system to write a computer check, you use the Payments and Adjustments screen. To access that screen, select Transaction from the main menu; choose option 3, Accounts Payable, from the Transaction menu; and select option 2, A/P Payments, from the Accounts Payable menu. Figure 7.10 shows the Payments and Adjustments screen as it appears when you first access it.

The information you enter to record or generate a check is exactly what you would expect.

Transaction #: This *transaction number* is the same as the transaction number on the Accounts Payable Transaction Entry screen. The Transaction # field identifies the payment or adjustment until you post it to the general ledger. Press Enter while the cursor is in this field, and the system automatically assigns the next sequential transaction number. If you want to edit a transaction you haven't posted yet, you can type the transaction's number to retrieve the transaction.

The Accounts Payable module uses transaction numbers on both A/P transactions and A/P payments and adjustments. Therefore, if you used the number

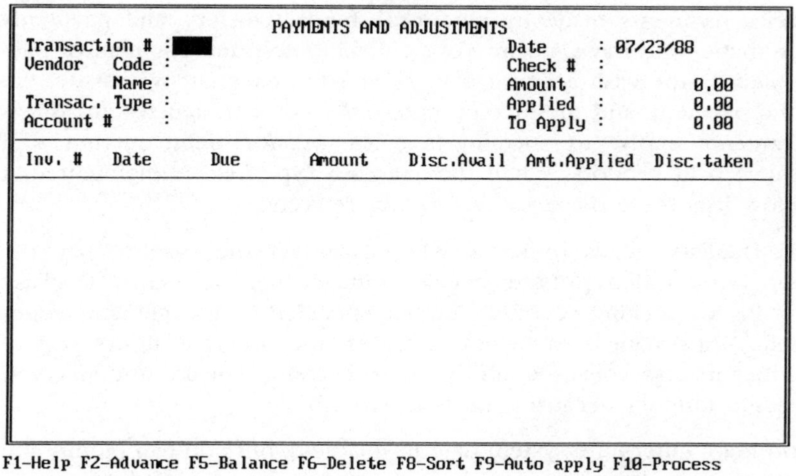

```
                        PAYMENTS AND ADJUSTMENTS
   Transaction # :█                          Date    : 07/23/88
   Vendor   Code :                           Check # :
            Name :                           Amount  :       0.00
   Transac. Type :                           Applied :       0.00
   Account #     :                           To Apply:       0.00

   Inv. #  Date      Due      Amount    Disc.Avail  Amt.Applied  Disc.taken




```

F1-Help F2-Advance F5-Balance F6-Delete F8-Sort F9-Auto apply F10-Process

Fig. 7.10

The Payments and Adjustments screen before you enter data.

00005 to identify an A/P transaction, you can't identify a payment or adjustment with that same number. Because the system usually assigns the transaction number, this situation isn't much of a concern unless you're on the Payments and Adjustments screen and trying to call up a transaction number that identifies an A/P transaction—or vice versa. You get an error message telling you that the transaction type is invalid. As with every other transaction in the system, you can't modify transactions you've previously posted.

Vendor Code: The *vendor code* identifies a vendor to the system and allows the Payments and Adjustments screen to retrieve information from the vendor master file. This information includes any message you've assigned to the vendor, your credit limit and current balance with the vendor, and the vendor's name and payment terms. The program also uses the vendor code to find any unpaid invoices you owe the vendor.

If you want to enter a transaction for a vendor you haven't already defined in the vendor master file, DacEasy allows you to enter these items directly from the Payments and Adjustments screen. All you have to do is enter a vendor code that hasn't been previously defined. A pop-up window then appears, alerting you that your entry is invalid and asking whether you want to add the entry to the master file. When you answer *Y*, another pop-up window appears, which allows you to access an abbreviated Vendor File Maintenance screen.

Transac. Type: You enter the *transaction type* to let the system know what kind of payment or adjustment you're entering. *K* designates a payment made with a check printed by the system. For system-printed checks, you identify only the open, or unpaid, invoices from this vendor, that you want to pay. DacEasy does the rest. *P* designates a manual payment, which includes handwritten checks, payments made by electronic funds transfers, and payments made by automatic withdrawals from your checking account. For manual payments, you identify the cash account from which the payment was made, the amount of the payment, and the invoice numbers paid. *A* designates an adjustment. Adjustments apply, to specific invoices, vendor debit memos and advances you've paid vendors. When the Transac. Type field is highlighted, a pop-up window lists these three codes for your reference.

Account #: DacEasy needs to know where you get the cash to pay the invoices. For both system-printed checks and manual payments, DacEasy retrieves the bank checking account number specified in the general ledger interface table. With manual payments, however, the program allows you to edit the number in case you used another cash account. For adjustments, you enter no account number because you used no cash.

Date: The program enters the system date in this field, but you can modify the field to show another date. This date isn't the check date, which you specify when you request the checks. Rather this field represents the date that appears on screens and reports as the date of the payment or adjustment.

Check #: You enter in this field the appropriate identifying number for the payment. Examples of this identifying number might include the manual check number, electronic funds transfer number, or automatic withdrawal receipt number.

Amount: The Amount field shows the amount of the payment or adjustment. For a *K* transaction type, you don't enter this amount, because the system generates a check equal to the total of the invoices you select. For *P* transactions, you do enter the amount—which makes sense because you're recording a transaction you've already made. For an *A* transaction, leave the Amount field as 0, because you're not recording a payment but applying a previously recorded payment or a debit memo against vendor invoices and credit memos.

Applied: The Applied field totals the invoices, debit memos, and credit memos you've selected to pay for this vendor. The Applied field must be positive, because you obviously can't pay a negative amount.

To Apply: The To Apply field shows the difference between the Amount and the Applied fields.

Inv. #, Date, Due, Amount, and Disc. Avail: The system lists in this section of the screen the unpaid invoices you owe the vendor, including the invoice number, the discount date, the due date, the invoice amount, and any early payment discount available. You don't change these values. You already entered them either in the Purchase Order module or on the Accounts Payable Transaction Entry screen.

Amt. Applied: In this field, enter the amount of an invoice you want to pay. If you're paying an invoice for which you will take a discount, enter only the net amount, which you calculate as the invoice amount minus the discount available. Enter the amount applied for any debit memo as a negative amount, just as debit memo amounts show as negative values. By entering an applied amount less than the invoice amount, you only partially pay an invoice. To apply the total amount of an invoice, press F9. (The F9 key works for vendor invoices and credit memos but not debit memos.)

Disc. Taken: This field shows any early payment discount you take. When you completely pay an invoice, the amount applied plus the discount taken should equal the invoice amount.

To delete a transaction, press F6. You can use this method to delete a payment or adjustment transaction but not an invoice. (To delete an invoice, you need to use the A/P Transaction Entry option from the Transaction Accounts Payable menu.)

After you finish recording the payment or adjustment, press F10, which saves the transaction, clears the screen, and positions the cursor at the Transaction # field. You're then ready to enter another payment or adjustment.

You can't save a payment or adjustment you haven't fully applied unless you use the F2 key, which allows you to classify the overpayment as an advance. Press F5 while the cursor is positioned on an invoice to see a pop-up window that shows the invoice number and balance, including the effect of any current applications. You may find this window easier to read than the Payments and Adjustments screen. Another special function key you can use on this screen is F8, which switches the sorting order for invoices—between sorting by discount date and sorting by due date.

Figure 7.11 shows the Payments and Adjustments screen completed so that a vendor's debit memo is applied to invoices and a computer check is automatically generated for the remaining balance.

Correcting Accounts Payable Payments

Most of the time, when you correct accounting or bookkeeping mistakes, you make adjustments to your books. But you may also have an overpayment or underpayment to your vendor to fix. In general, the preferred approach for correcting accounting system errors is to reverse the erroneous transactions and then reenter new transactions.

```
                        PAYMENTS AND ADJUSTMENTS
   Transaction # :0010                       Date     : 08/15/88
   Vendor   Code :J25                        Check #  :
            Name :Janitorial Excellence, Inc.  Amount   :      473.00
   Transac. Type :K                          Applied  :      473.00
   Account #     :                           To Apply :        0.00

   Inv. #   Date      Due        Amount   Disc.Avail  Amt.Applied  Disc.taken

   88-123   07/16/88  07/16/88    125.00     0.00       125.00        0.00
   88-128   07/23/88  07/23/88    125.00     0.00       125.00        0.00
   88-135   07/30/88  07/30/88    125.00     0.00       125.00        0.00
   88-145   08/06/88  08/06/88    125.00     0.00       125.00        0.00
   88-165C  08/10/88  08/10/88    -27.00     0.00       -27.00         .
```

```
F1-Help F2-Advance F5-Balance F6-Delete F8-Sort F9-Auto apply F10-Process
```

Fig. 7.11

The Payments and Adjustments screen with sample data.

If you haven't yet posted the transactions, retrieve the incorrect payment or adjustment by entering the transaction number and then make your corrections. This approach should prove satisfactory for most of your mistakes because you're probably exceedingly careful about disbursing money.

If you've already printed but haven't posted or mailed the checks, write in permanent ink the word "VOID" in big letters across the face of an erroneous check you printed. Then return to the Payments and Adjustments screen and make the changes to the incorrect payment transaction. Reprint the *checks to print journal* to ensure that the check is right, and then run the Print Checks option, printing only the transaction number of the payment you want to correct and this time using the new check number.

If you've already printed and mailed a check, you need to post the payment, because the payment has occurred and your books need to reflect that fact. Then you need to calculate the amount of the overpayment or underpayment, convince the vendor that your calculation is correct, and set up either a credit memo for the underpayment amount or a debit memo for the overpayment amount. Treat the credit or debit memo just as you would any other accounts payable transaction.

Using the Checks To Print Journal

Before you let the computer print checks for the *K* type payment transactions you enter, you should review the results of your work to verify that the payments you defined are accurate. Providing this review is precisely the purpose of the *checks to print journal*. To print the journal, select option 3, Checks to Print Journal, from the Transaction Accounts Payable menu (see fig. 7.12).

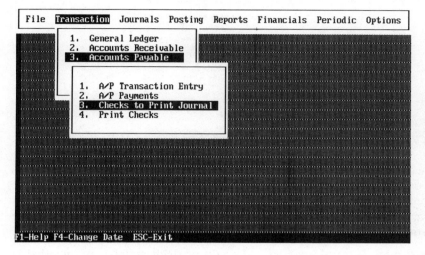

Fig. 7.12

The Transaction Accounts Payable submenu.

After you choose the Checks to Print Journal option, the screen shown in figure 7.13 appears. Enter the transaction numbers of the checks you want to print. If you want to print all the checks, press Enter when each field is highlighted, and the screen uses the first and last transaction numbers. Figure 7.14 shows an example of a checks to print journal.

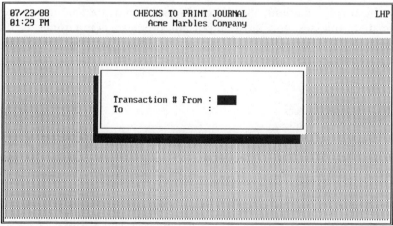

Fig. 7.13

The report request screen for the checks to print journal.

Fig. 7.14

A sample checks to print journal.

```
Date : 10/06/88                        Acme Marbles Company                      Page no. 1
Time : 01:25 PM                          512 Wetmore Street
                                         Seattle, Wa 98114
                             Tel: (206) 555-1234 Fax: (206) 555-6789

                          ACCOUNTS PAYABLE CHECKS TO PRINT JOURNAL

       Tran.
       No.  Vendor      Vendor Name         Invoice# Inv. Amount  Disc. Taken  Amt. to Pay
       ---- ------   -----------------       -------  ----------- ------------ ------------
       0004 H25     Jimmy Hughes, Attorney at law 983467      650.00      0.00       650.00
       0004 H25     Jimmy Hughes, Attorney at law ADVANCE   -1000.00      0.00     -1000.00
       0004 H25     Jimmy Hughes, Attorney at law ADVANCE   -1000.00      0.00     -1000.00
       0004 H25     Jimmy Hughes, Attorney at law APR 234    -750.00      0.00      -750.00
       0004 H25     Jimmy Hughes, Attorney at law JULY       3500.00      0.00      3500.00
                    Check Total: # of Transactions    5      1400.00      0.00      1400.00


                    Grand Total: # of Transactions    5      1400.00      0.00      1400.00
```

Note that this report corresponds closely to the Payments and Adjustments screen. For an individual vendor, the report includes each of the invoices, the invoice amounts, the discount taken, and the amount to pay on each invoice. The journal also totals the number of transactions included for a vendor and the invoice amounts, discounts taken, and amounts to pay.

For some vendors, several invoices and credit or debit memos are included in the calculation of the check. For example, figure 7.14 shows five transactions for Janitorial Excellence, Inc., only one for Walter's Wonders, and four for First Class Marble Mfg. Inc. Notice also that both Janitorial Excellence, Inc., and First Class Marble Mfg. Inc. include a debit memo (negative amount) in the calculation of the check amount.

At the bottom of the journal, DacEasy calculates grand totals for the number of transactions, the invoice amount, the discounts taken, and the amount to pay. For many small businesses, the most important of these grand totals is the amount to pay. You can examine these figures to determine how much cash you need in your checking account to write these checks.

Printing Checks

To print the checks shown on the checks to print journal, select the fourth option, Print Checks, from the Transaction Accounts Payable menu. The first time you access it, the Print Checks request screen looks similar to figure 7.15.

Notice that you need to complete several fields before your checks are printed.

Reprint Checks (Y/N): If you're printing a batch of checks for the first time, leave this answer as *N* for "no." If you're correcting a check because of an error in the definition of a *K* transaction, or because you had a problem when you

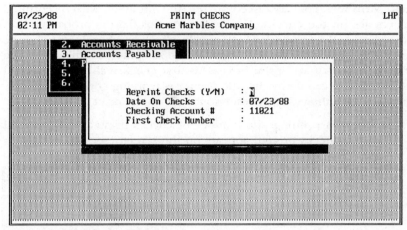

```
07/23/88                    PRINT CHECKS                         LHP
02:11 PM                 Acme Marbles Company

         2.  Accounts Receivable
         3.  Accounts Payable
         4.  P
         5.
         6.
                     Reprint Checks (Y/N)   : N
                     Date On Checks         : 07/23/88
                     Checking Account #     : 11021
                     First Check Number     :




F1-Help  F4-Change Date  ESC-Exit
```

Fig. 7.15

The Print Checks request screen.

previously printed a check (perhaps the checks became misaligned during the printing), you can use this parameter to reprint checks. If you do choose to reprint checks, a pop-up window appears and prompts you for the beginning and ending check numbers of the range you want to reprint. When you want to reprint just one check, specify that check's number as both the beginning and ending check number.

Date On Checks: In general, the date you want the system to write on your checks should be the date you're printing the checks. Because the system fills this field with the system date, you usually don't need to make changes. Businesses sometimes postdate checks, however, to force the check payee (in this example, your vendor) to wait until the check date to deposit the checks. You can use this parameter to postdate checks.

Checking Account #: Before DacEasy can print the checks, it needs to know from which account it should withdraw the cash to cover the checks. You identify the correct source of cash by entering the *checking account number* in this field. The system retrieves the bank checking account number specified in the general ledger interface table, but you can edit this number if you're going to use another detail account as the source of cash.

Note, however, that the checking account number you specify here is *not* the account number that the bank uses to identify your account for *its* records but rather is the Chart of Accounts number you use to identify the checking account for *your* records. Be careful not to confuse the two account numbers. One other related point is that if you use multiple checking accounts to write checks, you need to be especially careful. Don't write checks on one account and tell DacEasy you're writing the checks on another account.

First Check Number: You also need to tell the program what preprinted check numbers are on the checks. The reason for this field is probably clear: You want the check your accounting system calls check number 2456 to be the same payment the bank calls check number 2456. Enter in this field the number of the check that will print next. This first check will be test printed and voided so that you can verify that the printer is working correctly and perfectly aligned. DacEasy then asks whether you want to test print another check.

When the checks finish printing, the number of checks printed and the total dollar amount of the checks printed appears on the screen (see fig. 7.16).

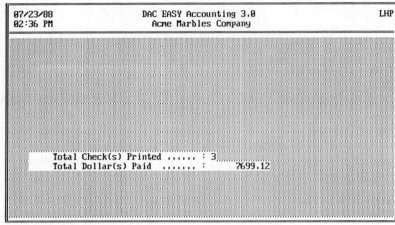

Fig. 7.16

The message that appears after you print checks.

| 07/23/88 | DAC EASY Accounting 3.0 | LHP |
| 02:36 PM | Acme Marbles Company | |

```
            Total Check(s) Printed ...... : 3
            Total Dollar(s) Paid  ....... :      7699.12
```

Press any key to continue...

Figure 7.17 shows an example of the remittance advice and check printed for Janitorial Excellence, Inc. Notice that basically the same information that was printed on the checks to print journal is printed on the remittance advice. The vendor can thus easily see which invoices you're paying with the check.

Printing and Using the Accounts Payable Journals

Both the accounts payable journal and the accounts payable payments journal show items you've entered but haven't yet posted. The A/P Transactions option, which you access from the Journals menu, prints an *accounts payable journal* that details the entries you've made using the A/P Transaction Entry screen. For each transaction, the journal specifies the transaction number, the vendor, the

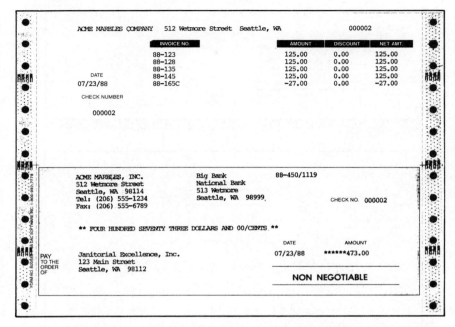

Fig. 7.17

A sample check generated by the Print Checks option.

accounts and amounts debited and credited, and other information you entered with the transaction. Figure 7.18 shows a page from the journal's detailed listing of transactions.

Fig. 7.18

The accounts payable journal.

The accounts payable journal also prepares a summary showing the total debits and credits made to each Chart of Accounts number (see fig. 7.19). This summary is printed at the end of the accounts payable journal.

The *accounts payable payments journal* provides the same kind of detailed information regarding your payments and adjustments. This journal corresponds to the check register you probably already maintain to record your manual checks. Figure 7.20 shows a sample accounts payable payments journal.

Fig. 7.19

The general ledger transfer summary.

```
Date : 11/02/88                        Acme Marbles Company                          Page no. 2
Time : 02:32 PM                          512 Wetmore Street
                                          Seattle, Wa 98114
                              Tel: (206) 555-1234 Fax: (206) 555-6789

                              GENERAL LEDGER TRANSFER SUMMARY
          Acct #    Acct. name        Description              Debit        Credit
          ------    --------------    --------------------     ------       ------

          2101     Accts Payable-Module Summary From AP Post                650.00
          52102    Legal                Summary From AP Post    650.00
                                        Summary Total :         650.00      650.00
```

Fig. 7.20

The accounts payable payments journal.

```
Date : 10/06/88                        Acme Marbles Company                          Page no. 1
Time : 01:27 PM                          512 Wetmore Street
                                          Seattle, Wa 98114
                              Tel: (206) 555-1234 Fax: (206) 555-6789

                              ACCOUNTS PAYABLE PAYMENTS JOURNAL

     Tran.
     No.   Acct # Vendor      Vendor Name          Invoice#  Date    Chk #  Type  Inv. Amount  Disc. Taken  Chk. Amount
     ----  ------ ------      -----------          --------  ------  ------  ----  -----------  -----------  -----------
     0003  11021  H25   Jimmy Hughes, Attorney at law  ADVANCE 07/23/88 1   PMT.    1000.00      0.00        1000.00
                        Acct. Total:                                                1000.00      0.00        1000.00

     0002  11022  H25   Jimmy Hughes, Attorney at law  ADVANCE 07/23/88 1   PMT.    1000.00      0.00        1000.00
                        Check Total: # of Transactions      2                       2000.00      0.00        2000.00

                        Acct. Total:                                                1000.00      0.00        1000.00


                        Grand Total: # of Transactions      2                       2000.00      0.00        2000.00
```

When you finish entering accounts payable transactions or payments, use these reports to check your work. By catching errors here, fixing mistakes will be much easier. But both journals serve as more than just error-checking tools. Each also represents an important part of your audit trail, so save the final, clean copies of the accounts payable journal and the accounts payable payments journal. They provide you with the details that support and explain the debits and credits posted to the general ledger.

Posting Accounts Payable Transactions and Payments

As with the other modules, you need to post information from the Accounts Payable module to the general ledger. Information from the Accounts Payable module updates the debts owed vendors, amounts incurred for various expenses and assets, and cash spent to pay debts. To post information from the Accounts Payable module to the general ledger, select the Posting option from the main menu and choose option 3, Accounts Payable, from the Posting menu.

DacEasy then displays a screen that warns you to back up files before you run the posting program (see fig. 7.21). If a hardware or power failure occurs during the posting process, you could lose your data files. Backing up your files before the posting allows you to recover easily from what could otherwise be a bookkeeping catastrophe. Press *Y* to continue. DacEasy then automatically posts all your accounts payable activity. If you press *N*, DacEasy returns you to the preceding menu level.

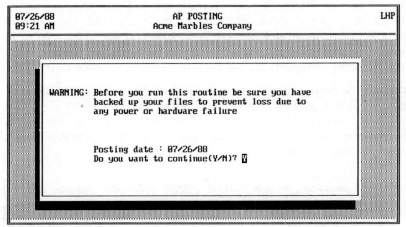

Fig. 7.21

The AP Posting warning screen.

A pop-up window appears when the posting program discovers errors or unusual conditions. For example, you need to print checks before you can post the checks to the general ledger. If the posting program identifies unprinted checks, it alerts you to this fact. If the posting program finds nothing to post —meaning that you've entered no accounts payable transactions or payments since the last posting—DacEasy alerts you to this fact. When posting is complete, a three-line message prints the totals of the amounts posted to the general ledger, as shown in figure 7.22.

```
Posted to G/L
   Total Debits   :    23719.44
   Total Credits  :    23719.44
```

Fig. 7.22

The total debits and credits message that appears after you post accounts payable.

Printing Other Accounts Payable Reports

One of the biggest benefits of using a computerized accounting system is that your system can easily generate many reports on all the information you've collected and stored in the system. In a sense, you're able to use the information as many times as you want.

The first time you use your data, both with a manual system and a computerized system, is usually when you keep your books. The second time may be for other financial or nonfinancial uses. For example, although the DacEasy accounts payable system's primary purpose is to maintain accounting records, the program prepares six other reports of vendor and accounts payable information. You can use these reports for much more than just keeping your books.

DacEasy prepares the following reports: accounts payable statements, accounts payable aging, accounts payable vendor directory, accounts payable vendor labels, accounts payable payments report, and vendor 1099 forms. You access these report-printing capabilities from the Reports Accounts Payable menu, which is shown in figure 7.23.

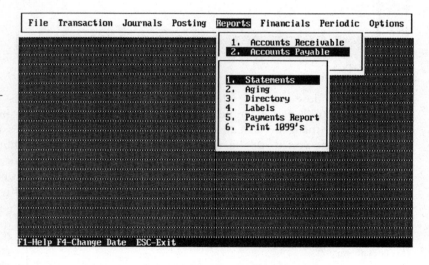

Fig. 7.23

*The Reports
Accounts Payable
options.*

Figure 7.24 shows an example of an *accounts payable statement*: a listing of the invoices, debit and credit memos, and payments to and from a specific vendor. Statements also show the transaction date, invoice number, due date, transaction description, reference number, debit or credit amounts, remaining amount due or past due, and the number of days past due. You might use this report to persuade a vendor who owes you money how you've arrived at this conclusion.

```
                        Acme Marbles Company
                         512 Wetmore Street
                         Seattle, Wa 98114
                Tel: (206) 555-1234 Fax: (206) 555-6789
                        S t a t e m e n t

        First Class Marble Mfg. Inc.
        Isaac Newton
        5150 Mukilteo Speedway              Page 1
        Mukilteo, WA   98210                Closing Date : 07/23/88

   --------------------------------------------------------------------------
   Date  Invoice#  Due Date CD  Description    Ref. #   Debits   Credits  Amount Due  Past Due  Days
   --------------------------------------------------------------------------
   07/22/88 00003  08/21/88  1  Purchase                          48.65
   07/23/88         07/23/88  4  Payment                          47.68
   07/23/88         07/23/88  6  Discount Taken                    0.97      0.00
   07/23/88 1001    07/23/88  4  Payment                        -1500.00
   07/20/88         08/19/88  5  Debit          NONE            1500.00      0.00
   06/10/88 234     07/10/88  1  Purchase       PO403   4750.00
   07/23/88         07/23/88  4  Payment                         4750.00      0.00
   07/20/88 238     08/19/88  1  Purchase       PO452   3200.11
   07/23/88         07/23/88  4  Payment                         3136.11
   07/23/88         07/23/88  6  Discount Taken                   64.00      0.00


                                                  Total       P a s t  D u e
                                                 Balance     Balance   Days
   --------------------------------------------------------------------------
                                                  0.00        0.00      0
```

Fig. 7.24

A sample accounts payable statement.

Figure 7.25 shows the second page of an *accounts payable aging report*. An aging shows the amounts you owe a vendor, categorized by the number of days since the transaction date. You can use the vendor aging to go beyond simply discovering how much you owe a vendor. You can examine the status of your accounts and determine whether you're completely current or have delinquent portions of your balance. The accounts payable aging report shows for each transaction the invoice number, the invoice date, the due date, the code identifying the type of transaction (invoice, credit memo, manual check, payment, debit memo, or discount taken), the amount, and the aging category in which the amount falls.

You can define up to seven aging categories, starting with those items that are due in the future and extending to those that are past due. The default aging categories provided for future dates are 9,999 to 61 days until an item is due, 60 to 31 days until an item is due, and 30 to 1 day until an item is due. For past due amounts, DacEasy provides default aging categories of 0 to 30 days since an item was due, 31 to 60 days since an item was due, 61 to 90 days since an item was due, and 91 to 9,999 days since an item was due.

An example of a *vendor directory* prepared from the Accounts Payable module's information is shown in figure 7.26. This report details the information retained in the vendor master file for each vendor: vendor code, name, address, phone number, type, territory, discount percent, discount days, due days, account type, credit limit, and current balance. You might want to have a current copy of the vendor directory available as you're entering purchasing and

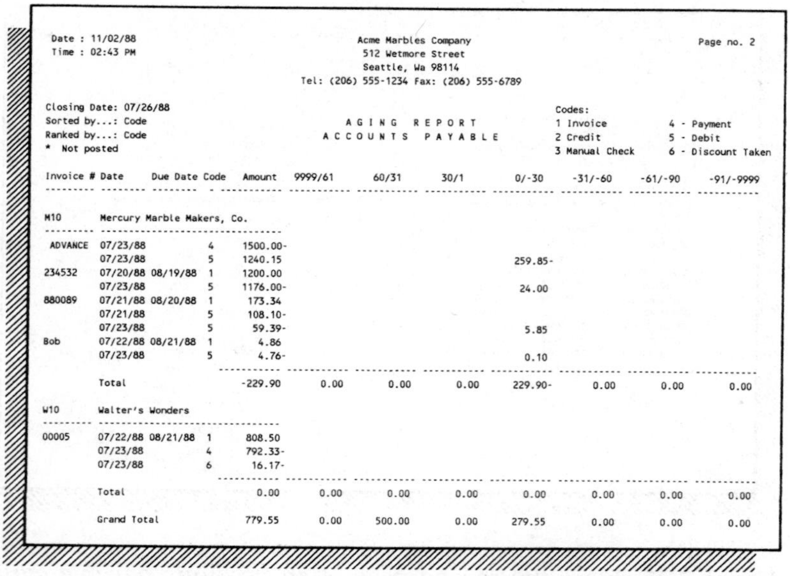

Date : 11/02/88
Time : 02:43 PM

Acme Marbles Company
512 Wetmore Street
Seattle, Wa 98114
Tel: (206) 555-1234 Fax: (206) 555-6789

Page no. 2

Closing Date: 07/26/88
Sorted by...: Code
Ranked by...: Code
* Not posted

A G I N G R E P O R T
A C C O U N T S P A Y A B L E

Codes:
1 Invoice
2 Credit
3 Manual Check
4 - Payment
5 - Debit
6 - Discount Taken

Invoice #	Date	Due Date	Code	Amount	9999/61	60/31	30/1	0/-30	-31/-60	-61/-90	-91/-9999
M10	Mercury Marble Makers, Co.										
ADVANCE	07/23/88		4	1500.00-							
	07/23/88		5	1240.15				259.85-			
234532	07/20/88	08/19/88	1	1200.00							
	07/23/88		5	1176.00-				24.00			
880089	07/21/88	08/20/88	1	173.34							
	07/21/88		5	108.10-							
	07/23/88		5	59.39-				5.85			
Bob	07/22/88	08/21/88	1	4.86							
	07/23/88		5	4.76-				0.10			
	Total			-229.90	0.00	0.00	0.00	229.90-	0.00	0.00	0.00
W10	Walter's Wonders										
00005	07/22/88	08/21/88	1	808.50							
	07/23/88		4	792.33-							
	07/23/88		6	16.17-							
	Total			0.00	0.00	0.00	0.00	0.00	0.00	0.00	0.00
	Grand Total			779.55	0.00	500.00	0.00	279.55	0.00	0.00	0.00

Fig. 7.25
A sample accounts payable aging report.

accounts payable transactions, because the directory provides a quick reference to the vendor code, which you often need to use to specify vendors. The directory also proves invaluable for writing manual checks.

With the accounts payable system, you can also generate *mailing labels* from the vendor master file (see fig. 7.27). All you need are standard-sized mailing label forms. These mailing labels are a real time-saver when you're preparing mass mailings to your vendors. You can also use these labels to identify file folders that hold the paid invoices for a vendor.

You select the sort order for printing accounts payable statements, the aging report, the vendor directory, and vendor mailing labels. Figure 7.28 shows the report request screen you must complete for statements. (The aging report, vendor directory, and mailing labels have identical request screens.)

For each of these four reports, you may sort the vendors by one of the following five fields from the vendor master file: code, name, type, territory, and ZIP code. This field is called your primary sort key, which you specify by entering the appropriate number at the end of the Sort By list on the request screen.

You also specify a secondary key to order vendors within the primary category. You can use as your secondary key one of these nine fields from the vendor master file: code, name, credit limit, credit available, balance, last purchase date, last payment date, purchase units, and purchase dollars. Specify the secondary key by entering the appropriate number at the end of the Rank By list. For both

```
Date : 10/06/88                              Acme Marbles Company                              Page no. 1
Time : 01:30 PM                               512 Wetmore Street
                                               Seattle, Wa 98114
                                   Tel: (206) 555-1234 Fax: (206) 555-6789

Sorted by: Code                              Vendor Directory                            Ranked by: Code

                           Area                          T e r m s                    Credit
Code   Name/Contact/Address  Code  Phone   Type Territory Disc % Days  Due Day Account Type   Limit      Balance
------ --------------------  ----  -------- ---- --------- ------ ----- -----  --------------- ---------- --------

F10    First Class Marble Mfg. Inc.  (206) 555-3212  1099          2.00   10    30  Open Invoice    5000.00   21565.95
       Isaac Newton
       5150 Mukilteo Speedway
       Mukilteo, WA   98210

G25    George's Service Station      (206) 555-1418                1.00    5    20  Open Invoice    2000.00     732.45
       Ms. Georgia George
       4300 Victoria Avenue
       Redmond, WA   98072

H25    Jimmy Hughes, Attorney at law (509) 555-3245                0.00    0    30  Open Invoice   10000.00    2750.00
       Jimmy Hughes
       1480 West Hume Blvd
       Portland, OR   98524-4391

J25    Janitorial Excellence, Inc.   (206) 555-1111                0.00    0     0  Open Invoice       0.00     500.00
       Bob
       123 Main Street
       Seattle, WA   98112

M10    Mercury Marble Makers, Co.    (206) 555-1159                2.00   10    30  Open Invoice    5000.00    -259.63
       Allison Mercury
       1401 Carmel Avenue
       Bellevue, WA   98052

S25    South Seattle Realty, Inc.    (206) 555-3210                0.00    0    10  Open Invoice       0.00    5000.00
       Walter Sugita
       2500 South Seattle Realty Bldg
       Tukwila, WA   98125

W10    Walter's Wonders              (206) 555-2626                2.00   10    30  Open Invoice   25000.00       0.00
       Bob Walters
       101 Washington Avenue
       Bellevue, WA   98072-1243


       Total Vendors : 7 records
```

Fig. 7.26

A sample vendor directory.

the primary and secondary keys, ascending ordering is used (*a* before *b*, and *1* before *2*).

You may find two other accounts payable reports helpful. Based on the information you've collected and stored in the Accounts Payable module, you can generate the payments report and the 1099 forms. The *payments report* lists, either by due date or by vendor name, the amounts due by discount dates and the amounts due by due date for each invoice. If you sort by vendor, you get vendor subtotals; if you sort by due dates, you get due date subtotals. Figure 7.29 shows the request screen you complete to generate a payments report. Figure 7.30 shows an example of a payments report sorted and subtotaled by vendor names.

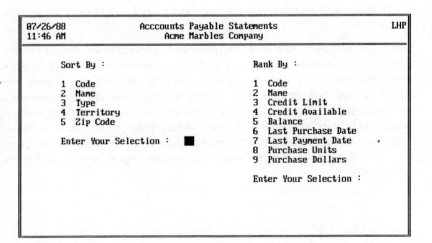

Fig. 7.27

Vendor mailing labels.

```
First Class Marble Mfg. Inc.
Isaac Newton
5150 Mukilteo Speedway
Mukilteo, WA   98210


George's Service Station
Ms. Georgia George
4300 Victoria Avenue
Redmond, WA   98072


Janitorial Excellence, Inc.
Bob
123 Main Street
Seattle, WA   98112

Mercury Marble Makers, Co.
Allison Mercury
1401 Carmel Avenue
Bellevue, WA   98052

South Seattle Realty, Inc.
Walter Sugita
2500 South Seattle Realty Bldg
Tukwila, WA   98125


Walter's Wonders
Bob Walters
101 Washington Avenue
Bellevue, WA   98072-1243




First Class Marble Mfg. Inc.
Isaac Newton
5150 Mukilteo Speedway
Mukilteo, WA   98210


George's Service Station
Ms. Georgia George
4300 Victoria Avenue
Redmond, WA   98072


Janitorial Excellence, Inc.
```

Fig. 7.28

The Accounts Payable Statements request screen.

```
07/26/88             Acccounts Payable Statements              LHP
11:46 AM                Acme Marbles Company


        Sort By :                        Rank By :

        1  Code                          1  Code
        2  Name                          2  Name
        3  Type                          3  Credit Limit
        4  Territory                     4  Credit Available
        5  Zip Code                      5  Balance
                                         6  Last Purchase Date
        Enter Your Selection :  ■        7  Last Payment Date
                                         8  Purchase Units
                                         9  Purchase Dollars

                                         Enter Your Selection :
```

```
07/26/88                  PAYMENTS REPORT                    LHP
11:50 AM                  Acme Marbles Company



              Report Options

              1  Sub-Totals by date
              2  Sub-Totals by vendor


              Enter Your Selection :  █


```

Fig. 7.29

The Payments Report request screen.

F1-Help F4-Change Date ESC-Exit

The Print 1099's option, the last option on the Reports Accounts Payable sub-menu, allows you to generate automatically the Internal Revenue Service form 1099 for vendors. To find out 1099 requirements, talk to either your tax advisor or preparer, or consult IRS publication circular E. In essence, however, you're required to report payments made to an unincorporated vendor if the payments total more than $600. The multipart form on which you report these payments is U.S. Treasury form 1099-MISC. You must send one copy of the form to the IRS, and another copy to the vendor. Most office supply stores carry the forms.

Figure 7.31 shows the report request screen you use to generate a 1099 either for a single vendor or for all your vendors. To generate a 1099 for a single vendor, simple specify the tax identification number for the vendor. To generate 1099s for all vendors, leave the Employer ID. NO field blank. By setting the minimum amount for which you'll generate a 1099, you save yourself the effort of printing and mailing 1099s for vendors for whom you're not required to prepare the forms. Figure 7.32 shows a sample 1099 screen printed with the Print 1099's option.

Chapter Summary

In this chapter, you learned about the accounts payable process in general and how to use DacEasy's Accounts Payable module to streamline the process in your business. The chapter also described how to record and correct errors in accounts payable transactions and payments, how to post accounts payable activity to the general ledger, and how to print and use the accounts payable journals and reports. In the next chapter, you learn about another of DacEasy's modules: Billing.

Fig. 7.30

A sample payments report.

Date : 11/02/88
Time : 02:57 PM

Acme Marbles Company
512 Wetmore Street
Seattle, Wa 98114
Tel: (206) 555-1234 Fax: (206) 555-6789

Page no. 1

PAYMENTS REPORT
Subtotals by Vendor

Vendor Code	Name	Invoice No.	Discount Available	Discount Date	Payment by Disc. Date	Due Date	Payment by Due Date	Remarks
F10	First Class Marble Mfg. Inc.	234	0.00	06/20/88	4750.00	07/10/88	4750.00	
		00003	-0.97		-47.68		-48.65	
		1001	0.00		1500.00		1500.00	
		234	0.00		-4750.00		-4750.00	
		238	-64.00		-3136.11		-3200.11	
		1001	0.00		-1500.00		-1500.00	
		238	64.00	07/30/88	3136.11	08/19/88	3200.11	
		00003	0.97	08/01/88	47.68	08/21/88	48.65	
		00006	431.32	08/17/88	21134.63	09/06/88	21565.95	
		Sub-totals:	431.32		21134.63		21565.95	
G25	George's Service Station	4972	0.00	07/27/88	732.45	08/11/88	732.45	
		Sub-totals:	0.00		732.45		732.45	
J25	Janitorial Excellence, Inc.	12345678	0.00	06/23/88	500.00	06/23/88	500.00	
		88-123	0.00	07/16/88	0.00	07/16/88	0.00	
		88-128	0.00	07/23/88	0.00	07/23/88	0.00	
		88-135	0.00		-125.00		-125.00	
		88-145	0.00		-125.00		-125.00	
		88-165C	0.00		27.00		27.00	
		88-135	0.00	07/30/88	125.00	07/30/88	125.00	
		88-145	0.00	08/06/88	125.00	08/06/88	125.00	
		88-165C	0.00		-27.00		-27.00	
		Sub-totals:	0.00		500.00		500.00	
M10	Mercury Marble Makers, Co.	ADVANCE	0.00		-259.85		-259.85	
		234532	0.00		-1176.00		-1176.00	
		880089	0.00		-59.39		-59.39	
		Bob	0.00		-4.76		-4.76	
		234532	24.00	07/30/88	1176.00	08/19/88	1200.00	
		880089	3.47	07/31/88	61.77	08/20/88	65.24	
		Bob	0.10	08/01/88	4.76	08/21/88	4.86	
		880089	3.47	11/12/88	61.77	12/02/88	65.24	
		Sub-totals:	31.04		-195.70		-164.66	
S25	South Seattle Realty, Inc.	AUG RENT	0.00	07/31/88	5000.00	08/10/88	5000.00	
		Sub-totals:	0.00		5000.00		5000.00	

Date : 11/02/88
Time : 02:57 PM

Acme Marbles Company
512 Wetmore Street
Seattle, Wa 98114
Tel: (206) 555-1234 Fax: (206) 555-6789

Page no. 2

PAYMENTS REPORT
Subtotals by Vendor

Vendor Code	Name	Invoice No.	Discount Available	Discount Date	Payment by Disc. Date	Due Date	Payment by Due Date	Remarks
W10	Walter's Wonders	00005	0.00	08/01/88	0.00	08/21/88	0.00	
		Sub-totals:	0.00		0.00		0.00	
	Totals :		462.36		27171.38		27633.74	

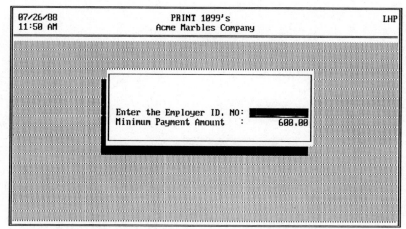

```
07/26/88                     PRINT 1099's                        LHP
11:50 AM                  Acme Marbles Company




          ┌─────────────────────────────────────────┐
          │                                         │
          │                                         │
          │                                         │
          │   Enter the Employer ID. NO:            │
          │   Minimum Payment Amount   :    600.00  │
          │                                         │
          │                                         │
          │                                         │
          └─────────────────────────────────────────┘




 F1-Help F4-Change Date   ESC-Exit
```

Fig. 7.31

The request screen to print 1099 forms.

	VOID	[X] CORRECTED			
PAYER'S name, street address, city, state, and ZIP code	1 Rents $	OMB No. 1545-0115		**Miscellaneous Income**	
Acme Marbles, Inc. 512 Wetmore Street Seattle, WA 98114	2 Royalties $	19**87** Statement for Recipients of			
PAYER'S Federal identification number XX–XXXXXXX	RECIPIENT'S identification number XXX–XX–XXXX	3 Prizes and awards $	4 Federal income tax withheld $	Copy C **For Payer or State Copy**	
RECIPIENT'S name, address, and ZIP code First Class Marble 5150 Mukilteo Speedway Mukilteo, WA 98210	5 Fishing boat proceeds $	6 Medical and health care payments $	For Paperwork Reduction Act Notice and instructions for completing this form, see Instructions for Forms 1099, 1098, 5498, 1096, and W-2G.		
	7 Nonemployee compensation $ 2,500.00	8 Substitute payments in lieu of dividends or interest $			
	9 Payer made direct sales of $5,000 or more of consumer products to a buyer (recipient) for resale . . . . . ▶ ☐				
Account number (optional)	10 The amount in Box 7 is crop insurance proceeds · · ▶ ☐				
Form **1099-MISC**	Approved I.R.S. Department of the Treasury—Internal Revenue Service 13-2678063				

Fig. 7.32

An example of a 1099 form.

Using the Billing Module

You use DacEasy's Billing module to prepare invoices for and record sales of goods or services to customers or clients. In addition, the Billing module passes information about customer invoices to the Accounts Receivable module, which makes monitoring and controlling customer collections and credit an easy job.

This chapter overviews the billing process and the reasons for using the tools DacEasy Accounting provides in the Billing module. The chapter also describes, for each billing menu selection, the event or transaction recorded, how to complete the menu selection, and how to handle common errors.

Reviewing the Billing Process

The billing process consists principally of preparing customer invoices. The process begins when you provide a customer or client with one of your products or services. You generally prepare an invoice detailing exactly what you have sold the customer, what the customer owes you as a result, and the payment terms. Additionally, if the sale involved merchandise, you need to record the decrease in units on hand of some items.

The last step in the billing process is to send the invoice to your customer and transfer the information to the accounts receivable system. That module performs the accounting for the sale, monitors the open invoices for customers, and records payments—steps that are described in more detail in Chapter 9, "Using the Accounts Receivable Module."

If you're in a business in which you sell merchandise, you can use the Billing module also to record sales returns. A sales return is the opposite of a customer invoice. You create a sales return to document that a customer has returned an item you originally sold to that customer. The Billing module passes information about the return to the Accounts Payable module, which then reduces the balance owed by the customer. Typically, that step completes the full cycle of the billing process.

Why Use the Billing Module?

The burden of billing your customers is usually not caused by the complexity of the process but by the number of transactions. Preparing dozens or hundreds of invoices each month can turn into an enormous job and prevent you from spending time on other important areas of your business, such as producing your products or services and marketing your firm. The alternative is to postpone billing until you have some slack time. Unfortunately, although it is often the only approach, deferring your billing delivers painful and sometimes crippling blows to your cash flow.

The DacEasy accounting system's billing tools dramatically lessen the burdens of billing your customers and recording accounts receivable information. Because of the width and depth of the information the system collects and stores, you benefit also from the many reports and statistical summaries that DacEasy prepares for you. These on-line statistical summaries and off-line reports may help you detect problems you might not have discovered until too late and see solutions you might have otherwise missed.

Accessing the Menu Options for Billing

You can find the billing menu selections in three places: the Transaction menu, the Journals menu, and the Posting menu. The Transaction Billing submenu provides you with four options with which you create and print invoices and sales returns (see fig. 8.1).

You use the Journals Sales Journal option, shown in figure 8.2, to print the report that lists your customer invoices and sales returns.

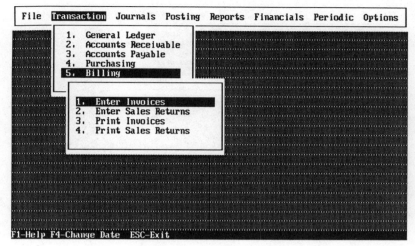

Fig. 8.1

The Transaction Billing submenu.

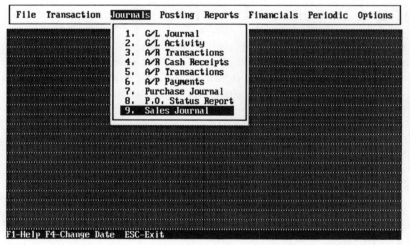

Fig. 8.2

The Journals Sales Journal option.

The Posting menu's Billing option (see fig. 8.3) posts, or passes, information to the general ledger to reflect sales and sales returns.

The remainder of this chapter addresses each of these menu options in detail.

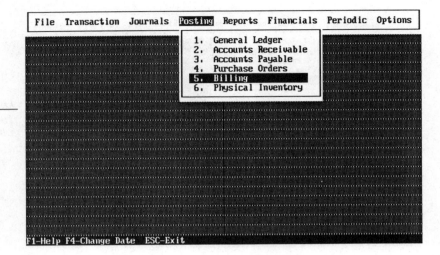

Fig. 8.3

The Posting Billing option.

Entering Customer Invoices

With the Enter Invoices option, you collect and calculate the information required to produce a customer or client invoice. First select the Transaction option from the main menu; choose option 5, Billing, from the Transaction menu; and then select option 1, Enter Invoices, from the Billing menu. Figure 8.4 shows the Customer Invoice screen as it appears before you begin entering data.

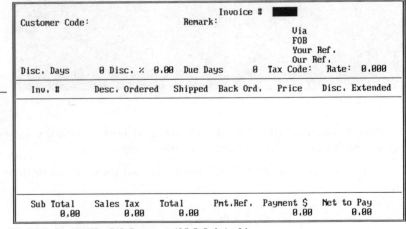

Fig. 8.4

The Customer Invoice screen before you enter data.

You must complete several fields on the Customer Invoice screen: Invoice #, Customer Code, Remark, Via, FOB, Your Ref., Our Ref., and for each product or service ordered the Inv. #, Ordered, and Disc. (discount) fields. You also have the option of editing the customer's name and address, discount days, discount percent, and due days (which DacEasy pulls from the customer master file) and the product or service price (which DacEasy pulls from the product master file, service master file, or billing codes file). The data you enter and edit is described in the following paragraphs.

Invoice #: You use the *invoice number* to identify the customer invoice. The system assigns this number by adding 1 to the last invoice number used. For the first customer invoice you create, the system adds 1 to the Last Invoice Number you entered as part of setting the system options and defaults, a process described in Chapter 3. If you enter an invoice number that has already been used, the Customer Invoice screen retrieves the invoice identified by that number—as long as you haven't posted the invoice. If the invoice has been posted, a pop-up window appears, telling you that you can't access a posted invoice.

Customer Code: The *customer code* is the abbreviation you assigned in the customer master file to the customer you're billing. If you specified a message code for this customer, that code's message, your credit limit for the customer, and the customer's current balance and available credit appear in a pop-up window (see fig. 8.5) when you enter the customer's code.

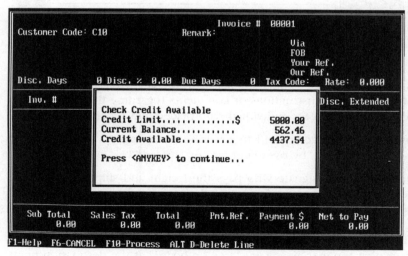

Fig. 8.5

The pop-up window that appears if you've specified a message for a customer.

When you enter the customer code, the Customer Invoice screen retrieves and places the following data in the corresponding fields: customer name and address, discount days, discount percent, due days, and sales tax code and rate.

You may edit these fields if, for this order, these values differ from the usual. If you want to skip to the Inv. # field next, press F10.

If you want to prepare an invoice for a customer that you haven't defined in the customer master file, enter an unused customer code. A pop-up window appears, telling you that the customer does not exist and asking whether you want to create one. If you press *Y* to answer "yes," another short window appears, which allows you to access an abbreviated Customer File Maintenance screen (see fig. 8.6). (You can't use this method if you've been assigned a password that doesn't allow you to add customers. For more information on passwords, see Chapter 5.)

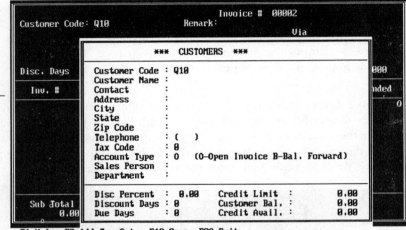

Fig. 8.6

The abbreviated Customer File Maintenance screen.

Remark: This area of the screen includes three 20-character fields in which you can enter any special instructions or comments regarding this invoice. You might, for example, record the individual who placed and received the order.

Via: You use this 15-character field to describe the method you use to ship merchandise, for example, "by overnight air" or "by land."

FOB: In this field, you designate who pays the freight and shipping insurance and who bears the risks of ownership while the merchandise is in transit. *FOB shipping point* indicates that the merchandise is "free on board" at the shipping point, which means the customer pays the freight and shipping insurance and bears the risks of ownership while the goods are in transit. *FOB destination point* indicates that the merchandise is "free on board" at the destination point and therefore that the seller bears the costs and risks. In addition to specifying the FOB point as either shipping or destination, you can use the actual location, as in "FOB Portland."

Your Ref.: The Your Ref. field provides up to six characters for entering any code or number the customer uses to identify this purchase. Usually, you type the customer's purchase order number in this field. You can use this field also to identify those sales for which the customer has issued no formal purchase order. For example, you might enter *verbal*.

Our Ref.: The Our Ref. field provides up to six characters for entering any special code or number you're using in addition to the invoice number to identify this order. The field is optional, but you may find it a useful place for recording the proposal, bid, or salesperson generating the sale.

Inv. #: You use the *inventory number* to tell the Customer Invoice screen what you're selling. If you're selling an item defined in the product or service master file, use the product or service code. If you're selling an item defined in the billing codes file, you can use one of the billing codes by entering the letter *C* (for codes), a space, and the billing code number. When you complete the Inv. # field, the Customer Invoice screen retrieves the description and price from the product, service, or billing codes file.

You can also include messages from the messages file by entering in the Inv. # field the letter *M* (for messages), a space, and the message number. DacEasy then retrieves the message text identified by that message code. To include your own description in the Desc. field, type in the Inv. # field the letter *D* (for descriptions) and then the text you want displayed (using as many as 40 characters).

If you want to include a product that you haven't defined in the product master file, service master file, or billing codes file, enter an unused inventory number in the Inv. # field. A pop-up window appears, telling you that the item does not exist and asking whether you want to create one (see fig. 8.7).

If you press *Y*, another short window appears (see fig. 8.8), which allows you to access an abbreviated Product/Service File Maintenance screen or the Billing Codes entry screen, or to return to the Customer Invoice screen. Figure 8.9 shows the abbreviated Product/Service File Maintenance screen. You can use this "on-the-fly" technique to add products to the product master file, service master file, or billing codes file as you construct first-time invoices for a product or service.

Ordered: In this field, you specify the quantity of the item for which you're billing the customer. If you specified fractional units in the product master file, you may enter a quantity that includes fractions of a unit. Otherwise, the system allows you to enter only whole numbers.

After you enter the ordered quantity, the Customer Invoice screen calculates the Shipped, Back Ord. (back ordered), and Extended fields. If the number in

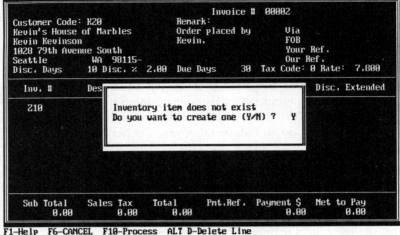

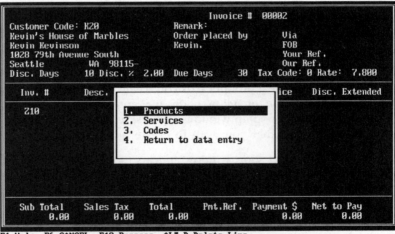

the Ordered field is less than or equal to the number of units on hand, the system copies the ordered quantity into the Shipped field. If you enter an ordered quantity that exceeds the number of units on hand, the screen calculates the back-ordered quantity as the ordered quantity minus the units on hand, and the shipped quantity as the number of units on hand. You can edit the Price, Disc. (purchase discount), and Extended fields if the system does not round these amounts to your satisfaction.

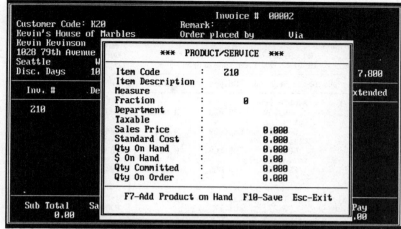

```
                               Invoice #  00002
 Customer Code: K20            Remark:
 Kevin's House of Marbles      Order placed by        Via
 Kevin Kevinson
 1028 79th Avenue         *** PRODUCT/SERVICE ***
 Seattle          W
 Disc. Days      10   Item Code      :   210                    7,000
                      Item Description :
  Inv. #      De      Measure        :                        xtended
                      Fraction       :      0
   210                Department     :
                      Taxable        :
                      Sales Price    :       0.000
                      Standard Cost  :       0.000
                      Qty On Hand    :       0.000
                      $ On Hand      :       0.00
                      Qty Committed  :       0.000
                      Qty On Order   :       0.000

                      F7-Add Product on Hand  F10-Save  Esc-Exit
 .
   Sub Total    Sa                                              Pay
       0.00                                                     .00

 F1-Help  F6-CANCEL  F10-Process  ALT D-Delete Line
```

Fig. 8.9

The abbreviated Product/Service File Maintenance screen.

You complete the Inv. # and Ordered fields for each item you want included on the invoice to the customer. To delete an item from the list of goods for which you're invoicing the customer, press Alt-D while the item you want to delete is highlighted. To delete the entire invoice, press F6. After you finish entering each of the items you want included on the customer invoice, press F10, which positions the cursor on the Pmt. Ref. field.

Pmt. Ref.: In this field, you record the *reference number* for any advance payment made by the customer for the items listed on the invoice. Because customers generally pay with checks, you can note the customer's check number in this field. Or if the customer uses cash, you can note that fact here.

Payment $: After you enter the payment reference number, you enter the *amount* of the advance payment on the invoice. To leave this field blank, press Enter.

To save the customer invoice, press F10. (You must press F10 twice if you have no payment reference number to enter and want to skip that field.) To save and print the invoice you've just created, press F7. To continue editing, press any other key. Figure 8.10 shows the Customer Invoice screen filled with sample data.

Correcting Customer Invoices

If you discover that you've entered an invoice incorrectly, your reaction depends on whether you've already posted or mailed the invoice. (Posting bill-

```
                                 Invoice #  00001
 Customer Code: C10          Remark:
 Columbus Glass Works, Inc.                    Via Overland
 Mr. Christopher Columbus                      FOB Seattle
 East 57th Avenue                              Your Ref. PO-561
 Seattle        WA  98104-                     Our Ref.
 Disc. Days    10 Disc. % 2.00  Due Days   30  Tax Code: 0 Rate: 7.000

  Inv. #       Desc. Ordered    Shipped  Back Ord.   Price   Disc. Extended

  B10          Bumble Bee
                500.000        500.000     0.000    0.035   0.00    17.50
  C10          Cat's Eye
                500.000        500.000     0.000    0.045   0.00    22.50
  C20          Cleary
                500.000        500.000     0.000    0.035   0.00    17.50
  Y10          Yellow Swirls
                250.000        250.000     0.000    0.040   0.00    10.00


  Sub Total   Sales Tax    Total     Pmt.Ref.  Payment $   Net to Pay
    76.00        5.27      81.27                   0.00       81.27

 F1-Help  F6-CANCEL  F10-Process   ALT D-Delete Line
```

Fig. 8.10

An example of a completed Customer Invoice screen.

ing transactions is discussed later in this chapter.) Correcting invoices you've neither posted nor mailed is easiest. To modify such an invoice, access the Customer Invoice screen and type the invoice's number to retrieve the invoice you want to change. Then change the wrong entries and resave the invoice. Because you've changed it, you also need to reprint it.

Don't edit the invoices you've already mailed—even if you haven't posted them. You want your accounting records to include the incorrect invoices, because those invoices are the ones the customer receives.

To correct an invoice you've already posted or mailed, you take two steps. First, using the next invoice number available, enter an entirely new invoice. The new invoice should mirror the incorrect one, but you should specify the new Ordered field as a negative amount. For example, if you originally created an invoice that ordered 10,000 cat's-eye marbles, enter −10,000 in the Ordered field of the new invoice. Saving and then posting this new invoice reverses your first, incorrect invoice.

Next, enter a third invoice. This time, use the data and amounts that you should have used for the first invoice.

C.P.A. Tip: Although you may be tempted to do so, don't combine these two correction steps and try to edit the incorrect mailed or posted transaction. When you review your books later, you'll more easily be able to understand two identical invoices that cancel each other and one independent invoice that represents the final correct bill you reissued the customer. Also, to clarify the situation in your records, use the *D* description feature to describe both the reversing invoice and the revised invoice.

Recording Sales Returns

You use the Enter Sales Returns option when a customer returns merchandise for which you previously billed the customer. To access the Sales Return screen, select the Transaction option from the main menu; choose option 5, Billing, from the Transaction menu; and select option 2, Enter Sales Returns, from the Billing menu. Figure 8.11 shows the Sales Return screen as it appears before you begin entering data.

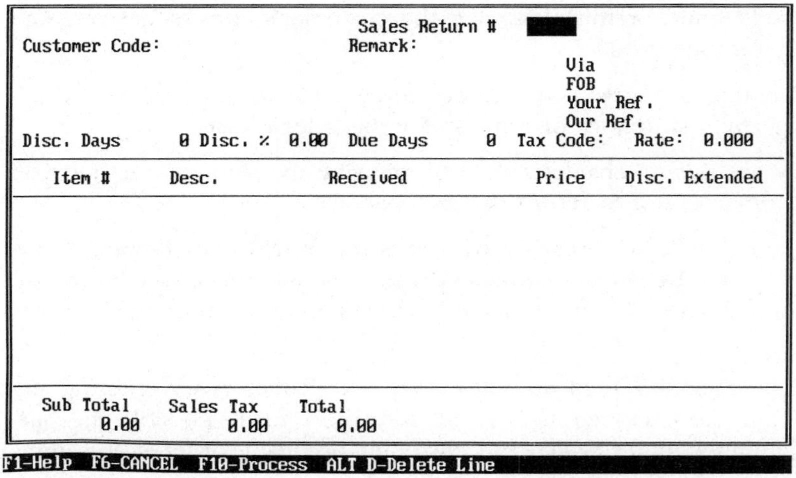

Fig. 8.11

The Sales Return screen before you enter data.

To complete the Sales Return screen, you enter data in several fields: Sales Return #, Customer Code, Remark, Via, FOB, Your Ref., Our Ref., and for each product returned the Item # and Received fields. You also have the option of editing the customer's name and address, discount days, discount percent, and due days (retrieved from the customer master file); the price (retrieved from the product master file, service master file, or billing codes file); and any discount you gave when you sold the items you're allowing the customer to return. The following paragraphs describe the fields in which you enter data.

Sales Return #: The system calculates the *sales return number* by adding 1 to the last sales return number used. Just as with the invoice number, the return number uniquely identifies the sales return for both you and the customer. For the first sales return you create, the system adds 1 to the Last Sales Order Return you entered as part of setting the system options and defaults (described in Chapter 3).

If you enter a number that has been used but not yet posted, the Sales Return screen retrieves the return previously identified by that number. If the transaction has been posted, a pop-up window alerts you that you cannot change a posted transaction.

Customer Code: The *customer code* is the abbreviation you assigned to the customer in the customer master file. When you enter this code, the Sales Return screen retrieves and places the following customer data in the corresponding fields: customer name and address, discount days, discount percent, due days, and sales tax code and rate. You may edit these fields if, for this sales return, these values differ from the usual. If you specified a message code for this customer in the messages file, a pop-up window displays the code's message, your credit limit for this customer, the customer's current balance, and the customer's unused credit.

Remark: This area of the screen includes three 20-character fields in which you can enter any instructions or remarks for this sales return.

Via: You may use this 15-character field to describe the shipping method you want the customer to use to return the merchandise.

FOB: You use this field to designate who pays the freight and shipping insurance and who bears the risks of ownership while the merchandise is in transit. The FOB field is described in more detail in the section on "Entering Customer Invoices."

Your Ref.: The Your Ref. field provides up to six characters for entering any code or number the customer uses to identify the return—possibly the purchase order number under which the customer originally ordered the items now being returned.

Our Ref.: The Our Ref. field provides up to six characters for entering any special code or number you're using in addition to the sales return number to identify this return. If you use return authorization numbers, for example you can enter that number in this field. Or you can enter the invoice number under which the items were originally billed.

Item #: You use the Item # field to tell the Sales Return screen what the customer is returning. When the customer returns a product defined in the product master file, you use the product code. When the customer returns an item defined in the billing codes file, you can use one of the billing codes by entering the letter *C* (for codes), a space, and the billing code number. When you complete the item number, the Sales Return screen retrieves the description and price from the product or service master file or the billing codes file.

You can also include messages from the messages file by entering in the Item # field the letter *M* (for messages), a space, and the message number. To include your own description (with as many as 40 characters) in the Desc. field, in the Item # field, type the letter *D* (for descriptions) and then the text of the description.

To create a sales return for a service, enter a service code rather than a product or billing code. Although this process may seem at first a little illogical, recording a return of a service adjusts the counter in the service master file that accumulates the units of a service provided.

You can accept a returned product or service that you haven't previously defined in the product or service master file or the billing codes file. As with the Customer Invoice screen, you simply enter an unused item number. A pop-up window appears, tells you that the item does not exist, and asks whether you want to create one. You probably shouldn't be using this feature, however, to record returns. Rarely will you be accepting a sales return of an item that you haven't previously defined for a customer invoice.

Received: You specify in this field the quantity of the item the customer is returning. If you specified fractional units in the product or service master file, you can enter a quantity that includes fractions of a unit. Otherwise, the system allows you to enter only whole numbers. After you indicate the received quantity, DacEasy calculates the Extended field. You can edit the Price, Disc. (purchase discount), and Extended fields if the system rounds these amounts incorrectly.

You enter an item number and a received quantity for each item the customer returns and you agree to accept. To delete an item from the list, press Alt-D while that item is highlighted. To delete the entire purchase return, press F6.

After you enter each of the items the customer is returning, press F10. To save the sales return, press F10 again. Or, to both save and print the sales return form you've just created, press F7. To continue editing, press any other key. Figure 8.12 shows the Sales Return screen filled with sample data.

C.P.A. Tip: Consider scheduling some date or time during the month to process your billing activity—perhaps at the end of every week or at the end of the month. Regular, frequent, and timely billing usually improves your cash flow and decreases your uncollectible receivables.

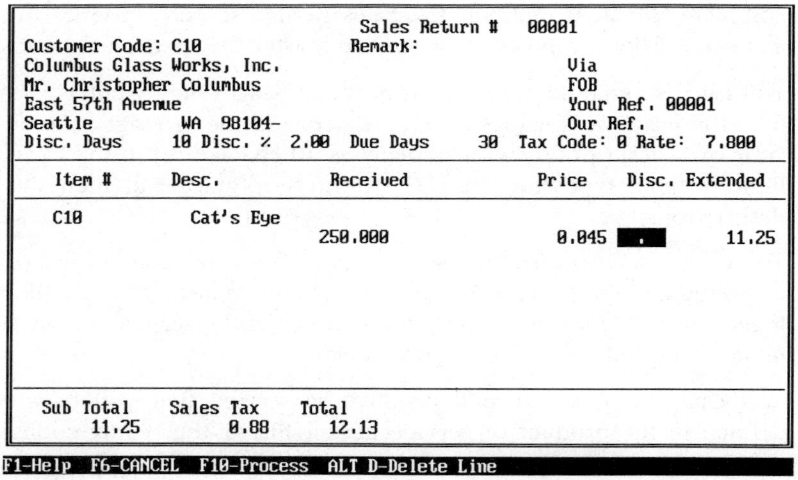

```
                              Sales Return #   00001
  Customer Code: C10          Remark:
  Columbus Glass Works, Inc.                   Via
  Mr. Christopher Columbus                     FOB
  East 57th Avenue                             Your Ref. 00001
  Seattle        WA  98104-                    Our Ref.
  Disc. Days    10 Disc. %  2.00  Due Days   30  Tax Code: 0 Rate:  7.800

    Item #       Desc.         Received           Price   Disc. Extended

    C10          Cat's Eye
                               250.000                    0.045  ▓ . ▓    11.25




  Sub Total    Sales Tax    Total
    11.25        0.88       12.13
```

F1-Help F6-CANCEL F10-Process ALT D-Delete Line

Fig. 8.12

An example of a completed Sales Return screen.

Correcting Sales Returns

As with customer invoices, if you incorrectly enter a sales return, your reaction depends on whether you've already posted the sales return (a process described at the end of this chapter). To correct a sales return you have not yet posted, access the Sales Return screen and type the sales return number to retrieve the sales return you want to change. Make your corrections and then save your work by pressing F10. You're done with the correction, but because you've changed the sales return, you also need to reprint it.

If you've already mailed the sales return to the customer, you should post the return even though it's incorrect. The transaction has in a sense become "real" and therefore should be recorded on your books exactly as the customer records it.

To correct a sales return you've already posted or mailed, first enter an entirely new sales return that mirrors the incorrect sales return. In the second return, however, specify the Received field as a negative amount. For example, if you originally created a sales return that showed a return of 3,700 Cleary marbles, enter a new sales return for − 3,700 Cleary marbles. Saving and then posting this new sales return reverses your first, incorrect sales return. Next, reenter the sales return you entered initially, but this time with no errors.

Printing Customer Invoices and Sales Returns

When you finish creating an invoice or return, you can print that single form by pressing F7. But the last two options on the Transactions Billing menu, Print Invoices and Print Sales Returns, allow you to print several invoices or returns at once, reprint previously printed invoices or returns, exclude certain data from printing, and modify the date that appears on the invoices or returns.

Because you use the same steps and the same print request fields to print both invoices and returns, I'll discuss the two procedures together. Figure 8.13 shows the Print Invoices screen. Figure 8.14 shows the Print Sales Return screen. Notice that only the title differs between the two screens. The parallel structure makes these options easier to use, because knowing how to use one option means you know also how to use the other. To simplify things even further, these two screens mirror the three purchase order screens you studied in Chapter 6. The identical structure used throughout the DacEasy accounting system represents just one more feature that makes the program easy to learn and use.

The fields you use to control the printing of invoices and sales returns are described in the following paragraphs.

Printing Packing Slips (Y/N)?: Answering this field *N* for "no" prints the invoice or sales return with the unit price and extended price. And, conversely, if you answer *Y*, DacEasy prints the form without the unit price and extended

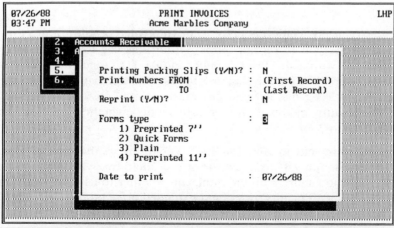

Fig. 8.13

The Print Invoices screen.

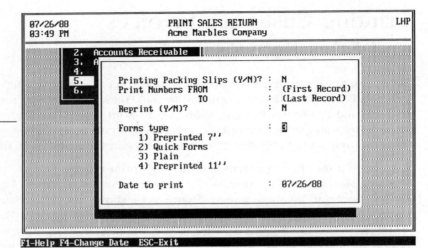

```
07/26/88                PRINT SALES RETURN                        LHP
03:49 PM                Acme Marbles Company

     2,  Accounts Receivable
     3,  A
     4,
     5,        Printing Packing Slips (Y/N)? :  N
     6,        Print Numbers FROM             :  (First Record)
                              TO             :  (Last Record)
               Reprint (Y/N)?                 :  N

               Forms type                     :  3
                  1) Preprinted 7''
                  2) Quick Forms
                  3) Plain
                  4) Preprinted 11''

               Date to print                  :  07/26/88




F1-Help F4-Change Date  ESC-Exit
```

Fig. 8.14

The Print Sales Return screen.

price. As the screen question implies, typically the only time you want to print an invoice or sales return without the unit price and extended price is when you want an abbreviated copy of the invoice or return to include with the shipment as a packing slip. Accordingly, DacEasy sets the default answer to this question at *N*.

Print Numbers FROM TO: By specifying the beginning and ending invoice or sales return numbers when you're generating either form, you control which forms print. If you don't complete these fields, the system assumes that you want all forms printed (except those you've previously printed). If you want to print only one form, type its invoice or sales return number in both the FROM and TO fields.

Reprint (Y/N)?: Typically, you produce or print an invoice or sales return only once. This field allows you to reprint forms. Setting this flag to *N* prints only those forms that fall within the Print Number FROM TO range and have not been previously printed. Setting this flag to *Y* prints all forms that fall within the Print Number FROM TO range. (If you previously printed an invoice or sales return but subsequently modified it, it reprints once whether you set the Reprint (Y/N)? field to *N* or *Y*.)

Forms Type: Use this field to alert DacEasy Accounting to the type of form you're using. The system needs to know the size of the form, whether to print your company name and address on the form, and whether to label information such as the item number, quantity, price, and extended price on the form. Enter the number that corresponds to the form type you're using.

Select the Preprinted 7″ or Preprinted 11″ form (options 1 and 4) if you've ordered custom business invoice or sales return forms with your name, address, and form labels. Quick Forms (option 2) refers to DacEasy's generic forms, which include form labels but not your company name or address. Choose Plain (option 3) if you're using plain, 8 1/2-inch-by-11-inch, continuous-form computer paper.

Date To Print: This date appears on the invoice or sales return as the date the form is generated. DacEasy automatically fills this field with the system date. You may substitute another date if you want a different date to print on the invoice or sales return.

Figure 8.15 shows a sample customer invoice, and figure 8.16 shows a sample sales return.

```
                              Acme Marbles Company
                               512 Wetmore Street
                               Seattle, Wa 98114
                        Tel: (206) 555-1234 Fax: (206) 555-6789
                                 I n v o i c e

      C10                                                    Ship to/Remarks
      Columbus Glass Works, Inc.
      Mr. Christopher Columbus
      East 57th Avenue
      Seattle WA 98104


                   Date 10/06/88      No. 00005 Page  1  Due Date   11/05/88
      ----------------------------------------------------------------------------
      Via Overland          FOB    Seattle      Disc.days 10 Disc.% 2.00 Net Days 30  Your #PO-561  Our #
      ----------------------------------------------------------------------------
      Inventory #   Description          Ordered     Shipped  Backorder Unit Price  Disc.%   Extended Price
      ----------------------------------------------------------------------------
      B10           Bumble Bee           500.000     500.000    0.000     0.035                      17.50
      C10           Cat's Eye            500.000     500.000    0.000     0.045                      22.50
      C20           Cleary            500000.000   36700.000  463300.000  0.035                    1284.50
      Y10           Yellow Swirls        250.000     250.000    0.000     0.040                      10.00
                    Freight                                                                           8.50




      ----------------------------------------------------------------------------
                                                           Sub-total      1343.00
                                                           Tax             104.09
                                                           Total          1447.09
                                                           Payment      (   500.00)
                                                           Net to Pay      947.09
                                                                        ------------
```

Fig. 8.15

A sample customer invoice.

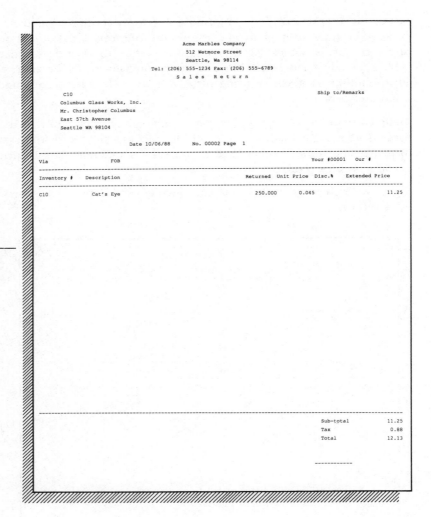

```
                        Acme Marbles Company
                         512 Wetmore Street
                          Seattle, Wa 98114
                  Tel: (206) 555-1234 Fax: (206) 555-6789
                        S a l e s   R e t u r n

     C10                                              Ship to/Remarks
  Columbus Glass Works, Inc.
  Mr. Christopher Columbus
  East 57th Avenue
  Seattle WA 98104

                Date 10/06/88       No. 00002 Page  1
  ----------------------------------------------------------------------
  Via              FOB                          Your #00001   Our #
  ----------------------------------------------------------------------
  Inventory #   Description          Returned  Unit Price  Disc.%  Extended Price
  ----------------------------------------------------------------------
  C10           Cat's Eye             250.000     0.045                11.25




  ----------------------------------------------------------------------
                                                Sub-total        11.25
                                                Tax               0.88
                                                Total            12.13

                                                ------------
```

Fig. 8.16

A sample sales return form.

Printing the Sales Journal

Choose the Journals option from the main menu and then select option 9, Sales Journal, to print the *sales journal*, a sample of which is shown in figure 8.17. The sales journal lists the customer invoices and sales returns you've created since the last time you posted billing transactions.

You can use the sales journal to review for possible errors in the customer invoices and sales returns you've created. If you do find errors, return to the screen you used to enter the transaction, make the necessary changes, and then

```
Date : 10/06/88                          Acme Marbles Company                        Page no. 1
Time : 02:55 PM                          512 Wetmore Street
                                         Seattle, Wa 98114
                              Tel: (206) 555-1234 Fax: (206) 555-6789

                                        SALES JOURNAL REPORT

          Cust.  Inv/Ret Customer
   Type   Dept.  Number  Code           Name          Date     Gross      Tax     Total    Amount Pd  Net To Pay
--------  -----  ------- ------   -------------------- -------- --------- -------- -------- --------- ----------
INVOICE          00005   C10    Columbus Glass Works, Inc 10/06/88  1343.00   104.09  1447.09   500.00    947.09
                                Invoice Total :                    1343.00   104.09  1447.09   500.00    947.09
RETURN           00002   C10    Columbus Glass Works, Inc 10/06/88   -11.25    -0.88   -12.13
                                Invoice Return Total :               -11.25    -0.88   -12.13     0.00    -12.13
                                Department Total :                  1331.75   103.21  1434.96   500.00    934.96

INVOICE   02     00006   Z10    Zebra Toys               10/06/88   562.50     0.00   562.50     0.00    562.50
                                Invoice Total :                     562.50     0.00   562.50     0.00    562.50
                                Department Total :                  562.50     0.00   562.50     0.00    562.50

                                Grand Totals :                     1894.25   103.21  1997.46   500.00   1497.46
```

Fig. 8.17

The sales journal.

print another copy of the sales journal to review. When you find no errors, you can post the customer invoices and sales returns. Save the last, error-free copy of the sales journal as your audit trail of billing transactions.

Most of the fields on the sales journal correspond directly to the fields you completed on the Customer Invoice and Sales Return screens. But two of the fields may be unfamiliar to you: Type and Cust. Dept.

The Type field identifies whether the transaction listed is an INVOICE or a RETURN. The Cust. Dept. field indicates the Type you entered for the customer in the customer master file. The sales journal uses the Type (of transaction) field as the primary sort key for ordering the transactions on the journal, and uses the Cust. Dept. (or the customer Type defined in the customer master file) as the secondary sort key. The sales journal also shows subtotals by Cust. Dept.

In addition, the sales journal prepares a summary of products and services sold. Figure 8.18 shows the sales journal summary.

On this portion of the journal, Type refers to those items you included on the customer invoice or sales return by specifying a product code from the product master file (labeled PRODUCT), a service code from the service master file (labeled SERVICE), or a billing code from the billing codes file (labeled CODE).

The summary's Dept. field refers to the revenue/cost department you defined in the product master file if you specified the revenue/cost department as INVEN-TORY. (You set the revenue/cost department as CUSTOMER, INVENTORY, or

```
Date : 10/06/88                          Acme Marbles Company                          Page no. 2
Time : 02:55 PM                           512 Wetmore Street
                                          Seattle, Wa 98114
                               Tel: (206) 555-1234 Fax: (206) 555-6789

                                         SALES JOURNAL REPORT
                                    SUMMARY BY INVENTORY AND CODE
 Dept.  Type   Item/Acct #   Description              Units       Amount    Avg./Unit  Sale Price  % Variance
 -----  ------ ------------  -------------------      ---------   --------   ---------  ----------  ----------
        CODE    4301         Freight                                  8.50
                             Code total :                             8.50
                             Department Total :                       8.50

 01    PRODUCT B10           Bumble Bee                500.000       17.50      0.04       0.03       16.67
 01    PRODUCT C10           Cat's Eye                 250.000       11.25      0.05       0.03       50.00
                             Product total :                         28.75
                             Department Total :                      28.75

 02    PRODUCT C20           Cleary                  36700.000     1284.50      0.04       0.04        0.00
 02    PRODUCT Y10           Yellow Swirls             250.000       10.00      0.04       0.01      207.69
                             Product total :                       1294.50
 02    SERVICE X10           Marble Consulting          10.000      562.50     56.25      75.00      -25.00
                             Service Total :                        562.50
                             Department Total :                    1857.00

                             Grand Totals :                        1894.25
```

Fig. 8.18

The sales journal report summary.

NONE as part of setting the system options and defaults, as described in Chapter 3.) The Dept. field is the primary sort key for ordering the items on the summary. Because the billing codes have no revenue/cost department, these items appear first on the summary with the Dept. field columns showing as blank. This summary also calculates totals by department (meaning here the revenue/cost department) and computes a grand total.

Posting Billing Transactions

Posting billing transactions means passing customer invoice and sales return information to the General Ledger module. You need to post the billing transactions to the general ledger before you can generate a balance sheet, income statement, and statement of changes in financial position. Accordingly, you should post billing information as frequently as you want to see up-to-date financial statements. To post the Billing module's customer invoices and sales returns, select the Posting option on the main menu and then choose option 5, Billing.

If you have not posted other modules with interrelated transactions, you may see a message similar to the one shown in figure 8.19. You must complete any related posting before you can post the billing transactions.

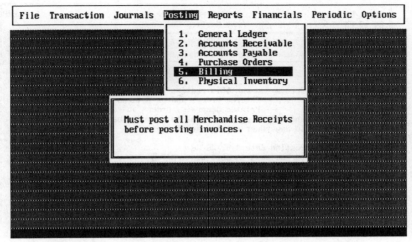

File Transaction Journals **Posting** Reports Financials Periodic Options

```
               1.  General Ledger
               2.  Accounts Receivable
               3.  Accounts Payable
               4.  Purchase Orders
               5.  Billing
               6.  Physical Inventory
```

Must post all Merchandise Receipts
before posting invoices.

Fig. 8.19

The screen that appears if you haven't posted all related transactions.

When you select the Posting Billing option (and after you've posted all related transactions), DacEasy displays a warning screen and asks you to be sure that you've entered the invoices and sales returns you want to post and that you've printed the sales journal, customer invoices, and sales returns (see fig. 8.20). The program suggests also that you back up your files before you post. (The procedures for backing up and restoring your files are discussed in Chapter 5, "Protecting Your System.") Press *Y* to continue with the posting process. DacEasy then automatically posts all your billing transactions to the General Ledger module.

Chapter Summary

This chapter examined the billing process in general and discussed why you might need to use the DacEasy Billing module. You learned how to use the Billing module to create and print customer invoices and sales returns and to post billing transactions to the general ledger. Chapter 9 describes the Accounts Receivable module, which takes up where the Billing module leaves off: monitoring the customer invoices and returns once you've created them.

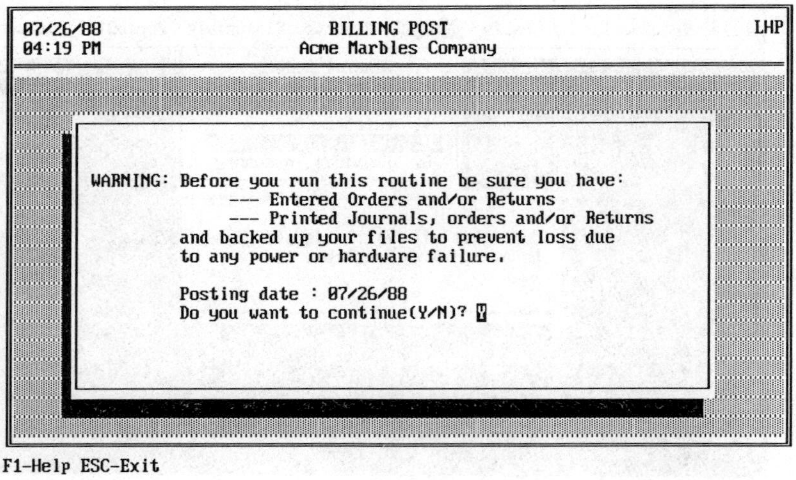

```
07/26/88                    BILLING POST                      LHP
04:19 PM                 Acme Marbles Company


        ┌─────────────────────────────────────────────────┐
        │                                                   │
        │  WARNING: Before you run this routine be sure you have: │
        │           --- Entered Orders and/or Returns       │
        │           --- Printed Journals, orders and/or Returns │
        │  and backed up your files to prevent loss due     │
        │  to any power or hardware failure.                │
        │                                                   │
        │  Posting date : 07/26/88                          │
        │  Do you want to continue(Y/N)? Y                  │
        │                                                   │
        └─────────────────────────────────────────────────┘



F1-Help ESC-Exit
```

Fig. 8.20

The warning screen that appears when you choose the Posting Billing option.

Using the Accounts Receivable Module

You use the DacEasy Accounts Receivable module to record amounts owed by customers or clients and to record their payments. The module's tools allow you to both account for and control customer receivables and collections.

This chapter reviews the accounts receivable process, illustrates some sample accounts receivable transactions that are probably similar to those you'll be recording, and explains why the Accounts Receivable module can be helpful to you. In addition, the chapter describes for each accounts receivable menu selection the event recorded or the report produced, the steps needed to complete each selection, and how to fix mistakes you make while using the Accounts Receivable module.

Reviewing the Accounts Receivable Process

The accounts receivable process amounts to no more than keeping records of the amounts customers owe and the payments they make on their accounts. The process begins when you provide some good or service to a customer. At that point, your books need to reflect two things:

1. Someone owes you money.
2. You've generated revenue.

201

(Sometimes, the customer pays you cash, which means your cash balance increases, and the customer doesn't owe you money. More often, however, customers want to pay you as part of their normal accounts payable cycle, which means you may not collect the cash for several days, or even weeks.)

If things go as planned, the customer eventually sends you payment for the owed amounts. Because you usually provide goods or services to a customer regularly, a customer may owe you for several purchases. Therefore, a check sometimes includes payment for several invoices.

When the customer pays, you deposit the check and then need to record the fact that one or several unpaid invoices have been paid. In a manual accounts receivable system, you must sort through your unpaid invoices for a customer and then mark (probably with the customer's check number) those invoices that the customer has paid. In the DacEasy Accounts Receivable module, the same thing happens, but the system does the work of sorting through the unpaid, or open, invoices for a customer and marking those that have been paid. Using the DacEasy accounting system doesn't change the accounts receivable process but just makes it easier and quicker.

Examining Some Sample Accounts Receivable Transactions

You'll find the Accounts Receivable module easier to use if you first understand the bookkeeping the module performs. Only three basic types of transactions are recorded in the Accounts Receivable module.

The first type is the recording of a sale when you sell some item on credit. You record both the asset you acquire (a receivable from your customer) and the revenue the sale provides. If you remember Chapter 1's discussion of debits and credits, the balance sheet, and the income statement, you may be able to construct the debits and credits for this type of transaction yourself. An increase in an asset is shown by a debit, so you must debit the accounts receivable balance. Because an increase in revenue is shown by a credit, you must credit the sales revenue account.

A couple of sample transactions may clarify this process for you. Suppose that you just sold some Bumble Bee marbles to Columbus Glass Works, Inc., one of your best customers, for $1,000. Columbus Glass Works now owes you $1,000, and you've also generated $1,000 in revenue. You need to make the following entry:

	Debit	*Credit*
Accounts Receivable	$1,000	
Sales		$1,000

In case you're interested, this transaction is the one that the Billing module automatically makes for you if you use that module to generate customer invoices. The Accounts Receivable account shows up on the asset portion of your balance sheet, and the Sales account on the income statement. When you enter the transaction in the Accounts Receivable Transaction Entry screen (see "Entering Accounts Receivable Transactions"), you enter the appropriate account number so that DacEasy posts the asset and revenue to the proper accounts.

You need to know about two other types of accounts receivable transactions. One type occurs when you accept the return of an item, the sale of which you previously recorded as a receivable and revenue. For example, what if you allow Columbus Glass Works to return the Bumble Bee marbles? Columbus Glass Works then no longer owes you the receivable, and you need to reduce the revenue you've recorded for the period as if the sale never occurred.

To reduce an asset, you credit the accounts receivable account; to reduce revenue, you debit sales. Once you know which accounts to credit and debit, completing the transaction is easy:

	Debit	*Credit*
Accounts Receivable		$1,000
Sales	$1,000	

Maybe you've noticed that this transaction looks identical to the one used to record the original sale except that the debits and credits are reversed. If you think about it, this transposition makes sense, because reversing the original sale is exactly what you're doing. (Although you can use this entry to record sales returns, you'll often want to keep specific track of sales returns. As noted in Chapter 3, "Defining the Chart of Accounts and System Options," you thus need to have a separate account number for sales returns. The DacEasy sample Chart of Accounts provides a special contrarevenue account called Sales Returns.)

The third and final type of accounts receivable transaction is probably the simplest: When a customer makes a payment to you, you record the increase in cash and the decrease in your accounts receivable. For example, suppose that a customer pays you $500 toward a debt. Your debit and credit should look like this:

	Debit	*Credit*
Accounts Receivable		$500
Cash	$500	

You credit the accounts receivable account to show the reduction in the amount the customer owes and debit the cash account to record the increase in cash. Because the transaction is simple and looks nearly the same each time it occurs, DacEasy records this transaction for you whenever you record a customer payment.

When To Use the Accounts Receivable Module

Do customer receivables comprise one of your major assets? Do you find tracking what customers owe you a major and never-ending headache? Do you ever find yourself with cash-flow problems because a customer's payment is late? If you answer any of these questions "yes," the Accounts Receivable module should prove itself a powerful tool to help you monitor and record customer receivables and collections.

Accessing the Menu Options for Accounts Receivable

The accounts receivable tools are grouped under five of the main DacEasy menu options: Transaction, Journals, Posting, Reports, and Periodic. From the Transaction menu, you choose the Accounts Receivable option to access two accounts receivable screens. The Accounts Receivable Transaction Entry screen allows you to enter amounts owed to you by customers when those amounts haven't been previously recorded in the Billing module. With the Cash Receipts and Adjustment screen, you can record customer payments and then indicate which invoices are satisfied by those payments. Figure 9.1 shows the Transaction menu.

Using the Journals menu, you can print two accounts receivable reports. The first is the *accounts receivable transaction journal*, which lists customer invoices, debit memos, and credit memos that you recorded with the Accounts Receivable Transaction Entry screen. The second is the *accounts receivable*

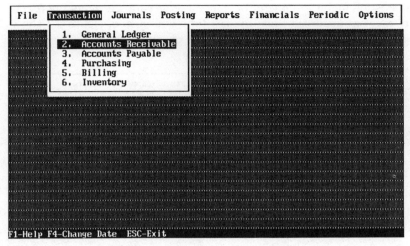

Fig. 9.1

The Transaction Accounts Receivable option.

payments journal, which lists the customer payments received and the invoices paid by the customer payments. These two journals provide the audit trail you need for documenting all the transactions recorded in the Accounts Receivable module.

Figure 9.2 shows the Journals menu with option 3, A/R Transactions, high-lighted. Choose this option to print the accounts receivable transaction journal. Option 4, A/R Cash Receipts Journal, accesses the accounts receivable payments journal.

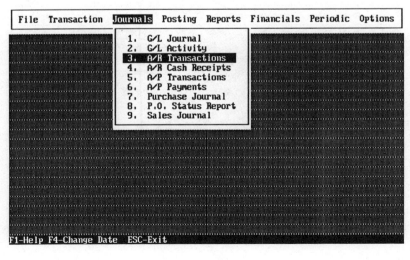

Fig. 9.2

The Journals A/R Transactions option.

You use the Posting menu to update the general ledger for the accounts receivable activity that has occurred since the last time you posted. Figure 9.3 shows the Posting menu with the Accounts Receivable choice selected.

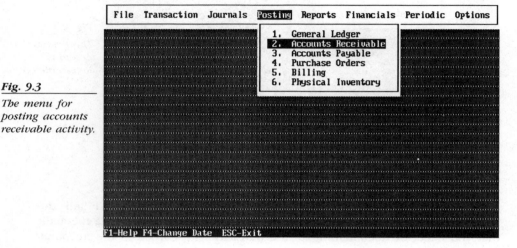

Fig. 9.3

The menu for posting accounts receivable activity.

On the Reports menu, you can use the Accounts Receivable option to print statements of what customers owe, an aging of the amounts customers owe, a directory of customers, and customer mailing address labels. Figure 9.4 reproduces the Reports menu with the cursor on the Accounts Receivable option.

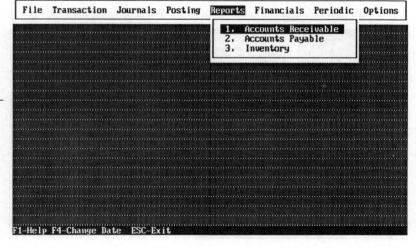

Fig. 9.4

The Reports Accounts Receivable option.

Finally, with the Periodic menu, you can run periodic routines monthly and annually to close out old accounts receivable transactions and to generate forecasts of next year's accounts receivable volumes and amounts. Because Chapter 12, "Using the Periodic Routines," describes these special features in detail, the periodic routines are not covered in this chapter. Figure 9.5 shows the Periodic menu with option 2, Accounts Receivable, selected.

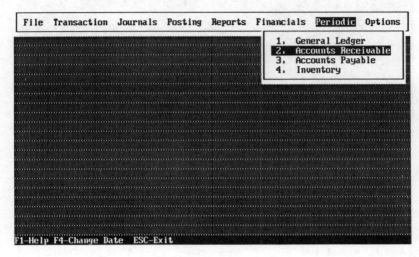

Fig. 9.5

The menu for running periodic accounts receivable routines.

The rest of this chapter is devoted to walking you through the steps of using—and profiting from—the first four sets of accounts receivable tools.

Entering Accounts Receivable Transactions

Use the Accounts Receivable Transaction Entry screen to record amounts customers owe—amounts for which you didn't use the Billing module to generate an invoice. To access this screen, first select the Transaction option from the main menu; choose option 2, Accounts Receivable, from the Transaction menu; and select option 1, A/R Transaction Entry from the Accounts Receivable menu. See figure 9.6 for the menu hierarchy.

Figure 9.7 shows the Accounts Receivable Transaction Entry screen before you begin entering data. The following paragraphs describe each of the fields in which you either must enter data or may edit data.

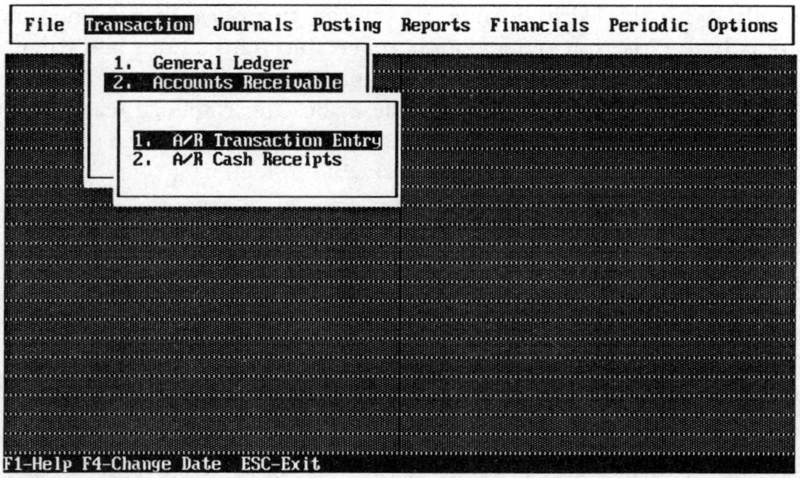

File **Transaction** Journals Posting Reports Financials Periodic Options

```
        1.  General Ledger
        2.  Accounts Receivable

           1.  A/R Transaction Entry
           2.  A/R Cash Receipts
```

Fig. 9.6

The options for entering accounts receivable transactions and cash receipts/ adjustments.

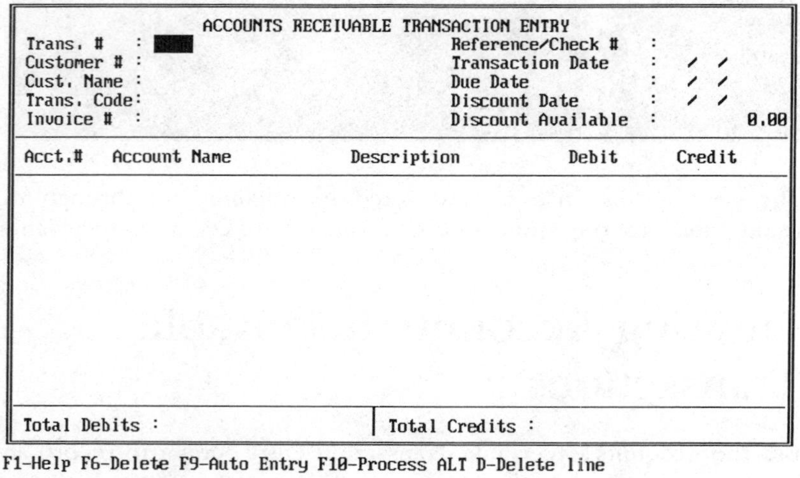

F1-Help F4-Change Date ESC-Exit

```
              ACCOUNTS RECEIVABLE TRANSACTION ENTRY
  Trans. #  :                    Reference/Check # :
  Customer #:                    Transaction Date  :    /  /
  Cust. Name:                    Due Date          :    /  /
  Trans. Code:                   Discount Date     :    /  /
  Invoice #  :                   Discount Available :        0.00

  Acct.#  Account Name          Description       Debit      Credit




  Total Debits :            │  Total Credits :
```

Fig. 9.7

The Accounts Receivable Transaction Entry screen before you enter data.

F1-Help F6-Delete F9-Auto Entry F10-Process ALT D-Delete line

Trans. #: The *transaction number* is the unique identifier that you use to reference the transaction until you post it to the general ledger. This method of identification is the same one used in the the Accounts Payable module.

If you want to edit a transaction that you haven't posted yet, you can type the transaction's number in the Trans. # field to have DacEasy retrieve the transaction for you. You can't modify transactions you've previously posted. In fact, the Accounts Receivable module resets the transaction number to 1 each time you post accounts receivable information to the general ledger.

Customer #: The *customer number* identifies a customer to the system and allows the Accounts Receivable Transaction Entry screen to retrieve the customer's name and payment terms (due date, discount date, and discount available) from the customer master file. (The Customer # field is what DacEasy on other screens calls the Customer Code.) After you enter a valid customer number, DacEasy displays also any message you specified for that customer, your credit limit for the customer, the customer's current balance, and the customer's unused credit.

As on the other screens in the DacEasy accounting system, if you find in the midst of entering a series of accounts receivable transactions that you need to create an invoice for a new customer, you can enter an unused customer code. A pop-up window then appears, tells you that the code doesn't exist, and asks whether you want to create the code. By answering *Y* for "yes," you access an abbreviated Customer File Maintenance screen and enter the new customer into the master file.

Trans. Code: You enter the *transaction code* to let the system know whether you're entering a normal accounts receivable invoice, a special accounts receivable debit memo, or an accounts receivable credit memo. You describe each transaction by using one of three codes: *I* for regular invoices, signifying a normal accounts receivable invoice; *D* for accounts receivable debit memos; and *C* for accounts receivable credit memos. To help you remember the three codes, DacEasy displays a pop-up window listing the codes whenever the Trans. Code field is highlighted.

When you're selecting the appropriate transaction code, you should keep one important consideration in mind: DacEasy calculates discounts only for transactions with codes of *I* (see the discussion of the Discount Available field).

Invoice #: The *invoice number* allows you to identify invoices, debit memos, and credits uniquely so that both you and the customer can specifically refer to transactions. You *cannot* move from the field without specifying some invoice number for a transaction. Later, the customer should use this number to identify amounts paid.

Reference/Check #: The system forces you to enter this six-character, alphanumeric field so that you reference the transaction to the source document that creates or authorizes the transaction. Most often, you use the customer's purchase order number or the name of the person who requested the good or service.

Transaction Date: The *transaction date* is the date you want to show the transaction as being recorded in the Accounts Receivable module. Because typically this date is the current date, DacEasy places the system date in this field. But you can modify the field.

Due Date: DacEasy calculates the *due date* by adding the transaction date to the due days specified for this customer in the customer master file. If payment isn't received from the customer by this date, you may assess finance charges and late payment penalties.

Discount Date: DacEasy calculates the *discount date* by adding the transaction date to the discount days specified for this customer in the customer master file. For the customer to be entitled to any early payment discount, the customer's payment must be received by this date.

Discount Available: This field shows the calculated early payment discount to which the customer is entitled if the invoice is paid by the discount date. You don't enter this field on the Accounts Receivable Transaction Entry screen. The system calculates the discount for you, based on the discount percent and the total invoice amount.

Acct. #: This field shows the Chart of Accounts number that should be debited or credited as part of the accounts receivable transaction. Because you are making debits and credits to these accounts, they must be detail accounts.

The system performs half of the transaction based on the transaction code you entered. For example, if you're creating a transaction with a code of *I* for invoice or *D* for miscellaneous debit, the Accounts Receivable module knows it should debit the accounts receivable account. The system therefore retrieves the accounts receivable account number and positions the cursor in the Debit field. If you're creating a transaction with a code of *C* for miscellaneous credit, DacEasy knows it should credit the accounts receivable account and so retrieves the accounts receivable account number and positions the cursor in the Credit field. (In either case, the accounts receivable account number credited or debited is the one you defined in the general ledger interface table. Setting up the general ledger interface table is described in Chapter 3.) You enter the account number or numbers for the other half of the transaction.

If you want to debit or credit an account that you haven't already set up in the Chart of Accounts, simply enter an account number that hasn't been previously defined. DacEasy then displays a pop-up window alerting you that your entry is invalid and asking whether you want to add the entry to the appropriate master file. If you answer *Y*, another pop-up window appears. This window provides an abbreviated Chart of Accounts File Maintenance screen.

Account Name: When you enter an account number, DacEasy retrieves the name of that account from the Chart of Accounts. This important feature helps you verify that you're debiting or crediting the correct accounts.

Description: The 24-character Description field allows you to describe briefly either the transaction or the debit or credit component of the transaction for that line. On reports, the transaction number is listed, so you can always use that number to return to the original transaction and examine the entry. But the description, which also appears on the accounts receivable reports, may save you the trouble.

Debit: If the account you've entered on a line represents the debit component of the transaction, you enter the amount of the debit in this field. If the account you've entered on a line represents the credit component, press Enter to move the cursor to the Credit field. For transaction codes of *I* and *D*, you can make your initial entry to the accounts receivable account only in the Debit column.

Credit: If the account you've entered on a line represents the credit component of the transaction, you enter the amount of the credit in this field. For transaction codes of *C*, you can make your initial entry to the accounts receivable account only in the Credit column.

You can enter as many debits and credits as you need to record the transaction. Remember that if you've correctly recorded the transaction, the total debits equal the total credits. The Accounts Receivable Transaction Entry screen reflects this balance at the bottom of the screen. To delete a debit or credit component in your transaction, press Alt-D while the cursor is highlighting one of the fields in that line. To delete a transaction, press F6. If you're not sure how to complete a transaction, press F9 to balance the difference between the total debits and total credits temporarily. DacEasy then lets you proceed with processing the accounts receivable transaction entry.

After you finish recording the accounts receivable transaction, press F10, which saves the transaction, clears the screen, and positions the cursor at the Trans. # field. You're then ready to enter another transaction. Unless you use F9, you can't save a transaction that doesn't balance. If you need to make any corrections, use the arrow keys to move through the fields on the screen.

Figure 9.8 shows the Accounts Receivable Transaction Entry screen completed to show the accounts receivable and revenue generated from a sale to Columbus Glass Works, Inc. The debit is to the accounts receivable detail account number from the sample Chart of Accounts. The credit is to the revenue detail account number.

Although DacEasy doesn't limit the number of debits and credits you can include in an accounts receivable transaction, if you begin to enter transactions with dozens of debits and credits, you may exceed the file size you previously established. You then need to use the File Rehash option to increase the number of accounts receivable transactions. If you have a large number of transactions to enter, check the status by choosing the Options Status option. If the number of currently used files is large in comparison to the number of

```
                ACCOUNTS RECEIVABLE TRANSACTION ENTRY
   Trans. #   : 0001              Reference/Check #  : po4592
   Customer # : C10               Transaction Date   : 07/27/88
   Cust. Name : Columbus Glass Works, Inc.  Due Date : 08/26/88
   Trans. Code: I                 Discount Date      : 08/06/88
   Invoice #  : 00001             Discount Available :     20.50

   Acct.#   Account Name        Description        Debit      Credit

   11051  Accts Rec'ble Modulesale of bumble bees  1025.00
   4101   Sales Dept. 01      sale of bumble bees             1000.00
   4301   Freight             sale of bumble bees               25.00
   ████████


   Total Debits :     1025.00   │   Total Credits :     1025.00
```

F1-Help F6-Delete F9-Auto Entry F10-Process ALT D-Delete line

Fig. 9.8

An example of a completed Accounts Receivable Transaction Entry screen.

defined files, choose File Rehash and increase the file size so that you won't run out of file space and thereby lose a transaction.

Correcting Accounts Receivable Transactions

Finding and correcting mistakes is part of the accounting and bookkeeping process, so knowing how to fix errors is as important as knowing how to use each screen and report. As is true elsewhere in the DacEasy accounting system, your approach to correcting errors depends on whether you've posted the transactions. If you enter an accounts receivable transaction incorrectly, you can retrieve it before you post it by typing the transaction number (in the Trans. # field) and then edit the fields you need to change.

If you've posted the accounts receivable transactions (a process described later in this chapter), you must take two steps to fix a mistake. First, reverse the incorrect entry by entering another transaction that looks exactly like the incorrect transaction but has the debits and credits reversed. For example, suppose that you debited accounts receivable and credited sales in the incorrect entry. When you reverse the first transaction, credit accounts receivable and debit sales for the same amounts you used in the incorrect transaction.

Because the Accounts Receivable Transaction Entry screen allows you to enter only a debit for a transaction with an *I* or *D* code, just enter a negative value in the debit column. A negative debit equals a credit. Similarly, because the program allows you to enter only a credit for a transaction with a *C* code, just enter a negative value in the credit column. A negative credit equals a debit. Use the Description field to document that this entry is a reversing transaction, and use the Reference/Check # field to tie this reversing transaction to the entry you're correcting. Save the transaction by pressing F10.

Your second step is to reenter the first transaction as you should have entered it the first time. Then save the new transaction. The next time you post the accounts receivable transactions, the reversing transaction cancels out the effects of your incorrect entry, and the third entry properly records the transaction.

If you've been moving through this book from front to back, you're probably getting tired of reading this warning, but here it is anyway: Always follow the two steps outlined to correct transactions that have already been posted. Don't combine the two steps, creating one transaction that merely adjusts the old entry so that it looks right. A few weeks or months from now, you'll be able to understand more easily both what the error was and what the correct transaction was if you completely cancel the incorrect entry with a reversing transaction and enter a third, accurate transaction.

Recording Accounts Receivable Cash Receipts and Adjustments

To record payments you receive from customers, you use the Cash Receipts and Adjustments screen. To access this screen, first select the Transaction option from the main menu; choose option 2, Accounts Receivable, from the Transaction menu; and select option 2, A/R Cash Receipts, from the Accounts Receivable menu. Figure 9.9 shows the Cash Receipts and Adjustments screen as it appears when you first access it.

The following paragraphs describe the fields in which you enter information to record customer collections.

Transaction #: This field is identical to the Trans. # field on the Accounts Receivable Transaction Entry screen. The *transaction number* identifies the cash receipt or adjustment until you post the transaction to the general ledger. Press Enter, and the system automatically assigns the next available transaction number.

As with every other transaction in the system, you can't modify transactions you've already posted. But if you want to edit a transaction you haven't posted yet, type that transaction's number, and the program retrieves the transaction.

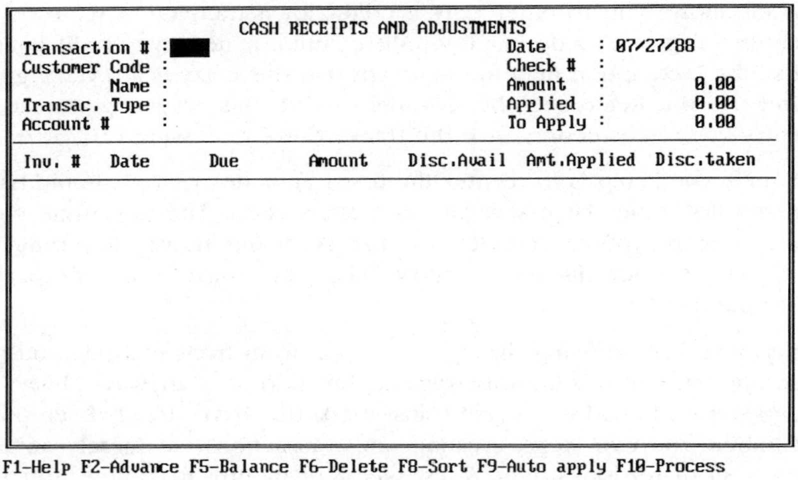

```
                        CASH RECEIPTS AND ADJUSTMENTS
        Transaction #  :███           Date      : 07/27/88
        Customer Code  :              Check #   :
                Name   :              Amount    :        0.00
        Transac. Type  :              Applied   :        0.00
        Account #      :              To Apply  :        0.00

        Inv. #   Date      Due       Amount   Disc.Avail  Amt.Applied  Disc.taken




```

Fig. 9.9

The Cash Receipts and Adjustments screen before you enter data.

F1-Help F2-Advance F5-Balance F6-Delete F8-Sort F9-Auto apply F10-Process

You can't use the same transaction number on both the Accounts Receivable Transaction Entry screen and the Cash Receipts and Adjustments screen. For example, if you used the number 00021 to identify an accounts receivable transaction, you can't use the same number to identify a cash receipt or adjustment. Because the system usually assigns the transaction number, this situation isn't much of a concern. But if you're on the Cash Receipts and Adjustments screen and enter a transaction number that identifies a transaction—or vice versa—you get an error message telling you that the transaction type is invalid.

Customer Code: The *customer code* identifies a customer to the system and allows the Cash Receipts and Adjustments screen to retrieve information from the customer master file (including any message you've assigned to a customer, your credit limit for and current balance with a customer, and the customer's name and payment terms) and to find any unpaid invoices the customer owes.

If you want to enter a cash receipt for a customer you haven't already defined in the customer master file, DacEasy allows you to enter these items directly from the Cash Receipts and Adjustments screen. Simply enter an unused customer code. A pop-up window appears, alerts you that your entry is invalid, and asks whether you want to add the entry to the master file. If you answer *Y*, another pop-up window appears, providing you with an abbreviated Customer File Maintenance screen.

Transac. Type: You enter the *transaction type* to tell the system what kind of payment or adjustment you're entering. *P* designates a customer payment, and *A* an adjustment. Adjustments apply to specific invoices those customer credit memos and advances that customers have previously paid or earned.

Account #: DacEasy needs to know where you deposit the cash received from the customer. The program retrieves the bank checking account number you specified in the general ledger interface table but allows you to edit the number in case you are using another cash account. Don't enter an account number for adjustments, because no cash is involved when you're netting credit memos and advance payments against invoices.

Date: The program puts the system date in this field, but you can modify the field to show another date. This date appears on screens and reports as the date of the payment or adjustment.

Check #: You enter in this field the appropriate identifying number for the payment—probably the customer's check number. You might also use an electronic funds transfer number or an automatic withdrawal receipt number. For adjustments, because you don't have a convenient external number, just assign your own number. For example, use ADJ01 for the first adjustment, ADJ02 for the second adjustment, and so on.

Amount: The Amount field shows the amount of the cash receipt. For *P* type transactions, you enter the amount because you're recording a collection. For an *A* type transaction, however, leave the Amount field set at 0.00, because you're not recording a payment but applying a previously recorded payment or a credit memo against customer invoices and debit memos.

Applied: The Applied field totals the invoices and debit memos the customer pays and the credit memos the customer wants you to apply against the invoices or debit memos. This field must display a positive amount because you can't record a negative cash receipt.

To Apply: The To Apply field shows the difference between the Amount and the Applied fields. The system's calculation of both these amounts is based on the cash received and the invoices, debit and credit memos, and unapplied cash receipts you select.

Inv. #, Date, Due, Amount, and Disc. Avail: DacEasy lists the customer's unpaid invoices in this section of the screen, showing the invoice number, the discount date, the due date, the invoice amount, and any early payment discount available. You don't change these values, because you entered them either in the Billing module or on the Accounts Receivable Transaction Entry screen.

Amt. Applied: Enter in this field the amount the customer pays on invoices and debit memos. If the customer includes with the check a remittance advice, it probably details the invoices and debit memos paid by the check. When a customer pays an invoice that includes a discount, enter in the Amt. Applied field only the net amount, calculated as the invoice total less the discount available. Enter the amount applied from any credit memos as negative amounts, just as credit memo amounts display as negative values. To make completion of this field easier, the Cash Receipts and Adjustments screen allows you to press F9 to apply the entire amount of an invoice or debit memo. The F9 technique does not work for credit memos.

Disc. Taken: This field shows any early payment discount the customer takes. To pay an invoice completely, the amount applied plus the discount taken must equal the invoice total.

To delete a transaction, press F6. You can use this key to delete a cash receipt or adjustment transaction but not an invoice, debit memo, or credit memo. (To delete these, you need to use the A/R Transaction Entry option from the Transaction Accounts Receivable menu.)

After you finish recording the payment or adjustment, press F10, which saves the transaction, clears the screen, and positions the cursor at the Transaction # field. You're then ready to enter another cash receipt or adjustment. You can't save a cash receipt or adjustment you haven't fully applied unless you use the F2 key, which allows you to classify the unapplied portion of the payment as an advance.

If you press F5 while the cursor is positioned on one of the invoices in the lower half of the screen, DacEasy displays a pop-up window that shows the invoice number and invoice balance, including the effect of any current applications. You may find this window easier to read than the list of horizontal invoices on the Cash Receipts and Adjustments screen. Another special function key you can use on this screen is F8, which switches the order in which invoices are sorted. If you press F8 when the invoices are sorted by discount date, DacEasy re-sorts them by due date. Conversely, pressing F8 when the invoices are sorted by due date re-sorts them by discount date.

Figure 9.10 shows the Cash Receipts and Adjustments screen completed so that a customer's credit memos are applied to an invoice and a $375.00 check is applied to the remaining balance.

C.P.A. Tip: To write off, or record as uncollectible, an amount from a customer, you can create a credit memo with a credit to the Accounts Receivable account and a debit to the Bad Debt Expense account. Then, within the Cash Receipts and Adjustments program, you can enter an adjustment that applies the credit memo against the uncollectible invoices and debit memos. If you use an allowance account to estimate uncollectible accounts receivable before you can identify specific invoices as uncollectible, you follow the same steps, but debit the Allowance for Bad Debts account rather than the Bad Debt Expense account. Both accounts are included on the DacEasy sample Chart of Accounts.

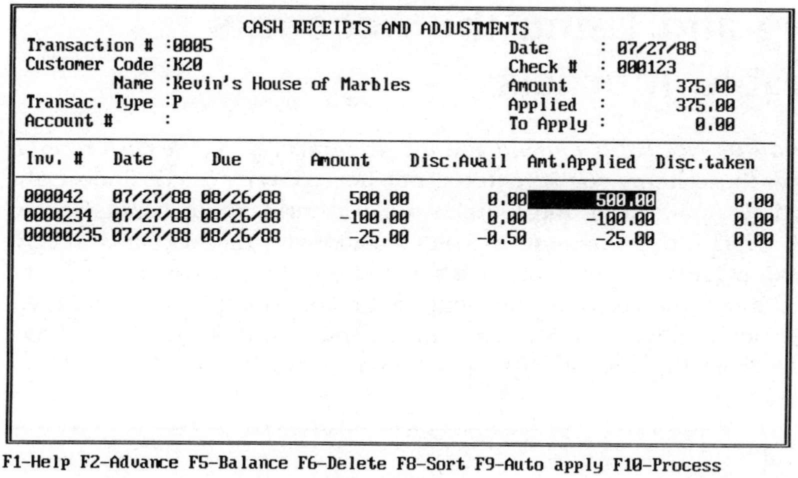

```
                    CASH RECEIPTS AND ADJUSTMENTS
  Transaction # :0005                        Date    : 07/27/88
  Customer Code :K20                          Check # : 000123
          Name :Kevin's House of Marbles      Amount  :      375.00
  Transac. Type :P                            Applied :      375.00
  Account #    :                              To Apply:        0.00

  Inv. #   Date      Due       Amount   Disc.Avail  Amt.Applied  Disc.taken

  000042   07/27/88 08/26/88    500.00      0.00        500.00        0.00
  0000234  07/27/88 08/26/88   -100.00      0.00       -100.00        0.00
  00000235 07/27/88 08/26/88    -25.00     -0.50        -25.00        0.00
```

Fig. 9.10

An example of a completed Cash Receipts and Adjustments screen.

F1–Help F2–Advance F5–Balance F6–Delete F8–Sort F9–Auto apply F10–Process

Correcting Accounts Receivable Cash Receipts and Adjustments

If you want to correct a transaction that you haven't yet posted, you can retrieve the incorrect cash receipt or adjustment transaction, using the transaction number, and make your corrections.

If you've already posted the accounts receivable cash receipts and adjustments, correcting the effects of a mistake is more difficult because you can't *unapply* previously applied cash receipts and adjustments. Accordingly, you need to modify the standard two-step correction procedure outlined in this and preceding chapters. First, reverse the incorrect entry. Use the Accounts Receivable Transaction Entry screen to set up for the customer a new debit memo that debits accounts receivable and then credits cash for the amount of the payment. Second, reenter the payment or adjustment, this time without mistakes, and apply the cash payment to the new debit memo. The first entry reverses the effect of the incorrect entry, and the second entry correctly records the receipt or adjustment.

As always, you should document well the incorrect original entry, the reversing entry, and the final correct entry. You may want to write messages to yourself on the accounts receivable journals, noting which entry was incorrect, which entry was the reversing one, and which entry was the final corrected transaction. Such descriptions may save you from later confusion about what a series of accounts receivable transactions records.

Printing and Using the Accounts Receivable Journals

Both the *accounts receivable journal* and the *accounts receivable cash receipts journal* show those items you've entered but haven't yet posted. Choose the A/R Transactions option from the Journals menu to print the accounts receivable journal, which details the entries you've made with the Accounts Receivable Transaction Entry screen. For each transaction, the journal indicates the transaction number, the customer, accounts and amounts debited and credited, and the other information you entered with the transaction. Figure 9.11 shows a sample page from the journal's listing of transactions.

Fig. 9.11

The accounts receivable journal.

```
Date : 07/27/88                                    Acme Marbles Company                                Page no. 1
Time : 12:37 PM                                      512 Wetmore Street
                                                     Seattle, Wa 98114
                                        Tel: (206) 555-1234 Fax: (206) 555-6789


                                               Accounts Receivable Journal


  Tran Custom.                               Ref. #   Due      Discount   Discount   Trans.
  No.  Code    Customer name      Invoice#  Date  Chk. #  Date     Date      Available  Type      Debit         Credit
  ---- ------  ----------------   --------  ------  ------  -------  --------  ---------  ------   --------      --------
  0001 C10    Columbus Glass Works,  00001  07/27/88 po4592 08/26/88 08/06/88          INVOICE
       11051   Accts Rec'ble Module                  sale of bumble bees                          1025.00
       4101    Sales Dept. 01                        sale of bumble bees                                        1000.00
       4301    Freight                               sale of bumble bees                                          25.00
                                                     Totals:   TRANSACTION    3         1025.00       1025.00

  0002 K20    Kevin's House of Marbl 000042  07/27/88 Frank  08/26/88 08/06/88          DEBIT
       11051   Accts Rec'ble Module                  Yellow Swirls Rush                            500.00
       4101    Sales Dept. 01                        Yellow Swirls Rush                                          500.00
                                                     Totals:   TRANSACTION    2          500.00        500.00

  0003 K20    Kevin's House of Marbl 0000234 07/27/88 Inv#42 08/26/88 08/06/88          CREDIT
       11051   Accts Rec'ble Module                                                                             100.00
       4101    Sales Dept. 01                        Yellow Swirls Error                          100.00
                                                     Totals:   TRANSACTION    2          100.00        100.00

  0004 K20    Kevin's House of Marbl 00000235 07/27/88 rvrse 08/26/88 08/06/88          INVOICE
       11051   Accts Rec'ble Module                  error reverse                                 -25.00
       4101    Sales Dept. 01                        error reverse                                              -25.00
                                                     Totals:   TRANSACTION    2          -25.00        -25.00


                                                     Grand Total :   TRANSACTIONS   9   1600.00       1600.00
```

The accounts receivable journal also prepares a summary showing the total debits and credits made to each Chart of Accounts account number (see fig. 9.12).

The accounts receivable cash receipts journal provides the same kind of detailed information for cash receipts transactions (see fig. 9.13). To print this journal, choose the A/R Cash Receipts option from the Journals menu.

```
Date : 07/27/88                          Acme Marbles Company                      Page no. 2
Time : 12:37 PM                            512 Wetmore Street
                                           Seattle, Wa 98114
                                 Tel: (206) 555-1234 Fax: (206) 555-6789

                         GENERAL LEDGER TRANSFER SUMMARY
      Acct #     Acct. name        Description           Debit        Credit
      ------  --------------------  ------------------  -----------   -----------

      11051   Accts Rec'ble Module  Summary From AR Post   1400.00
      4101    Sales Dept. 01        Summary From AR Post                1375.00
      4301    Freight               Summary From AR Post                  25.00
                                    Summary Total :        1400.00     1400.00
```

Fig. 9.12

The general ledger transfer summary.

```
Date : 07/27/88                          Acme Marbles Company                      Page no. 1
Time : 01:01 PM                            512 Wetmore Street
                                           Seattle, Wa 98114
                                 Tel: (206) 555-1234 Fax: (206) 555-6789

                         ACCOUNTS RECEIVABLE CASH RECEIPTS JOURNAL

      Tran.
      No.   Acct # Cust.        Customer Name       Invoice#  Date     Chk #  Type  Inv. Amount  Disc. Taken  Chk. Amount
      ----  ------ ------  --------------------------  --------  --------  ------  -----  ------------  ------------  -----------
      0001  11021  K20    Kevin's House of Marbles    000042   07/27/88 000123 PMT.     500.00        0.00       500.00
      0001  11021  K20    Kevin's House of Marbles    0000234  07/27/88 000123 PMT.    -100.00        0.00      -100.00
      0001  11021  K20    Kevin's House of Marbles    00000235 07/27/88 000123 PMT.     -25.00        0.00       -25.00
                          Acct. Total:                                                  375.00        0.00       375.00

                          Grand Total: # of Transactions     3                         375.00        0.00       375.00
```

Fig. 9.13

The accounts receivable cash receipts journal.

When you finish entering accounts receivable transactions or cash receipts, use these reports to review your work. Catching errors at this point makes correcting mistakes much easier. But both journals serve as more than just error-checking tools. Each also represents an important part of your audit trail, so you should save the final, clean copies of both journals. They provide you with the detail to support and explain the debits and credits posted to the general ledger from the Accounts Receivable module.

Posting Accounts Receivable Transactions and Cash Receipts

Information from the Accounts Receivable module updates both the receivables from customers and the amounts collected from customers. To post information from the Accounts Receivable module to the general ledger, you select the Posting option from the main menu, and then choose option 2, Accounts Receivable. When you select the Posting Accounts Receivable option, DacEasy displays a screen that warns you to back up files before you run the posting program (see fig. 9.14). A hardware or power failure during the posting process can damage your data files. So that you can recover easily from what can otherwise turn into a minor catastrophe, back up your files before posting.

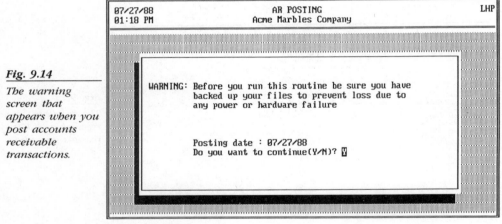

Fig. 9.14

The warning screen that appears when you post accounts receivable transactions.

```
07/27/88                        AR POSTING                        LHP
01:18 PM                   Acme Marbles Company


        WARNING: Before you run this routine be sure you have
                 backed up your files to prevent loss due to
                 any power or hardware failure



                 Posting date : 07/27/88
                 Do you want to continue(Y/N)? Y



F1-Help ESC-Exit
```

If the posting program locates nothing to post—which may result if you've entered no accounts receivable transactions, cash receipts, or adjustments since the last posting—DacEasy alerts you to this fact. When posting is complete, your printer prints a three-line message indicating the totals of the amounts posted to the general ledger (see fig. 9.15).

```
       Posted to G/L
       Total Debits   :      1975.00
       Total Credits  :      1975.00
```

Fig. 9.15

The message that appears after DacEasy posts the accounts receivable.

Printing Other Accounts Receivable Reports

Because you've collected and stored all your accounts receivable information in the system, it can easily generate reports on that data. In a sense, you can use your information as many times as you want. The first time you use the information, both with manual and computerized systems, is for everyday bookkeeping. The second time may be for other financial or nonfinancial uses. From the accounts receivable files, DacEasy's Accounts Receivable module prepares four other useful reports: customer statements, agings, a customer directory, and mailing labels. You can access these reports from the Reports Accounts Receivable menu, as shown in figure 9.16.

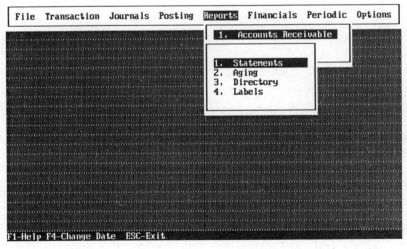

Fig. 9.16

The options for printing the accounts receivable reports.

Figure 9.17 shows an example of a *customer statement*, which lists the invoices, debit and credit memos, and payments to and from a specific customer. The customer statements show also the transaction date, invoice number, due date, transaction description, reference number, debit or credit amounts, remaining amount due or past due, and, for past due amounts, the number of days past due. Some companies send customers a statement monthly. If you do so, you can use this report to detail for a customer the amount owed.

Acme Marbles Company
512 Wetmore Street
Seattle, Wa 98114
Tel: (206) 555-1234 Fax: (206) 555-6789
S t a t e m e n t

C10
Columbus Glass Works, Inc.
Mr. Christopher Columbus
East 57th Avenue   Page 1
Seattle, WA 98104   Closing Date : 07/27/88

Date	Invoice#	Due Date	CD	Description	Ref. #	Debits	Credits	Amount Due	Past Due	Days
07/26/88	00001	08/25/88	1	Invoice	PO-561	947.09				
07/27/88		08/26/88	1	Invoice	po4592	1025.00				
07/26/88		08/25/88	5	Credit	00001		12.13	1959.96		
06/09/88	234198	07/09/88	1	Invoice	test	10000.00		10000.00	10000.00	18
07/20/88	88001	08/19/88	1	Invoice	PO9056	235.78		235.78		
07/15/88	88002	08/14/88	2	Debit	PO9001	450.13		450.13		
07/10/88	88003	08/09/88	5	Credit	verbal		123.45	-123.45		

	Total Balance	Past Due Balance	Days
	12522.42	10000.00	18

Thank you for your business, but it
seems that your payment is past due

Fig. 9.17

An accounts receivable customer statement.

An example of an *accounts receivable aging report* is featured in figure 9.18. An aging shows the amounts customers owe classified by the number of days since the transaction date. Often businesses use agings to check on the financial health of a customer before extending additional credit, or as part of deciding what tactics to use to improve collections from a customer.

The aging report shows for each transaction the invoice number, the invoice date, the due date, a code identifying the type of transaction (invoice, debit

```
Date : 07/23/88                        Acme Marbles Company                         Page no. 1
Time : 03:59 PM                         512 Wetmore Street
                                         Seattle, Wa 98114
                            Tel: (206) 555-1234 Fax: (206) 555-6789

Closing Date: 07/27/88                                          Codes:
Sorted by...: Code                    A G I N G   R E P O R T   1 Invoice         4 - Payment
Ranked by...: Code               A C C O U N T S   R E C E I V A B L E   2 Debit  5 - Credit
* Not posted                                                    3 Finance Charge 6 - Discount Taken

Invoice # Date     Due Date Code  Amount   9999/61     60/31     30/1     0/-30    -31/-60   -61/-90   -91/-9999

C10      Columbus Glass Works, Inc.
-------- --------------------------
00001    07/26/88 08/25/88  1     947.09
         07/27/88 08/26/88  1    1025.00
         07/26/88           5      12.13-                                1959.96
234198   06/09/88 07/09/88  1   10000.00                       10000.00
88001    07/20/88 08/19/88  1     235.78                                  235.78
88002    07/15/88           2     450.13                                  450.13
88003    07/10/88           5     123.45-                                 123.45-
                                  ----------  -------   -------  -------- -------  -------   -------   --------
         Total                  12522.42      0.00      0.00   10000.00  2522.42   0.00      0.00      0.00

K20      Kevin's House of Marbles
-------- --------------------------
00000235 07/27/88 08/26/88  1      25.00-
         07/27/88           4      25.00
0000234  07/27/88           4     100.00
         07/27/88           5     100.00-
000042   07/27/88           2     500.00
         07/27/88           4     500.00-
                                  ----------  -------   -------  -------- -------  -------   -------   --------
         Total                      0.00      0.00      0.00      0.00     0.00    0.00      0.00      0.00

Z10      Zebra Toys
-------- ----------
00002    07/26/88 08/25/88  1     562.50                                  562.50
                                  ----------  -------   -------  -------- -------  -------   -------   --------
         Total                    562.50      0.00      0.00      0.00    562.50   0.00      0.00      0.00

         Grand Total            13084.92      0.00      0.00   10000.00  3084.92   0.00      0.00      0.00
```

Fig. 9.18

An accounts receivable aging report.

memo, finance charge, payment, credit memo, or discount taken), the amount, and the aging category for the amount. You can define up to seven aging categories, starting with those items that aren't due yet and ranging to those most overdue. The default aging categories are

9,999 to 61 days until an item is due
60 to 31 days until an item is due
30 to 1 day until an item is due
0 to 30 days since an item was due
31 to 60 days since an item was due
61 to 90 days since an item was due
91 to 9,999 days since an item was due

Figure 9.19 shows a sample *customer directory* prepared from the Accounts Receivable module's information. The directory lists the information sorted in the customer master file for each customer: customer code, name, address, phone number, department, salesperson, discount percent, discount days, due days, account type, credit limit, and current balance. You'll probably want to have a current copy of the customer directory while you're entering billing and accounts receivable transactions, because the directory gives you the customer code at a glance.

```
Date : 07/23/88                          Acme Marbles Company                        Page no.  1
Time : 03:59 PM                            512 Wetmore Street
                                           Seattle, Wa 98114
                                  Tel: (206) 555-1234 Fax: (206) 555-6789

Sorted by: Code                          Customer Directory                          Ranked by: Code

                              Area              Sales      T e r m s                 Credit
Code  Name/Contact/Address    Code  Phone  Dept. Person Disc % Days  Due Day Account Type    Limit      Balance
----  --------------------    ----- ------ ----- ------ ------ ----- ------ --------------   --------   --------

C10   Columbus Glass Works, Inc.  (206) 555-9000    Juan   2.00    10    30  Open Invoice    5000.00    95516.10
      Mr. Christopher Columbus
      East 57th Avenue
      Seattle, WA   98104

K20   Kevin's House of Marbles    (206) 555-8080    Juan   2.00    10    30  Open Invoice    5000.00        0.00
      Kevin Kevinson
      1028 79th Avenue South
      Seattle, WA   98115

S10   Specialty Products, Inc.    (206) 555-5534    Coco   2.00    10    30  Open Invoice    5000.00        0.00
      Francis Drake
      1620 Silver Lake Drive
      Seattle, WA   98072

Z10   Zebra Toys                  (206) 555-4444  02        2.00    10    30  Open Invoice    1000.00      562.50
      Blaise Pascal
      2325 NE 20th Place
      Redmond, WA   98053


      Total Customers : 4 records
```

Fig. 9.19

A sample customer directory.

The accounts receivable system also allows you to generate *mailing labels* from the customer master file (see fig. 9.20). All you need are standard-sized mailing forms. You'll find these labels a real time-saver for preparing mass mailings to your customers or for organizing file folders for your paperwork.

For the four accounts receivable reports, you select the first and second sort keys you want DacEasy to use—and thereby choose how to order the customers on the reports. Figure 9.21 shows the report request screen that appears after you choose Reports Accounts Receivable Statements. The aging report, customer directory, and mailing labels have identical request screens.

For each of these four reports, you may use as your primary sort key one of the following five fields from the customer master file: code, name, department, salesperson, and ZIP code. You specify also a secondary key, which sorts those customers that have the same primary key value. For the secondary sort key, you use one of these fields from the customer master file: code, name, credit limit, credit available, balance, last sales date, last payment date, sales units, sales dollars, and profit. For both the primary and the secondary keys, DacEasy uses ascending order—*a* before *b*, and *1* before *2*. You specify the primary and

```
Columbus Glass Works, Inc.
Mr. Christopher Columbus
East 57th Avenue
Seattle, WA   98104


Kevin's House of Marbles
Kevin Kevinson
1028 79th Avenue South
Seattle, WA   98115


Specialty Products, Inc.
Francis Drake
1620 Silver Lake Drive
Seattle, WA   98072


Zebra Toys
Blaise Pascal
2325 NE 20th Place
Redmond, WA   98053




Columbus Glass Works, Inc.
Mr. Christopher Columbus
East 57th Avenue
Seattle, WA   98104


Kevin's House of Marbles
Kevin Kevinson
1028 79th Avenue South
Seattle, WA   98115


Specialty Products, Inc.
Francis Drake
1620 Silver Lake Drive
Seattle, WA   98072


Zebra Toys
Blaise Pascal
2325 NE 20th Place
Redmond, WA   98053
```

Fig. 9.20

Customer mailing labels.

```
07/27/88                 Accounts Receivable Statements              LHP
01:34 PM                    Acme Marbles Company


     Sort By :                        Rank By :

     1  Code                          1  Code
     2  Name                          2  Name
     3  Department                    3  Credit Limit
     4  Sales Person                  4  Credit Available
     5  Zip Code                      5  Balance
                                      6  Last Sales Date
     Enter Your Selection :  ■        7  Last Payment Date
                                      8  Sales Units
                                      9  Sales Dollars
                                      10 Profit

                                      Enter Your Selection :
```

Fig. 9.21

The request screen for printing accounts receivable statements.

secondary keys by entering in each Enter Your Selection field the number that corresponds to the appropriate key description.

After you've specified the sort keys, DacEasy queries for some additional information. The nature of the query depends on the report you're printing. For customer statements, a pop-up window asks whether you want the customer code to appear above the customer name. You answer this question by pressing *Y* for "yes" or *N* for "no." The Default is *N*.

When you're creating an aging report, DacEasy queries whether you want a detail or summary report and allows you to specify what aging categories you want to use. Figure 9.22 shows the default entries for the type of report and the aging categories. A detail report shows each invoice for a customer, but a summary report shows only the invoice totals. Aging category 1 is for the most overdue, and aging category 7 is for the most current.

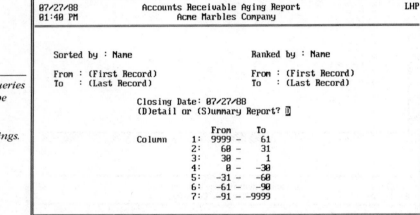

Fig. 9.22

Additional queries concerning the printing of accounts receivable agings.

For the customer labels, DacEasy displays a pop-up window that asks whether you want the customer code and phone number on the label and prompts you to indicate the number of lines on the label. This screen is shown in figure 9.23. If you're using the labels for mailing, you probably want neither the phone number nor the customer code, but if you're creating labels for file folders, you might want both. (The default for both fields is *Y*.) The default answer to the number of lines on a label is 6, which is the number of lines that fit on a one-inch label.

```
07/27/88                    Customer Labels                   LHP
01:47 PM                  Acme Marbles Company


    Sorted by : Name                  Ranked by : Name

    From : (First Record)             From : (First Record)
    To   : (Last Record)              To   : (Last Record)

                Include the code on label(Y/N)?  N
                Include the phone on label(Y/N)?  N
                Lines per label...:  6
```

Fig. 9.23

Additional queries concerning the printing of customer labels.

Chapter Summary

This chapter reviewed the basic accounts receivable process, discussed when you might need to use the DacEasy Accounts Receivable module, and provided some sample standard accounts receivable transactions. The chapter described also how to record accounts receivable transactions and customer payments, how to correct errors in these items, and how to post accounts receivable information to the general ledger. The chapter concluded with an overview of the special reports the Accounts Receivable module provides.

10

Using the Inventory Module

If you're in wholesaling, retailing, or manufacturing, you can use the Inventory module to maintain a perpetual inventory system and to monitor closely your inventory purchasing, balances, costs, and pricing. This chapter overviews the importance of using a perpetual inventory system, describes when you might want to use the DacEasy Inventory module, and explains how to complete each inventory menu selection and use each inventory report.

Using a Perpetual Inventory System

You can use one of two basic approaches to track both the units and dollars of inventory you hold: the *periodic* method or the *perpetual* method. Most businesses start with the periodic approach, which is the easiest to apply. With the periodic inventory system, you calculate your inventory on hand and the cost of the inventory sold, usually called *cost of goods sold*, only periodically. Some businesses calculate the inventory figures only once a year, while others take inventory many times throughout a year. No matter how often you compute your inventory and cost of goods sold, however, the main characteristic of this inventory system—and its big disadvantage—is that only on the calculation date do you know exactly what you're holding and what you've sold throughout the period.

The basic calculations are easy. To determine the value of the inventory you're holding in your warehouse or on store shelves, you count the quantity of each item you're holding, figure out what you paid for the item, and then use these two numbers to calculate the dollars of inventory. Both the beginning and ending inventory figures are determined this way. For example, for Acme Marbles, you might count the number of each kind of marble held in the warehouse and multiply these quantities by the purchase price to calculate both beginning and ending inventory.

To calculate the value of the inventory you sold during the year, the only other information you need to know is the total marble purchases made during the year. With this information, you calculate the cost of the inventory sold as the beginning inventory plus the purchases during the period minus the inventory held at the end of the period. For example, if you counted the inventory at both the beginning and the end of the year, assigned a price, and then flipped through your checkbook to total your marble purchases, you can calculate Acme's cost of goods sold as follows:

Beginning inventory	$ 300
Plus: Total marble purchases	+ 1000
Less: Total ending inventory	− 400
Cost of goods sold	$ 900

The advantage of this method is that it requires effort only once a year or once a month—whenever you want or need to calculate the inventory held and the inventory sold. The disadvantage of a periodic system is that between calculations of the inventory balances you can't get much of an idea about whether you're holding too much of one item and too little of another. And you can never determine the units and dollars of inventory lost to spoilage, theft, and obsolescence, because you calculate only the beginning and ending inventory and the purchases between the two periods. The cost of goods sold amount is a calculated amount. It includes not only the inventory that went out the front door as part of sales to customers, or returns to vendors, but also the inventory that goes out the back door as part of a shoplifter's booty, or into the trash because of damage or spoilage. For these reasons, your best bet in an inventory system is the perpetual method.

Clearly, the secret to obtaining inventory information at any time and having more detail about what costs comprise the cost of goods sold is to track every change in inventory level and cost when the change occurs. By definition, a perpetual inventory system does exactly that. Every time you purchase inventory, you increase your counts of both inventory units and inventory dollars. Every time you sell inventory, you decrease your counts of both inventory units and inventory dollars.

The advantage of a perpetual inventory system is that you always know both the number of units and the dollar value of the inventory you're holding. The disadvantage of a perpetual system is that recording every increase and decrease in both the units and dollars of inventory requires a great deal of work. In practice, you need a computer to keep up, but then that may be why you bought DacEasy.

Examining Some Sample Inventory Transactions

The Inventory module keeps track of not only the basic dollar changes in inventory—the focus of bookkeeping—but also the unit changes in inventory, which are just as important. Understanding the bookkeeping process, however, can help you understand how the Inventory module works with other modules in the system to manage your inventory. The next few paragraphs briefly describe the bookkeeping mechanics of inventory accounting in a perpetual inventory system.

Only three types of inventory transactions are recorded. The first type is the purchase of inventory items. Suppose that you purchase $2,000 worth of inventory. To record the effect on your books, you make a $2,000 debit to inventory to reflect the increase in inventory, and a $2,000 credit to accounts payable (if you purchase the items on credit) or to cash (if you purchase the items with cash).

	Debit	Credit
Inventory	$2,000	
Accounts Payable or Cash		$2,000

The Purchase Order module automatically makes the preceding entry for you whenever you record the receipt of merchandise. If you don't use the Purchase Order module, you need to make this entry through either the Accounts Payable or General Ledger module.

A second type of transaction occurs when you sell inventory. From the preceding chapter, you may remember that to record a sales transaction you need to debit accounts receivable and credit sales revenue for the amount of the sale. But another important part of the transaction involves the reduction in inventory and the cost of the inventory being sold. To record a sale completely, you must record the fact that your inventory decreases and your cost of goods sold increases. If the cost of the inventory sold is $1,000, your entry looks like this:

	Debit	*Credit*
Cost of Goods Sold	$1,000	
Inventory		$1,000

If you use the Billing module, it automatically records this transaction. If you don't use that module, you need to make such an entry with either the Accounts Receivable or General Ledger module.

A third transaction you make in a perpetual inventory system is called a *book-to-physical adjustment*. In essence, this adjustment corrects the perpetual inventory system's count and balance of inventory so that those figures correspond to the actual physical count of the inventory. You may wonder how, if you're recording every transaction, the perpetual inventory system's counts and balances can be wrong. Most of the reasons for such a discrepancy are unpleasant to think about. You may have shoplifters or employees who steal inventory. You may have inventory that either spoils or becomes damaged and therefore is discarded. Or you may have just forgotten to record an increase or decrease in inventory.

Imagine that your inventory records indicate you should have $10,000 of inventory, but a careful physical count reveals only $9,500 of inventory. You need to make the following book-to-physical adjustment to recognize that you have had a $500 decrease that was not previously recorded:

	Debit	*Credit*
Cost of Goods Sold	$500	
Inventory		$500

When To Use the Inventory Module

Do you find yourself running out of inventory items? Do you wonder about the inventory you lose to shoplifting or employee theft? Do you ever have in inventory more of a product than you can possibly sell? Closely managing your inventory investment with the DacEasy system should alleviate all these problems—for two reasons. First, by using a computer, you can begin to implement a perpetual inventory system and have information about your inventory counts and balances literally at your fingertips. This characteristic alone justifies using the module.

But the DacEasy inventory management tools go beyond maintaining a simple perpetual inventory system. A second advantage of using the Inventory module is that because it automatically collects all sorts of information on the products you're buying and selling, DacEasy can provide you with reports showing detailed historical information about almost every facet of your inventory. You receive information that can give you insights and perspectives you've never had before. And the "cost" of receiving the information is only the time required to request the report you want—a few seconds at most.

Accessing the Menu Options for Inventory Management

DacEasy's inventory tools are grouped under four of the main menu options: Transaction, Posting, Reports, and Periodic. Choosing the Inventory option from the Transaction menu allows you to access both the Price Assignment screen, which you use to set sales prices for items, and the Physical Inventory screen, which you use to record your physical counts of inventory. Figure 10.1 shows the Transaction Inventory submenu.

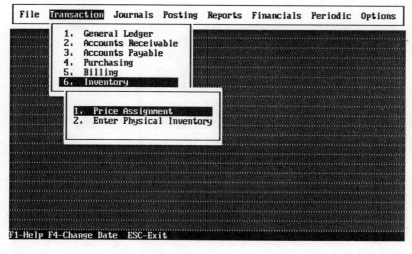

Fig. 10.1

The Transaction Inventory menu.

You use the Posting menu to update the general ledger with the changes to the inventory counts and balances. The posting program updates both the product master file and the general ledger with the item counts entered on the Physical

Inventory screen since the last time you posted inventory transactions. Figure 10.2 shows the Posting menu with the Physical Inventory option selected.

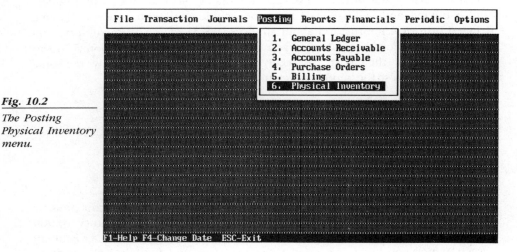

Fig. 10.2

The Posting Physical Inventory menu.

From the Reports Inventory menu, you can print several reports and worksheets useful for managing and monitoring your inventory investments. These reports include a product listing report, a product price list, a product activity report, a product alert report, a service report, a physical inventory count sheet, and a physical-perpetual comparison report. Figure 10.3 shows the menu from which you access all these reports.

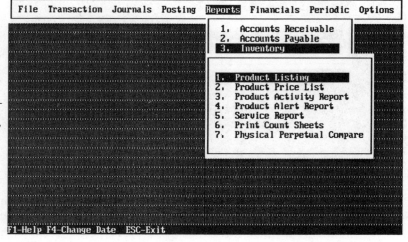

Fig. 10.3

The options for printing inventory reports.

The fourth and final location for inventory tools is the Periodic menu. Figure 10.4 shows this menu with option 4, Inventory, selected. The instructions and suggestions for using the inventory periodic routines are discussed in Chapter 12, "Using the Periodic Routines."

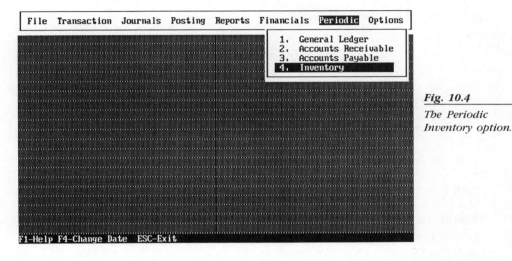

Fig. 10.4
The Periodic
Inventory option.

The rest of this chapter walks you through the steps for using—and profiting from—the inventory tools you find in the Transaction, Posting, and Reports menus.

Entering Inventory Price Changes

To set sales prices for inventory items, choose the Transaction option from the main menu; select option 6, Inventory, from the Transaction menu; and then choose option 1, Price Assignment. The Price Assignment program uses two screens. The first screen, which is shown in figure 10.5, closely resembles the report request screen used to generate many of the DacEasy reports. In this case, however, you use it to sort the products that will appear on the second Price Assignment screen.

On this screen, you order the products that will be listed on the second screen by using one of five primary sort keys: inventory number (called also the product code), description, department, bin, and vendor. To sort products that have the same primary key, you can indicate one of these fields as the secondary sort key: inventory number, description, sales units, sales dollars, last sales date, purchase units, purchase dollars, last purchase date, on-hand units, on-hand dollars,

```
07/31/88                      PRICE ASSIGNMENT                        LHP
01:10 PM                     Acme Marbles Company


        Sort By :                          Rank By :

        1  Inventory #                     1   Inventory #
        2  Description                     2   Description
        3  Department                      3   Sales Units
        4  Bin                             4   Sales Dollars
        5  Vendor                          5   Last Sales Date
                                           6   Purchase Units
                                           7   Purchase Dollars
        Enter Your Selection :  ■          8   Last Purchase Date
                                           9   On Hand Units
                                           10  On Hand Dollars
                                           11  Profit
                                           12  Turns
                                           13  Gross Profit

                                           Enter Your Selection :



F1-Help F4-Change Date  ESC-Exit
```

Fig. 10.5

The first Price Assignment screen.

profit, turns, and gross profit. If you've forgotten the meanings of any of these fields, refer to the sections in Chapter 3 that describe loading the product master file. Each of these possible primary and secondary sort keys originates in the product master file. To select the primary and secondary sort keys, type at each of the Enter Your Selection prompts the number that appears beside the sorting option you want to use.

After you select a primary and secondary sort order, the second Price Assignment screen appears, as shown in figure 10.6. The products in your master file, sorted according to your primary and secondary keys, appear on the screen.

```
07/31/88                      PRICE ASSIGNMENT                        LHP
01:14 PM                     Acme Marbles Company



     Product #    Description      Price    Last Cost    % OR $   New Price
     ----------   -----------      -----    ---------    ------   ---------
     B10          Bumble Bee       0.025    0.015
     C10          Cat's Eye        0.020    0.020
     C20          Cleary           0.030    0.025
     Y10          Yellow Swirls    0.025    0.003




F1-Help ALT P-Print  ESC-Exit
```

Fig. 10.6

The second Price Assignment screen before you enter data.

Figure 10.6 shows only four products, but more can fit on one screen. As with other screens in the DacEasy system, you press Enter or use the arrow keys to move from field to field. The following paragraphs describe both the fields that automatically appear on the screen and those you enter or edit.

Product #, Description, Price, Last Cost: DacEasy retrieves these four fields for each product from the product master file. These fields show the product code, the product name, the current assigned sales price for the item, and the last unit purchase cost for the item.

% or $: You have two possible approaches for defining sales prices for inventory items. One alternative is to set the gross margin (the difference between the sales price and the cost of the good) as a dollars-and-cents amount. For example, if you last purchased an item for $.02 a unit, you might assign the price change as $.01 plus the last purchase price, which results in a new unit price of $.03 a unit.

The other alternative is to set the gross margin on a product as a percentage of the sales price. For example, you may decide that you want a 33 percent gross margin on inventory items costing $.02. The Price Assignment screen calculates the price that will result in a 33 percent gross margin, using this formula:

unit cost/(1 − gross margin percent)

For an item costing $.02 and for which you want a 33 percent margin, the calculation is $.02/(100% − 33%), or $.03. You specify either a dollar-and-cents gross margin or a percentage gross margin by toggling back and forth with the space bar between the % and $ flags that appear in the narrow unmarked column to the right of the Last Cost column. If the unmarked column shows %, you enter the gross margin percent in the % or $ field. If the unmarked column shows $, you enter the dollars and cents of gross margin in the % or $ field.

In figure 10.6, the price changes have not yet been entered. Figure 10.7 shows the screen after you set the gross margin for the Bumble Bee marbles as a percent (50.000 for a 50 percent gross margin), and the gross margins for each of the other marbles as a dollars-and-cents figure (0.010 for $.01 of gross margin).

New Price: DacEasy calculates the new price for the product, based on the last cost and your specification of the gross margin, and places this price in the New Price column.

When you finish setting the prices for the products whose prices need to change, you use the Esc key to leave the Price Assignment screen and to save your new prices. To exit the Price Assignment screen without saving your new prices, press F6. If you make a mistake when setting a product price and then leave the screen before correcting the error, all you have to do is return to this screen and correct your price.

```
07/31/88                    PRICE ASSIGNMENT                     LHP
01:15 PM                  Acme Marbles Company


Product #      Description       Price    Last Cost    % OR $   New Price
-----------    ------------      -----    ---------    ------   ---------
B10            Bumble Bee        0.025    0.015 %      50.000   0.030
C10            Cat's Eye         0.020    0.020 $      0.010    0.030
C20            Cleary            0.030    0.025 $      0.010    0.035
Y10            Yellow Swirls     0.025    0.003 $      0.010    0.013




F1-Help ESC-Exit   <SPACE>-USE THE SPACE BAR TO SELECT ANSWER
```

Fig. 10.7

The second Price Assignment screen filled with sample data.

Entering Physical Inventory Adjustments

Even when you're using a perpetual inventory system, you should periodically count your inventory and then compare the physical counts to the perpetual inventory system's counts. Discrepancies in the two counts, for such reasons as shoplifting, employee theft, and bookkeeping errors, are inevitable in many businesses. Accordingly, you need some way of identifying these count differences.

The Physical Inventory screen provides what amounts to an on-line scratch pad, which you can use to collect and total your counts of the number of units of inventory items you're holding. By using this screen, the physical-perpetual comparison report, and the Posting Physical Inventory option, you can record and reconcile disagreements between the perpetual inventory records and your physical counts of the inventory. To access the Physical Inventory screen, select the Transaction option from the main menu; choose option 6, Inventory, from the Transaction menu; and then select option 2, Enter Physical Inventory. Figure 10.8 shows the Physical Inventory screen before you begin entering the results of your physical counts.

The information you enter to record physical inventory counts is described in the following paragraphs.

Product #, Description, Previous Count: The *product number* is the unique identifier you assigned in the product master file to the product for which you want to record a physical inventory count. After you enter a valid product

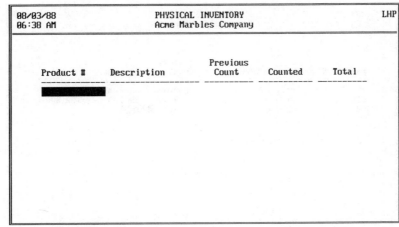

```
88/03/88                    PHYSICAL INVENTORY                      LHP
06:38 AM                    Acme Marbles Company


                                        Previous
         Product #    Description         Count      Counted      Total
         ------------ ------------------- ---------- ------------ --------
         ████████████
```

```
F1-Help F6-Delete  ESC-Exit
```

Fig. 10.8

The Physical Inventory screen before you enter data.

number, DacEasy displays the description and the previous count for this item. The description comes from the product master file. The previous count is the total counted units you've entered since the last time you posted physical inventory counts to the general ledger.

Counted: You enter in this field the number of units counted.

Total: The Counted field plus the Previous Count field equals the Total field, which DacEasy calculates automatically. The Total field is what is posted to the general ledger. Thus you can enter the count from one warehouse or store in the Counted field one day, and the count from another warehouse or store the next day. On the second day, the first day's count appears in the Previous Count field, and the total for the first and second counts shows in the Total field.

Figure 10.9 shows the Physical Inventory screen after two products have been counted. On the screen, you can see that a previous Bumble Bee count for 2,000 marbles was recorded. Neither the cat's-eye or Cleary marbles were previously counted.

To delete a transaction before you enter the current count, press F6. If you discover that the Previous Count amount is too large, you can adjust the count on hand by entering a negative amount in the Counted column. Always be sure to document changes in inventory counts.

```
07/31/88                    PHYSICAL INVENTORY                      LHP
01:43 PM                    Acme Marbles Company


                                        Previous
               Product #   Description  Count      Counted    Total
               ─────────   ───────────  ────────   ────────   ────────
               B10         Bumble Bee   2000.000   2000.000   4000.000
               C10         Cat's Eye       0.000   2500.000   2500.000
               C20         Cleary          0.000████████




F1-Help F6-Delete  ESC-Exit
```

Fig. 10.9

The Physical Inventory screen after you enter data.

C.P.A. Tip: Rather than count all your inventory once a year, consider dividing the task into several smaller partial counts that you can perform at different times throughout the year. This method, called *cycle counting*, has become popular with larger businesses as an alternative to the traditional once-a-year, physical inventory.

By reducing the counting process into smaller efforts, it should be less disruptive. What's more, if you can perform a physical inventory without having to close your business for several days or hours, you may be able to take physical inventories of your most valuable items several times a year.

Posting Physical Inventory Adjustments to the General Ledger

The price assignments you make don't affect the inventory balances carried in the general ledger. But you do need to adjust the inventory counts and balances if a physical count indicates that your perpetual system's count is incorrect. (The physical-perpetual comparison report shows discrepancies between the physical counts and the perpetual system's counts. See the section on "Using the Physical-Perpetual Comparison Report.") To adjust both the counts and the balances, you must post the physical inventory counts to the general ledger. First, select the Posting option from the main menu and then choose option 6, Physical Inventory.

When you select the Posting Physical Inventory option, a screen appears, warning you to back up your files before you run the posting routine (see fig. 10.10). If you've already backed up your files and want DacEasy to complete the posting process, press *Y*. If not, press *N*.

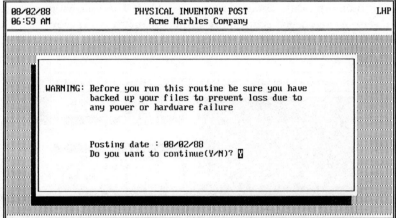

```
08/02/88                 PHYSICAL INVENTORY POST                    LHP
06:59 AM                   Acme Marbles Company


        WARNING: Before you run this routine be sure you have
                 backed up your files to prevent loss due to
                 any power or hardware failure


                 Posting date : 08/02/88
                 Do you want to continue(Y/N)? Y




F1-Help ESC-Exit
```

Fig. 10.10

The warning screen that appears before DacEasy posts physical inventory.

The posting program increases or decreases the perpetual inventory count so that it corresponds to the physical count. In other words, if the Total field on the Physical Inventory screen is less than the number of units on hand according to the perpetual inventory records, DacEasy decreases the inventory counts and balances when you choose the Posting Physical Inventory option. If the Total field is greater than the number of units on hand listed in the perpetual inventory records, DacEasy increases the inventory counts and balances as part of the posting procedure. In either case, the offsetting debit or credit is made to the cost of goods sold detail account specified in the general ledger interface table.

When DacEasy is finished posting the physical inventory, a three-line message prints the totals of the amounts that were posted to the general ledger.

Reviewing the Inventory Reports

While you're using the Purchase Order and Billing modules, the Inventory module collects information about inventory being purchased, inventory being sold, costs and prices, and a wealth of other data. And the inventory reports provide the windows with which you can view this information.

To print these reports, choose the Reports option from the main menu and then select option 3, Inventory, from the Reports menu. The menu shown in figure 10.11 appears. Six product reports (options 1 through 4 and options 6 and 7 on the Reports Inventory menu) list product and statistical information collected from the Purchase Order and Billing modules. One service report (option 5 on the Reports Inventory menu) provides statistical information collected from the Billing module about services provided. The following sections examine the various inventory reports, describe the many ways you can use them, and explain the printing procedure for the reports.

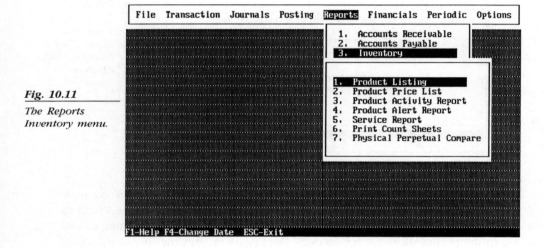

Fig. 10.11

The Reports Inventory menu.

Using the Product Listing Report

Figure 10.12 shows an example of a *product listing report* sorted by the inventory number. This report shows for each product the inventory number (on some screens and other reports called the product code), product description, revenue/cost department code, bin, preferred vendor, units of measure, fractional units, price, minimum on-hand quantity, minimum reorder quantity, last sales date, last purchase date, last purchase price, standard cost, and average cost. You entered this data as part of defining a product in the product master file or when using the Billing module, the Purchase Order module, and the Price Assignment screen. If you forget how to use this data or why you entered it, review the portion of Chapter 2 that describes loading the product master file.

The product listing report provides the most detailed listing of the contents of the product master file. You may therefore want to use this report as a

```
Date : 07/23/88                        Acme Marbles Company                    Page no. 1
Time : 04:07 PM                         512 Wetmore Street
                                         Seattle, Wa 98114
                               Tel: (206) 555-1234 Fax: (206) 555-6789

Sorted by: Inventory #                     Product Listing                   Ranked by: Inventory #
              Description            Unit                 Last Sales Last Pur Last Pur  Standard  Average
Inventory #  Dept  Bin  Vendor      Frac   Price  Minimum Reorder  Date      Date      Price     Cost      Cost
-----------  ----  ---  ------      ----   -----  ------- -------  ---------  --------  -------   -------   -------
B10          Bumble Bee             each   0.030  10000   1000    08/07/88   08/07/88  0.015     0.000     0.015
             01    E13  F10         1
C10          Cat's Eye              each   0.030  10000   1000    08/07/88   08/07/88  0.020     0.000     0.020
             01    E12  F10         1
C20          Cleary                 each   0.035  5000    500     08/07/88   08/07/88  0.025     0.000     0.025
             02    F10              1
Y10          Yellow Swirls          each   0.013  7500    1500    08/07/88   08/07/88  0.003     0.000     0.003
             02    F12              1

             Total Products : 4 records
```

Fig. 10.12

The product listing report.

review of the contents of the master file, as a resource when placing purchase orders and preparing invoices, and as a detailed report of the components and quantities that comprise your inventory.

Using the Product Price Listing Report

Figure 10.13 shows a sample *product price listing report*, which provides a subset of the information shown on the product listing report. The product price listing report includes the inventory number or product code, product description, units of measure and allowable fractional units, revenue/cost department, bin, preferred vendor, sales tax flag, and unit sales price. Because it details products and their prices, you may want to give copies of this report to the people in your firm who sell your products or take sales orders.

```
Date : 07/23/88                        Acme Marbles Company                    Page no. 1
Time : 04:07 PM                         512 Wetmore Street
                                         Seattle, Wa 98114
                               Tel: (206) 555-1234 Fax: (206) 555-6789

Sorted by: Inventory #                  Product Price Listing              Ranked by: Inventory #

             Inventory #  Description     Unit  Frac  Dept  Bin   Vendor Tax Sales Price
             -----------  -----------     ----  ----  ----  ----  ------  -  -----------
             B10          Bumble Bee      each  1     01    E13   F10     Y    0.030
             C10          Cat's Eye       each  1     01    E12   F10     Y    0.030
             C20          Cleary          each  1     02    F10           Y    0.035
             Y10          Yellow Swirls   each  1     02    F12           Y    0.013

             Total Products : 4 records
```

Fig. 10.13

The product price listing report.

Using the Product Activity Report

Figure 10.14 shows the *product activity report*, which includes basic information about each product, such as the inventory number, description, revenue/cost department, bin, vendor, units of measure for the product, number of fractional units, and the unit sales price.

Fig. 10.14

The product activity report.

```
Date : 07/23/88                           Acme Marbles Company                              Page no. 1
Time : 04:07 PM                            512 Wetmore Street
                                           Seattle, Wa 98114
                               Tel: (206) 555-1234 Fax: (206) 555-6789

Sorted by: Inventory #                      Product Activity Report              Ranked by: Inventory #
             Description          Unit  Unit Price                                           Turns
Inventory #  Dept  Bin   Vendor   Frac  Unit Cost   On Hand    Purch YTD   Sales YTD   Cost YTD   Profit YTD   G.R.O.I.
-----------  ----------  ------   ----  ----------  ---------  ----------  ----------  --------  ----------  ----------
B10          Bumble Bee          each   0.030       4000.000   503000.000  450500.000                          112.625
             01    E13   F10     1      0.015       60.000     7545.000    22517.500   6757.500  15760.000   15760.000
C10          Cat's Eye           each   0.030       4500.000   254000.000  245250.000                          54.500
             01    E12   F10     1      0.020       90.000     5080.000    9811.250    4905.000   4906.250    4906.250
C20          Cleary              each   0.035       36700.000  316700.000  286700.000                          7.812
             02    F10           1      0.025       917.500    7917.500    13784.500   7167.500   6617.000    6617.000
Y10          Yellow Swirls       each   0.013       9750.000   401500.000  400250.000                          41.051
             02    F12           1      0.003       45.750     1204.500    20010.000   1201.250   18808.750   18808.750

             Grand Total :                          1113.250   21747.000   66123.250   20031.250  46092.000
```

The product activity report also displays purchasing and sales statistical information that the Inventory module has collected about each product from the Billing and Purchase Order modules. This information for the current year includes the unit cost, on-hand units and on-hand dollars of inventory, units and dollars of an item purchased, units and dollars of an item sold, the costs of units sold, and the gross profit on the units sold. All amounts are calculated as the year-to-date balance. These figures allows you to assess how purchasing, holding, and selling a particular product affects your business.

Note in the last column of figure 10.14 that the report calculates two financial ratios: the inventory turns (computed as the unit sales divided by the number of units on hand) and the gross return on investment (computed as the units on hand multiplied by the profit and divided by the inventory turns). As mentioned in Chapter 4, you can use these financial calculations to compare your business to similar businesses and to compare products. In general, the higher the number of inventory turns, the better. A higher number means that you're getting more dollars of sales for each dollar of inventory. Similarly, a higher gross return on inventory investment indicates that you're getting more dollars of gross profit for the dollars of inventory you're holding.

Be careful, however, to make only apples-to-apples comparisons. Remember that you're using year-to-date numbers. If your ratios are calculated with 2 months of sales, and you compare these ratios to a competitor's that are calculated with 12 months of sales, your ratios will look poor. But you may be doing much better than the comparison suggests.

Using the Product Alert Report

The *product alert report* helps you identify products you need to replenish and, perhaps, those you need to return to the vendor. A sample report is shown in figure 10.15. This report provides some basic product information, including the inventory number, description, revenue/cost department, bin, preferred vendor, units of measure, and fractional units that comprise a whole unit—all of which you need to know and should find helpful as you consider which inventory items you need to purchase. The real value of the product alert report, however, is in the other information it either calculates or retrieves.

```
Date : 07/23/88                          Acme Marbles Company                      Page no. 1
Time : 04:08 PM                           512 Wetmore Street
                                          Seattle, Wa 98114
                                 Tel: (206) 555-1234 Fax: (206) 555-6789

Sorted by: Inventory #                   Product Alert Report              Ranked by: Inventory #
                     Description       Unit
       Inventory #   Dept  Bin  Vendor Frac  Available Minimum    Under    On Order  Reorder   Price    Purchase
       -----------   ----  ---  ------ ----  --------- -------   -------   --------  -------   -----    --------
         B10         Bumble Bee         each  4000.000  10000    6000.000    0.000    1000     0.015     15.000
                      01    E13  F10    1
         C10         Cat's Eye          each  4500.000  10000    5500.000  1000.000   1000     0.020     20.000
                      01    E12  F10    1

                     Grand Total :                                                                      35.000
```

Fig. 10.15

The product alert report.

The report lists the available number of units of an item (calculated as the number of units on hand minus the units that have been billed but not yet posted), the minimum number of units you set in the product master file for this item, the number of units by which you fall short of the minimum, the on-order quantity retrieved from the purchasing records, and the reorder quantity you set in the product master file for this item. The report shows also the unit purchase price and the minimum purchase amount, calculated as the unit price multiplied by the reorder quantity.

You'll probably want to print this report regularly, perhaps even daily or weekly. Doing so may help you avoid overstocking and understocking inventory items.

Using the Service Report

The *service report* is similar to the product listing report. You are given basic information about the services you defined in the service master file, including the service number or code, description, units and fractional units of the service, revenue/cost department, and sales price per unit. Like the product listing report, the service report may be valuable to your salespeople, because it lists both the services provided and the sales price per unit. Figure 10.16 shows an example of the service report without the units and dollars of sales showing. In figure 10.17, this information is displayed. You can request the service report either with or without this information included.

Fig. 10.16

The service report without units and dollars of sales.

```
Date : 07/23/88                        Acme Marbles Company                         Page no. 1
Time : 04:10 PM                          512 Wetmore Street
                                         Seattle, Wa 98114
                               Tel: (206) 555-1234 Fax: (206) 555-6789

Sorted by: Department                       Service Report                     Ranked by: Service #

              Service #    Description        Unit  Frac  Dept   Price
              ---------    -----------        ----  ----  ----   -----
              C30          consulting         hour   4    01     75.000
              P10          polish marbles     each   1    01      0.050

              Subtotal 01   : 2

              X10          Marble Consulting  hour   4    02     75.000

              Subtotal 02   : 1


              Total Services : 3 records
```

Fig. 10.17

The service report with units and dollars of sales.

```
Date : 07/23/88                        Acme Marbles Company                         Page no. 1
Time : 04:09 PM                          512 Wetmore Street
                                         Seattle, Wa 98114
                               Tel: (206) 555-1234 Fax: (206) 555-6789

Sorted by: Department                       Service Report                     Ranked by: Service #

              Service #    Description        Unit  Frac  Dept   Price     Sales Units   Sales $
              ---------    -----------        ----  ----  ----   -----     -----------   -------
              C30          consulting         hour   4    01     75.000       0.000       0.000
              P10          polish marbles     each   1    01      0.050       0.000       0.000

              Total : 01                                                                  0.000

              X10          Marble Consulting  hour   4    02     75.000      10.000     562.500

              Total : 02                                                               562.500

              Grand Total :                                                            562.500
```

Using Inventory Count Sheets

As shown in figure 10.18, the *inventory count sheet* lists the basic information about a product. The purpose of the count sheet is to provide a convenient preprinted list you can use to keep track of the number of units you hold of each inventory item. The count sheet provides space for you to record the units and fractional units counted and to remark on those counts or units. You might, for example, note in this report that certain units appear damaged and should be reexamined after the physical count is completed. You should retain these count sheets, because they provide supporting documentation for the book-to-physical adjustment that will be made.

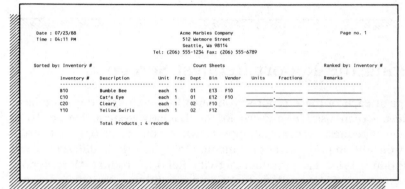

Fig. 10.18

The inventory count sheet.

C.P.A. Tip: You may want to have your employees work in pairs when counting your inventory. One employee can count, and the other can write down the units, fractions, and any remarks. This method speeds up the inventory counting process. You should also have the individuals initial and date each page of the count sheet as part of your records.

Using the Physical-Perpetual Comparison Report

Before you post the physical inventory counts to the general ledger and the product master file, you should review the *physical-perpetual comparison report* (see fig. 10.19). For each product for which you entered a physical count, the report shows both the perpetual inventory system's count and the physical inventory count of the units and fractional units on hand. The report also provides space for you to note any comments or document any assumptions regarding the products listed and the discrepancies observed. You should retain this report as an audit trail because it explains, product-by-product, the reasons for a book-to-physical adjustment.

Fig. 10.19

The physical-perpetual comparison report.

Completing the Report Request Screen

Before you print each of these reports, you must first complete the same basic report request screen used elsewhere in the DacEasy system. Figure 10.20 shows the report request screen that appears when you select option 1, Product Listing, from the Reports Inventory menu. Only the title is different if you select the Product Price List, Product Activity Report, Product Alert Report, Print Count Sheets, or Physical Perpetual Compare option.

Fig. 10.20

The product report request screen.

You specify both primary and secondary keys for sorting products on a report. DacEasy uses ascending sorting order, meaning that *a* appears before *b*, and *1* before *2*. To specify the primary and secondary keys, you enter in the Enter Your Selection field the number of the field by which you want to sort. DacEasy uses the primary key to order the products or services printed. The secondary key—what DacEasy labels a ranking—affects sorting only when two or more products or services have the same primary key.

For each of the six product reports, you can use as your primary key one of the following five fields from the product master file: inventory number (product code), description, revenue/cost department, bin, and preferred vendor. You can use as a secondary key one of these fields: inventory number, description, sales units, sales dollars, last sales date, purchase units, purchase dollars, last purchase date, on-hand units, on-hand dollars, profit, turns, and gross profit. If you don't remember how you use or how the system calculates these fields, refer to the section in Chapter 4 on loading the product master file.

For the product price listing report, the request screen also asks whether you want to print only the products with a certain cost code. If you set the revenue/cost department code to INVENTORY when you defined the general ledger interface table (see Chapter 3), you can limit the products printed on the product price listing report to those with a specific revenue/cost department code.

Figure 10.21 shows the report request screen that appears when you select the Service Report option from the Reports Inventory menu. This screen is slightly different from the request screens for the product reports.

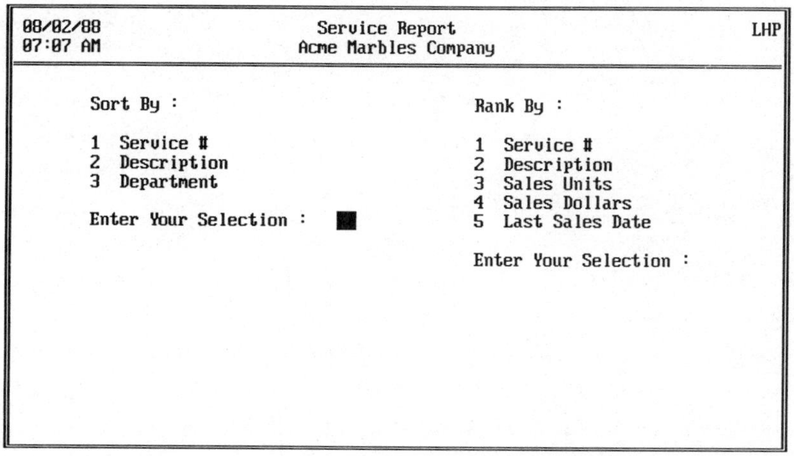

```
08/02/88                    Service Report                         LHP
07:07 AM                 Acme Marbles Company

        Sort By :                      Rank By :

        1 Service #                    1 Service #
        2 Description                  2 Description
        3 Department                   3 Sales Units
                                       4 Sales Dollars
        Enter Your Selection :  █      5 Last Sales Date

                                       Enter Your Selection :
```

Fig. 10.21

The service report request screen.

For the service report, you can use either the service number, the description, or the revenue/cost department as the primary key; and the service number, description, sales units, sales dollars, or last sales date as the secondary key. A pop-up window appears also, asking whether you want to see units of sales and dollars of sales information on the report. You simply answer *Y* or *N*.

Chapter Summary

This chapter described the tools DacEasy provides to allow you to manage your inventory investments more profitably and to maintain a perpetual inventory system. The chapter explained the perpetual inventory system—an inventory accounting method that can often have a dramatic positive effect both on business profits and cash flows. In this chapter, you learned also about the two on-line tools for controlling inventory—the Price Assignment screen and the Physical Inventory screen—and the seven powerful reports that can help you better manage each step in the process of buying, holding, and selling products and services. In the next chapter, you learn about a module that has been mentioned many times throughout this book: the General Ledger module.

CHAPTER 11

Using the General Ledger Module

The General Ledger module collects information from the other DacEasy modules and then uses this information to construct financial statements: a balance sheet, an income statement, and a statement of changes in financial position. If you want to prepare any of these financial statements, you need to use the General Ledger module. With this module, you can record the entries you may need but haven't recorded through one of the other modules.

This chapter illustrates some standard general ledger transactions you'll be making and details the instructions for completing each of the general ledger menu selections. The chapter also describes how to fix mistakes you make while using the General Ledger Transaction Entry screen and how to use the reports generated by the General Ledger module.

Examining Some Sample General Ledger Transactions

Most of the bookkeeping entries involving the financial activities and events of your business are recorded in one of DacEasy's other subsidiary modules. The Purchase Order and Accounts Payable modules record the changes in assets and liabilities, the expenses, and the cash outflows that stem from your purchases of goods and services. The Billing and Accounts Receivable modules record the revenues, the expenses, and any increases in costs of goods sold and decreases in inventory resulting from sales.

Small businesses usually don't have many other transactions. But five general categories of transactions are *not* recorded in one of the other modules: asset depreciation, contributions and reductions in the owner's equity account, loans provided by creditors, prepaid expenses, and adjusting entries. For these transactions you need to use the General Ledger module. (Incidentally, the first three types of entries are illustrated in some detail in Chapter 1.)

Recording Asset Depreciation

Often, the cost of a fixed asset, such as furniture or equipment, is high. Because you usually will use such an asset for several years, you can use an asset depreciation entry to prorate the purchase price over the number of years you will use the asset. One key difference between this and other expense entries is that the asset depreciation entry does not involve paying cash to a vendor every month. You pay once and then spread your cost over the period of use.

With this entry, you debit an expense account called Depreciation Expense and credit an asset account called Accumulated Depreciation. On the income statement, depreciation expense is treated just like any other expense. On the balance sheet, the accumulated depreciation, because it holds a credit balance, reduces the asset balance reported. (If you're a little unclear about exactly why or how this depreciation business works, review the accounting primer in Chapter 1.)

For example, suppose that you want to make an asset depreciation entry to record the expense of furniture costing $5,000. You plan to use the furniture over the next five years. Several depreciation methods are available, but suppose that you use the straight-line method, which spreads the cost of the expense equally over the years of use. This method involves dividing the cost of the asset by the number of periods in which you will use the asset. You therefore need to show $1,000 of depreciation expense in each year ($5,000/5 years). Here's the bookkeeping entry to record the transaction:

	Debit	Credit
Depreciation Expense	$1,000	
Accumulated Depreciation		$1,000

If you think you can sell the furniture for $500 at the end of the five years, you need to include this residual, or salvage, value in your calculations. For example, the amount to be depreciated would be $4,500 ($5,000 − $500), and the annual depreciation expense would be $900 ($4500/5 years).

In theory, depreciation is simply an application of economic common sense: over time, even long-lived assets are used up, and therefore an expense must be recognized. In practice, however, depreciation can be more complex. If you're figuring depreciation for the calculation of taxable income, you must follow specific tax accounting laws. In these cases, you probably should consult your tax advisor. If you're calculating depreciation to prepare financial statements in accordance with generally accepted accounting principles, the standards pro-scribe both general and specific rules for calculating depreciation. In these cases, you probably should consult your certified public accountant. (For more information on depreciation, refer to Chapter 1 of *Using DacEasy* and to an introductory college accounting text like *Fundamentals of Financial Accounting,* written by Glenn A. Welsch and Robert N. Anthony and published by Richard D. Irwin, Inc.

Adjusting the Owner's Equity Account

A second type of transaction you record with the General Ledger module involves contributions of capital by investors or partners. Typically, an investor or partner contributes cash, so you debit cash. The credit portion of the entry is to the owner's equity or net worth account. For example, if you originally contributed $5,000 to start your business, you record the transaction this way:

	Debit	*Credit*
Cash	$5,000	
Owner's Equity		$5,000

You might also contribute something other than cash to start the business. If you invest $5,000 of inventory, for example, your entry should include a debit to inventory rather than cash.

In practice, both corporations and partnerships divide the owner's equity account into smaller accounts to show more detail. If you're going to be show-ing your balance sheet to people outside your business, or you want more spe-cific information yourself, you need to use more detailed owner's equity accounts. Unfortunately, this area is often complex enough that you may need to review the accounting with your certified public accountant.

Recording Loans

When a creditor provides you with a loan, you record in the General Ledger module a third type of bookkeeping entry. The debit in this entry is usually to cash, because a loan generally involves cash. If the creditor loans you some other asset, you debit the account for that asset. You must also credit the appropriate liabilities account. Suppose that you borrow $10,000 from the bank to purchase a delivery truck. Remember that the Purchase Order and Accounts Payable modules record the actual purchase of the truck. You use the General Ledger module to record the liability that gives you the cash to make the purchase. To record the liability, you make the following entry:

	Debit	Credit
Cash	$10,000	
Loan from Bank		$10,000

Recording Prepaid Expenses

A prepaid expense, which is similar to depreciation, is a fourth type of general ledger transaction. Suppose that you enter into a maintenance agreement with a local equipment service company. The company agrees to provide on-site maintenance service on your computers and printers for the next 12 months for $1,200. You need to debit an expense account and credit accounts payable for the amount of the expenditure. But because the maintenance agreement covers more than one month and you're preparing monthly financial statements, you need to record 1/12 of the contract as an expense each month. Here are the entries:

	Debit	Credit
Prepaid Computer Maintenance	$1,200	
Accounts Payable		$1,200
Repair and Maintenance Expense	$100	
Prepaid Computer Maintenance		$100

Note that you handle the prepaid expense account the same way you do accumulated depreciation: you debit the entire amount at the time of purchase and offset that amount with monthly credits over the time period.

Adjusting the General Ledger

Another type of entry that you often encounter in the operation of a general ledger is called an adjusting entry. You make adjusting entries at the end of an accounting period to adjust the general ledger accounts so that their balances agree with the balances of the underlying detail accounts. Some common adjusting journal entries (AJE) involve recording the following:

1. Bank service charges
2. State and local business taxes
3. Payroll taxes for unemployment or industrial insurance
4. The interest portion of payments on a bank loan
5. Interest earned on your business savings account

For example, you might record bank service charges with this entry:

	Debit	Credit
Bank Service Charge Expense	$5	
Cash		$5

Accessing the Menu Options for the General Ledger

The menu selections involving the general ledger are located in five places on the main menu: the Transaction, Journals, Posting, Financials, and Periodic options. The Transaction General Ledger option provides you with the screen you use to enter general ledger transactions, recording such things as asset depreciation, contributions of capital, loans from creditors, prepaid expenses, and adjusting entries. Figure 11.1 shows the Transaction menu with the General Ledger option highlighted.

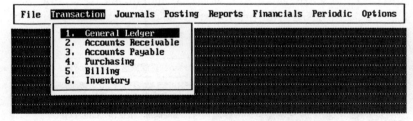

Fig. 11.1

The Transaction General Ledger option.

From the Journals menu, you can print two journals: the general ledger journal and the general ledger activity report. These journals provide audit trails of the bookkeeping entries recorded with the General Ledger Transaction Entry screen and those entries posted to the general ledger from other modules. Figure 11.2 shows the Journals menu with the first option, G/L Journal, highlighted. Notice that the second option on the Journals menu is G/L Activity.

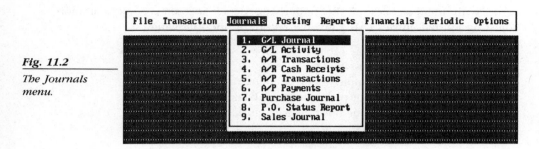

Fig. 11.2

The Journals menu.

The Posting General Ledger option (see fig. 11.3) updates the general ledger for both the bookkeeping entries posted from other modules and those entries made with the General Ledger Transaction Entry screen.

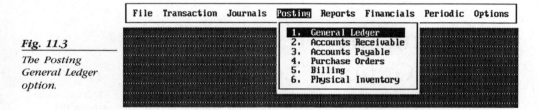

Fig. 11.3

The Posting General Ledger option.

The Financials menu lists several reports you can print: the Chart of Accounts, a trial balance (which is a Chart of Accounts with account balances included), a balance sheet, an income statement, and a statement of changes in financial conditions. All these reports are generated from the information that is contained in the general ledger, even though the general ledger name does not appear on the menu.

The fifth option on the Financials menu, Financial Statements Generator, provides you with tools to design and print custom-tailored financial statements. Figure 11.4 shows the Financials menu.

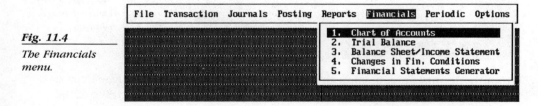

Fig. 11.4

The Financials menu.

You choose the Periodic General Ledger option (see fig. 11.5) to run the general ledger periodic routines at the end of each accounting period. The periodic routines for all DacEasy's modules are discussed in Chapter 12, "Using the Periodic Routines."

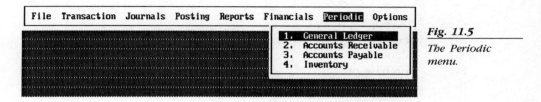

File	Transaction	Journals	Posting	Reports	Financials	Periodic	Options

```
1. General Ledger
2. Accounts Receivable
3. Accounts Payable
4. Inventory
```

Fig. 11.5

The Periodic menu.

The rest of this chapter is devoted to discussing each of these general ledger menu selections in detail.

Entering General Ledger Transactions

You use the General Ledger Transaction Entry screen to create necessary bookkeeping entries that weren't recorded in another module. To access this screen, select the Transaction option from the main menu and choose option 1, General Ledger, from the Transaction menu. Figure 11.6 shows the General Ledger Transaction Entry screen before you begin entering data.

```
                   GENERAL LEDGER TRANSACTION ENTRY
 Journal.. :█            Transaction #..:           Date..:

 Acct.#   Account Name          Description        Debit     Credit





















 Total Debits :                  Total Credits :
```

F1-Help F2-Difference F6-Delete F9-Auto Entry F10-Process ALT D-Delete line

Fig. 11.6

The General Ledger Transaction Entry screen before you begin entering data.

You enter data in six fields to complete a general ledger transaction. These fields and the instructions for completing them are described in the following paragraphs.

Journal: In this field, you enter a two-letter code to classify the transaction. DacEasy, which classifies transactions in the same way, reserves the following seven codes for the program's use:

Code	Journal Type
AP	Accounts payable
AR	Accounts receivable
PO	Purchase order
BI	Billing
IN	Inventory
PY	Payroll system
SU	Setup initial entries

You can use any other combination of letters. You may decide to use the two characters *GL* to represent all general ledger transactions. Or maybe you want to use codes that more specifically identify general ledger transactions. For example, you can use *FA* for fixed asset transactions such as depreciation, *CE* for creditor's equity transactions, *OE* for owner's equity transactions, and so on.

Transaction #: Just as on the other data entry screens, the *transaction number* uniquely identifies the transaction. On this screen, however, the system doesn't assign the next available transaction for you. You type the number you want to use. If you enter a previously used transaction number, the General Ledger Transaction Entry screen retrieves the bookkeeping entry identified by that number. Unlike other modules, the General Ledger module allows you to retrieve entries you've posted. You can add debits and credits to these entries, but you can't change the existing debits and credits.

Date: As soon as you enter a new transaction number, DacEasy places the current system date in the Date field. You can edit this field if you prefer. This date, labeled as the transaction date, appears on the general ledger audit trails.

Acct. #: The *account number* identifies the detail general ledger account you want to debit or credit. You can't debit or credit the accounts payable, accounts receivable, revenue, cost of goods sold, and inventory accounts that the other modules debit and credit. When you enter the Chart of Accounts number, the screen retrieves the account description from the Chart of Accounts file and places this description in the Account Name field. If you enter an account number that hasn't been previously defined in the Chart of Accounts, a pop-up window appears, asking whether you want to add the account number. By answering this question *Y* for "yes," you access an abbreviated Chart of Accounts File Maintenance screen, which you can use to create a new detail account number. Because you can't debit or credit a general account, you can't use this method to create a general account number.

Description: For each debit or credit, the screen provides a 24-character field you can use to document the debit or credit. Because usually the description for any one of the debits or credits matches the others, the General Ledger Transaction Entry screen (like the Accounts Receivable Transaction Entry and the Accounts Payable Transaction Entry screens) repeats the description you type for the first debit or credit as the description for the debits and credits that follow. You can, however, edit these descriptions.

If you're typing adjusting entries, you may want to enter each of them separately under one transaction number but reference the number of the adjustment in the Description field.

Debit, Credit: You use these fields to enter the amount of the debit or credit to the account. After the description is entered, the cursor moves to the Debit field. Type the debit amount and then press Enter to move to the next line. If you want to enter a credit rather than a debit, press Enter to move the cursor from the Debit field to the Credit field. Then type your credit amount and press Enter to move to the next line.

You enter an account number, a description, and a debit or credit amount for each debit or credit you need to make. (Remember that after you type the description for the first debit or credit, DacEasy fills the Description fields for the remaining debits and credits with that same description.)

If you enter a debit or credit and later discover a mistake, use the arrow keys to move backward through your entries to the incorrect field. Then simply modify the field. To delete a debit or credit you've already listed, press Alt-D while the item you want to delete is highlighted. To delete the entire general ledger transaction, press F6. (You can delete only unposted transactions.) After you enter all the debits and credits you want to include in the general ledger transaction, press F10 to save the transaction.

Two other handy function keys that make using the General Ledger Transaction Entry screen easier are the F2 and the F9 keys. By pressing F2, you can temporarily complete the general ledger transaction entry even if your total debits don't equal your total credits. DacEasy temporarily posts the difference between the debits and credits to the *journal difference account* (labeled *D*), which is also known as a suspense account. You must review the journal difference account and properly record the amounts to the correct accounts before DacEasy allows you to post your general ledger transactions.

You can use the F9 key to debit or credit the most recently entered account for the amount of the remaining needed debit or credit. For example, suppose that you're recording a bank loan for $5,000 and have already entered the $5,000 debit to cash. To finish the transaction, you can enter the correct liability account number and then press F9. DacEasy automatically credits the liability account number with the amount necessary to balance the debits and credits: $5,000.

Figures 11.7 through 11.11 show the General Ledger Transaction Entry screen with some sample journal entries. Figure 11.7 features the entries to record $1,000 of asset depreciation. Figure 11.8 displays the entries you use to record a $500 investment made by a shareholder for 500 shares of stock, each with a par value of $1.00. In figure 11.9, you can examine the entries to record a $5,000 loan from a bank. Figure 11.10 provides examples of three adjusting journal entries entered on one General Ledger Transaction Entry screen: one entry to record a bank service charge, one to record dividends paid, and another to record interest expense that the bank directly deducted from an account. Figure 11.11 shows the use of the F2 key to balance those adjusting entries, as you might do when you don't know the bank account that was credited for interest expense.

Fig. 11.7

The General Ledger Transaction Entry screen with sample entries to record asset depreciation.

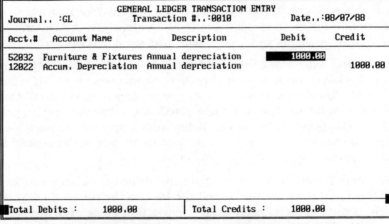

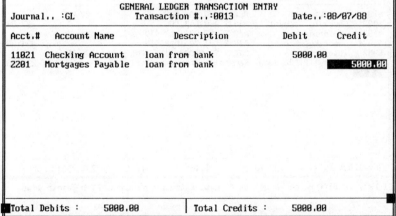

```
                    GENERAL LEDGER TRANSACTION ENTRY
 Journal.. :GL            Transaction #..:0011          Date..:08/07/88

 Acct.#   Account Name         Description          Debit      Credit

 11023   Savings Account    Initial investment     5000.00
 31011   Par Value          Initial investment                  500.00
 31012   Surplus            Initial investment                 4500.00
 ▆▆▆▆▆




















 ▌Total Debits :    5000.00    │ Total Credits :   5000.00        ▆
 F1-Help F2-Difference F6-Delete F9-Auto Entry F10-Process ALT D-Delete line
```

Fig. 11.8

The General Ledger Transaction Entry screen with sample entries to record an initial capital contribution.

```
                    GENERAL LEDGER TRANSACTION ENTRY
 Journal.. :GL            Transaction #..:0013          Date..:08/07/88

 Acct.#   Account Name         Description          Debit      Credit

 11021   Checking Account   loan from bank         5000.00
 2201    Mortgages Payable  loan from bank                    5000.00




















 ▌Total Debits :    5000.00    │ Total Credits :   5000.00        ▆
 F1-Help F2-Difference F6-Delete F9-Auto Entry F10-Process ALT D-Delete line
```

Fig. 11.9

The General Ledger Transaction Entry screen with sample entries to record a loan.

Fig. 11.10

The General Ledger Transaction Entry screen with sample adjusting entries.

```
                    GENERAL LEDGER TRANSACTION ENTRY
   Journal.. :AJ            Transaction #..:0001        Date..:08/30/88

   Acct.#   Account Name        Description         Debit      Credit

   5303   Bank Charges       AJE 1 AUG BAN CHG       27.00
   11021  Checking Account   AJE 1 AUG BAN CHG                   27.00
   4403   Dividends          AJE 2 XYZ CO JULY DIV  434.00
   11021  Checking Account   AJE 2 XYZ CO JULY DIV              434.00
   5302   Interest           AJE 3 TO RECORD INT BANK 276.78
   2202   Notes Payable      AJE 3 TO RECORD INT BANK            276.78



   Total Debits :    737.78   |   Total Credits :    737.78
```

F1-Help F2-Difference F6-Delete F9-Auto Entry F10-Process ALT D-Delete line

Fig. 11.11

The General Ledger Transaction Entry screen with an entry posted to the journal difference account.

```
                    GENERAL LEDGER TRANSACTION ENTRY
   Journal.. :AJ            Transaction #..:0001        Date..:08/30/88

   Acct.#   Account Name        Description         Debit      Credit

   5303   Bank Charges       AJE 1 AUG BAN CHG       27.00
   11021  Checking Account   AJE 1 AUG BAN CHG                   27.00
   4403   Dividends          AJE 2 XYZ CO JULY DIV  434.00
   11021  Checking Account   AJE 2 XYZ CO JULY DIV              434.00
   5302   Interest           AJE 3 TO RECORD INT BANK 276.78
   D      Journal Difference Reconcile Trans. Differ.           276.78



   Total Debits :    737.78   |   Total Credits :    737.78
```

F1-Help F2-Difference F6-Delete F9-Auto Entry F10-Process ALT D-Delete line

Correcting General Ledger Transactions

As elsewhere in DacEasy, to correct bookkeeping entries you haven't posted, access the General Ledger Transaction Entry screen and then type the transaction number to retrieve the transaction you want to change. Make your corrections and press F10 to save your work.

To correct a bookkeeping entry you've already posted, first enter a new transaction that mirrors the old, incorrect entry with only one exception: the debits and credits should be reversed. For example, if you need to correct a general ledger transaction that debited depreciation expense $5,000 and credited accumulated depreciation $5,000, reverse this entry by crediting depreciation expense $5,000 and debiting accumulated depreciation $5,000. Saving and then posting this new transaction reverses your first, incorrect general ledger transaction. Next, reenter the original general ledger transaction, but this time use the correct accounts, descriptions, and amounts.

C.P.A. Tip: Don't combine the two steps outlined to correct transactions that have already been posted. Later, you'll more easily be able to understand two identical transactions that cancel each other and one independent transaction that represents the final, correct entry. Also, you need to realize that if you're correcting an entry made in a previous accounting period, the net effect of the reversing entry and revised entry will show up not in the previous period but in the current period. Accordingly, if this change is material, you may need to follow specific tax accounting and financial accounting procedures to restate and correct the previous period's financial statements. See your tax advisor or certified public accountant if you need assistance.

Printing the General Ledger Journals

You use the Journals option from the main menu to print both the general ledger journal and the general ledger activity report. From the Journals menu, choose option 1, G/L Journal, to print the general ledger journal; and option 2, G/L Activity, to print the general ledger activity report.

The General Ledger Journal

The *general ledger journal* lists both the bookkeeping entries you entered with the General Ledger Transaction Entry screen and those entries created by the other modules. You use this journal to review for errors the transactions you entered on the General Ledger Transaction Entry screen. (If you do find errors, follow the procedures outlined in the section on "Correcting General Ledger Transactions" to correct the mistakes.)

Figure 11.12 shows the report request screen you use to print the general ledger journal. The Journal Code From and To fields allow you to limit the journal entries printed. In these fields, you enter the two-character codes that you and DacEasy have used to identify journal entries. You might, for example, set the From code to AP and the To code to AR. If you have given some journal entries the code AQ, DacEasy then prints all the general ledger transactions with codes equal to AP, AQ, and AR. (DacEasy looks at the codes alphabetically.) Using the Transaction Date From and To fields, you can choose to print only transactions created within a range of dates. The transaction date for bookkeeping entries constructed by any other module—Purchase Order, Accounts Payable, Billing, Accounts Receivable, or Inventory—is that module's posting date.

Fig. 11.12

The request screen for the general ledger journal.

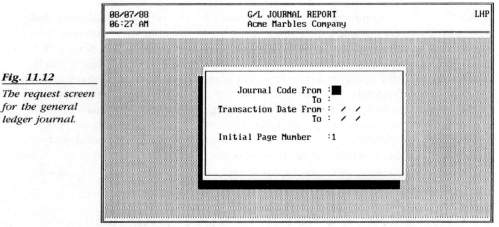

The G/L Journal Report request screen also allows you to set the initial page number. Although the default initial page number is 1, in some cases you may want to begin printing on another page. For example, if you're printing the general ledger journal for the second month of the year, and the journal for the first month had 10 pages, you can set the starting page number for the second month's journal to 11. Using this approach, you can combine the journals from each month into a master journal for the entire year and have all the pages correctly numbered.

Figure 11.13 shows a sample general ledger journal with several transactions posted from other modules and the three sample general ledger transactions shown in figures 11.7, 11.8, and 11.9.

The Journal Trans. # column identifies the transaction code. If the transaction is from one of the other modules, the system fills in this column. The four-digit number displayed beside the transaction code identifies the date the posting was made. The first code, *AP 0723*, for example, identifies an accounts payable transaction posted on July 23. If the transaction is from the General Ledger Transaction Entry screen, you entered the transaction number and date on that screen (or allowed DacEasy to set the date as the system date).

The number and name of the account being debited or credited are retrieved from the Chart of Accounts. The description is either retrieved from the other modules or from the description you created with the General Ledger Transac-

```
Date : 08/03/88                        Acme Marbles Company                     Page no. 1
Time : 11:49 AM                          512 Wetmore Street
                                         Seattle, Wa 98114
                               Tel: (206) 555-1234 Fax: (206) 555-6789

                                  General Ledger Journal Report

        Journal
        Trans.#  Date     Acct. #  Account Name      Description           Debits      Credits   Posted?
        -------  -------- -------  ----------------- ----------------   ----------  ---------- --------
        AP 0723  07/23/88 2101     Accts Payable-Module Payments Summ.-AP Post  9309.99                 NO
                          52025    Building          Summary From AP Post    973.00                 NO
                          52055    Building          Summary From AP Post   4000.00                 NO
                          52072    Transportation    Summary From AP Post    732.45                 NO
                          52102    Legal             Summary From AP Post   2750.00                 NO
                          5214     Utilities         Summary From AP Post   1000.00                 NO
                          11021    Checking Account  First Class Marb-fs                 4750.00   NO
                          11021    Checking Account  First Class Marb-000001             1683.79   NO
                          11021    Checking Account  Janitorial Excel-000002             473.00   NO
                          11021    Checking Account  Walter's Wonders-000003             792.33   NO
                          11021    Checking Account  Mercury Marble M-CK4561            1500.00   NO
                          2101     Accts Payable-Module Summary From AP Post              9455.45   NO
                          4404     Purchase Discounts Payments Summ.-AP Post               110.87   NO

                                            TOTAL TRANSACTION  :    18765.44    18765.44


        AR 0727  07/27/88 11021    Checking Account  Payments Summ.-AR Post    500.00                 NO
                          11021    Checking Account  Payments Summ.-AR Post   -100.00                 NO
                          11021    Checking Account  Payments Summ.-AR Post    -25.00                 NO
                          11051    Accts Rec'ble Module Summary From AR Post    1400.00                 NO
                          11051    Accts Rec'ble Module Payments Summ.-AR Post             375.00   NO
                          4101     Sales Dept. 01    Summary From AR Post               1375.00   NO
                          4301     Freight           Summary From AR Post                 25.00   NO

                                            TOTAL TRANSACTION  :     1775.00     1775.00


        BI 0727  07/27/88 11021    Checking Account  Billing Summary          500.00                 NO
                          11051    Accts Rec'ble Module Billing Summary        1497.46                 NO
                          4201     Returns Dept. 01  Billing Summary           11.25                 NO
                          5101     COGS Dept. 01     Billing Summary           12.50                 NO
                          5102     COGS Dept. 02     Billing Summary          918.75                 NO
                          11071    Inventory - Module Billing Summary                    931.25   NO
                          21042    Sales Tax Payable Billing Summary                     103.21   NO
                          4101     Sales Dept. 01    Billing Summary                      40.00   NO
                          4102     Sales Dept. 02    Billing Summary                    1857.00   NO
                          4301     Freight           Billing Summary                       8.50   NO

                                            TOTAL TRANSACTION  :     2939.96     2939.96


        GL 0001  08/03/88 52032    Furniture & Fixtures Annual depreciation   1000.00                 YES
                          12022    Accum. Depreciation Annual depreciation               1000.00   YES

                                            TOTAL TRANSACTION  :     1000.00     1000.00


        GL 0002  08/03/88 11023    Savings Account   Initial investment      5000.00                 YES
                          31011    Par Value         Initial investment                  500.00   YES
                          31012    Surplus           Initial investment                 4500.00   YES

                                            TOTAL TRANSACTION  :     5000.00     5000.00


        GL 0003  08/03/88 11021    Checking Account  Loan from Finance Compny 5000.00                 YES
```

Fig. 11.13

The general ledger journal.

```
Date : 08/03/88                          Acme Marbles Company                          Page no. 2
Time : 11:49 AM                          512 Wetmore Street
                                         Seattle, Wa 98114
                               Tel: (206) 555-1234 Fax: (206) 555-6789

                                    General Ledger Journal Report

         Journal
         Trans.#    Date    Acct. #   Account Name          Description          Debits     Credits   Posted?
         -------   -------- -------   ---------------------  --------------------- ----------- ----------- -------
         GL 0003  08/03/88 2201      Mortgages Payable      Loan from Finance Compny            5000.00   YES

                                                            TOTAL TRANSACTION  :   5000.00    5000.00

         IN 0802  08/02/88 5101      COGS Dept. 01          Physical Inventory Post  420.00              YES
                           11071     Inventory - Module     Physical Inventory Post            420.00    YES

                                                            TOTAL TRANSACTION  :    420.00     420.00

         PO 0721  07/21/88 11071     Inventory - Module     Purchase Order Summary    40.00              NO
                           52081     Freight                Purchase Order Summary    20.00              NO
                           52082     Insurance              Purchase Order Summary     2.00              NO
                           52091     Sales Tax/Purchases    Purchase Order Summary     3.24              NO
                           2101      Accts Payable-Module   Purchase Order Summary              65.24    NO

                                                            TOTAL TRANSACTION  :     65.24      65.24

         PO 0726  07/26/88 11071     Inventory - Module     Purchase Order Summary   799.50              NO
                           52091     Sales Tax/Purchases    Purchase Order Summary    62.51              NO
                           2101      Accts Payable-Module   Purchase Order Summary             862.01    NO

                                                            TOTAL TRANSACTION  :    862.01     862.01

         SU 0717  07/17/88 520119    Officer's Salaries     Chart of Accts Setup       0.00              YES
                           D         Journal Difference     Chart of Accts Setup                 0.00    YES

                                                            TOTAL TRANSACTION  :      0.00       0.00

         SU 0720  07/20/88 11051     Accts Rec'ble Module   Summ. Customer Setup     562.46              YES
                           11071     Inventory - Module     Summ. Products Setup     667.50              YES
                           D         Journal Difference     Summ. Vendor Setup      7650.11              YES
                           2101      Accts Payable-Module   Summ. Vendor Setup                 7650.11   YES
                           D         Journal Difference     Summ. Customer Setup                562.46   YES
                           D         Journal Difference     Summ. Products Setup                667.50   YES

                                                            TOTAL TRANSACTION  :   8880.07    8880.07

                                                            TOTAL TRANSACTION  :  44707.72   44707.72

         # OF ENTRIES PRINTED  : 55
```

Fig. 11.13-Continued*

tion Entry screen. The debits and credits columns show the amount debited or credited to the account.

The entire DacEasy posting process involves two steps. The first post is from the Purchase Order, Accounts Payable, Billing, Accounts Receivable, and Inventory modules to the general ledger. The second post takes these transactions—and those entries created with the General Ledger Transaction Entry screen—and posts them to the Chart of Accounts. The last column on the general ledger journal, titled "Posted?", indicates whether this entry has been posted from the general ledger to the Chart of Accounts (the entry may already have been posted from another module to the general ledger).

Save the last error-free copy of the general ledger journal as your audit trail of the bookkeeping entries made with the General Ledger Transaction Entry screen and with other modules.

The General Ledger Activity Report

The *general ledger activity report* lists the same information as the general ledger journal, but with the debits and credits sorted by account number. (In comparison, the general ledger journal sorts the debits and credits by journal code and transaction number.) The general ledger activity report also totals the debits and credits made to an account. Being able to see in one place all the debits and credits made to an account helps you explain the changes in an account balance over an accounting period.

Figure 11.14 shows the report request screen you use to print the general ledger activity report. The Print Account # From and To fields allow you to print a range of accounts rather than all the accounts. The Transaction Date From and To fields and the Initial Page Number fields affect printing the same way as they do on the report request screen for the general ledger journal. The Print by Page (Y/N) field allows you to print each account on its own page. If you set the flag to *Y*, the printer advances to a new page before printing the debits and credits to an account. With the Rank by Date or by Jrn/Trans. # (D/J) field, you can specify a secondary sort key within each account. A *D* sets the secondary key to the transaction date, and a *J* sets the secondary key to the journal code and transaction number. Remember that because the transaction date is used for the transaction number for the entries constructed by other modules, you may not notice much difference between these two secondary sorting options.

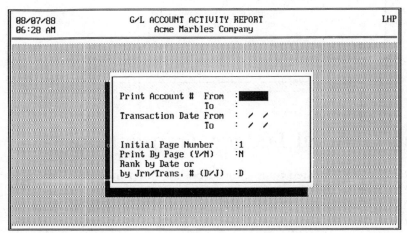

Fig. 11.14

The request screen for the general ledger activity report.

F1-Help ESC-Exit

Figure 11.15 shows the first page from a sample general ledger activity report.

```
Date : 08/03/88                           Acme Marbles Company                    Page no. 1
Time : 11:56 AM                            512 Wetmore Street
                                           Seattle, Wa 98114
                                   Tel: (206) 555-1234 Fax: (206) 555-6789

                                     G/L Account Activity Detail Report
                                        From : 07/20/88 To : 08/03/88

     Journal
     Trans.#   Date     Acct. #   Account Name        Description            Debits      Credits   Posted?
     -------  --------  --------  ----------------    ----------------    ----------  ----------  -------
                        11021  Checking Account    BEGINNING BALANCE       25167.48
     AP 0723  07/23/88                             First Class Marb-fs                   4750.00   NO
     AP 0723  07/23/88                             First Class Marb-000001               1683.79   NO
     AP 0723  07/23/88                             Janitorial Excel-000002                473.00   NO
     AP 0723  07/23/88                             Walter's Wonders-000003                792.33   NO
     AP 0723  07/23/88                             Mercury Marble M-CK4561               1500.00   NO
     AR 0727  07/27/88                             Payments Summ.-AR Post    500.00                NO
     AR 0727  07/27/88                             Payments Summ.-AR Post   -100.00                NO
     AR 0727  07/27/88                             Payments Summ.-AR Post    -25.00                NO
     BI 0727  07/27/88                             Billing Summary           500.00                NO
     GL 0003  08/03/88                             Loan from Finance Compny 5000.00                YES
                                                   CURRENT BALANCE         21843.36

                        11023  Savings Account     BEGINNING BALANCE       10000.00
     GL 0002  08/03/88                             Initial investment       5000.00                YES
                                                   CURRENT BALANCE         15000.00

                        11051  Accts Rec'ble Module BEGINNING BALANCE      82951.64
     SU 0720  07/20/88                             Summ. Customer Setup      562.46                YES
     AR 0727  07/27/88                             Summary From AR Post     1400.00                NO
     BI 0727  07/27/88                             Billing Summary          1497.46                NO
     AR 0727  07/27/88                             Payments Summ.-AR Post                 375.00   NO
                                                   CURRENT BALANCE         86036.56

                        11071  Inventory - Module  BEGINNING BALANCE        1097.50
     SU 0720  07/20/88                             Summ. Products Setup      667.50                YES
     PO 0721  07/21/88                             Purchase Order Summary     40.00                NO
     PO 0726  07/26/88                             Purchase Order Summary    799.50                NO
     BI 0727  07/27/88                             Billing Summary                        931.25   NO
     IN 0802  08/02/88                             Physical Inventory Post                420.00   YES
                                                   CURRENT BALANCE          1253.25

                        12022  Accum. Depreciation BEGINNING BALANCE       -2000.00
     GL 0001  08/03/88                             Annual depreciation                   1000.00   YES
                                                   CURRENT BALANCE         -3000.00

                        2101  Accts Payable-Module BEGINNING BALANCE                    29216.06
     SU 0720  07/20/88                             Summ. Vendor Setup                    7650.11   YES
```

Fig. 11.15

The general ledger activity report.

Posting General Ledger Transactions

You've probably already posted transactions from the other modules to the general ledger. To post to the Chart of Accounts the transactions you created with the General Ledger Transaction Entry screen, select the Posting option from the main menu and then choose option 1, General Ledger. (Remember to review the general ledger journals before posting general ledger transactions to ensure that you have made no data entry errors when creating these transactions.)

After you choose Posting General Ledger, a warning screen appears and asks you to be sure that you've backed up your files to protect them from a loss of power or a hardware failure that might occur during the posting process (see fig. 11.16). (The process for backing up and restoring your files is discussed in Chapter 5, "Protecting Your System.")

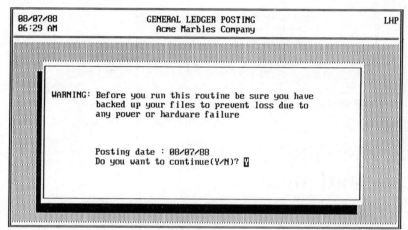

Fig. 11.16

The warning screen that appears when you choose the Posting General Ledger option.

You specify the accounting period for which you want to post the general ledger transactions. When you provide the posting date on the General Ledger Posting screen, DacEasy calculates the posting month. For example, if the posting date is 08/04/88, DacEasy assumes that the posting month is 08, which is August. (Accounting periods are identified by the month number: January equals 01, February equals 02, and so on.)

This helpful feature means that you can begin entering the current month's general ledger transactions even if you haven't posted the preceding month's transactions. You may want to take advantage of this feature if a new accounting period has begun and you need to begin making bookkeeping entries for it, but you still haven't finished all the bookkeeping entries for the preceding period. For example, suppose that you haven't yet posted July's activity and want to do so. Press the up arrow, and the screen displays the month to be posted rather than the posting date, as shown in figure 11.17. You can change the posting month to July by simply typing *07* in the field.

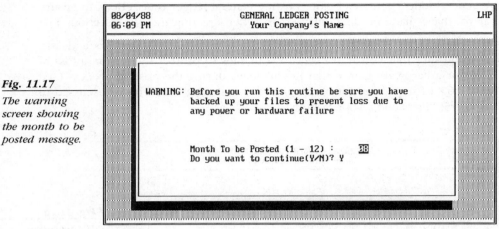

Fig. 11.17

The warning screen showing the month to be posted message.

```
08/04/88                  GENERAL LEDGER POSTING                    LHP
06:09 PM                   Your Company's Name


        WARNING: Before you run this routine be sure you have
                 backed up your files to prevent loss due to
                 any power or hardware failure



                 Month To be Posted (1 - 12) :      08
                 Do you want to continue(Y/N)? Y




F1-Help ESC-Exit
```

Printing the General Ledger Financial Statements

The general ledger includes several options for printing financial statements. These statements, which you access from the Financials menu, include the Chart of Accounts, a trial balance, a balance sheet, and a statement of changes in financial conditions. The last option on the Financials menu accesses a financial statements generator, which allows you to design and print custom financial statements.

Printing the Standard Financial Statements

You use the first option on the Financials menu to print the Chart of Accounts and the second option to print a trial balance. The Chart of Accounts simply lists the accounts, or classifications, you use to collect and categorize financial data. Figure 11.18 shows the report request screen you use to print such a listing.

A trial balance is like the Chart of Accounts, except that the trial balance shows the total debits or credits made to an account. The report request screen for printing a trial balance is exactly like the Chart of Accounts version, with only a different title. You must complete five fields to request either report.

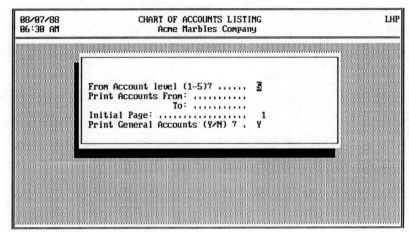

```
From Account level (1-5)? ......  5
Print Accounts From: ...........
             To: ...........
Initial Page: ..................  1
Print General Accounts (Y/N) ? .  Y
```

Fig. 11.18

The Chart of Accounts report request screen.

F1-Help F4-Change Date ESC-Exit

From Account Level (1-5)?: First, specify the account levels you want. If you type *1*, only level 1 accounts appear on the listing. If you type *2*, both level 1 and 2 accounts appear on the listing. If you specify *3*, perhaps you've already guessed that level 1, 2, and 3 accounts appear on the listing. If you want all accounts to show on the listing, type *5*, which is the default.

Print Accounts From, To: Next you must specify (by account number) the range of accounts you want to include on the listing. If you don't select a range but instead just press Enter to move past these two fields, all the accounts are printed.

Initial Page: You use this field to specify the starting page number of the report you're requesting.

Print General Accounts (Y/N)?: This last field allows you to include or exclude general accounts. Remember that general accounts are those you can't directly debit or credit but can use only for subtotals and totals on your financial statements.

After you've completed the report request screen and pressed Enter, a pop-up window appears, asking whether you want inactive accounts included on the report. Inactive accounts are those that have a zero balance. Figure 11.19 shows an extract of the sample Chart of Accounts DacEasy provides. If you don't remember what the Chart of Accounts columns represent, return to Chapter 3's section on "Defining the Chart of Accounts."

Figure 11.20 shows a sample trial balance listing. The DacEasy accounting system uses the asset, liability, and owner's equity accounts from the trial balance

```
Date : 08/07/88            Acme Marbles Company              Page no. 1
Time : 02:24 PM             512 Wetmore Street
                            Seattle, Wa 98114
                  Tel: (206) 555-1234 Fax: (206) 555-6789

                           CHART OF ACCOUNTS

                                         Acct.
         Acct. # Account Name            Type  Level  Type    General
         ------- -------------------------- ----- ----- ------- --------
         1       Assets                      ASSET 1     GENERAL
         11         Current Assets           ASSET 2     GENERAL 1
         1101         Petty Cash             ASSET 3     DETAIL  11
         1102         Cash In Banks          ASSET 3     GENERAL 11
         11021          Checking Account     ASSET 4     DETAIL  1102
         11022          Payroll Account      ASSET 4     DETAIL  1102
         11023          Savings Account      ASSET 4     DETAIL  1102
         1103         Cash Register Fund     ASSET 3     GENERAL 11
         11031          Cash Register # 1    ASSET 4     DETAIL  1103
         11032          Cash Register # 2    ASSET 4     DETAIL  1103
         1104         Mktable Securities     ASSET 3     GENERAL 11
         11041          Cert. of Deposit     ASSET 4     DETAIL  1104
         11042          US Gover. Securities ASSET 4     DETAIL  1104
         11043          Other Securities     ASSET 4     DETAIL  1104
         1105         Accounts Receivable    ASSET 3     GENERAL 11
         11051          Accts Rec'ble Module ASSET 4     DETAIL  1105
         11052          Allow Doubtful Accts ASSET 4     DETAIL  1105
         1106         Other Receivable       ASSET 3     GENERAL 11
         11061          Affiliated Company   ASSET 4     DETAIL  1106
         11062          Employee Loans       ASSET 4     DETAIL  1106
         11063          Officers Loans       ASSET 4     DETAIL  1106
         11064          Other Receivable     ASSET 4     DETAIL  1106
         1107         Inventory              ASSET 3     GENERAL 11
         11071          Inventory - Module   ASSET 4     DETAIL  1107
         11072          Allow Damage/Obsol.  ASSET 4     DETAIL  1107
         12         Fixed Assets             ASSET 2     GENERAL 1
         1201         Autos & Trucks Net     ASSET 3     GENERAL 12
         12011          Original Value       ASSET 4     DETAIL  1201
         12012          Accum. Depreciation  ASSET 4     DETAIL  1201
         1202         Furniture & Fixt.Net   ASSET 3     GENERAL 12
         12021          Original Value       ASSET 4     DETAIL  1202
         12022          Accum. Depreciation  ASSET 4     DETAIL  1202
         1203         Office Equipment Net   ASSET 3     GENERAL 12
         12031          Original Value       ASSET 4     DETAIL  1203
         12032          Accum. Depreciation  ASSET 4     DETAIL  1203
         1204         Machinery & Eq. Net    ASSET 3     GENERAL 12
         12041          Original Value       ASSET 4     DETAIL  1204
         12042          Accum. Depreciation  ASSET 4     DETAIL  1204
         1205         Building Net           ASSET 3     GENERAL 12
         12051          Original Value       ASSET 4     DETAIL  1205
         12052          Accum. Depreciation  ASSET 4     DETAIL  1205
         1206         Other Fixed Assets     ASSET 3     GENERAL 12
         12061          Original Value       ASSET 4     DETAIL  1206
         12062          Accum. Depreciation  ASSET 4     DETAIL  1206
         1207         Land-Original Value    ASSET 3     DETAIL  12
         13         Deferred Assets          ASSET 2     GENERAL 1
         1301         Organization Expense   ASSET 3     GENERAL 13
         13011          Original Value       ASSET 4     DETAIL  1301
         13012          Accum. Amortization  ASSET 4     DETAIL  1301
```

Fig. 11.19

An extract from the Chart of Accounts.

to prepare the balance sheet; and the revenue and expense accounts to prepare the income statement. The trial balance helpfully includes three columns of debits and credits. The first column shows the debit and credit balances at the beginning of the accounting period, the second column shows the debit and credit changes during the current period, and the last column combines the beginning balance with the current period change to show the current balance.

One important use for this report is to verify that you don't have a balance in the journal difference account (labeled *D* in the account number column) after

```
Date : 08/04/88                    Acme Marbles Company                      Page no. 1
Time : 10:39 AM                     512 Wetmore Street
                                    Seattle, Wa 98114
                           Tel: (206) 555-1234 Fax: (206) 555-6789

                                      TRIAL BALANCE

                          BEGINNING BALANCE        THIS MONTH           CURRENT BALANCE
      Acct #  Account Name       Debits   Credits     Debits   Credits     Debits   Credits
      ------  ------------       ------   -------     ------   -------     ------   -------
      1      Assets                0.00               1229.96              1229.96
      11       Current Assets      0.00               1229.96              1229.96
      1105       Accounts Receivable 0.00              562.46               562.46
      11051        Accts Rec'ble Module 0.00           562.46               562.46
      1107       Inventory         0.00                667.50               667.50
      11071        Inventory - Module 0.00             667.50               667.50
      0        Journal Difference  0.00               6420.15              6420.15
      2      Liabilities                     0.00               7650.11              7650.11
      21       Short Term Liability          0.00               7650.11              7650.11
      2101       Accts Payable-Module        0.00               7650.11              7650.11

                                  ============ ============  ============ ============  ============ ============
                                    0.00        0.00          7650.11      7650.11       7650.11      7650.11
           Number of Accounts printed 10
```

Fig. 11.20

A sample trial balance.

defining and setting up your Chart of Accounts and loading your master files. If the journal difference account shows a balance, you've omitted an asset, liability, owner's equity, revenue, or expense account balance. First, review the assets listed to make sure that you didn't forget to enter some item. Then, check the trial balance's listing of liability, owner's equity, revenue, and expense accounts to make sure that you didn't omit one of these accounts. When you discover which account you missed, you must use the Chart of Accounts File Maintenance screen to update the account balance of that account.

Option 3 on the Financials menu allows you to print balance sheets and income statements. Option 4 prints a statement of changes in financial conditions. Figure 11.21 shows the report request screen you complete to print either the balance sheet, the income statement, or the statement of changes in financial conditions. The fields you complete are the same as previously described for the Chart of Accounts and the trial balance. Here again, a pop-up window appears and asks whether you want to include inactive accounts.

Figures 11.22 and 11.23 show a sample balance sheet and income statement, both generated by selecting option 3 on the Financials menu.

Examine the statement of changes in financial conditions shown in figure 11.24. If you compare this report to the trial balance, you can see that the statement of changes in financial conditions acts as a summary of the trial balance, showing the summary sources and uses in accounts rather than the debit and credit changes in detail accounts. Sources are credits, and uses are debits.

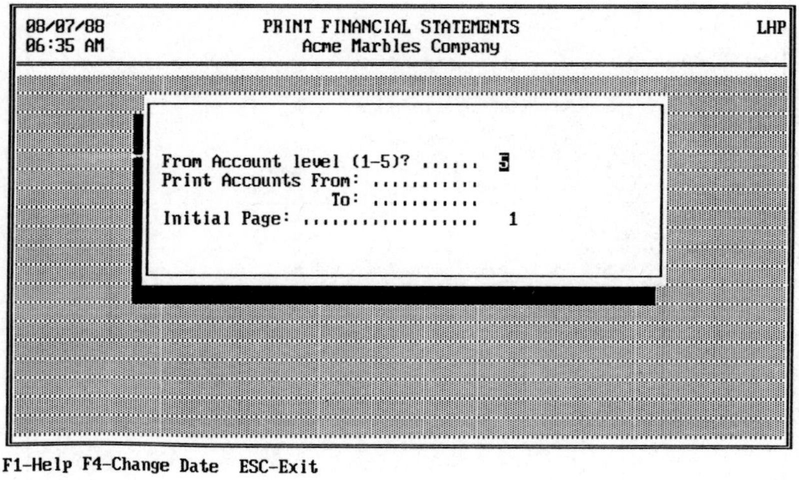

```
        From Account level (1-5)? ......  5
        Print Accounts From: ...........
                         To: ...........
        Initial Page: ................    1
```

F1-Help F4-Change Date ESC-Exit

Fig. 11.21

The Print Financial Statements report request screen.

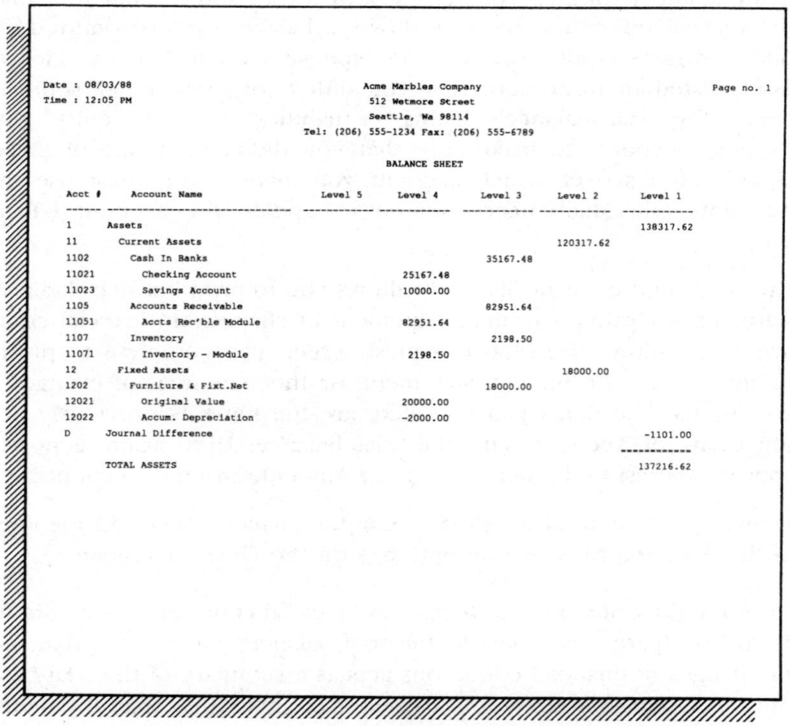

Fig. 11.22

The balance sheet.

```
Date : 08/03/88                     Acme Marbles Company                      Page no. 1
Time : 12:05 PM                       512 Wetmore Street
                                       Seattle, Wa 98114
                          Tel: (206) 555-1234 Fax: (206) 555-6789

                                      BALANCE SHEET

Acct #   Account Name          Level 5      Level 4      Level 3      Level 2      Level 1
------   -------------------   ----------   ----------   ----------   ----------   ----------
1        Assets                                                                    138317.62
11          Current Assets                                              120317.62
1102        Cash In Banks                                  35167.48
11021          Checking Account              25167.48
11023          Savings Account               10000.00
1105        Accounts Receivable                            82951.64
11051          Accts Rec'ble Module          82951.64
1107        Inventory                                       2198.50
11071          Inventory - Module             2198.50
12          Fixed Assets                                                 18000.00
1202        Furniture & Fixt.Net                           18000.00
12021          Original Value                20000.00
12022          Accum. Depreciation          -2000.00
D        Journal Difference                                                        -1101.00
                                                                                 ------------
         TOTAL ASSETS                                                             137216.62
```

```
Date : 08/03/88                          Acme Marbles Company                              Page no. 2
Time : 12:05 PM                           512 Wetmore Street
                                          Seattle, Wa 98114
                              Tel: (206) 555-1234 Fax: (206) 555-6789

                                          BALANCE SHEET

Acct #    Account Name              Level 5      Level 4      Level 3      Level 2      Level 1
------    ---------------------     ----------   ----------   ----------   ----------   ----------
2         Liabilities                                                                   89270.46
21           Short Term Liability                                          34270.46
2101            Accts Payable-Module                          29216.06
2104            Taxes Payable                                 5054.40
21042              Sales Tax Payable              5054.40
22           Long Term Liability                                           55000.00
2201            Mortgages Payable                             55000.00
                                                                                       ------------
          TOTAL LIABILITIES                                                             89270.46

3         Stockholders Equity                                                           10000.00
31           Capital Stock                                                 10000.00
3101            Common Stock                                  10000.00
31011              Par Value                      1000.00
31012              Surplus                        9000.00
             CURRENT EARNINGS                                                           37946.16

                                                                                       ------------
          TOTAL EQUITY                                                                  47946.16

                                                                                       ------------
          TOTAL LIABILITIES PLUS EQUITY                                                137216.62
```

Fig. 11.22-Continued

```
Date : 08/03/88                          Acme Marbles Company                              Page no. 3
Time : 12:05 PM                           512 Wetmore Street
                                          Seattle, Wa 98114
                              Tel: (206) 555-1234 Fax: (206) 555-6789

                                          INCOME STATEMENT

Acct #    Account Name              Level 5      Level 4      Level 3      Level 2      Level 1
------    ---------------------     ----------   ----------   ----------   ----------   ----------
4         Revenues                                                                      77334.78
41           Sales                                                         77334.78
4101            Sales Dept. 01                                44834.78
4102            Sales Dept. 02                                32500.00
                                                                                       ------------
          TOTAL REVENUE                                                                 77334.78

5         Total Expenses                                                                39388.62
51           Cost of Goods Sold                                            19520.00
5101            COGS Dept. 01                                 12070.00
5102            COGS Dept. 02                                 7450.00
52           Gen & Admin Expenses                                          19868.62
5201            Payroll                                       1200.00
52011              Wages                          1200.00
520118                Contract Labor   1200.00
5202            Maintenance                                   500.00
52025              Building                        500.00
5203            Depreciation                                  2000.00
52032              Furniture & Fixtures           2000.00
5205            Rents and Leases                              750.00
52055              Building                        750.00
5207            Travel & Entertain                            326.87
52072              Transportation                 326.87
5208            Shipping                                      76.30
52081              Freight                         76.30
5209            Taxes (other)                                 1672.82
52091              Sales Tax/Purchases            1672.82
5210            Consulting Fees                               543.00
52102              Legal                           543.00
5214            Utilities                                     453.92
5219            Advertising                                   3500.12
52191              Broadcast Advert.              3500.12
5220            Promotion                                     1300.52
52201              Catalogues                     1300.52
5221            Public Relations                              4700.00
5222            Marketing Research                            2845.07

                                                                                       ------------
          NET INCOME                                                                    37946.16
```

Fig. 11.23

The income statement.

Date : 08/07/88
Time : 07:09 AM

Acme Marbles Company
512 Wetmore Street
Seattle, Wa 98114
Tel: (206) 555-1234 Fax: (206) 555-6789

Page no. 1

STATEMENT OF CHANGES IN FINANCIAL CONDITIONS

Acct #	Account Name	Last Yr - Yr. Bef. Last Sources	Uses	This Yr. - Last Yr. Sources	Uses	Current Period Sources	Uses
1	Assets		0.00		137216.62		137216.62
11	Current Assets		0.00		119216.62		119216.62
1102	Cash In Banks		0.00		35167.48		35167.48
11021	Checking Account		0.00		25167.48		25167.48
11023	Savings Account		0.00		10000.00		10000.00
1105	Accounts Receivable		0.00		82951.64		82951.64
11051	Accts Rec'ble Module		0.00		82951.64		82951.64
1107	Inventory		0.00		1097.50		1097.50
11071	Inventory - Module		0.00		1097.50		1097.50
12	Fixed Assets		0.00		18000.00		18000.00
1202	Furniture & Fixt.Net		0.00		18000.00		18000.00
12021	Original Value		0.00		20000.00		20000.00
12022	Accum. Depreciation		0.00	2000.00		2000.00	
2	Liabilities		0.00	89270.46		89270.46	
21	Short Term Liability		0.00	34270.46		34270.46	
2101	Accts Payable-Module		0.00	29216.06		29216.06	
2104	Taxes Payable		0.00	5054.40		5054.40	
21042	Sales Tax Payable		0.00	5054.40		5054.40	
22	Long Term Liability		0.00	55000.00		55000.00	
2201	Mortgages Payable		0.00	55000.00		55000.00	
3	Stockholders Equity		0.00	10000.00		10000.00	
31	Capital Stock		0.00	10000.00		10000.00	
3101	Common Stock		0.00	10000.00		10000.00	
31011	Par Value		0.00	1000.00		1000.00	
31012	Surplus		0.00	9000.00		9000.00	
4	Revenues		0.00	77334.78		77334.78	
41	Sales		0.00	77334.78		77334.78	
4101	Sales Dept. 01		0.00	44834.78		44834.78	
4102	Sales Dept. 02		0.00	32500.00		32500.00	
5	Total Expenses		0.00		39388.62		39388.62
51	Cost of Goods Sold		0.00		19520.00		19520.00
5101	COGS Dept. 01		0.00		12070.00		12070.00
5102	COGS Dept. 02		0.00		7450.00		7450.00
52	Gen & Admin Expenses		0.00		19868.62		19868.62
5201	Payroll		0.00		1200.00		1200.00
52011	Wages		0.00		1200.00		1200.00
520118	Contract Labor		0.00		1200.00		1200.00
5202	Maintenance		0.00		500.00		500.00
52025	Building		0.00		500.00		500.00
5203	Depreciation		0.00		2000.00		2000.00
52032	Furniture & Fixtures		0.00		2000.00		2000.00
5205	Rents and Leases		0.00		750.00		750.00
52055	Building		0.00		750.00		750.00
5207	Travel & Entertain		0.00		326.87		326.87
52072	Transportation		0.00		326.87		326.87
5208	Shipping		0.00		76.30		76.30
52081	Freight		0.00		76.30		76.30
5209	Taxes (other)		0.00		1672.82		1672.82
52091	Sales Tax/Purchases		0.00		1672.82		1672.82
5210	Consulting Fees		0.00		543.00		543.00
52102	Legal		0.00		543.00		543.00

Fig. 11.24

The statement of changes in financial conditions.

```
Date : 08/07/88                          Acme Marbles Company                      Page no. 2
Time : 07:09 AM                            512 Wetmore Street
                                           Seattle, Wa 98114
                              Tel: (206) 555-1234 Fax: (206) 555-6789

                        STATEMENT OF CHANGES IN FINANCIAL CONDITIONS

                          Last Yr - Yr. Bef. Last   This Yr. - Last Yr.     Current Period
   Acct #   Account Name      Sources     Uses       Sources      Uses      Sources      Uses
   ------   ------------   -----------  --------    ----------  ---------   ----------  ---------
   5214     Utilities                     0.00                   453.92                 453.92
   5219     Advertising                   0.00                  3500.12                3500.12
   52191      Broadcast Advert.           0.00                  3500.12                3500.12
   5220     Promotion                     0.00                  1300.52                1300.52
   52201      Catalogues                  0.00                  1300.52                1300.52
   5221     Public Relations              0.00                  4700.00                4700.00
   5222     Marketing Research            0.00                  2845.07                2845.07

          Totals :           ==========  ========    ==========  =========   ==========  =========
                              0.00        0.00      176605.24  176605.24   176605.24  176605.24
```

Fig. 11.24-Continued

You'll find this report particularly helpful when you want to look at the total increase or decrease in cash stemming from changes in an account. For example, on figure 11.24, you can look down the list of accounts to account 11071, Inventory. This account is listed as a use of cash amounting to $1,097.50, meaning that the changes in the inventory account over the period resulted in $1,097.50 of cash being used.

Creating Custom Reports

DacEasy provides a powerful feature that you usually see only in expensive accounting systems running on larger computers: a *report writer* you can use to design and print customized financial statements. You can use the Chart of Accounts and the account balances it collects as the foundation for custom-tailored financial statements, or accounting reports, that more closely meet your information needs. You may not ever use this feature, because it involves learning computer programming conventions, which requires some time and can be a challenge. But if you want financial statements that follow a special format, and you think writing a simple computer program to generate your own custom-designed financial statements sounds like fun, you can use the report writer to your advantage.

Figure 11.25 shows the two options that appear when you choose Financial Statements Generator from the Financials menu. You use the first option, Edit Financial Reports, to create the specifications for a new custom financial statement. The second option allows you to print your custom statements. When you select the Edit Financial Reports option, the screen shown in figure 11.26 appears.

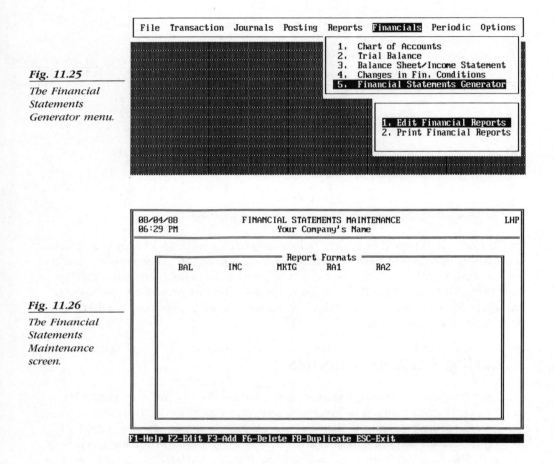

Fig. 11.25

The Financial Statements Generator menu.

Fig. 11.26

The Financial Statements Maintenance screen.

The Financial Statements Maintenance screen lists the names of the four sample custom report formats provided by DacEasy and any custom formats you've already created. With your system, DacEasy provides four reports, based on the sample Chart of Accounts: a balance sheet (BAL), an income statement (INC), and two reports that calculate several financial ratios (RA1 and RA2). See Appendix B for examples and descriptions of these sample report formats.

To begin defining a new custom format report, press F3. Or to use one of the existing report formats as the basis of the new report you're creating, use the arrow keys to move the cursor to one of the previously defined report formats and then press F8. When you press F3, the screen shown in figure 11.27 appears.

```
08/07/88                                                              LHP
07:17 AM                      Acme Marbles Company

  Enter Report Name :  ▓▓▓

  Print                              Amount Amount To       Lines
  (Y/N) Acct.# Description           From     1  2  3   %   99=pg.
  ─────  ─────  ──────────────       ─────                   ─────
```

F1-Help ALT I-Insert ALT D-Delete ALT P-Print F10-Process ESC-exit

Fig. 11.27

The custom report definition screen.

You need to complete several steps to define a report format. Take a look at figure 11.28. These headings automatically appear on any custom-tailored report format. You must tell DacEasy what information you want added. As you build the report, keep in mind that DacEasy offers three Alt-key combinations that can help you:

Alt-I   Inserts a line into the report format immediately above the line on which the cursor rests

Alt-D   Deletes the report format line on which the cursor rests

Alt-P   Prints the report format on which you're working

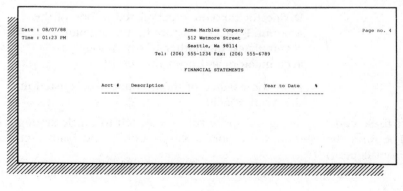

```
Date : 08/07/88              Acme Marbles Company              Page no. 4
Time : 01:23 PM               512 Wetmore Street
                              Seattle, Wa 98114
                      Tel: (206) 555-1234 Fax: (206) 555-6789

                             FINANCIAL STATEMENTS

          Acct #   Description                    Year to Date    %
          ──────   ────────────────────          ──────────── ───────
```

Fig. 11.28

The custom report headings.

The following paragraphs describe each of the fields you use to add information to the report.

Enter Report Name: The first item you define is the report name. You can use up to four alphanumeric characters to name a report format. Suppose that you're creating a special report that just shows marketing expenses. You might name the report *MKTG*.

Print (Y/N): A custom report format pulls account balances from the Chart of Accounts and then displays these account balances on a report, includes them in some calculation, or both displays and includes the balances in some calculation. For those account balances you want to display, set the Print (Y/N) field to *Y*. For those you don't want to display, set the code to *N*.

Acct. #: For every account balance you want to display on the report or include in a calculation, you must specify an account number. DacEasy prints accounts and includes them in calculations in the order in which you list them on this screen. To include blank lines or descriptions in your report, leave the Acct. # field blank.

Description: The Description field is a 20-character field you can use to describe the parts of the report. Typically, you might use this field to describe the account balance or the total amount that will appear to the right of the description text.

Amount From: You use the Amount From field to tell the report writer where to get the dollars-and-cents information that should be printed on the line you're defining. Here's a list of the Amount From codes and how they affect what prints on the report:

Amount From Code	Instructs Program To
0	Print the text only (no account balance)
1, 2, or 3	Print the amount accumulated in the Amount To 1, 2, or 3 accumulator
/	Divide the amount accumulated in one of the Amount To accumulators by the amount accumulated in another of the Amount To accumulators and print the result
99	Print the balance of the account that is listed in the Acct. # field

You select these codes by using the space bar as a switch to toggle among the choices. For lines that should show only a description or be blank, set the Amount From code to 0.

Amount To 1, 2, 3, %: These four fields are called the accumulator registers. Each accumulator acts as a memory stack from and to which you can add and subtract. The first column is labeled 1, the second is 2, the third is 3, and the special fourth register is labeled %.

You use the space bar to toggle through the five possible values for an accumulator column: +, −, 0, N, or D. By specifying a plus sign (+) in the accumulator column for a specific account, you tell DacEasy to add the balance in that account to the accumulator. By specifying a minus sign (−), you tell DacEasy to subtract the balance in that account from the accumulator. If you want to zero out, or clear, an accumulator at some point in the report, put a zero (0) in the accumulator column or columns on the line in the report where you want the accumulator zeroed.

If you used the / code in the Amount From field, you need to indicate in the Amount To field what you want DacEasy to use as the numerator and denominator. Use *N* in the accumulator column for the account that holds the numerator for the calculation, and use *D* for the account that holds the denominator. DacEasy then divides the N value by the D value and prints that amount on the line.

The Amount To % accumulator field is a special accumulator column. You use it to calculate a total amount for which you can show other amounts printed on the report as percentages. For example, if you want to create a simple list of marketing expenses and show each of these expenses as a percent of the total sales, you can calculate the total sales in the Amount To % accumulator column. The second column that appears on every report shows the percentage of the amount accumulated in the Amount To % accumulator column that each individual line amount represents. (If you're still a little unsure of how the Amount To fields work, see the marketing expense example that is described in subsequent paragraphs.)

Lines 99 = pg.: This field allows you to do several things, including specifying page breaks, line spacing, and the placement of dividing lines and double dividing lines on a report. Here are the entries you can make in this field and their results in your report:

Lines Code	Instructs Program To
−	Print a single row of lines under the dollar amount and percentage columns below the line for which the underlining is specified
=	Print a double row of lines, using the equal sign, under the dollar amount and percentage columns below the line for which the underlining is specified

C	Center the text contained in the Description field
1	Single-space the report
2	Double-space the report
99	Skip to new page (enter page break)

With these six codes, you can create either a simple or a complex report. To continue the preceding example, suppose that you want to produce a report that lists marketing expenses. Looking through your Chart of Accounts, you can identify four marketing level 4 expense accounts. (Note that these accounts are detail, not general, accounts.) By listing the four accounts in the order you want them to appear and setting the Print (Y/N) flag to Y, you've defined a simple report format that lists these accounts and their balances. You may notice that for accounts, DacEasy fills the Description field with the account name from the general ledger. You can edit this field, however, if you want a different description of an amount. Figure 11.29 shows the report format definition screen completed to print the report shown in figure 11.30.

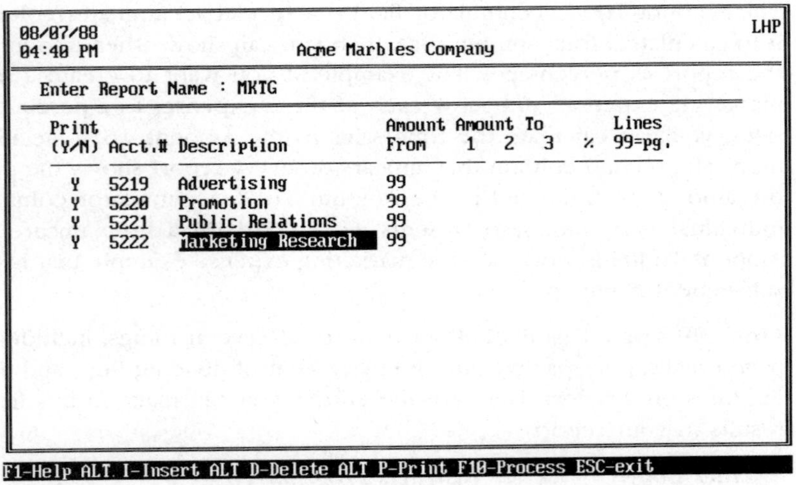

Fig. 11.29

A simple report format that lists marketing expenses.

```
08/07/88                                                           LHP
04:40 PM                    Acme Marbles Company

   Enter Report Name : MKTG

   Print                         Amount Amount To        Lines
   (Y/N) Acct.# Description       From    1  2  3  %    99=pg.
          Y    5219  Advertising          99
          Y    5220  Promotion            99
          Y    5221  Public Relations     99
          Y    5222  Marketing Research   99




F1-Help ALT I-Insert ALT D-Delete ALT P-Print F10-Process ESC-exit
```

```
Date : 08/07/88                          Acme Marbles Company                    Page no. 1
Time : 02:22 PM                           512 Wetmore Street
                                          Seattle, Wa 98114
                              Tel: (206) 555-1234 Fax: (206) 555-6789

                                       FINANCIAL STATEMENTS


                  Acct #    Description                    Year to Date      #
                  ------    --------------------           --------------  -------


                  5219      Advertising                      3,500.12
                  5220      Promotion                        1,300.52
                  5221      Public Relations                 4,700.00
                  5222      Marketing Research               2,845.07
```

Fig. 11.30

A simple report that lists marketing expenses.

Although you might have use for such a simple report, you can easily amass a total by using the Amount To 1 column. To sum the four marketing expenses and then include a line that totals these four expenses, you can modify the format as shown in figure 11.31. Figure 11.32 shows how the report looks after the modification.

```
08/07/88                                                              LHP
04:40 PM                    Acme Marbles Company

  Enter Report Name : MKTG

  Print                           Amount Amount To        Lines
  (Y/N) Acct.# Description        From   1   2   3   %    99=pg.
        Y   5219  Advertising        99     +
        Y   5220  Promotion          99     +
        Y   5221  Public Relations   99     +
        Y   5222  Marketing Research 99     +
        Y         Total Marketing     1




F1-Help ALT I-Insert ALT D-Delete ALT P-Print F10-Process ESC-exit
```

Fig. 11.31

A report format that lists and totals marketing expenses.

Fig. 11.32

A report that lists and totals marketing expenses.

The report, with this enhancement, probably begins to have real value, but you can add even more improvements. For example, you can show what percentage of total sales each of the marketing expenses represents, by adding the first two lines shown on the report format definition in figure 11.33 and accumulating the total in the Amount To % column. You can also easily add underlining and double-underlining to improve the report's readability. Figure 11.34 shows the resulting report. Remember that by using an *N* in the Print (Y/N) column for the total sales figures (see fig. 11.33), the base that accumulates to calculate the percentages is not printed.

Fig. 11.33

A report format that lists and totals marketing expenses and shows what percentage of sales each marketing expense represents.

At this point, you've created a rather sophisticated report that allows you to monitor a special category of expenses. But you can make even more additions

```
Date : 08/07/88                          Acme Marbles Company                    Page no. 1
Time : 02:16 PM                           512 Wetmore Street
                                          Seattle, Wa 98114
                              Tel: (206) 555-1234 Fax: (206) 555-6789

                                         FINANCIAL STATEMENTS

              Acct #   Description                    Year to Date      %
              ------   --------------------           --------------  ------

               5219    Advertising                        3,500.12     4.5
               5220    Promotion                          1,300.52     1.7
               5221    Public Relations                   4,700.00     6.1
               5222    Marketing Research                 2,845.07     3.7
                                                     --------------  ------

                       Total Marketing                   12,345.71    16.0
                                                     --------------  ------
```

Fig. 11.34

A report that lists and totals marketing expenses and shows what percentage of sales each marketing expense represents.

to this custom-tailored report. Suppose that you believe you can gain some insight into your firm's marketing activities by looking at the ratio of advertising expenses to total marketing expenses. By using the Amount To 2 accumulator column to store the advertising expenses, placing a / code in the Amount From field for the marketing ratio, and adding the extra lines shown in figure 11.35, you can produce a report like the one shown in figure 11.36.

```
08/07/88                                                                    LHP
04:40 PM                    Acme Marbles Company

    Enter Report Name : MKTG

 Print                              Amount  Amount To        Lines
 (Y/N) Acct.# Description           From    1    2    3   %  99=pg.

    N   4101   Sales Dept. 01         99                  +
    N   4102   Sales Dept. 02         99                  +
    Y   5219   Advertising            99     +    +
    Y   5220   Promotion              99     +
    Y   5221   Public Relations       99     +
    Y   5222   Marketing Research     99     +              -
    Y          Total Marketing         1                   =
    Y          ******************* 0
    Y          Advertising to Total 0
    Y          Marketing Ratio        /     D    N         =
    Y          ******************* 0

F1-Help ALT I-Insert ALT D-Delete ALT P-Print F10-Process ESC-exit
```

Fig. 11.35

A report format that adds a financial ratio to the report on marketing expenses.

```
Date : 08/07/88                          Acme Marbles Company                      Page no. 1
Time : 02:02 PM                           512 Wetmore Street
                                         Seattle, Wa 98114
                              Tel: (206) 555-1234 Fax: (206) 555-6789

                                        FINANCIAL STATEMENTS

              Acct #   Description                      Year to Date      %
              ------   -----------------------          ------------    ------

              5219     Advertising                         3,500.12       4.5
              5220     Promotion                           1,300.52       1.7
              5221     Public Relations                    4,700.00       6.1
              5222     Marketing Research                  2,845.07       3.7
                                                         ------------    ------
                       Total Marketing                    12,345.71      16.0
                                                         ------------    ------
              *********************
              Advertising to Total
              Marketing Ratio                                 0.28
                                                         ------------    ------
              *********************
```

Fig. 11.36

A report that includes a financial ratio.

Printing Custom Reports

To print your custom reports, you use the second option on the Financial Statements Generator menu: Print Financial Reports. When you select this option, a screen similar to the one shown in figure 11.37 appears. To select the report for printing, move the cursor to each of the report formats you want to print, and press F2. Note that an asterisk appears beside the format name when you press F2 on that name. To "unmark" a report, press F3. Once you've marked all the reports you want to print, press F10.

After you press F10, two pop-up windows appear. The first asks whether you want to see year-to-date amounts, both year-to-date and last-year amounts, or year-to-date and budgeted amounts. You select one of these three by toggling to your choice with the space bar.

The second pop-up window asks whether you want to include the account numbers on your report. Press either *Y* for yes or *N* for no.

Chapter Summary

This chapter described the steps for using the general ledger menu options, correcting any mistakes you make when using the data entry screens, using the

```
08/07/88              PRINT FINANCIAL STATEMENTS                    LHP
07:56 AM                  Acme Marbles Company

            ┌──────────────── Report Formats ────────────────┐
            │   BAL  *    INC  *    MKTG    RA1  *    RA2  *   │
            │                                                 │
            │                                                 │
            │                                                 │
            │                                                 │
            │                                                 │
            │                                                 │
            │                                                 │
            │                                                 │
            │                                                 │
            │                                                 │
            │                                                 │
            └─────────────────────────────────────────────────┘
 F1-Help F2-Select F3-Unselect F10-Print Statements ESC-Exit
```

Fig. 11.37

The custom financial statement report request screen.

reports generated by these options, posting general ledger transactions to the Chart of Accounts, and printing standard and custom-tailored financial statements.

Using the Periodic Routines

This final chapter describes the menu options available for running periodic routines and printing forecasting reports for the General Ledger, Accounts Receivable, Accounts Payable, and Inventory modules. All these options, which you access from the Periodic menu (see fig. 12.1), operate almost identically.

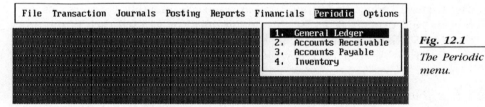

File Transaction Journals Posting Reports Financials Periodic Options

1.	General Ledger
2.	Accounts Receivable
3.	Accounts Payable
4.	Inventory

Fig. 12.1

The Periodic menu.

Before I even begin discussing the periodic routines, I want to issue three important warnings, which cannot be stressed enough:

1. Run all forecasting procedures first. If you run year-end closing routines before asking DacEasy to calculate forecasts, you lose all the information needed to generate the forecasts.

2. Be sure to produce all the reports you need for audit trails before you run either the monthly or annual closing routines.

3. Although this chapter discusses the periodic routines in the order in which they appear on the Periodic menu, you need to run the accounts receivable, accounts payable, and inventory routines before you run the routines for the general ledger. If you don't take care of those routines first, your general ledger will not include accounts receivable, accounts payable, and inventory activity.

289

Using the Periodic General Ledger Options

When you choose the Periodic General Ledger option, DacEasy displays the menu shown in figure 12.2. You can choose either End Month, End Year, or Forecasting.

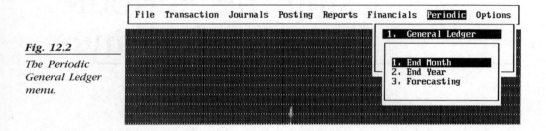

Fig. 12.2

The Periodic General Ledger menu.

Running the End-of-Month Routine

The General Ledger End Month option resets the monthly counters that tally revenue and expense. You use this option *after* you've used each of the other three End Month options—Accounts Receivable, Accounts Payable, and Inventory—and *before* you post new general ledger transactions to the Chart of Accounts.

When you choose End Month, a warning screen like the one in figure 12.3 appears to tell you that you should post all transactions, print all reports, and back up your files before running the periodic routine. If you want to continue with the routine, press *Y*. DacEasy then resets all the monthly counters to 0. If you've forgotten to do something and want to exit from the routine, press *N*.

Running the End-of-Year Routine

The General Ledger End Year option closes, or zeros out, the current year's revenue and expense accounts and adds the result, representing either a profit or loss, to the owner's equity account. Before you run the general ledger end-of-year routine, you should run each of the other modules' end-of-year routines, the general ledger's end-of-month routine for the last month of the accounting

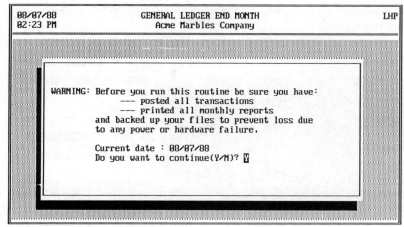

```
08/07/88                    GENERAL LEDGER END MONTH              LHP
02:23 PM                      Acme Marbles Company



      WARNING: Before you run this routine be sure you have:
                --- posted all transactions
                --- printed all monthly reports
              and backed up your files to prevent loss due
              to any power or hardware failure.

              Current date : 08/07/88
              Do you want to continue(Y/N)? Y




F1-Help ESC-Exit
```

Fig. 12.3

The warning you see before running the general ledger end-of-month routine.

year, and any forecasts. You should also print your audit trails and the annual financial statements before you select this option.

As with the End Month option, choosing the End Year option displays a warning screen that reminds you to complete and post all bookkeeping transactions for the year you are, in effect, telling the system you've completed. After you press *Y* to confirm that you want to continue with the routine, DacEasy asks to which capital or equity account you want to post the current year's profit or loss. If you're using the DacEasy sample Chart of Accounts, type *33* in response to the Current Year Profit/Loss prompt. When a new accounting year begins, you move the balance in this Current Year Profit/Loss account to retained earnings by debiting Current Year Profit/Loss and crediting Retained Earnings for the year's profit or loss.

Additionally, you may remember that the Chart of Accounts keeps not only the current year's account balances but also the account balances for the preceding year and the year before the preceding year. When you run the general ledger end-of-year routine, the preceding year's balance is moved to the balance for the year before the preceding year, the current year's balance is moved to the preceding year's balance, and the current year's balance is zeroed.

Forecasting for the Chart of Accounts

The General Ledger Forecasting option calculates budgeted or forecasted amounts for the Chart of Accounts (using one of four forecasting methods) and prints reports on these forecasts. Figure 12.4 shows the Periodic General Ledger Forecasting menu with its three options: Automatic Calculations, Print Forecast, and Print Statistical YTD.

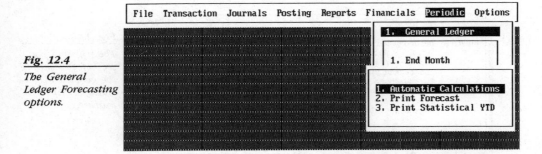

File   Transaction   Journals   Posting   Reports   Financials   Periodic   Options

Fig. 12.4

The General Ledger Forecasting options.

(Remember that to have DacEasy generate a forecast for the next year, you need to retain the current year's balances. If you close the year and then ask DacEasy to calculate the forecast, the program has no current information from which to make the calculation.)

Using Automatic Calculations for Forecasts

The first option, Automatic Calculations, allows you to select one of four methods for DacEasy to use to forecast account balances for the coming year. Figure 12.5 shows the four available automatic calculation methods as they are listed on the General Ledger Forecast Calculation screen. (This screen displays after you choose the Automatic Calculations option.) You don't have to use one of these methods to enter forecast amounts. In fact, you can enter a forecast amount for each Chart of Accounts account number individually. If you find that any of the automatic calculation options closely matches any of your budgeting assumptions, however, you'll find DacEasy's automatic forecasting a great help. The four forecasting methods are described in the following paragraphs.

Previous Year: You may decide to forecast the coming year's account balance as simply the current year's balance. For example, if sales for the current year total $250,000, you can select this method to forecast the coming year's sales as $250,000.

Previous Year +/− **Pct:** You may decide to forecast the coming year's account balance as the current year's balance increased or decreased by some percentage. For example, suppose that sales for the current year total $250,000, and you think sales will increase by 10 percent in the coming year. You can select this method and specify the percentage change as + *10* to forecast the coming year's sales as $275,000 ($250,000 plus 10 percent).

```
┌──────────────────────────────────────────────────────────────┐
│ 08/07/88              GL Forecast Calculation            LHP   │
│ 02:28 PM ·              Acme Marbles Company                   │
│ ┌────────────────────────────────────────────────────────────┐│
│ │                                                            ││
│ │                                                            ││
│ │   Calculation Method :        Sorted by : Account number   ││
│ │                                                            ││
│ │   1  Previous Year                                         ││
│ │   2  Previous Year +/- Pct                                 ││
│ │   3  Previous Year + Trend                                 ││
│ │   4  Trend Line Analysis                                   ││
│ │                                                            ││
│ │   Enter Your Selection :  ■                                ││
│ │                                                            ││
│ │                                                            ││
│ │                                                            ││
│ │                                                            ││
│ │                                                            ││
│ └────────────────────────────────────────────────────────────┘│
└──────────────────────────────────────────────────────────────┘
```

Fig. 12.5

Selecting the automatic calculation method for forecasting.

Previous Year + Trend: You may decide to forecast the change from the current year's balance as equal to the same percentage that the current year changed from the preceding year. For example, if an expense account totaled $10,000 for last year, and $11,000 for the current year, this method calculates that the $1,000 change amounts to a 10 percent change (calculated as the $1,000 change divided by the $10,000 amount). The forecast amount, therefore, is the current year's amount plus 10 percent, which equals $12,100.

Obviously, you need two years of data to calculate forecasts with this method. Additionally, this method will not calculate a forecast equal to a percentage change of less then 0. If the change from the last year to the current year is less than 0 percent, DacEasy forecasts the coming year as equal to the current year.

Trend Line Analysis: You can use this method only if you've collected three years of data. The trend line analysis method uses a statistical forecasting tool called the *least squares method* to plot a line that best fits the three years of data you already have. Figure 12.6 shows a simple line graph with a straight line representing the best fitting line, given the three data points. The least squares method fits a straight line that minimizes the variances between the actual data points and the line.

To calculate the fourth year's amount, or the forecast, the program extends the straight line calculated by the least squares method. Figure 12.7 extends the straight line drawn in figure 12.7 to the fourth data point, the forecast. The dashes show the portion of the straight line that is being extended.

Once you select an automatic calculation method, you need to specify the range of accounts to which the automatic calculation should be applied. For the

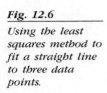

Fig. 12.6

Using the least squares method to fit a straight line to three data points.

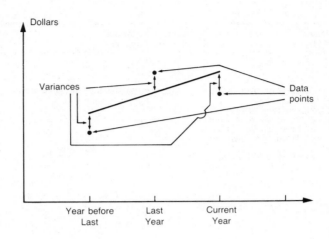

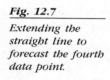

Fig. 12.7

Extending the straight line to forecast the fourth data point.

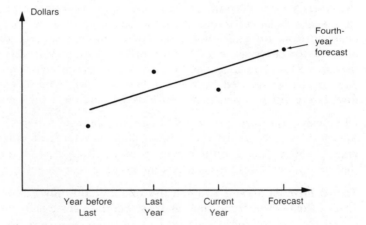

Previous Year +/− Pct method, you also must specify the percentage change. Figure 12.8 shows the screen you complete to specify the range of accounts to which an automatic calculation method should be applied and, for the Previous Year +/− Pct method, a percentage change. (DacEasy automatically completes the Sorted by field.) The capability to limit the accounts to which an automatic calculation is applied provides you with a high degree of flexibility in developing forecasts of various account balances.

DacEasy then moves from account to account in the Chart of Accounts, calculating the forecast amounts. The program informs you as it calculates the forecast for each account (see fig. 12.9).

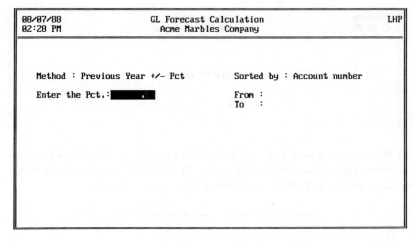

```
08/07/88                    GL Forecast Calculation                    LHP
02:28 PM                      Acme Marbles Company



   Method : Previous Year +/- Pct        Sorted by : Account number

   Enter the Pct.:█        .            From :
                                        To   :
```

Fig. 12.8

Specifying the percentage increase and the range of accounts.

```
09/30/88                    GL Forecast Calculation                    LHP
05:40 AM                      ACME MARBLE COMPANY

       Please wait while calculating.............

                    Account....: 12041

                    Yr Bef Last:           0.00
                    Last Year..:           0.00
                    YTD........:           0.00
                    Forecast...:           0.00
```

Fig. 12.9

DacEasy's message while calculating the forecast for an account.

Printing the Forecast

After you've instructed DacEasy to generate forecasts, you can print the general ledger forecast by choosing option 2, Print Forecast, from the Periodic General Ledger Forecasting menu. A report request screen like the one shown in figure 12.10 appears. When you specify the range of accounts, the program generates the Yr. Bef. Last, Last Year, This Year, and Forecast amounts and the variance—both in dollars and as a percentage—between the This Year and Forecast amounts.

```
08/07/88                    GL Forecast Report                        LHP
02:45 PM                    Acme Marbles Company


                      Sorted by : Account number

                      From : 5219
                      To   : 52202
```

Fig. 12.10

The report request screen for the general ledger forecast.

Figure 12.11 shows an example of the general ledger forecast generated with the Print Forecast option. On this example, the Yr. Bef. Last and Last Year fields are zero because only one year of accounting data was entered.

```
Date : 08/07/88                        Acme Marbles Company                    Page no. 1
Time : 12:43 PM                          512 Wetmore Street
                                        Seattle, Wa 98114
                            Tel: (206) 555-1234 Fax: (206) 555-6789

                               General  Ledger  Forecast
Account    Description               Yr.Bef.Last  Last Year  This Year   Forecast   Variance     %
--------   -----------------------   ----------   ---------  ---------   --------   --------   -----
5219       Advertising                     0.00       0.00    3500.12    3850.13     350.01     10
52191      Broadcast Advert.               0.00       0.00    3500.12    3850.13     350.01     10
52192      Print Advertising               0.00       0.00       0.00       0.00       0.00      0
5220       Promotion                       0.00       0.00    1300.52    1430.57     130.05     10
52201      Catalogues                      0.00       0.00    1300.52    1430.57     130.05     10
52202      Brochures                       0.00       0.00       0.00       0.00       0.00      0
52203      Other Promotions                0.00       0.00       0.00       0.00       0.00      0
```

Fig. 12.11

The general ledger forecast report.

Printing the Statistical YTD

With the third option on the Forecasting menu, Print Statistical YTD, you can print the general ledger statistical YTD report. The request screen for this report matches the one for the general ledger forecast. You specify a range of accounts for which you want to see a report. Figure 12.12 shows an example of the general ledger statistical YTD for the same range of accounts included in the general ledger forecast in figure 12.11.

```
Date : 08/07/88                        Acme Marbles Company                    Page no. 1
Time : 12:50 PM                          512 Wetmore Street
                                        Seattle, Wa 98114
                            Tel: (206) 555-1234 Fax: (206) 555-6789

                            General  Ledger  Statistical  YTD
Account    Description               Yr.Bef.Last  Last Year  This Year   Forecast   Variance     %
--------   -----------------------   ----------   ---------  ---------   --------   --------   -----
5219       Advertising                     0.00       0.00    3500.12    3850.13    -350.01     -9
52191      Broadcast Advert.               0.00       0.00    3500.12    3850.13    -350.01     -9
52192      Print Advertising               0.00       0.00       0.00       0.00       0.00      0
5220       Promotion                       0.00       0.00    1300.52    1430.57    -130.05     -9
52201      Catalogues                      0.00       0.00    1300.52    1430.57    -130.05     -9
52202      Brochures                       0.00       0.00       0.00       0.00       0.00      0
```

Fig. 12.12

The general ledger statistical YTD report.

The only difference between these two reports is the method of calculating the variance. The general ledger forecast calculates the variances from the This Year amount, and the general ledger statistical YTD bases the variance calculations on the Forecast amount. The difference amounts to only a simple change in perspective.

Using the Periodic Accounts Receivable Options

When you choose the Periodic Accounts Receivable option, DacEasy displays the menu shown in figure 12.13. You can choose either End Month, End Year, Forecasting, or Generate Fin. Chgs.

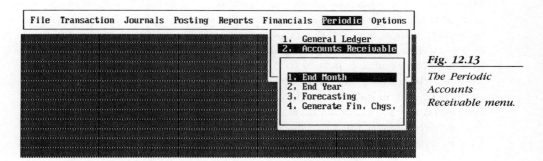

Fig. 12.13

The Periodic Accounts Receivable menu.

Running the End-of-Month Routine

You use the accounts receivable end-of-month routine to clean the open customer invoices list in the DacEasy system. Because you lose detail about customer invoices when you complete the end-of-month routine, you must print any end-of-period reports you need for audit trails—and should also back up your files—*before* you select the End Month option.

The accounts receivable end-of-month routine is like the monthly routine for the general ledger. When you choose End Month, a warning screen identical to the general ledger warning screen appears; you press *Y* to continue, and DacEasy cleans the accounts receivable files by removing customer invoice details. As with the general ledger end-of-month routine, with the accounts receivable routine you can limit the customers to whom the End Month option is applied. You simply press the up arrow while you're on the warning screen and then specify a range of customers (identified by code) to which the end-of-month routine should be run.

The method DacEasy uses to clean the list depends on which invoice method you selected when setting up a customer: balance forward or open invoice. If you're using the balance forward method, running the accounts receivable end-of-month routine sums all the invoices owed by the customer and subtracts any credit memos and unapplied payments to get the total amount owed by the customer. This total then becomes the new balance forward. All the details that supports the calculation of this balance forward—invoices, debit and credit memos, and payments—are deleted. If you're using the open invoice method, DacEasy removes only paid invoices from the list of open customer invoices.

Running the End-of-Year Routine

The operation and purpose of the Accounts Receivable End Year option are the same as those of the General Ledger End Year version, except that the accounts receivable option acts on the customer master file rather than the Chart of Accounts. The Last Year balance is moved to the Year Before Last balance, the Current Year balance is moved to the Last Year balance, and the Current Year amount field is changed to zero so that the field can begin tallying the current year's data. As you did with the general ledger, you want to run any forecasting before you run the accounts receivable end-of-year routine, because the end-of-year program resets the Current Year balance to zero, and you may lose the Year Before Last amounts.

Forecasting Accounts Receivable Activity

Similar to the general ledger's Forecasting options, the options on the Accounts Receivable Forecasting menu allow you to forecast accounts receivable activity, using one of the four automatic calculation methods: Previous Year, Previous Year +/− Pct, Previous Year + Trend, and Trend Line Analysis. Figure 12.14 shows the screen you use to select an automatic calculation method for forecasting.

You can also limit the effect of your forecast. After you choose the calculation method, you can select the customers, revenue/cost departments, or salespersons to which DacEasy should apply the forecast calculation. You have three fields you can use to limit the forecast. First, you specify the sorting order in the Sorted By field on the AR Forecast Calculation screen. DacEasy then asks you to indicate in the From and To fields the range of customers you want

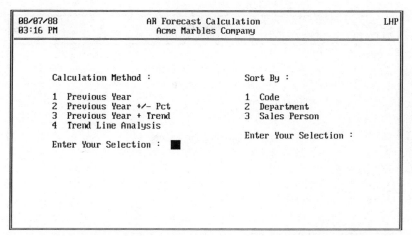

```
08/07/88                    AR Forecast Calculation                    LHP
03:16 PM                     Acme Marbles Company


        Calculation Method :              Sort By :

        1  Previous Year                  1  Code
        2  Previous Year +/- Pct          2  Department
        3  Previous Year + Trend          3  Sales Person
        4  Trend Line Analysis
                                          Enter Your Selection :
        Enter Your Selection :  █
```

Fig. 12.14

Selecting the automatic calculation method and the customers for whom forecasts will be calculated.

forecast. For example, if you choose to sort by *code*, as shown in figure 12.15, you need to indicate the From and To *codes*.

```
09/30/88                    AR Forecast Calculation                    LHP
06:07 AM                     ACME MARBLE COMPANY


        Method : Previous Year            Sorted By : Code

                                          From :  ████
                                          To   :
```

Fig. 12.15

Specifying the range of customers for whom forecasts will be calculated.

The reports generated by the Print Forecast and Print Statistical YTD options on the Accounts Receivable Forecasting menu look similar to the reports generated by the same general ledger options. Figure 12.16 shows the report request screen on which you select the sort order for each report. DacEasy then gives you the opportunity to limit the customers printed. (Your range of customers can be different from the range you specified when calculating forecasts.)

Figure 12.17 shows an example of an accounts receivable forecast, and figure 12.18 shows a sample accounts receivable statistical YTD report. As with the

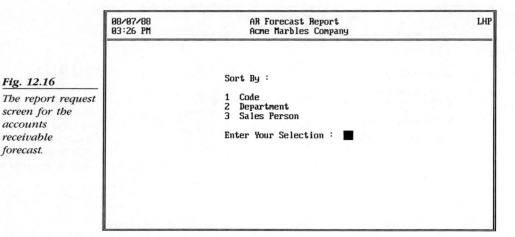

```
08/07/88                    AR Forecast Report                        LHP
03:26 PM                    Acme Marbles Company


                        Sort By :

                        1  Code
                        2  Department
                        3  Sales Person

                        Enter Your Selection :  ■
```

Fig. 12.16

The report request screen for the accounts receivable forecast.

general ledger, the only difference between these two reports is that the accounts receivable forecast calculates the dollar and percentage variances with the This Year amount as the benchmark, and the accounts receivable statistical YTD calculates the variances with the Forecast amount as the benchmark. On both accounts receivable reports, you have the option of including the costs and profits.

```
Date : 08/07/88                        Acme Marbles Company                      Page no. 1
Time : 12:59 PM                         512 Wetmore Street
                                        Seattle, Wa 98114
                            Tel: (206) 555-1234 Fax: (206) 555-6789

                      A c c o u n t s   R e c e i v a b l e   F o r e c a s t
Sorted by: Code
Code         Name                        Yr.Bef.Last  Last Year  This Year  Forecast   Variance     %
------------ ------------------------    -----------  ---------  ---------  ---------  ---------  -----
C10          Columbus Glass Works, Inc.  # Invoices         0         0           7          8          1     14
                                         $ Sales            0         0       91026     100128       9102     10
                                         $ Costs            0         0       21147      23261       2114     10
                                         $ Profit           0         0       69879      76867       6988     10

K20          Kevin's House of Marbles    # Invoices         0         0           1          1          0      0
                                         $ Sales            0         0         375        412         37     10
                                         $ Costs            0         0           0          0          0      0
                                         $ Profit           0         0         375        412         37     10

S10          Specialty Products, Inc.    # Invoices         0         0           0          0          0      0
                                         $ Sales            0         0           0          0          0      0
                                         $ Costs            0         0           0          0          0      0
                                         $ Profit           0         0           0          0          0      0

Z10          Zebra Toys                  # Invoices         0         0           2          2          0      0
                                         $ Sales            0         0        1125       1237        112     10
                                         $ Costs            0         0           0          0          0      0
                                         $ Profit           0         0        1125       1237        112     10


             Grand Total                 # Invoices         0         0          10         11          1     10
                                         $ Sales            0         0       92526     101777       9251     10
                                         $ Costs            0         0       21147      23261       2114     10
                                         $ Profit           0         0       71379      78516       7137     10
```

Fig. 12.17

The accounts receivable forecast report.

```
Date : 08/07/88                          Acme Marbles Company                        Page no. 1
Time : 12:59 PM                            512 Wetmore Street
                                           Seattle, Wa 98114
                                Tel: (206) 555-1234 Fax: (206) 555-6789

                       A c c o u n t s   R e c e i v a b l e   S t a t i s t i c a l   Y T D
     Sorted by: Code
     Code           Name                        Yr.Bef.Last  Last Year  This Year  Forecast   Variance      %
     -------------- -----------------------------------------  ---------- ---------- ---------- ----------  -----
     C10            Columbus Glass Works, Inc.  # Invoices           0          0          7          8         -1    -12
                                                $ Sales              0          0      91026     100128      -9102     -8
                                                $ Costs              0          0      21147      23261      -2114     -8
                                                $ Profit             0          0      69879      76867      -6988     -8

     K20            Kevin's House of Marbles    # Invoices           0          0          1          1          0      0
                                                $ Sales              0          0        375        412        -37     -8
                                                $ Costs              0          0          0          0          0      0
                                                $ Profit             0          0        375        412        -37     -8

     S10            Specialty Products, Inc.    # Invoices           0          0          0          0          0      0
                                                $ Sales              0          0          0          0          0      0
                                                $ Costs              0          0          0          0          0      0
                                                $ Profit             0          0          0          0          0      0

     Z10            Zebra Toys                  # Invoices           0          0          2          2          0      0
                                                $ Sales              0          0       1125       1237       -112     -8
                                                $ Costs              0          0          0          0          0      0
                                                $ Profit             0          0       1125       1237       -112     -8


                    Grand Total                 # Invoices           0          0         10         11         -1     -8
                                                $ Sales              0          0      92526     101777      -9251     -8
                                                $ Costs              0          0      21147      23261      -2114     -8
                                                $ Profit             0          0      71379      78516      -7137     -8
```

Fig. 12.18

The accounts receivable statistical YTD report.

Generating Finance Charges

When you choose Generate Fin. Chgs., the last option on the Periodic Accounts Receivable menu, the program examines your customer master file and calculates finance charges for those customers with past due balances. Figure 12.19 shows the screen that appears when you select the Generate Fin. Chgs. option.

The screen warns you to back up your files and enter and post all transactions before running the Generate Finance Charges routine. The posting date that shows on the screen is the system date, but you can edit it.

The precise calculation for a finance charge depends on the invoice method you've chosen. If you're using the balance forward method, the program takes the customer's beginning-of-the-month balance and subtracts payments made and credit memos entered. If the result is a negative amount, no finance charge is generated. If the result is a positive amount, DacEasy calculates the finance charge by multiplying the calculated amount by the monthly interest rate specified for the customer. For example, if a customer had a beginning balance of $10,150, made no payments and received no credit memos during the month, and the monthly interest rate you specified for the customer was 1.5 percent

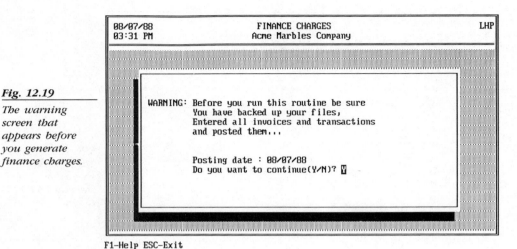

Fig. 12.19

The warning screen that appears before you generate finance charges.

```
08/07/88                    FINANCE CHARGES                    LHP
03:31 PM                  Acme Marbles Company


        WARNING: Before you run this routine be sure
                 You have backed up your files,
                 Entered all invoices and transactions
                 and posted them...


                 Posting date : 08/07/88
                 Do you want to continue(Y/N)? Y
```

F1-Help ESC-Exit

per month, the program calculates a finance charge of $152.25 (1.5 percent of $10,150).

If you're using the open invoice method, the program takes those invoices that are more than 30 days past due and multiplies each invoice by the monthly interest rate to calculate the finance charge. For invoices that are less than 30 days past due, DacEasy prorates the monthly interest to reflect a partial month. For example, if the invoice is 15 days past due, the program calculates the finance charge as if the invoice were 30 days past due and then multiplies this result by 15/30.

As part of running the Generate Finance Charges routine, DacEasy prints a journal of the finance charges calculated and added to customer invoices. Figure 12.20 shows an example of this accounts receivable finance charges journal. For each finance charge, DacEasy also creates an accounts receivable transaction that records a debit to accounts receivable and a credit to the finance charges account specified in the general ledger interface table.

Fig. 12.20

The accounts receivable finance charges journal.

```
Date : 08/07/88                    Acme Marbles Company                    Page no. 1
Time : 01:05 PM                     512 Wetmore Street
                                    Seattle, Wa 98114
                        Tel: (206) 555-1234 Fax: (206) 555-6789

                        ACCOUNTS RECEIVABLE FINANCE CHARGES JOURNAL

        Cust. #.        Name          Invoice #  Inv.Date Due Date  Balance   Fin. Charge
        -------  ------------------------  --------  -------- --------  --------  -----------
        C10      Columbus Glass Works, Inc.  234198   06/09/88 07/09/88  10302.25    149.38
                 Total for Customer :                                    10302.25    149.38

                 Grand Totals :                                          10302.25    149.38
```

Using the Periodic Accounts Payable Options

The Periodic Accounts Payable menu offers three options, which are shown in figure 12.21. These options mirror the first three options of the Periodic Accounts Receivable menu in both purpose and operation.

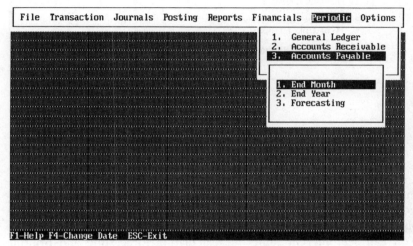

Fig. 12.21

The Periodic Accounts Payable menu.

Remember that before you select either End Month or End Year, you should print any end-of-period audit trails and reports you need, calculate forecasts, and back up your files. Because the periodic routines close and zero out income statement balances, you lose the detail needed to generate reports and calculate forecasts.

The Forecasting options (Automatic Calculations, Print Forecast, and Print Statistical YTD) are also similar to the accounts receivable forecasting options. Automatic Calculations allows you to forecast accounts payable activity by using one of the four automatic calculation methods: Previous Year, Previous Year +/− Pct, Previous Year + Trend, and Trend Line Analysis.

As with both the general ledger and the accounts receivable forecasts, you can limit your accounts payable forecasts. You have three fields you can use to restrict the effect of your forecast: vendor code, type, and territory. Figure 12.22 shows the screen you use to choose the automatic calculation method and to select the vendors, types, or territories to which you want DacEasy to apply the forecast calculation. If you forget the definition of any of these vendor master file fields, refer to the section in Chapter 4 on "Loading the Vendor Master File."

```
┌─────────────────────────────────────────────────────────────────┐
│ 08/09/88              AP Forecast Calculation               LHP   │
│ 07:12 PM                Acme Marbles Company                      │
├─────────────────────────────────────────────────────────────────┤
│                                                                   │
│                                                                   │
│         Calculation Method :              Sort By :               │
│                                                                   │
│         1  Previous Year                  1  Code                 │
│         2  Previous Year +/- Pct          2  Type                 │
│         3  Previous Year + Trend          3  Territory            │
│         4  Trend Line Analysis                                    │
│                                           Enter Your Selection :  │
│         Enter Your Selection :  ■                                 │
│                                                                   │
│                                                                   │
│                                                                   │
│                                                                   │
│                                                                   │
│                                                                   │
└─────────────────────────────────────────────────────────────────┘
   F1-Help F4-Change Date  ESC-Exit
```

Fig. 12.22

Selecting the automatic calculation method and the vendors for which forecasts will be calculated.

The accounts payable reports generated by the Print Forecast and Print Statistical YTD menu options look similar to those generated by the same general ledger and accounts receivable options. Figure 12.23 shows the report request screen you use to select the sort order for the report and to limit the vendors printed. You can set different limits for calculating forecasting and printing reports.

```
┌─────────────────────────────────────────────────────────────────┐
│ 08/09/88                AP Forecast Report                  LHP   │
│ 07:18 PM                Acme Marbles Company                      │
├─────────────────────────────────────────────────────────────────┤
│                                                                   │
│                                                                   │
│                                                                   │
│                Sort By :                                          │
│                                                                   │
│                1  Code                                            │
│                2  Type                                            │
│                3  Territory                                       │
│                                                                   │
│                Enter Your Selection :  ■                          │
│                                                                   │
│                                                                   │
│                                                                   │
│                                                                   │
└─────────────────────────────────────────────────────────────────┘
```

Fig. 12.23

The report request screen for the accounts payable forecast.

Figure 12.24 shows a sample accounts payable forecast, and figure 12.25 shows a sample accounts payable statistical YTD. The only difference between these two reports is that the accounts payable forecast calculates the variances with the This Year amount as the benchmark, and the accounts payable statistical YTD calculates the variances with the Forecast amount as the benchmark.

```
Date : 08/07/88                        Acme Marbles Company                      Page no. 1
Time : 01:07 PM                         512 Wetmore Street
                                        Seattle, Wa 98114
                            Tel: (206) 555-1234 Fax: (206) 555-6789

                         A c c o u n t s   P a y a b l e   F o r e c a s t
Sorted by: Code
Code          Name                           Yr.Bef.Last  Last Year  This Year  Forecast  Variance    %
------------  --------------------------------------      ---------  ---------  ---------  --------  --------- -----
F10           First Class Marble Mfg. Inc.  # Invoices          0          0          2         2         0       0
                                            $ Purchases         0          0      19995     21994      1999      10

G25           George's Service Station      # Invoices          0          0          0         0         0       0
                                            $ Purchases         0          0        732       805        73      10

H25           Jimmy Hughes, Attorney at law # Invoices          0          0          1         1         0       0
                                            $ Purchases         0          0       2750      3025       275      10

J25           Janitorial Excellence, Inc.   # Invoices          0          0          5         6         1      20
                                            $ Purchases         0          0        973      1070        97      10

M10           Mercury Marble Makers, Co.    # Invoices          0          0          2         2         0       0
                                            $ Purchases         0          0         66        73         7      11

S25           South Seattle Realty, Inc.    # Invoices          0          0          1         1         0       0
                                            $ Purchases         0          0       5000      5500       500      10

W10           Walter's Wonders              # Invoices          0          0          1         1         0       0
                                            $ Purchases         0          0        750       825        75      10


              Grand Total                   # Invoices          0          0         12        13         1       8
                                            $ Purchases         0          0      30266     33292      3026      10
```

Fig. 12.24

The accounts payable forecast report.

```
Date : 08/07/88                        Acme Marbles Company                      Page no. 1
Time : 01:07 PM                         512 Wetmore Street
                                        Seattle, Wa 98114
                            Tel: (206) 555-1234 Fax: (206) 555-6789

                      A c c o u n t s   P a y a b l e   S t a t i s t i c a l   Y T D
Sorted by: Code
Code          Name                           Yr.Bef.Last  Last Year  This Year  Forecast  Variance    %
------------  --------------------------------------      ---------  ---------  ---------  --------  --------- -----
F10           First Class Marble Mfg. Inc.  # Invoices          0          0          2         2         0       0
                                            $ Purchases         0          0      19995     21994     -1999      -8

G25           George's Service Station      # Invoices          0          0          0         0         0       0
                                            $ Purchases         0          0        732       805       -73      -8

H25           Jimmy Hughes, Attorney at law # Invoices          0          0          1         1         0       0
                                            $ Purchases         0          0       2750      3025      -275      -8

J25           Janitorial Excellence, Inc.   # Invoices          0          0          5         6        -1     -16
                                            $ Purchases         0          0        973      1070       -97      -8

M10           Mercury Marble Makers, Co.    # Invoices          0          0          2         2         0       0
                                            $ Purchases         0          0         66        73        -7      -9

S25           South Seattle Realty, Inc.    # Invoices          0          0          1         1         0       0
                                            $ Purchases         0          0       5000      5500      -500      -8

W10           Walter's Wonders              # Invoices          0          0          1         1         0       0
                                            $ Purchases         0          0        750       825       -75      -8


              Grand Total                   # Invoices          0          0         12        13        -1      -7
                                            $ Purchases         0          0      30266     33292     -3026      -8
```

Fig. 12.25

The accounts payable statistical YTD report.

Using the Periodic Inventory Options

The Periodic Inventory menu offers only two options for the Inventory module. These options are shown in figure 12.26.

Fig. 12.26

The Periodic Inventory menu.

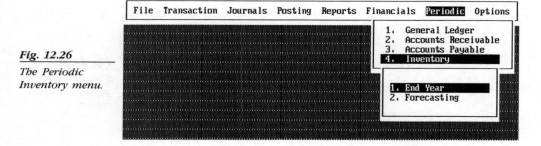

Running the End-of-Year Routine

The End Year option does the same thing that the accounts receivable and accounts payable year-end routines do, except that the inventory routine adjusts the product and service master files rather than the customer and vendor master files. The Last Year amounts are moved to the Year Before Last amounts, the Current Year amounts are moved to the Last Year amounts, and the Current Year amount field is reset to zero so that it can begin tallying the current year's data. As with the other modules, you want to calculate forecasts *before* you run the inventory year-end program.

Forecasting Inventory Activity

Choosing the Forecasting option from the Periodic Inventory menu produces the same three options that appear for the General Ledger, Accounts Receivable, and Accounts Payable modules (see fig. 12.27).

When you select any of the three Forecasting options (Automatic Calculations, Print Forecast, or Print Statistical YTD), DacEasy asks whether you're working on the inventory or services forecasts (see fig. 12.28).

You choose option 1, Automatic Calculations, to forecast inventory and services activity with one of the four automatic calculation methods: Previous Year, Previous Year +/− Pct, Previous Year + Trend, and Trend Line Analysis. And, as

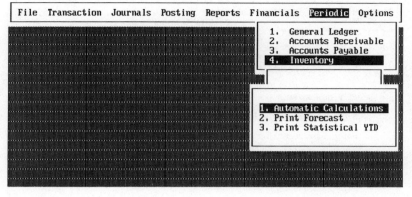

Fig. 12.27

The Periodic Inventory Forecasting options.

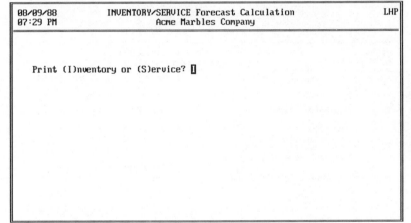

Fig. 12.28

The screen you use to tell DacEasy whether you want to forecast for the product or the service master file.

with the other modules' forecasts, you can limit your inventory forecasts. Here, however, you have four fields from which to choose to limit the effect of your forecast on products: inventory number (or product code), revenue/cost department, bin, and vendor. Figure 12.29 shows the screen you use to choose the automatic calculation method for the forecast and to limit the product records for which the automatic calculation forecasts amounts.

For services, you have two fields with which you can limit the effect of your forecast on services: inventory number or (service code) and revenue/cost department. Figure 12.30 shows the screen you use to choose the automatic calculation method for the forecast and to limit the service records for which the automatic calculation forecasts amounts.

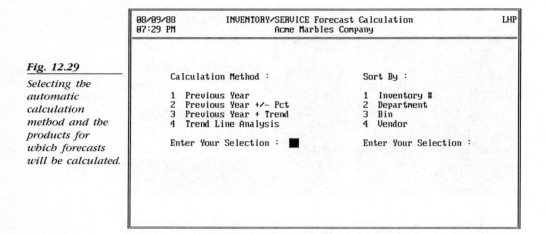

```
08/09/88              INVENTORY/SERVICE Forecast Calculation           LHP
07:29 PM                       Acme Marbles Company


        Calculation Method :                    Sort By :

        1  Previous Year                        1  Inventory #
        2  Previous Year +/- Pct                2  Department
        3  Previous Year + Trend                3  Bin
        4  Trend Line Analysis                  4  Vendor

        Enter Your Selection :  ■               Enter Your Selection :
```

Fig. 12.30

Selecting the automatic calculation method and the services for which forecasts will be calculated.

```
08/09/88              INVENTORY/SERVICE Forecast Calculation           LHP
07:33 PM                       Acme Marbles Company


        Calculation Method :                    Sort By :

        1  Previous Year                        1  Inventory #
        2  Previous Year +/- Pct                2  Department
        3  Previous Year + Trend
        4  Trend Line Analysis
                                                Enter Your Selection :
        Enter Your Selection :  ■
```

The inventory and services reports generated by the Print Forecast and Print Statistical YTD menu options look similar to those generated by the same menu options within the other modules. Figure 12.31 shows the report request screen you use to select the sort order for the report and to limit the product or service records printed.

After you specify the range of products you want to print on the report, a pop-up window appears and asks whether you want to include costs and profits on the report. You press *Y* for "yes" or *N* for "no."

```
08/10/88              INVENTORY/SERVICE Forecast Report           LHP
03:09 PM                    Acme Marbles Company


             Sort By :

             1   Inventory #
             2   Department
             3   Bin
             4   Vendor

             Enter Your Selection : ■
```

Fig. 12.31

The report request screen for the inventory forecast.

Figure 12.32 shows an example of an inventory forecast, and figure 12.33 shows a sample inventory statistical YTD report. Again, the only difference between these two reports is the method of calculating variance. The inventory forecast uses the This Year amount as the benchmark, and the inventory statistical YTD uses the Forecast amount as the benchmark. The forecast reports for services are the same as the reports for products.

Chapter Summary

This chapter concludes *Using DacEasy* with an explanation of and instructions for using the DacEasy Periodic menu for the General Ledger, Accounts Receivable, Accounts Payable, and Inventory modules. For each of these modules, the periodic options include special routines you need to run at the end of a month or year—or both—to reset the counts and total the amounts. In addition, each of the periodic routines includes a powerful set of forecasting tools you can use to build budgets for general ledger, customer, vendor, and inventory and services data. This flexible feature should allow you to become much better at planning for your business's future.

Fig. 12.32

The inventory forecast report.

```
Date : 08/07/88                           Acme Marbles Company                          Page no. 1
Time : 01:10 PM                            512 Wetmore Street
                                           Seattle, Wa 98114
                                 Tel: (206) 555-1234 Fax: (206) 555-6789

                                      I n v e n t o r y   F o r e c a s t

Sorted by: Inventory #
Product #      Description                     Yr.Bef.Last  Last Year  This Year   Forecast    Variance      %
-------------  ------------------------------  -----------  ---------  ---------   --------    --------    -----
B10            Bumble Bee         # Units Sold           0          0     451100     496210       45110     10
                                  $ Sales               0          0      22538      24791        2253     10
                                  $ Costs               0          0       6766       7443         677     10
                                  $ Profit              0          0      15771      17348        1577     10
                                  # Units Pur.          0          0     503000     553300       50300     10
                                  $ Purchases           0          0       7545       8299         754     10


C10            Cat's Eye          # Units Sold          0          0     245500     270050       24550     10
                                  $ Sales               0          0       9822      10804         982     10
                                  $ Costs               0          0       4910       5401         491     10
                                  $ Profit              0          0       4912       5403         491     10
                                  # Units Pur.          0          0     252000     277200       25200     10
                                  $ Purchases           0          0       5040       5544         504     10


C20            Cleary             # Units Sold          0          0     323400     355740       32340     10
                                  $ Sales               0          0      15069      16576        1507     10
                                  $ Costs               0          0       8269       9095         826     10
                                  $ Profit              0          0       6800       7480         680     10
                                  # Units Pur.          0          0     280000     308000       28000     10
                                  $ Purchases           0          0       7000       7700         700     10


Y10            Yellow Swirls      # Units Sold          0          0     400500     440550       40050     10
                                  $ Sales               0          0      20020      22022        2002     10
                                  $ Costs               0          0       1202       1322         120     10
                                  $ Profit              0          0      18818      20699        1881     10
                                  # Units Pur.          0          0     401500     441650       40150     10
                                  $ Purchases           0          0       1204       1324         120     10


               Grand Total        # Units Sold          0          0    1420500    1562550      142050     10
                                  $ Sales               0          0      67449      74193        6744     10
                                  $ Costs               0          0      21147      23261        2114     10
                                  $ Profit              0          0      46302      50932        4630     10
                                  # Units Pur.          0          0    1436500    1580150      143650     10
                                  $ Purchases           0          0      20789      22867        2078     10
```

```
Date : 08/07/88                         Acme Marbles Company                    Page no. 1
Time : 01:10 PM                          512 Wetmore Street
                                         Seattle, Wa 98114
                             Tel: (206) 555-1234 Fax: (206) 555-6789

                       I n v e n t o r y   S t a t i s t i c a l   Y T D
  Sorted by: Inventory #
  Product #   Description                     Yr.Bef.Last  Last Year   This Year  Forecast   Variance     %
  ---------   ------------------------------------------   ----------  ----------  ----------  ----------  ----------  -----
  B10         Bumble Bee              # Units Sold      0          0     451100     496210     -45110      -8
                                      $ Sales           0          0      22538      24791      -2253      -8
                                      $ Costs           0          0       6766       7443       -677      -8
                                      $ Profit          0          0      15771      17348      -1577      -8
                                      # Units Pur.      0          0     503000     553300     -50300      -8
                                      $ Purchases       0          0       7545       8299       -754      -8

  C10         Cat's Eye               # Units Sold      0          0     245500     270050     -24550      -8
                                      $ Sales           0          0       9822      10804       -982      -8
                                      $ Costs           0          0       4910       5401       -491      -8
                                      $ Profit          0          0       4912       5403       -491      -8
                                      # Units Pur.      0          0     252000     277200     -25200      -8
                                      $ Purchases       0          0       5040       5544       -504      -8

  C20         Cleary                  # Units Sold      0          0     323400     355740     -32340      -8
                                      $ Sales           0          0      15069      16576      -1507      -8
                                      $ Costs           0          0       8269       9095       -826      -8
                                      $ Profit          0          0       6800       7480       -680      -8
                                      # Units Pur.      0          0     280000     308000     -28000      -8
                                      $ Purchases       0          0       7000       7700       -700      -8

  Y10         Yellow Swirls           # Units Sold      0          0     400500     440550     -40050      -8
                                      $ Sales           0          0      20020      22022      -2002      -8
                                      $ Costs           0          0       1202       1322       -120      -8
                                      $ Profit          0          0      18818      20699      -1881      -8
                                      # Units Pur.      0          0     401500     441650     -40150      -8
                                      $ Purchases       0          0       1204       1324       -120      -8


              Grand Total             # Units Sold      0          0    1420500    1562550    -142050      -8
                                      $ Sales           0          0      67449      74193      -6744      -8
                                      $ Costs           0          0      21147      23261      -2114      -8
                                      $ Profit          0          0      46302      50932      -4630      -8
                                      # Units Pur.      0          0    1436500    1580150    -143650      -8
                                      $ Purchases       0          0      20789      22867      -2078      -8
```

Fig. 12.33

The inventory statistical YTD report.

DacEasy Accounting 3.0 Files

Your DacEasy Accounting 3.0 package includes two program disks. You'll find the following files on those two disks:

Disk 1	*Disk 2*
DEA3.EXE	DA3-00.EXE
DEAU.EXE	SETUP.EXE
DA3-F00.DA1	DA3-HLP2.DAT
DA3-HLP1.DAT	INSTALL.TXT
DA3-F17.DA1	DA3-HLP2.KEY
DA3-RA2.REP	INSTALL.BAT
DA3-INC.REP	READ.ME
DA3-BAL.REP	
DA3-F00.KA1	
DA3-RA1.REP	
DA3-HLP1.KEY	

The files with the .REP extension are the sample report formats DacEasy provides. The .EXE files are, of course, the DacEasy programs. The DA3-HLP files are for DacEasy's on-line, context-sensitive help feature. INSTALL.TXT and INSTALL.BAT are the program and instructions for installing DacEasy. READ.ME contains additonal information and instructions that may be helpful to you as you install and begin using DacEasy. To view the contents of the READ.ME file, insert program disk 2 in floppy drive A and enter *type read.me* at the A› prompt.

If you're using a dual floppy disk system, DacEasy prompts you when you need to swap disks. Depending on the main menu option you choose, DacEasy prompts you to insert the appropriate program disk, as follows:

Menu Option	Insert
File	Program Disk 2
Transaction	Program Disk 2
Journals	Program Disk 2
Posting	Program Disk 2
Reports	Program Disk 1
Financials	Program Disk 1
Periodic	Program Disk 1
Options	Program Disk 1

Once you've installed DacEasy and defined the data files, DacEasy creates the following files:

File	Contents
DA3-F00.KEY	General ledger accounts
DA3-F00.DAT	
DA3-F01.KEY	Customer files
DA3-F01.DAT	
DA3-F02.KEY	Vendor files
DA3-F02.DAT	
DA3-F03.KEY	Product files
DA3-F03.DAT	
DA3-F04.KEY	A/R open invoices
DA3-F04.DAT	
DA3-F05.KEY	A/R transactions
DA3-F05.DAT	
DA3-F06.KEY	A/P open invoices
DA3-F06.DAT	
DA3-F07.KEY	A/P transactions
DA3-F07.DAT	
DA3-F08.KEY	G/L transactions
DA3-F08.DAT	
DA3-F09.KEY	Sales invoices
DA3-F09.DAT	
DA3-F10.KEY	Purchase orders
DA3-F10.DAT	
DA3-F11.KEY	Physical inventory
DA3-F11.DAT	
DA3-F17.DAT	General file
DA3-F18.DAT	Sort file

Reviewing DacEasy's Sample Custom Report Formats

As part of the program's package, DacEasy includes four sample custom report formats (BAL, INC, RA1, and RA2). You can use these custom reports only if you've made no additions or deletions to the sample Chart of Accounts. Any time you modify the Chart of Accounts, you need to edit the provided financial statement formats to include the changes (either adding or deleting accounts).

Even if you decide not to use the sample Chart of Accounts, these reports provide a useful starting point for you, because they are well-conceived examples of the types of reports and styles you can create with the Financial Statements Generator. (For more information on creating custom reports, see the section in Chapter 11 on "Creating Custom Reports.")

The BAL report format generates a more summary-level balance sheet than the standard balance sheet (see fig. B.1).

The INC report format generates a summary-level income statement. A sample report produced with this format is displayed as figure B.2.

The RA1 and RA2 report formats generate financial statements that calculate a series of financial ratios. Financial ratios, which are mathematical comparisons of amounts from the balance sheet and the income statement, provide insights into the relative financial strengths, weaknesses, and performance of a company. Most often, you can't interpret financial ratios alone but must compare them to the ratios of competitors and business peers or to your company's historical data (a trend analysis).

Fig. B.1

An extract from DacEasy's BAL custom report format.

```
Date : 08/07/88                      Acme Marbles Company                          Page no. 1
Time : 01:23 PM                        512 Wetmore Street
                                        Seattle, Wa 98114
                              Tel: (206) 555-1234 Fax: (206) 555-6789

                                     FINANCIAL STATEMENTS

            Acct #   Description                      Year to Date        %
            ------   --------------------             -------------     -------

                                    ** Balance Sheet **

                                           ASSETS
                     Current Assets:
            1101     Petty Cash                            0.00
            1102     Cash In Banks                     35,167.48          25.4
            1103     Cash Register Fund                    0.00
            1104     Mktable Securities                    0.00
            1105     Accounts Receivable               82,951.64          60.0
            1106     Other Receivable                      0.00
            1107     Inventory                          2,198.50           1.6
                                                   ---------------      -------
                     Total Current                   120,317.62          87.0
                     Fixed Assets:
            12011    Autos & Trucks                        0.00
            12021    Furniture & Fixtures              20,000.00          14.5
            12031    Office Equipment                      0.00
            12041    Machinery & Equip.                    0.00
            12051    Building                              0.00
            12061    Other Fixed Assets                    0.00
                                                   ---------------      -------
                     Total Original Value            20,000.00          14.5
                     Accum. Depreciation             -2,000.00          -1.4
                                                   ---------------      -------
                     Net Value                       18,000.00          13.0
            1207     Land                                  0.00
                                                   ---------------      -------
                     Total Fixed                     18,000.00          13.0
                     Deferred Assets:
            13011    Organization Expense                  0.00
            13021    Leasehold Improv.                     0.00
                                                   ---------------      -------
                     Original Investment                   0.00
                     Accum. Amortization                   0.00
                                                   ---------------      -------
                     Net Value                             0.00
            1303     Prepaid Expenses                       0.00
                                                   ---------------      -------
                     Total Deferred                        0.00
                     Other Assets:
            1401     Deposits                               0.00
            1402     Long Term Investment                   0.00
                     Total Other                            0.00
                                                   ===============      =======
                     TOTAL ASSETS                    138,317.62         100.0
                                                   ===============      =======
```

```
Date : 08/07/88                          Acme Marbles Company                    Page no. 2
Time : 01:23 PM                            512 Wetmore Street
                                           Seattle, Wa 98114
                              Tel: (206) 555-1234 Fax: (206) 555-6789

                                       FINANCIAL STATEMENTS

              Acct #   Description                      Year to Date      %
              ------   --------------------            --------------- -------

                                         LIABILITIES
                       Short Term:
              2101     Accounts Payable                     29,216.06    21.1
              2102     Notes Payable                             0.00
              2103     Accrued Payable                          0.00
              2104     Taxes Payable                         5,054.40     3.7
              2105     Other Pyroll Payable                      0.00
              2106     Dividends Payable                         0.00
              2107     Other Payable                             0.00
                                                       --------------- -------
                       Total Short Term                    34,270.46    24.8
                       Long Term:
              2201     Mortgages Payable                    55,000.00    39.8
              2202     Notes Payable                             0.00
              2204     Other Long Term Liab                      0.00
                                                       --------------- -------
                       Sub-Total                           55,000.00    39.8
              2203     Current L/Term Liab.                      0.00
                                                       --------------- -------
                       Total Long Term                     55,000.00    39.8
                       Deferred:
              2301     Commit & Contingenc                       0.00
              2302     Deferred Income                           0.00
              2303     Profit/Instalm.Sales                      0.00
              2304     Unearned Interest                         0.00
                                                       --------------- -------
                       Total Deferred                           0.00
                                                       --------------- -------
                       TOTAL LIABILITIES                   89,270.46    64.5
                                       STOCKHOLDERS EQUITY
                       Capital Stock:
              3101     Common Stock                        10,000.00     7.2
              3102     Preferred Stock                          0.00
                                                       --------------- -------
                       Sub-Total                           10,000.00     7.2
              3103     Treasury Stock                           0.00
                                                       --------------- -------
                       Total Capital Stock                 10,000.00     7.2
                       Retained Earnings                        0.00
                       Current Earnings                    37,946.16    27.4
                                                       --------------- -------
                       Total Equity                        47,946.16    34.7
                                                       --------------- -------
                       TOTAL LIABILITIES
                       PLUS EQUITY                        137,216.62    99.2
                                                       --------------- -------
```

Fig. B.1-Continued

Fig. B.2

An extract from DacEasy's INC custom report format.

```
Date : 08/07/88                      Acme Marbles Company                    Page no. 1
Time : 01:23 PM                       512 Wetmore Street
                                       Seattle, Wa 98114
                          Tel: (206) 555-1234 Fax: (206) 555-6789

                                     FINANCIAL STATEMENTS

                  Acct #   Description                    Year to Date     %
                  ------   --------------------           ------------   -------

                                  * Income Statement *

                                     GROSS MARGIN:

                                     Department 01

                  4101     Sales                              44,834.78    58.0
                  4201     Returns                                 0.00
                                                             ------------   -------
                           Net Sales                          44,834.78    58.0

                  5101     Cost of Goods Sold                 12,070.00    15.6
                                                             ------------   -------
                           Gross Margin Dept.01              32,764.78    42.4

                                     Department 02

                  4102     Sales                              32,500.00    42.0
                  4202     Returns                                 0.00
                                                             ------------   -------
                           Net Sales                          32,500.00    42.0

                  5102     Cost of Goods Sold                  7,450.00     9.6
                                                             ------------   -------
                           Gross Margin Dept.02              25,050.00    32.4

                           GROSS MARGIN:                      57,814.78    74.8
                                                             ------------   -------
```

```
Date : 08/07/88                        Acme Marbles Company                      Page no. 2
Time : 01:23 PM                        512 Wetmore Street
                                         Seattle, Wa 98114
                              Tel: (206) 555-1234 Fax: (206) 555-6789

                                       FINANCIAL STATEMENTS


         Acct #    Description                           Year to Date    %
         ------    --------------------                  ------------    -------


                   GROSS MARGIN:                          57,814.78      74.8
                   Less:
                                       GENERAL AND
                                      ADMINISTRATIVE
                                        EXPENSES:

         5201      Payroll                                 1,200.00       1.6
         5202      Maintenance                               500.00       0.6
         5203      Depreciation                            2,000.00       2.6
         5204      Amortization                                0.00
         5205      Rents and Leases                          750.00       1.0
         5206      Assets Insurance                            0.00
         5207      Travel & Entertain                        326.87       0.4
                   Net Shipping Expense                       76.30       0.1
         5209      Taxes (other)                           1,672.82       2.2
         5210      Consulting Fees                            543.00       0.7
         5211      Office Supplies                             0.00
         5212      Telephone & Telegrph                        0.00
         5213      Mail/Postage                                0.00
         5214      Utilities                                  453.92       0.6
         5215      Alarms                                      0.00
         5216      Contribution/Donat.                         0.00
         5217      Licenses/Permits                            0.00
         5218      Memships/Dues/Subscr                        0.00
         5219      Advertising                              3,500.12       4.5
         5220      Promotion                                1,300.52       1.7
         5221      Public Relations                         4,700.00       6.1
         5222      Marketing Research                       2,845.07       3.7
         5223      Bad Debt Loss                               0.00
         5224      Inventory Losses                            0.00
         5299      Other Expenses                              0.00
                                                         ------------   -------
                   Total G&A Expenses                     19,868.62      25.7
                                                         ------------   -------
                   OPERATIVE PROFIT
                   OR (LOSS)                               37,946.16      49.1
                                                         ------------   -------
```

Fig. B.2-Continued

```
Date : 08/07/88                    Acme Marbles Company                    Page no. 3
Time : 01:23 PM                      512 Wetmore Street
                                     Seattle, Wa 98114
                          Tel: (206) 555-1234 Fax: (206) 555-6789

                                   FINANCIAL STATEMENTS

        Acct #   Description                        Year to Date      %
        ------   -------------------                ----------------  -------


                 OPERATIVE PROFIT
                 OR (LOSS):                              37,946.16    49.1
                                      FINANCIAL OPERATION
                 Financial Revenues
        4401     Ints. Investments                           0.00
        4402     Finance Charges                             0.00
        4403     Dividends                                   0.00
        4404     Purchase Discounts                          0.00
                                                     ----------------  -------
                 Total Financial Rev.                        0.00
                 Financial Expenses
        5301     Credit Card Discount                        0.00
        5302     Interest                                    0.00
        5303     Bank Charges                                0.00
        5304     Sales Discounts                             0.00
        5305     Agents Commisions                           0.00
        5399     Other Financial Exp.                        0.00
                                                     ----------------  -------
                 Total Financial Exp.                        0.00
                                                     ----------------  -------
                 Net Financial Oper.                         0.00
                                                     ----------------  -------
                 FINANCIAL PROFIT
                 OR (LOSS)                               37,946.16    49.1
                                                     ----------------  -------
                                       OTHER REVENUE
                                       AND EXPENSES:
                 Other Revenues
        4501     Recovery Bad Debt                           0.00
        4502     Gain in Sale/Assets                         0.00
        4503     Miscellaneous                               0.00
                                                     ----------------  -------
                 Total Other Revenue                         0.00
                 Other Expenses
        5401     Cash Short                                  0.00
        5402     Loss on Sale/Assets                         0.00
        5403     Miscellaneous Losses                        0.00
                                                     ----------------  -------
                 Total Other Expenses                        0.00
                                                     ----------------  -------
                 Net Other Revenue
                 and Expenses                                0.00
                                                     ----------------  -------
                 NET PROFIT OR (LOSS)                   37,946.16    49.1
        55       Income Tax                                  0.00
                                                     ----------------  -------
                 NET PROFIT OR (LOSS)
```

Fig. B.2-Concluded

Figures B.3 and B.4 show extracts from the sample financial ratios statements produced by the RA1 and RA2 report formats. You should consult a good intermediate accounting textbook or your certified public accountant for more information regarding ratio and trend analyses. They can be beneficial for highlighting areas of your business that need attention.

Fig. B.3

An extract from DacEasy's RA1 custom report format.

```
Date : 08/07/88                        Acme Marbles Company                      Page no. 1
Time : 01:24 PM                         512 Wetmore Street
                                        Seattle, Wa 98114
                            Tel: (206) 555-1234 Fax: (206) 555-6789

                                      FINANCIAL STATEMENTS

         Acct #   Description                              Year to Date      %
         ------   --------------------                     ------------- -------

                              FINANCIAL RATIOS
                              ANALYSIS:

                   Acid Test:


                   The ratio determines
                   the relation between
                   Cash availability
                   and Short Term Debt:

                              Arithmetic Ratio:

         1101      Petty Cash                                    0.00
         1102      Cash In Banks                             35,167.48
         1103      Cash Register Fund                             0.00
         1104      Mktable Securities                            0.00
         1105      Accounts Receivable                       82,951.64
         1106      Other Receivable                              0.00
                                                         --------------- ------
                   Total Cash available                     118,119.12
                   minus:
         21        Short Term Liability                      34,270.46
                                                         --------------- ------
                   Net Cash Available                        83,848.66
                                                         =============== ======


                              Geometrical Ratio:

                   Cash Available                           118,119.12
                                                         --------------- ------
                   Short Term Liability                     34,270.46

                   Ratio:                                        3.45
                                                         =============== ======
```

Fig. B.3-Continued

```
Date : 08/07/88                        Acme Marbles Company                    Page no. 2
Time : 01:24 PM                          512 Wetmore Street
                                         Seattle, Wa 98114
                             Tel: (206) 555-1234 Fax: (206) 555-6789
                                       FINANCIAL STATEMENTS

              Acct #   Description                        Year to Date      %
              ------   -----------------------            ---------------  -------

                             Current Liquidity:
                      This Ratio gives the
                      position between
                      Current Assets and
                      Short Term Debt:


                             Arithmetic Ratio:

                11    Current Assets                        120,317.62
                21    Short Term Liability                   34,270.46
                                                          ---------------  -------
                      Ratio                                  86,047.16
                                                          ---------------  -------


                             Geometrical Ratio:

                11    Current Assets                        120,317.62
                                                          ---------------  -------
                21    Short Term Liability                   34,270.46

                      Ratio                                       3.51
                                                          ---------------  -------
```

```
Date : 08/07/88                    Acme Marbles Company                    Page no. 1
Time : 01:24 PM                     512 Wetmore Street
                                    Seattle, Wa 98114
                          Tel: (206) 555-1234 Fax: (206) 555-6789

                                  FINANCIAL STATEMENTS

        Acct #   Description                     Year to Date     %
        ------   ---------------------           ---------------  -------

                              FINANCIAL RATIOS
                                 ANALYSIS:


                             L I Q U I D I T Y



                                 Acid Test:

                 Cash Available                   118,119.12
                                                 ---------------  -------
        21       Short Term Liability              34,270.46
                                                 ---------------  -------
                 Ratio:                                 3.45
                                                 ---------------  -------


                             Current Liquidity:

        11       Current Assets                   120,317.62
                                                 ---------------  -------
        21       Short Term Liability              34,270.46
                                                 ---------------  -------
                 Ratio                                  3.51
                                                 ---------------  -------
```

Fig. B.4

An extract from DacEasy's RA2 custom report format.

```
Date : 08/07/88                    Acme Marbles Company                    Page no. 2
Time : 01:24 PM                     512 Wetmore Street
                                    Seattle, Wa 98114
                          Tel: (206) 555-1234 Fax: (206) 555-6789

                                  FINANCIAL STATEMENTS

        Acct #   Description                     Year to Date     %
        ------   ---------------------           ---------------  -------

                             L E V E R A G E



                              Debt to Total Assets


        2        Total Debt                        89,270.46
                                                 ---------------  -------
        1        Total Assets                     138,317.62
                                                 ---------------  -------
                 Ratio                                  0.65
                                                 ---------------  -------


                                 Times Interest
                                     Earned:

                 Profit before Tax                 37,946.16
        5302     Plus:Interest Paid                     0.00
                 Total                             37,946.16
                                                 ---------------  -------
        5302     Interest Paid                          0.00
                                                 ---------------  -------
                 Ratio                                  0.00
                                                 ---------------  -------
```

```
Date : 08/07/88                    Acme Marbles Company                    Page no. 3
Time : 01:24 PM                      512 Wetmore Street
                                     Seattle, Wa 98114
                          Tel: (206) 555-1234 Fax: (206) 555-6789

                               FINANCIAL STATEMENTS

        Acct #   Description                    Year to Date      %
        ------   --------------------           ---------------  ------
                               T U R N O V E R S

                               Inventory:

        51       Cost of Goods Sold                19,520.00
                                                ---------------  ------
        11071    Inventory                          2,198.50
                                                ---------------  ------
                 Times turn                             8.88
                                                ---------------  ------

                            Accounts Receivable:

                 Net Sales                         77,334.78
                                                ---------------  ------
        11051    Accounts Receivable               82,951.64
                                                ---------------  ------
                 Times Turn                             0.93
                                                ---------------  ------

                               Fixed Assets:

                 Net Sales                         77,334.78
                                                ---------------  ------
        12       Fixed Assets                      18,000.00
                                                ---------------  ------
                 Times Turn                             4.30
                                                ---------------  ------

                               Total Assets:

                 Net Sales                         77,334.78
                                                ---------------  ------
        1        Total Assets                     138,317.62
                                                ---------------  ------
                 Times Turn                             0.56
                                                ---------------  ------
```

Fig. B.4-Continued

```
Date : 08/07/88                    Acme Marbles Company                    Page no. 4
Time : 01:24 PM                     512 Wetmore Street
                                    Seattle, Wa 98114
                          Tel: (206) 555-1234 Fax: (206) 555-6789

                                  FINANCIAL STATEMENTS

            Acct #   Description                    Year to Date      %
            ------   --------------------           ---------------  -------

                                    PROFITABILITY


                          Profit on Revenues:


                     Profit After Tax                37,946.16
                                                     ---------------  -------
               4     Revenues                        77,334.78
                                                     ---------------  -------
                     Margin                              0.49
                                                     ---------------  -------


                           Profit on Assets:


                     Profit After Tax                37,946.16
                                                     ---------------  -------
               1     Assets                         138,317.62
                                                     ---------------  -------
                     Margin                              0.27
                                                     ---------------  -------

                          Profit on Net Worth:

                     Profit After Tax                37,946.16
                                                     ---------------  -------
                     Equity before Profit           -27,946.16
                                                     ---------------  -------
                     Margin                             -1.36
                                                     ---------------  -------
```

Fig. B.4-Concluded

Converting Your Current DacEasy Accounting Files to DacEasy Release 3.0

Release 3.0 of DacEasy Accounting includes a utility that converts to Release 3.0 the accounting files created with an earlier version of DacEasy—Release 1.0 or Release 2.0. If you've been using DacEasy 1.0 or 2.0, you'll find the conversion utility invaluable because it will save you from having to load the master files.

Note: If you want to convert 1.0 files to 3.0, you must print and post all outstanding billing invoices and merchandise received reports before you run the conversion routine. If you don't do so, you'll have to reenter all billing invoices and merchandise receipts after the conversion is complete.

To run the file conversion utility after you've installed DacEasy 3.0, first back up your accounting files. Then type *DEAU* at the C› prompt while you're in the DacEasy program directory. As soon as you do, a warning screen appears, reminding you to run the install program and back up your files before running the conversion utility (see fig. C.1).

You can press Esc if you haven't backed up your accounting files or installed the DacEasy program. If you want to continue with the file conversion, however, press Enter to produce the screen shown in figure C.2. This screen gives you information you need in order to run the conversion utility for a floppy disk system or a hard disk system.

```
┌────────────────────────────────────────────────────────────┐
│                                                              │
│    This utility program will convert your current DAC-EASY   │
│  Accounting files to DAC-EASY 3.0 accounting files. Before   │
│  continuing with the upgrade process, please be sure that    │
│  you have done the following :                               │
│                                                              │
│                                                              │
│      1. Run the install program to correctly install the     │
│         DAC-EASY 3.0 program files.                          │
│                                                              │
│                                                              │
│      2. Make a backup copy of your current data files.       │
│                                                              │
│                                                              │
│  Press any key to continue or ESC to abort.                  │
│                                                              │
│                                                              │
│                                                              │
└────────────────────────────────────────────────────────────┘
```

Fig. C.1

The warning screen that appears when you start the file conversion utility.

```
┌────────────────────────────────────────────────────────────┐
│                                                              │
│  The following screen will prompt you for the drive or path- │
│  name of your current and upgraded 3.0 accounting files.     │
│                                                              │
│  For floppy drive usage enter :                              │
│                                                              │
│     A: for your 3.0 program files                            │
│     B: for your 3.0 accounting data files                    │
│     A: for your current accounting data files                │
│                                                              │
│  For hard drive usage enter     :                            │
│                                                              │
│     C: plus the pathname for your 3.0 program files          │
│     C: plus the pathname for your 3.0 accounting files       │
│     C: plus the pathname for your current accounting files   │
│                                                              │
│  < Press any key to continue >                               │
│                                                              │
└────────────────────────────────────────────────────────────┘
```

Fig. C.2

The information screen that tells you how to identify the old and new locations of your accounting files.

For a floppy disk system, you must have the program disk for DacEasy Release 3.0 in drive A, and the disk for the DacEasy 3.0 accounting files in drive B. When prompted, replace the program disk in drive A with the disk for the current accounting files—those you've been maintaining with DacEasy Release 1.0 or 2.0. For a hard disk system, specify the complete path name, including the drive letter, the directory name, and any subdirectory names. Press Enter to continue to the next screen, on which you specify the drives for a floppy disk or hard disk system (see fig. C.3.).

```
┌─────────────────────────────────────────────────────────────┐
│              DAC EASY 3.0 Conversion Utility            LHP   │
│                                                               │
│                                                               │
│                                                               │
│    Enter Drive or Directory for the Dac-Easy 3.0 Program      │
│    --> C:\DEA3                                                 │
│                                                               │
│    Enter Drive or Directory for Dac-Easy 3.0 Files            │
│    --> C:\DEA3\FILES                                           │
│                                                               │
│    Enter Drive or Directory for your current Dac-Easy Files   │
│    --> C:\DEA3\FILES                                          │
│                                                               │
│                                                               │
│                                                               │
│                                                               │
└─────────────────────────────────────────────────────────────┘
```

Fig. C.3

The screen on which you specify the old and new locations of your accounting files.

(Fig. C.3 shows the screen completed for a hard disk system and uses the default program and file directory names supplied by the installation program. DEA3 is the name of the DacEasy 3.0 program directory, DEA is the name of the DacEasy 2.0 program directory, and FILES is the name of the subdirectory in which the accounting files are stored for both Releases.)

After you've specified the drives and path names for both the old and new locations of the accounting files, press Enter. The conversion utility then converts your Release 1.0 or 2.0 DacEasy accounting files to the DacEasy Release 3.0 format. When the conversion is complete, another message appears. The screen informs you that if you're converting from Release 1.0 of DacEasy, you need to reset the printer codes and passwords.

APPENDIX D

Using This Book for DacEasy Release 2.0

If you're working with DacEasy Release 2.0, you should find *Using DacEasy* helpful even though the book is written for DacEasy Release 3.0. To use this book for Release 2.0, you simply need to be aware of the differences between 2.0 and 3.0 menu structure, the two new options that DacEasy 3.0 provides, and a couple of minor cosmetic differences between the two Releases.

Reconciling the Menu Differences

The only major change from Release 2.0 to Release 3.0 is the menu structure—the way the options are grouped. In Release 2.0, menu options are arranged by accounting activity. Accounts receivable options are together, accounts payable options are together, general ledger options are together, and so on. In Release 3.0, menu options are grouped by function. The transaction options are together, the journal options are together, the posting options are together, and so on. Although the design is different, the detailed menu options are the same in both Releases and have either identical or similar names. If you have trouble finding a specific option or the screen to request a certain report, the menu maps in the back of this book provide a quick reference source.

If you have trouble finding a specific option or the screen to request a certain report, the menu maps in the back of this book provide a quick reference source.

331

A couple of other points about the menus deserve attention. First, DacEasy 3.0 includes the file utilities options in the menu structure, and Release 2.0 has you access the file utilities options by pressing F3. (The file utilities are those options you use to set the printer- and monitor-color parameters, view the file status, and change the defined file sizes.) The options work the same way in either Release—you just access them differently.

Another difference between DacEasy 2.0 and 3.0 menu structure isn't apparent on the menu maps but is discussed in several places in this book. In Release 3.0, you can add customers, vendors, products, services, and Chart of Accounts numbers directly on the transaction screens. When you're entering an accounting transaction, you can simply use an invalid customer, vendor, product, service, or Chart of Accounts number to access an abbreviated master file maintenance screen. Unfortunately, you don't get this timesaving feature with DacEasy 2.0.

DacEasy 3.0's Two New Options

The menu maps show another difference between Releases 2.0 and 3.0. If you look carefully at both menu maps, you can see that Release 3.0 includes two extra options: a tax table that allows you to store commonly used sales tax rates, and a feature that allows you to print 1099 forms for vendors. To facilitate both the 1099 and the tax table features, Release 3.0 also includes a couple of new fields in the vendor and customer master files: the tax identification number and the tax table code. If you're using DacEasy 2.0, just pass over the discussions of these new features.

Other Miscellaneous Changes

If you're using this book for Release 2.0, you need to be aware of two remaining minor differences between Release 2.0 and Release 3.0. First, in Release 3.0, you access the purchase order codes table separately from the billing codes table. But in Release 2.0 you can access either codes table and then flip between the two tables by using F2. In addition, Release 2.0 lets you use only 20 purchase order codes and 20 billing codes. Release 3.0 extends these limits to 40 codes for each category.

The one other small change from Release 2.0 to Release 3.0 concerns the Current Balance field in the Chart of Accounts file. Release 3.0 not only shows the total current balance for an account but also breaks the current balance into two separate amounts: the This Period Balance and the Current Period Balance. Release 2.0 shows only the total Current Balance.

Knowing about these differences not only helps you use this book for DacEasy Release 2.0 but also can help you decide whether to upgrade from Release 2.0 to Release 3.0. (If you *are* thinking about upgrading, see Appendix C, which describes a feature not discussed in the Release 3.0 documentation: a file conversion utility. This program converts Release 1.0 and Release 2.0 accounting files to the Release 3.0 accounting file format.)

Index

More Computer Knowledge from Que

SELECT QUE BOOKS TO INCREASE
YOUR PERSONAL COMPUTER PRODUCTIVITY

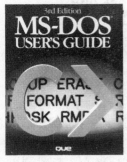

MS-DOS User's Guide, 3rd Edition

by Chris DeVoney

This classic guide to MS-DOS is now better than ever! Updated for MS-DOS, Version 3.3, this new edition features several new extended tutorials and a unique new command reference section. The distinctive approach of this text lets you easily reference basic command syntax, while comprehensive tutorial sections present indepth DOS data. Appendixes provide information specific to users of DOS on COMPAQ, Epson, Zenith, and Leading Edge personal computers. Master your computer's operating system with *MS-DOS User's Guide*, 3rd Edition—the comprehensive tutorial/reference!

Using PC DOS, 2nd Edition

by Chris DeVoney

DOS master Chris DeVoney has updated his classic *Using PC DOS* to include information on PC DOS 3.3. Critically acclaimed, this book is a combination of step-by-step tutorial and lasting reference. This new edition adds up-to-date information on IBM's PS/2 computers and shows how to work with 3 1/2-inch disks. Also featured is a comprehensive beginning tutorial and the popular Command Reference—an easy-to-use consolidation of essential DOS commands. No IBM microcomputer user should be without a copy of *Using PC DOS*, 2nd Edition!

Using 1-2-3, Special Edition

Developed by Que Corporation

Acclaimed for its wealth of information and respected for its clear and concise style, *Using 1-2-3* is required reading for more than one million 1-2-3 users worldwide. This Special Edition of the classic text has more than 900 pages of up-to-date information and features, including comprehensive Command Reference and Troubleshooting sections, hands-on practice sessions, and information on Lotus HAL and other add-in/add-on programs. Discover for yourself why *Using 1-2-3*, Special Edition, is the ultimate tutorial and reference to 1-2-3, Release 2!

Using WordPerfect 5

by Charles O. Stewart III, et al.

WordPerfect 5 is the latest version of the popular word processor and Que's new *Using WordPerfect 5* is the perfect WordPerfect guide. This comprehensive text introduces you to WordPerfect basics; helps you learn to use macros, Styles, and other advanced features; presents information on outlining, referencing, and text columns; and shows you how to use WordPerfect for desktop publishing. Also included are numerous Quick Start tutorials, a tear-out command reference card, and an introduction to WordPerfect 5 for 4.2 users. Become a WordPerfect expert with *Using WordPerfect 5*!

ORDER FROM QUE TODAY

Item	Title	Price	Quantity	Extension
838	MS-DOS User's Guide, 3rd Edition	$22.95		
807	Using PC DOS, 2nd Edition	22.95		
805	Using 1-2-3, Special Edition	24.95		
843	Using WordPerfect 5	24.95		

Book Subtotal _____

Shipping & Handling ($2.50 per item) _____

Indiana Residents Add 5% Sales Tax _____

GRAND TOTAL _____

Method of Payment

☐ Check   ☐ VISA   ☐ MasterCard   ☐ American Express

Card Number _____ Exp. Date _____

Cardholder's Name _____

Ship to _____

Address _____

City _____ State _____ ZIP _____

If you can't wait, call **1-800-428-5331** and order TODAY.

All prices subject to change without notice.

Place
Stamp
Here

Que Corporation
P.O. Box 90
Carmel, IN 46032

REGISTRATION CARD

Register your copy of *Using DacEasy* and receive information about Que's newest products. Complete this registration card and return it to Que Corporation, P.O. Box 90, Carmel, IN 46032.

Name _____ Phone _____

Company _____ Title _____

Address _____

City _____ State _____ ZIP _____

Please check the appropriate answers:

Where did you buy *Using DacEasy*?
- ☐ Bookstore (name: _____)
- ☐ Computer store (name: _____)
- ☐ Catalog (name: _____)
- ☐ Direct from Que _____
- ☐ Other: _____

How many computer books do you buy a year?
- ☐ 1 or less   ☐ 6–10
- ☐ 2–5   ☐ More than 10

How many Que books do you own?
- ☐ 1   ☐ 6–10
- ☐ 2–5   ☐ More than 10

How long have you been using DacEasy?
- ☐ Less than 6 months
- ☐ 6 months to 1 year
- ☐ 1–3 years
- ☐ More than 3 years

What influenced your purchase of *Using DacEasy*?
- ☐ Personal recommendation
- ☐ Advertisement   ☐ Que catalog
- ☐ In-store display   ☐ Que mailing
- ☐ Price   ☐ Que's reputation
- ☐ Other: _____

How would you rate the overall content of *Using DacEasy*?
- ☐ Very good   ☐ Satisfactory
- ☐ Good   ☐ Poor

How would you rate the overall content of *Using DacEasy*?
- ☐ Very good   ☐ Satisfactory
- ☐ Good   ☐ Poor

How would you rate *Chapter 1: Review of Small-Business Accounting*?
- ☐ Very good   ☐ Satisfactory
- ☐ Good   ☐ Poor

How would you rate the *tear-out menu charts*?
- ☐ Very good   ☐ Satisfactory
- ☐ Good   ☐ Poor

What do you like *best* about *Using DacEasy*?

What do you like *least* about *Using DacEasy*?

How do you use *Using DacEasy*?

What other Que products do you own?

For what other programs would a Que book be helpful?

Please feel free to list any other comments you may have about *Using DacEasy*.

_____

_____

_____

_____

_____

_____

_____

_____

FOLD HERE

Place
Stamp
Here

Que Corporation
P.O. Box 90
Carmel, IN 46032